Through the fiction of Phebe Gibbes (1764–90)

Manchester University Press

Through the fiction of Phebe Gibbes (1764–90)

Women, alienation, and prodigality in the long eighteenth century

Kathryn S. Freeman

MANCHESTER UNIVERSITY PRESS

Copyright © Kathryn S. Freeman 2025

The right of Kathryn S. Freeman to be identified as the author of this work has been asserted in accordance with the Copyright, Designs and Patents Act 1988.

Published by Manchester University Press
Oxford Road, Manchester, M13 9PL

www.manchesteruniversitypress.co.uk

British Library Cataloguing-in-Publication Data
A catalogue record for this book is available from the British Library

ISBN 978 1 5261 7500 7 hardback

First published 2025

The publisher has no responsibility for the persistence or accuracy of URLs for any external or third-party internet websites referred to in this book, and does not guarantee that any content on such websites is, or will remain, accurate or appropriate.

EU authorised representative for GPSR:
Easy Access System Europe, Mustamäe tee 50, 10621
Tallinn, Estonia
gpsr.requests@easproject.com

Typeset by Newgen Publishing UK

To Jane, Linda, Elizabeth, and Jory
With love and gratitude for your creative spirit and support

Contents

Acknowledgments   viii
Abbreviations   ix

Introduction   1

1 *The Life and Adventures of Mr. Francis Clive* (1764): "A marriage, where love is wanting, is only a legal prostitution"   21
2 *The American Fugitive: or, Friendship in a Nunnery* (1778, 1784): transnationalism between the Seven Years' War and the American Revolution   72
3 Transnationalism in the Anglo-Indian novels: *Zoriada, or, Village Annals* (1786) and *Hartly House, Calcutta: A Novel of the Days of Warren Hastings* (1789)   115
4 *Elfrida; or Paternal Ambition* (1786): "fled from Arcadia, she could not fly from the apprehended disease"   154

Conclusion: affect, globalism, and modernity from the Seven Years' War to Waterloo   208

Bibliography   224
Index   234

Acknowledgments

I thank the following people and institutions for generous support at various stages in the evolution of this book:

Colleagues at the International Conference on Romanticism and the "Adventurous Wives" Conference at Chawton House shared valuable insights about early versions of Chapters 3 and 4.

The University of Miami offered fellowship support over several summers of my work on this project.

I am grateful to Manchester University Press for recognizing the importance of Gibbes as a novelist worthy of scholarly attention; to Manchester's editorial staff and external reviewers whose support and suggestions have proven invaluable in the revision process; and to the production staff for meticulous care in preparing the manuscript.

I appreciate the following for granting permission to use two previously published articles:

Bucknell University Press for material in Chapter 3, section 1 on *Zoriada*, from my 2020 essay, " 'A little earthly idol to contract your ideas': Global Hermeneutics in Phebe Gibbes's *Zoriada, or, Village Annals* (1786)" [*Romantic Automata: Exhibitions, Figures, Organisms*. Ed. Clason and Demson. 146–64].

European Romantic Review for material in Chapter 3, section 2 on *Hartly House, Calcutta*, from my essay, " 'She had eyes and chose me': Ambivalence and Miscegenation in Phebe Gibbes's Hartly House, Calcutta (1789)" [Vol. 22, 2011. 35–47].

Eighteenth Century Collections Online has been an essential resource in making available archival materials including the texts of Gibbes and her contemporaries.

Michael Franklin for his pioneering research and scholarship on Gibbes and for his collegiality in sharing his insights about her life and literature.

Finally, I thank my readers. Because Gibbes's intricately plotted fiction may be unfamiliar, this monograph contextualizes its discussion of the novels to aid in following elaborate plot developments. My hope is that more modern editions of Gibbes's fiction will be forthcoming.

Abbreviations

ECCO	*Eighteenth Century Collections Online*
FID	free indirect discourse
HHC	*Hartly House, Calcutta*
OED	*Oxford English Dictionary*
VRW	*Vindication of the Rights of Woman*

Introduction

> Would she would go with me into England; though to say truth, there's plenty of whores already. But a pox on 'em, they are such mercenary prodigal whores, that they want such a one as this, that's free and generous, to give 'em good examples.
>
> *(Aphra Behn, The Rover, III. ii. 22–26)*

> All women together ought to let flowers fall upon the tomb of Aphra Behn, for it was she who earned them the right to speak their minds.
>
> *(Virginia Woolf, A Room of One's Own, chapter 4)*

The legacy of Aphra Behn has proven more ambivalent than Virginia Woolf would have known in the 1920s, when curiosity about the writings of women in history sent her to the British Museum. As Jane Spencer notes, despite her influence on early eighteenth-century women writers, known as the "Daughters of Behn," Behn's inheritance by writers of the later eighteenth and nineteenth centuries is "an uneasy one" (1). A half century after Woolf's rallying cry, scholarship began taking up her mantle with a reimagining of literary history known as the "long eighteenth century," whose aim is to bridge the late seventeenth to the early nineteenth centuries by challenging the exclusivity of traditional periodization founded on a small number of English male poets.[1] Though the scholarly revolution brought about through the recovery of noncanonical writers has been extant for nearly a half century, its repercussions continue today.[2]

Though the process of recovering women writers has suggested a matriarchal line beginning with Behn, the murkiness of Behn's legacy speaks to a gap that has remained between the early and late ends of the long eighteenth century. This polarization between the two ends of the period has created a stalemate in attempting to move beyond the ideological paradigm of traditional historical divisions: the Renaissance, Neoclassical, and Romantic periods.[3] One of the most important insights to emerge from the challenge to traditional periodization, discussed later in this Introduction, involves remapping the revolutionary period beginning with the Seven Years' War in the mid-eighteenth century (1756–63) rather than the French or even American Revolution.[4]

This study focuses on the literary career of Phebe Gibbes, whose prolific body of fiction, from 1764 to 1790, coincides with the pivotal era constituting the global revolutionary period that historians have recently begun tracing back to the Seven Years' War.[5] Spanning the revolutionary period at the heart of the long eighteenth century, Gibbes's career bridges the traditionally polarized ends of the period that this study represents respectively by Behn and, in the final chapter, Jane Austen. Gibbes's novels have only recently—and continue to—come to light.[6] It is not surprising that Gibbes's name has not been better known. Most of her novels were discovered in the past thirty years, some having been attributed to contemporaries or remaining anonymous until recently. Six more novels that she claimed have yet to be discovered. Gibbes's best known novel, *Hartly House, Calcutta*, first became known because of the 1984 publication of the Royal Literary Fund archive.[7]

Through the lens of Gibbes, this study traces a trajectory from the broader strokes of seventeenth-century comedy and such early anti-sentimental fiction as that of Eliza Haywood and Charlotte Lennox to Austen's increasingly nuanced narrative voice, irony, and female subjectivity.[8] To challenge the literary history born of the old canon, this study positions Gibbes at the pivotal center of the shift into the modern, situating her fiction as it echoes and modulates seventeenth-century writers, and as it anticipates those writers who have been subsumed into the Romanticism paradigm. She can thus be seen as a lynchpin in a lineage of women writers represented by Behn in the seventeenth century; Eliza Haywood in the early eighteenth century; Wollstonecraft in the late eighteenth century; and Austen in the early nineteenth century.

Gibbes populates her fiction with a range of transgressive female subjectivities: cross-dressing duelists, chambermaids, fugitives, prostitutes, bigamists, and women of color, whose transgressive agency has repercussions for their community, their nation, and a new world order that comes to be associated with modernity.[9] Equally revolutionary, however, are Gibbes's less colorful characters who refuse to fill their mothers' roles in the patriarchal family, themselves pioneering a new world order that, in turn, looks ahead to late Austen. Behind Gibbes's range of female characters, she develops a subversive authorial voice that in turn looks ahead to the free indirect discourse of Austen's late narrative voice.[10]

Struggling to navigate the complexities of modernity, Gibbes's female characters can be seen as a bridge from the colorful women of Behn's drama and the writings of the "Daughters of Behn" to Austen. Thus, the transgressive voices of female authority in Gibbes's fiction have their origins in Behn's drama, where the complication of narrative voice paradoxically begins even before Behn herself turned to writing narrative.[11] As seen in the epigraph at the start of this Introduction, Behn uses satire to condemn misogyny by reproducing it, not only through her male characters but even through the *dramatis personae* that, for instance, lists Lucetta as a "jilting wench" (2). In the passage above from *The Rover*, Blunt, "an English country gentleman," claims authority to judge the Italian Lucetta as "free and generous" by contrast to the "mercenary prodigal whores" in England. Behn's "Restoration" era male contemporaries—the traditional periodization giving primacy to the male writers—connect the prodigal son story to profligacy in "tales that emphasized the importance of paternal or fraternal forgiveness of the spendthrift or greedy child" (Barclay 316). Behn enacts a revolution in gender even on the linguistic level by embedding the popular story in the context of Blunt, a British man, using the term with swaggering authority to describe an English woman as a prodigal whore.[12] Blunt's assessment of Lucetta as a good woman because she is free with her sexuality thus reflects a historical shift away from the story of the prodigal son who has squandered his wealth, redeeming himself when he returns home repentant. At its foundation, gendering prodigality female reflects the double bind of a woman who is expected to embody virtue by staying within the domestic sphere rather than wandering in the way of the prodigal son. Behn's usage thus underscores the double standard behind the "prodigal" British woman, chastised for being "mercenary" with her sexuality. The shift in gendering prodigality from a man squandering his wealth to a woman driving a hard bargain in selling her sexual wealth, hence degrading her value, deepens the paradox at the heart of Behn's portrayal of Blunt as "an object only of scorn and laughter" (Spencer, "Introduction" to *The Rover*, xv). Satirizing misogyny's double standard that makes prodigality a female condition, Behn heralds the women writers after her who echo this female prodigality well into the nineteenth century. The Conclusion to this study returns to Behn's gendering of prodigality from the hindsight of Gibbes's developing voice and as it anticipates Austen's own gendering of prodigality.[13]

Bridging the divide: women writers polarized by periodization

Centralizing Gibbes's career at the pivotal point of the long eighteenth century helps to rethink two interrelated ways that scholarship has been stymied in recontouring this literary history. The first involves scholarship's polarized view of Behn's legacy. Beyond Woolf's celebration of her legacy, Behn has more recently been seen as a "colossal and enduring embarrassment to the generations of women who followed her into the literary marketplace" (Gallagher 65). By extension, focusing on Gibbes at the center of the period addresses a second scholarly impasse between those who focus on the female agency of the "Daughters of Behn"—largely one of sexual empowerment— against those who position Mary Wollstonecraft's *Vindication of the Rights of Woman* (*VRW*) as pioneering modern feminism by offering the first analysis of patriarchy's systemic repression of women's intellect. However, the conflicting lineages that these two positions create—one of sexual empowerment, the other of sexual repression—can be addressed by considering Wollstonecraft's literary career as beginning and ending with fiction that struggled to balance her biographical embrace of erotic empowerment as opposed to *VRW*'s polemical repression of female desire.

Two studies illustrate this implicit historical division between the eras of Behn and of Wollstonecraft. In her 1995 article, "Aphra Behn—Whom Mary Wollstonecraft Did Not Read," Janet Todd ponders the apparent 100-year lacuna between Behn's representation of female subjectivity amid a culture of misogynistic attacks on women writers as "whores"—as seen in the passage above from *The Rover*—and Wollstonecraft's late eighteenth-century advocacy of women's rights in a culture defined by "the sentimental construction of woman"; Todd speculates about how Wollstonecraft's writing might have changed had she known Behn's strategy of using "the image of the seducing and manipulating woman ... to advantage, realizing its constructed quality" (153).[14] In the second study, five years later, Jane Spencer provides a path to addressing Todd's question. Spencer suggests that, though by the latter half of the period, Behn's influence waned following the "Daughters of Behn" who were writing in the earlier part of the eighteenth century, from "our perspective it is easy to see a kind of parallel between Behn and Wollstonecraft: both were challenging the limits on women's cultural role imposed in their time"; Spencer continues, "[W]omen writers were no longer looking back to Behn" by the latter end of the long eighteenth century (*Afterlife* 184).

Through Gibbes's fiction, this study challenges the notion that Behn was an embarrassment to later women writers. This point may best be illustrated through Behn's endowing prostitutes with subjectivity, one of many elements of Behn's writing that Gibbes and others both inherited and shaped in their own fiction. As Catherine Gallagher has noted, Behn "managed to create the effect of an inaccessible authenticity of the very image of prostitution. In doing so, she capitalized on a commonplace slur that probably kept many less ingenious women out of the literary marketplace" (69). Though Gallagher argues that Behn may have become "a problematic figure for later women writers" for her "bawdiness and the author-whore metaphor she celebrated," Behn's influence can be seen in Gibbes's own pattern of giving creative agency to female characters who are either literally prostitutes or are seen by their community as tainted sexually for reasons this study takes up in the chapters that follow (Gallagher 84).[15]

At the other end of the Behn/Wollstonecraft polarization is the traditional focus on *VRW* as representative of Wollstonecraft's impact on the path towards modern feminism, as noted above. To make such a case, scholarship has divorced Wollstonecraft from both her precursors and her contemporaries by focusing on *VRW*'s argument for a "revolution in female manners" that extols the "virtue" of the chaste, educated wife devoted to her domestic duties (49). *VRW* has thus been taken out of its context in the middle of Wollstonecraft's career cut short by her early death. Wollstonecraft's two novels, *Mary, A Novel* and the posthumously published *Maria or the Wrongs of Woman*, frame her literary life.[16] Thus, scholarship has tended to use large brushstrokes to contrast Wollstonecraft and women writers who both preceded her and were her contemporaries. However, several important elements of Wollstonecraft's life and her unfinished or unpublished writing suggest that the persona of *VRW* represents a moment—albeit an important one—in Wollstonecraft's complex and ambivalent literary life. Though before her death at thirty-eight Wollstonecraft was at work on several manuscripts, she had not yet navigated the divide between her private embrace of free love and the polemical voice of chaste rationalism aimed at a repressive patriarchy.[17] As Clemit and Walker note, Wollstonecraft "could no more deny her sensuality than repress her intellect" (18, 28).[18] Wollstonecraft and other polemicists were more cognizant of earlier writers who had embraced female authority in a spectrum of contexts—creative, sociopolitical, and epistemological, as well as in a spectrum of tonalities—satirical, ironic, sentimental, and polemical than has been acknowledged.

No fewer than forty years before *VRW* attacked the sentimental novel's marriage plot for its role in keeping women subjugated, Gibbes's fiction came to represent a range of women struggling for financial independence to liberate themselves from abusive marriages. This study's focus on Gibbes as a precursor to modern feminism thus aims to qualify the monolithic role often accorded *VRW*, with the hope that the gap between Wollstonecraft's public persona that she fabricated in her polemical prose and the private persona of her memoirs and personal letters can be addressed vis-à-vis Wollstonecraft's growing awareness of the novel's potential significance in bringing about a new agency for women. While Wollstonecraft felt the need in *VRW* to denounce sentimental novels appears to have been a strategy to make a stronger case for a more rigorous education for women, her positive review of Gibbes's fiction implicitly distinguishes novels working against the sentimental tradition from those perpetuating it.[19] Despite *VRW*'s categorical reversal of the reason/sensibility gender binary, with its argument that it is male sensibility that sexualizes women and thereby represses female reason, Wollstonecraft's praise of Gibbes's fiction suggests that what she finds admirable in Gibbes is her nuanced and frank representation of patriarchy's oppression of women, as the following chapters detail. That Gibbes does so through female characters representing a spectrum of social classes, nationalities, and moral dilemmas regarding the stigma of the unchaste woman calls for a more nuanced response to the Behn/Wollstonecraft polarity. Gibbes's fiction refuses the constraints to which Wollstonecraft held her persona in *VRW* whose aim is twofold: to persuade her male readers to educate women and to scold women away from passivity in dallying with sentimental novels. By contrast, Gibbes's fiction challenges a range of masculine expressions of misogyny, including a pattern of scenes of rape or attempted rape by men who euphemistically refer to their exploits as "seduction."

Theorizing the long eighteenth century

The various methodologies revolving around cultural studies and new historicism have contributed to the potential for a reimagined historical, epistemic, and literary bridge into modernity. Of the recent approaches to scholarship on eighteenth-century fiction, affect theory has been a productive means to study the contemporaneity of an emerging sensibility and the erosion of patrimony.[20] For example, Katie Barclay discusses the "strict settlement" debate as it relates to the history of emotions beginning in the seventeenth century:

> In a legal context where long-term entails (restrictions on the use and inheritance of land) were prohibited, the strict settlement was a legal device that allowed landowners to limit their heirs' control of the family estate. Like an entail, it established the appropriate heir and removed many of her or, typically his, rights to the use and disposal of property, protecting the long-term family interest over that of the individual. (309)

Most relevant for this study, Barclay notes that "the English family saw a reduction of patriarchal power due to the rise of the 'affective family'" (309). This approach promises a means to bridge Behn's authorial creativity to that of later writers of the revolutionary period, as the patriarchal family gives way to what Stuart Curran, pioneering the recovery of women's writing during the period, has called the "cult of sensibility" (195).

Nevertheless, even scholarship founded on affect theory has largely elided the center of the period, maintaining satire and sentiment as mutually exclusive categories. Within her own career, Behn exhibits a complex interplay of these apparent binaries. As Adrienne Eastwood notes in her nuanced approach to Behn's 1670 *The Forced Marriage*, this earliest of Behn's plays is "the human damage caused when parents forced their children, particularly their daughters, to marry against their free choice"; yet, as Eastwood notes, this theme is "present in many of her later plays as well" (8).[21] A concern voiced about affect theory—true for any theoretical construct—is that it is often been applied without historical context.[22] Relevant for the present study, for instance, Stephen Ahern warns that, "as readers of cultural artifacts or of social practices, we are beckoned to articulate a more complete phenomenology of the aesthetic and of lived experience"; Ahern is concerned that "such a focus may vacate potentials for political agency beyond mere celebration of immediate (unmediated) affective engagement, and so in the end reinforce rather than interrogate a metaphysics of presence that both the writer of sensibility 200 years ago and the affect theorist now would seem to embrace" (281).[23] This study too underscores the importance of attending to the relationship between historical context and affect during this revolutionary period as the intersection of the sociopolitical and the development of subjectivity, particular through women writers.

Though scholarship founded on new historicism and cultural studies has been instrumental to this study, it reintegrates textual analysis, an element of scholarship jettisoned with the upending of both formalism and deconstruction. A return to the study of textuality free from the hermeticism of those earlier approaches adds greater nuance to cultural and historical studies. For instance, the question raised earlier of how Behn might have transformed Wollstonecraft and other late eighteenth- and early nineteenth-century writers need not be rhetorical: tracing the permutations of language—particularly as it is gendered, as in the case of female prodigality—exposes a common concern with the double standard embedded in the patriarchal structures of the period.[24]

Gibbes, literary matriarchy, and the evolution of a female authorial voice

Gibbes's fiction portrays female characters whose sensibility does not preclude but rather inflects their rational revolt against a range of patriarchal institutions, including patrimony, marriage, jurisprudence, colonialism, nationalism, and religion. Gibbes creates a diffuse authorial voice whose relationship to the subjectivities of its characters and its complex narrative structures represents a literary historical transformation involving female resistance to these forms of patriarchy. With the premise that two of the defining characteristics of the long eighteenth century are the twin masculinist phenomena of sexual aggression and economic exploitation, then, Gibbes's fiction provides a link in the chain of women's writing that represents female agency. Complicating her position in this legacy, Gibbes's representations of women's agency evolve within and throughout her career. Gibbes inherited the satire of her forebears, including Behn's drama as well as the subsequent novels of such writers as Eliza Haywood and Charlotte Lennox, both of whom pilloried sentimental fiction. Gibbes's fiction transmutes their representation of misogyny in increasingly nuanced representations of gender and sexuality that, in turn, anticipate Austen's late fiction. Throughout her career, Gibbes represents sexual aggression towards women by men across social classes, her female characters exhibiting shrewdness in extricating themselves from misogynistic attacks.[25] That Wollstonecraft reviewed Gibbes positively, that Gibbes builds on Behn, and that Austen appears to have admired Wollstonecraft all suggest a legacy of women's voices as stepping stones towards modernity.[26] Especially in the early novels, Gibbes echoes Behn in often direct ways, suggesting that the relationship between nineteenth-century writers to their female precursors is more complex than might have appeared even in the not-too-distant past of the 1990s.

Gibbes's career exposes another important dimension of scholarship of the long eighteenth century: the revolutionary period beginning with the Seven Years' War (1756–63) and continuing with global revolutions traditionally associated with the Romantic era. As Hamish Scott notes of this history, scholars must

> return to viewing the Seven Years' War through the eyes of those who lived through it, sometimes fought in it, and above all struggled to cope with its legacies. We need to think about the war's long-term consequences, as well as its short-term impact and medium-term results which have often monopolized attention, in other words to view its repercussions from the perspective of the next political generation. (425)[27]

In literary studies, this historical reassessment entails shifting the focus to the center of the long eighteenth century, during that critical transition globally, nationally, and in all the ways that such revolutionary upheaval manifests, including gender, sexuality, the sociopolitical, and literary form from genre to linguistics. Gibbes's career is a complex intersection of evolving female subjectivities and a patriarchal world transformed by sociopolitical revolution.

At the chronological center of this lineage of women writing during the long eighteenth century, Gibbes is thus more than Janus-faced. Gesturing both back to literature of the late seventeenth century and ahead to that of the early nineteenth century, Gibbes's fiction also shapes and is shaped by the continuities and developments of the period. Her novels offer a fresh perspective on Britain's role in shifting economic and social structures globally during this pivotal time, her novels ushering in the emergence of female subjectivity new to the literature of the mid-eighteenth century and, therefore, revealing the roots of modernity traditionally attributed to canonical Romanticism. Anticipating the ambivalence of nineteenth-century writers, Gibbes represents masculinist revolutions of the period as substitutions of one form of patriarchy for another, from the weakening of patrilineal entitlement to British imperialism.[28]

The recurring figure of the female outcast in Gibbes's fiction embodies a creative and often subversive energy. Gibbes aligns these characters with the authorial while representing them as at odds with the narrators who judge them. The first of these female outcasts in Gibbes's fiction is the complex figure of Penelope the prostitute in *The Adventures of Francis Clive*, the subject of Chapter 1. Behind the narrator's platitudes regarding Penelope's immorality that ultimately spins out of control when she murders her husband, Penelope has an irresistible gift for colorful self-fashioning as she scorns her johns and their wives. As a mid-eighteenth-century female writer, Gibbes seems to find liberation in granting Penelope's voice power over the narrative; in this sense, she is a parody of Homer's Penelope, who weaves and unweaves her shroud to keep her would-be suitors at bay till Odysseus can return home to rescue her and reassert his patriarchal rule. Penelope—the name itself most likely an alias—takes on a dizzying number of personae during the novel, a ploy of female self-fashioning reminiscent of *Fantomina*, Haywood's satire of the generic sentimental novel. Though Haywood's nameless protagonist also assumes a sequence of personae, beginning with that of a prostitute named Fantomina, she does not do so out of desperation due to poverty. Instead, Fantomina is an aristocrat, curious about what she observes below of the far more colorful drama in the theater's "pit" where wealthy young men dally with prostitutes rather than stay aloft in the expensive seats with the insipid belles Fantomina soon abandons. For Haywood's character, curiosity gives way to an obsession with keeping her lover satisfied through a variety of personae, and then turning her personae against each other. She is ultimately punished for her fall as only a woman can be: her pregnancy is the *deus ex machina* that ends her charade with her mother confining her to a convent. Gibbes's Penelope appears to build on Fantomina's dazzling creativity, though Penelope is more psychologically prismatic, both abused by and abuser of a social structure that has impoverished her and denied her an education until she learns to use the fraudulent methods of the men who have exploited her, exploiting men in turn for money. By the end of the novel, her greed leads to her murder of her husband, then to her execution. Though the narrator offers the story as a morality tale, in the larger context of the novel, as Chapter 1 of this study details, Gibbes creates a counterpoint between Penelope and Charlotte Clive, the wife of the eponymous Francis, Penelope's john, thus complicating the facile moralizing of the narrator.

Penelope is one of a range of Gibbes's female characters who use their wits in a world of oppressive patriarchy. In her later novel, *Zoriada*, Gibbes creates a redeemed figure of female self-fashioning through the paradoxically nameless eponymous protagonist who withholds her identity even from the reader, as discussed in Chapter 3. Between *Francis Clive* and *Zoriada*, Gibbes's writing evolves in tandem with a complicating world order, her representation of female authorial power increasingly inflected during her career. The study traces this arc, from the prostitute who literally spars with the cross-dressing wife of the eponymous Francis Clive; the young women of *The American Fugitive* who use their wits to escape the abuses of priests in the convent; a young English woman in Anglo-India who falls in love with a Brahmin priest in *Hartly House, Calcutta*; the Indian Zoriada, upon whom English villagers project their moral judgments and desires; to the eponymous Elfrida, who inadvertently commits bigamy, forcing her to rise above the shame that her hypocritical and entitled first husband exacts upon her.

Diffusing the authorial voice

Through a range of modalities characterizing her career, Gibbes complicates what Janet Todd has identified as the stock characters of sentimental fiction: women as "archetypal victims" who are the "chaste and suffering woman ... elevated into redemptive death" and the "sensitive, benevolent man whose feelings are too exquisite for the acquisitiveness, vulgarity and selfishness of his world" (*Sensibility* 4). As noted earlier, Gibbes anticipates and complicates Wollstonecraft's indictment of sentimental fiction as responsible for so many young women's influence by "the reveries of the stupid novelists" (*VRW* 192). Wollstonecraft gives the example of the daughter of an acquaintance who "affected a simplicity bordering on folly; and with a simper would utter the most immodest remarks and questions, the full meaning of which she had learned whilst secluded from the world" (194). Of course, Wollstonecraft was not the first to articulate the dangerous influence of sentimental novels on young women. Charlotte Lennox's 1752 *The Female Quixote* satirizes women's desire for romantic adventure through her protagonist, Arabella, "supposing Romances were real Pictures of Life" due to the "perfect Retirement she lived in" (4). Arabella takes the illusion of romance novels' worlds literally to the point of imperiling herself: "[S]he was taught to believe, that Love was the ruling Principle of the World" (4). While the novel has been read as a precursor to Wollstonecraft's warning against the danger of novel-reading in *VRW*, Lennox's authorial voice suggests her sly enjoyment at calling the reader's bluff, as though to say that we are under her authorial spell in imagining Arabella's plight brought on by her imaginative act of literalizing her reading. This metanarrative sleight of hand is an important aspect of the literary legacy that Gibbes carries forward, though Gibbes's metanarrative deepens overt satire into a more oblique irony. Thus, by shifting the trajectory away from Wollstonecraft's *VRW*, we can posit an emergent voice of female authorial agency that in turn complicates Wollstonecraft's own place in this legacy.[29]

Gibbes's place in the evolution of British fiction can thus be seen through her fashioning of an authorial voice distinct from that of her narrators and letter writers. She endows with metanarrative authority her female protagonists as well as minor female characters including not only pariahs such as the prostitute Penelope in *Francis Clive* discussed earlier but caretakers such as *Elfrida*'s illiterate storyteller, Hannah. Such an authorial strategy can be seen to anticipate free indirect discourse, the hallmark of modernity because of its prismatic power to shift in and out of omniscience and limited subjectivities.[30] Throughout her career, Gibbes embraces the modulated voice of irony over that of satire. Her authorial voice emerges behind those of her unreliable narrators and letter writers through two devices connected through female creativity: first, Gibbes uses metanarrative to undermine the authority of her narrators, characters referring to a providential power or describing themselves as actors in a theatrical production; second, Gibbes's heroines face a conflict between identity imposed by external forces, such as ancestry and culture, and their own subjectivity.

In the third phase of her career, Gibbes's fiction culminates with the courageous, self-created agency of her late protagonists that she aligns with her own authorial creativity. Gibbes thus anticipates the interiority of narrative voice traditionally attributed to Romanticism. Ultimately, such connection between the female protagonist and the authorial voice at the expense of an unreliable narrator is characteristic of modernity as the world grows larger, more complex, and more fraught with perils for women regarding their subject position.[31] In the course of her career, therefore, Gibbes creates female characters who inhabit a fragile space as they struggle for autonomy. Gibbes endows them with increasing psychological depth amid Britain's growing global empowerment and shifting social structure.

Yet despite the growth of Gibbes's authorial voice, even her earliest novels anticipate a post-Enlightenment interest in the mind as both creative and at times self-subverting, characteristics of modernity. Gibbes can be seen as a pioneer in representing the psychology of her characters, delving deeper into the subject of the perverse than her precursors had. Though the term "perverse" had existed in English long before the eighteenth century with a plethora of meanings revolving around immorality and particularly its noun form, "pervert," as one who behaves with sexual impropriety, Gibbes's use has a central, psychological component. The perverse in Gibbes's fiction suggests the tendency to incriminate oneself that predates even Coleridge's interest in psychoanalysis—a term he coined—particularly as it manifests through the self-incriminating act, a psychology that further evolves into Poe's "imp of the perverse" and, in the twentieth century, to *parapraxis*, or the "Freudian slip."[32] Gibbes's novels dissect the perverse with a deepening sense of the connection between the hypocrisy of those labeling others as perverse, exemplified in even her earliest fiction and becoming yet more nuanced as her career developed. Thus, in *Francis Clive*, the Irish lord who is employer of the newly married Clive attempts to rape Clive's wife. When he fails, he "curse[s] his perverse stars for admiring a little obstinate girl, whose education alone was the bar to his success" (I. 64). As the authorial voice behind her narrator, Gibbes is that providential fate that the lord sees as "perverse," for she creates a world in which an educated woman outsmarts an entitled man, liberating herself from his assumption that he is entitled to dominate her.[33] In the same novel, Gibbes also explores the perverse as it comes to be known later through Poe's "imp of the perverse," when Clive, later having gotten involved with Penelope, the prostitute, mixes up letters to his wife and to his cousin whom he is asking to lie for him, the *parapraxis* forcing him to confess his adultery to his wife.

Mapping Gibbes's career: metanarrative as providence in the margins

Because Gibbes's fiction engages political issues of global reach, from the Seven Years' War (1756–63) to the spread of revolution and colonialism, studying her career contributes to a reassessment of British literary dissent commonly characterized as instigated by the 1789 liberation of political prisoners in the Bastille. Following Gibbes's evolving concerns with the intersection of empire, nationalism, and female creative authority, this study traces three major periods of Gibbes's fiction that reflect the parallel between the growing intricacy of her craft and her representation of an increasingly complicated socioeconomic world. Chapter 1 examines Gibbes's first phase through focus on one of her first two novels, *The Adventures of Francis Clive* (1764).[34] Through often pointed references, the novel reveals its influence by both Behn's drama and such fiction satirizing the sentimental tradition as Haywood's *Fantomina* and Lennox's *Female Quixote*. Gibbes's early novels can be characterized through their influence by the theatricality of early fiction seen through their use of metanarrative, including direct allusions to Restoration-era theater and plots involving characters watching performances. Characters even watch other characters watching performances, as in Gibbes's later novel, *Elfrida*, in which Wilmot, the man who loves the eponymous heroine, studies her face as she watches a play whose subject is a man who, much like Wilmot's rival, Elfrida's husband, Ellison, sells her to pay his gambling debts. Just as Behn had complicated the stock characters of the comedy of her day by having women engineer marriage plots, Gibbes destabilizes not just the plotting of the narrative line but the romantic hero himself. Thus, for instance, Gibbes refers to Behn's *Lucky Chance* through both Francis Clive's gambling and through a subplot in which a minor character tries to sell his sister for military advancement. The theme becomes relevant again in Gibbes's later novels such as *Elfrida*, with Ellison's attempt to pay back his gambling debts by offering his creditor the sexual favors of his wife, Elfrida.[35]

Even in this earliest phase, Gibbes exhibits a sophistication that looks ahead to her own subsequent fiction as well as to that of Austen. While Gibbes's satire echoes Behn's repudiation of misogyny, Gibbes's career can be described as developing an increasingly complex spectrum of women's varied responses to the predations of men in power. Gibbes's early novels thus look ahead to the yet more nuanced subjectivity of her transatlantic novels, the subjects of Chapters 3 and 4. The 1764 *Francis Clive* is multilayered in tone, from broadly drawn satire to the more nuanced irony that becomes the hallmark of Gibbes's later fiction. *Francis Clive* subverts the sentimental genre with a darker narrative of female subjugation, beginning with Clive's father impregnating the young nurse of his dying wife. The young woman dies after attempting to abort the pregnancy. This act haunts the novel through to its hollow comedic resolution. All the men are tinged to varying degrees by their oppression of women whose responses, from cross-dressing to prostituting themselves, accord with their social class and education.

Gibbes's 1778 novel, *The American Fugitive: or, Friendship in a Nunnery*, the subject of Chapter 2, is a turning point in her career. Through the novel's transatlantic scope as it reflects the upheaval of the period between the Seven Years' War and the American Revolution, Gibbes expands the parameters of her earlier novels, globally and intellectually. Gibbes here dissects nationalism and revolution in relation to gender, representing the repressive forces of patriarchy through the microcosm of a French convent. The novel is pivotal generically as well, Gibbes subverting the marriage plot through the intricate double perspective reflected in the title. Each woman in the convent makes a different choice when liberated from the predations they have endured there. In this novel, the French Catholic convent represents the larger intersection of women ostracized, scared, duped, punished, under the guise of paternalistic protection. Though the novel culminates with the marriage of two of the central characters, Gibbes balances them with the third central character who chooses not to marry. The novel represents the centrality of gender during the pivotal period leading to the French Revolution, particularly in the relationship among England, France, and America, as the title of the novel suggests. Gibbes connects the title's two halves (the order of which changed in its two editions) by relating the English perspective of the war in America to the Catholic Relief Act of the same year.

Chapter 3 focuses on Gibbes's Anglo-Indian novels, *Zoriada* (1786) and *Hartly House, Calcutta* (1789), as the culmination of Gibbes's engagement with the intellectual, philosophical, and political concerns of this watershed period in Anglo-India. The two novels portray British colonialism in India from two perspectives: in *Hartly House*, a young English woman arrives in India intending to marry an East India Company man but, witnessing the predations inflicted on the indigenous Indians by the English, decries colonialism, embracing the Vedic philosophy she learns from a young Hindu priest. In *Zoriada*, Gibbes reverses course by representing England from the perspective of a young Indian woman. Objectified, demonized, and eroticized by provincial English villagers, Zoriada tells the horrific story of her family's massacre and her own escape from colonial India. The novel is thus a powerful demonstration of Gibbes's anticipation of modern feminism and indictment of British imperialism from a non-western perspective.

Chapter 4 focuses on *Elfrida*, written the same year as *Zoriada*, the two novels sharing a contrast between provincialism and global expanse. *Elfrida* includes voyages to the East and West Indies and to America. While *Zoriada* sets indigenous Indian culture against English provincialism, however, *Elfrida* represents British colonialism without the perspective of the subaltern present in *Zoriada* and *Hartly House*. *Elfrida* instead represents the continuity of patriarchy across generations, from provincial entitlement to the masculinist aggression underlying nation building and colonialism. Whereas Zoriada is an Indian woman who appears in an English village for reasons Gibbes withholds from the reader, Elfrida, of English and Welsh ancestry, represents the English/Welsh woman as an instrument of patriarchy in its interrelated guises surrounding lineage and economic exploitation. In *Elfrida*, the distinction between provincial life and globalism is gendered: Elfrida's rival lovers, Ellison and Wilmot, travel back and forth between the East and West Indies and America, Ellison engaging in war to escape his crimes, Wilmot, pursuing fame, wealth, and retribution across the globe. Elfrida's orbit is between London and the two areas of her patriarchal home in Wales: "The Grange," where her mother grew up, and a place her mother's two evil cousins call "Arcadia," where they raise Elfrida. Despite the two novels' differences, however, Zoriada and Elfrida are acted upon not only by fathers and husbands, but by children and those of the lower class for whom the two protagonists represent an unattainable ideal, these women fulfilling their dreams and expectations.

The Conclusion to the study synthesizes the preceding chapters' exploration of Gibbes's evolving relationship to her literary forebears with her anticipation of the writing traditionally categorized as Romantic. Perhaps most important in Gibbes's prolepsis of late Austen is her representation of female interiority amid sociopolitical unrest; Gibbes's 1786 *Elfrida*, set during the French and Indian War, gestures ahead to Austen's 1817 *Persuasion*, set between the 1805 Battle of Trafalgar and the 1815 Battle of Waterloo. Both protagonists navigate a British patriarchy shifting from aristocratic entitlement to nautically driven military engagement and colonialism. Gesturing back to Behn's comedy, *The Lucky Chance*, the Conclusion explores how Gibbes complicates the potential for inadvertent bigamy by deepening the crisis for Elfrida, who commits bigamy, raising a family before she discovers that her first husband is alive. *Elfrida* simultaneously gestures ahead to Austen through uncanny similarities in literary devices, including anticlimax and the love triangle; the sociopolitical importance of the navy; and wordplay, such as the ubiquitous appearances in both novels of the gendered double meanings of the economic terms, "tender" and "alienation." These parallels challenge the traditional reading of Austen's last novel as embracing the new canonical Romanticism through its subjectivity.

Notes

1 Beyond the parameters of this study, the recovery of noncanonical writers extends back to scholarship on the "early Modern" period that challenges the traditional eras of the Middle Ages and Renaissance founded on early canonical literature.
2 The new periodization has explored ways to examine literary connections among canonical and noncanonical writers rather than segregate them from the previously canonized writers. Though the name "Daughters of Behn" plays upon the "Sons of Ben," a lineage of male writers influenced by Ben Jonson, Spencer complicates Behn's legacy in her chapter on the "Sons of Behn" (*Afterlife*, 102–42). I explore the later connections among Mary Robinson, S.T. Coleridge, and Mary Shelley in *Rethinking the Romantic Era*.
3 Discussion of Behn's legacy has typically focused on the generation or two immediately following Behn. Jeslyn Medoff writes that the women writing in "the generation after Aphra Behn were strongly affected by society's reception (or rejection) of her, well aware that they were writing in a new era that required different methods for coping with the problem of combining femaleness and fame" (35), and Jacqueline Pearson discusses Behn's influence on "women writers of the late seventeenth and early eighteenth centuries" (234). For more on

the scholarship of the long eighteenth century see Judith Hawley, who identifies the parameters of the long eighteenth century (1660–1830) beginning with Behn's *The Rover*, and Jane Spencer, who details Behn's context in Restoration England (Introduction, *The Rover*, xvi–xix). The dearth of studies focusing on the bridge between the two ends of the period is implicit in the historical ranges of two studies, Michael McKeon's, 1600–1740, and Edward Copeland's *Women Writing About Money*, focusing on women's fiction from 1790–1820.

4 As Hamish Scott notes, "The eighteenth century has conventionally been seen as the final phase of early modern Europe, an epoch when the forces of tradition remained stronger than the elements of change. Modernity, whether political, social, economic, cultural, or indeed military, began during its final decades in the Enlightenment and French Revolution" (424). See the discussion later in this Introduction of Scott's study.

5 See Franklin's Introduction and Bibliography for a detailed account of what is known regarding Gibbes's authorship (2019). In the bibliography, I have added to his entries those that are now available on *ECCO*. Regarding the novels on which this study focuses, *Friendship in a Nunnery: or, The American Fugitive* was published in 1778 and again in 1784, the latter reversing title and subtitle; *Elfrida* was published anonymously, but Joseph Johnson attested to her authorship of the novel. *Zoriada* was misattributed to Anne Hughes. *Hartly House* was misattributed to the narrator, Sophia Goldbourne. The only edition of *HHC* included here is Franklin's, whose bibliography not only gives the most current status of archival research on Gibbes's fiction but includes her letter to the Royal Literary Fund: BL MSS (2:74).

6 See the first section of this study's bibliography for information currently known about her corpus. Gibbes claimed over twenty novels, at least six more than are now known. Though this study focuses on Gibbes's prolific output of novels representing the exploitation of women on multiple levels, others are worthy of inclusion, such as Frances Sheridan, whose 1764 novel, *Memoirs of Miss Sidney Bidulph*, has significant plot elements that anticipate Gibbes and work as well in counterpoint to the novels Wollstonecraft decries in *VRW*.

7 Michael Franklin's Introduction to his edition of *Hartly House* gives a detailed biography as well as discussion of Gibbes's anticipation of "the social protest of novelist such as Mary Hays, Mary Robinson, Anna Maria Bennett, and Mary Wollstonecraft herself" (xv). Jennie Batchelor argues that Gibbes used the Royal Literary Fund to advantage: "Using her refusal to put her name to her novels as evidence that she was a 'domestic woman' of a 'withdrawing turn of temper', Gibbes made several successful claims on the Royal Literary Fund's generosity, although ironically she had to enjoin Joseph Johnson to confirm her authorship of her novel *Elfrida* (1786) before the charity would release any monies" (*Women's Work* 227–28, n. 88).

8 Among recent new perspectives of the relationship of economics and fiction, or the converging of "sentimentalism and capitalism" in the eighteenth century, see Binhammer's engagement with "critical finance studies" in *Downward Mobility* (7). Binhammer connects the contemporary interest in tales of

profligacy to narrative techniques themselves, many of which are central to this study's discussion of Gibbes's fiction, including the use of embedded narrative. Binhammer's third chapter gives a detailed discussion of embedded narratives in sentimental novels (pp. 85ff).

9 Though in the twenty-first century, the terms "sex-worker" and "sex-work" are preferred, I use the terms "prostitute" and "prostitution" as they were used during the long eighteenth century to reflect the stigma that they held for women.

10 See the section later in this Introduction, "Diffusing the authorial voice," for a more detailed discussion of the evolution of free indirect discourse (FID).

11 Though issues of gender and sexuality shift over the long eighteenth century, Behn's career itself complicates the static label of Restoration satire vis-à-vis authorial voice, a topic outside the parameters of this study. It is worth noting, however, that Behn's late works draw on her earliest social satire, as seen, for instance, in *The Forced Marriage* (1670). Adrienne Eastman observes that the theme of children forced "to marry against their free choice" deepens in Behn's late works, the tragicomedy, *The Widow Ranter* and Behn's prose narrative, *Oroonoko*, both expanding her social consciousness with a new interest in the relationship between "imperial power and revolt" in "the colonized Americas" (Eastman 8–9).

12 For the biblical parable, see Luke 15:11–23.

13 As detailed in this study's Conclusion, Austen's *Persuasion* thematizes the idea of the daughter's refusal to return home. As its example of the nineteenth-century usage of the term, the *OED* uses Austen's letter to her sister in which she refers to her own prodigality from her father's perspective: "My father will be so good as to fetch home his prodigal daughter from town."

14 For more on Wollstonecraft's conflict regarding affect, see Temple on Wollstonecraft's "agitation": "Wollstonecraft both seemed to capitalize on the association of genius and agitation and to have been instrumental in constructing the relation" (372). Although outside the parameters of this study, one means of addressing the apparent gap between Behn and Wollstonecraft regarding affect is by attending to the mutual antipathy of Wollstonecraft and Anna Barbauld, as seen in the sequence of Wollstonecraft's criticism of Barbauld's "To a Lady" as shameful coming from the pen of an educated woman, followed by Barbauld's "The Rights of Woman," attacking Wollstonecraft for claiming that woman can be a better companion to her husband if she is educated: "[s]eparate rights are lost in mutual love." While Barbauld sees in the Wollstonecraft of *VRW* a rigid anti-sensualist, Wollstonecraft's subjectivity is an amalgam of the voices of her prose that suggests a writer more ambivalent and fluid than the single text of *VRW*.

15 This representation of prostitution is true for many other writers during the period, outside the parameters of this study though significant to the larger discussion, from the satire of Eliza Haywood's earlier novella, *Fantomina*, to William Blake's empathic representations of the figures of Wollstonecraft in the poem "Mary" and of Oothoon in *Visions of the Daughters of Albion*; both

women embrace their sexuality but neither can rise above the social norms of female chastity and the virgin/whore binary. Blake represents both female figures as self-divided: a visionary woman tragically confined by the oppression of British patriarchy. For more on Blake's relationship to Wollstonecraft, see various entries in my *Guide to Blake's Cosmology* (196–99, 222–23, 225–26).

16 Though beyond the scope of this study, this argument about Wollstonecraft as novelist as well as prose polemicist recurs at various points in the study to demonstrate the important strands of this matriarchal legacy extending from Behn to Austen.

17 As Godwin notes in discussing the contrast between Wollstonecraft's *Vindication* and her *Letters from Norway*, "The occasional harshness and ruggedness of character, that diversify her Vindication of the Rights of Woman, [sic] here totally disappear. If ever there was a book calculated to make a man in love with its author, this appears to me to be the book" (95). Godwin's publication of her memoirs scandalized their contemporaries despite his intention to share and explain the complex subjectivity behind the writer. In the words of one contemporary review, Wollstonecraft had "erred fatally—but it is an error too common with her sex: and to which women of sensibility and intellect are peculiarly liable" (qtd. in Clemit and Luria 33).

18 That Wollstonecraft visited Helen Maria Williams in France is further evidence that the authorial voice Wollstonecraft projects in *VRW* does not speak to the complexity of a persona that was evolving at the time of her death. Williams herself was condemned in misogynistic terms for her continued support of the Revolution even by her earlier admirers, most famously Sir Horace Walpole who called her a "scribbling trollop" (Gravil 64). Once extolled in England for her poetry and whose *Letters from France* had been read in the early phase of the French Revolution, Williams was denounced in misogynistic terms for her support of the Revolution.

19 See Franklin on the reviews of Gibbes's work ("Introduction" xx–xxii). Though Wollstonecraft would not have known Gibbes as author of *Hartly House*, as Franklin remarks, Wollstonecraft's "appreciative review" of the novel, appearing in Joseph Johnson's *Analytical Review,* praises the letters as "written with a degree of vivacity which renders them very amusing, even when they are merely descriptive, and the young reader will see, rather than listen to the instruction they contain" (qtd. in Franklin xxii).

20 See, for instance, the special issue of *The Eighteenth Century*, 58:3 (Fall 2017), entitled *Emotion, Affect, and the Eighteenth Century*, particularly Hultquist's "Introductory Essay," 273–80. www.jstor.org/stable/10.2307/90013398.

21 Michael McKeon observes the connection between the sexual violence and economic exploitation in "forced marriages," as Behn and Haywood represent them, and "the threat of aristocratic rape as violent [expression] of corruption" (258). The section of McKeon's book, "Gendering of Ideology," includes discussion of Behn's and Haywood's depictions of forced marriages vis-à-vis his dialectical reading of literary history (258–65). It is therefore important to qualify such recent criticisms of McKeon as perpetuating a masculinist representation of the period as in Batchelor and Kaplan's Introduction to their 2005 essay

collection on the long eighteenth century where discussion of early scholarship on the literary "all-male pantheon" includes McKeon's "influential Marxist revision"; Batchelor and Kaplan set these earlier studies against such treatments as Nancy Armstrong's 1987 argument for an "alternative geology of women's fiction" to the current trend of "imbrication in the philosophical debates of the period" (13). For Tiffany Potter, Behn's comedies offer "a glimpse into the ugly underbelly of the wit and seduction that was the typical focus of Restoration comedy"; noting that *The Rover*'s courtesan Angellica Bianca shares Behn's initials, Potter suggests Behn's authorial point of view when Angellica "asserts the similarity between the courtesan's selling of her body and the entirely respectable selling of virgins through property marriage" (9).

22 Beginning in the early 1980s, the rejection of formalism and deconstruction as ahistorical heralded the shift towards new historicism and cultural studies. Hua Hsu discusses the importance of Berlant's *Cruel Optimism* to affect theory: "A New Critic might have scrutinized form and irony, explicating the interplay between overt and actual meaning; a deconstructionist might have been attuned to the way the metaphors and propositions in a passage undermined each other; a historicist to the way the meanings of a text might be situated within larger political or social tensions" (61). This study supports the way affect theory complicates our understanding of this period of change. As will be discussed throughout the subsequent chapters, Gibbes's use of metanarrative brings into focus the shift from providential thinking as religious to socioeconomic in patriarchal society, the female writer emerging albeit peripherally to create a new social order through metanarrative.

23 See Ahern's detailed discussion of affect theory as eighteenth-century studies has applied it to the "cultural significance of the triad *passion / feeling / emotion* [that] has been ongoing for decades," Ahern noting that "from mid-century onwards polite society throughout Europe and the Anglo-Atlantic world was preoccupied with feeling" (283).

24 Following the segregated treatment of women writers that characterizes the pioneering recovery discussed above, the next stage in the scholarly trajectory is beginning to integrate them into the canon, a strategy upon which I have based my monograph, *Rethinking the Romantic Era*. To introduce Gibbes into the new canon, the current study returns to a focus on women writers to explore Gibbes's centrality to a new vision of the revolutionary period.

25 For an early example, see Chapter 1's discussion of the Irish Lord's attempted rape of Charlotte Clive. Even in this early novel, Gibbes has Charlotte use her wits to escape his attempts.

26 Regarding Austen's admiration of Wollstonecraft, see Mellor.

27 As Chapter 2 discusses, Gibbes provides a critical perspective of the transitional period between the two wars in her novel, *The American Fugitive*. That Gibbes's career spans this period offers rare insight into such a historical development.

28 See Andrew Cayton's discussion of the rise of the novel during the Revolutionary period as fiction writers urge "transnational" community over upheaval (10).

29 This shift complicates Wollstonecraft's career from the scholarly focus on *VRW*. From her 1788 novel, *Mary*, to her unfinished *Maria* (published posthumously

in 1798), she wrestles with the potential of fiction to do more than perpetuate women's participation in their subjugation.

30 Central to the question of narrative and subjectivity developing during this period is the use of free indirect discourse (FID). Though rightly associated with the rise of modernity in fiction because of its complex representation of subjectivity, it is commonly assumed to begin with Austen: "FID has been a crucially important technique for the representation of consciousness in the English novel, particularly in the tradition which runs from Jane Austen through George Eliot to Henry James, Virginia Woolf, and James Joyce" (Gunn). See Anna Kornbluh's useful summary of critical views on FID: "Critics of many persuasions, ranging from feminist to narratological to historicist to Marxist, consider FID a technique for the relay of thoughts and feelings that results in unprecedented intensification of interiority ... FID appears central to the rendering of the psychological subject and to the empathogenic function of literature ... Quite opposed to all this, many other critics, including especially prominent ones like D.A. Miller, Deidre Lynch, Franco Moretti, and Mark Seltzer, propose that FID is better understood as a cunning *de*personalization" (35–36).

31 See my Introduction to *Rethinking Romanticism* for a detailed discussion of the problematic label of Romanticism for this quality of interiority as it was earlier in the twentieth century attributed to the male canonical poets who were subsequently discovered to have been influenced by women poets such as Charlotte Smith and others.

32 Gibbes anticipates this lineage from the "mobile without motive [t]hrough [whose] promptings ... we act," shared among Coleridge, Mary Robinson, and Mary Shelley, extending to Poe's "self-subverting impulse," and Freud's *parapraxis* (see Coleridge and Poe qtd. in my study, *Rethinking the Romantic Era* 18).

33 The etymology of *perverse*, according to the *OED*: < Anglo-Norman and Middle French *pervers*, *parvers* (French *pervers*) inclined to do evil, wicked, unnatural, deformed, abnormal (late 12th cent. in Anglo-Norman and Old French; 1st half of the 12th cent. in Anglo-Norman as *purvers*, noun), mistaken, wrong, contrary (*c*1370) and its etymon classical Latin *perversus* turned the wrong way, awry, unnatural, abnormal, wrong-headed, misguided, perverted, use as adjective of past participle of *pervertere* PERVERT *v*. Compare Old Occitan *pervers* (early 13th cent.; Occitan *pervèrs*), Catalan *pervers* (first half of the 14th cent.), Spanish *perverso* (first half of the 13th cent.), Portuguese *perverso* (15th cent.), Italian *perverso* (13th cent.). OED, "perverse, adj." *OED Online*, Oxford University Press, June 2022. www.oed.com/view/Entry/141672. Accessed June 29, 2022.

34 Gibbes's other known 1764 novel, *Lady Caroline Stretton*, uses an epistolary exchange between two young women whose argument about marriage and virtue includes a revisionist reading of the biblical Eve's desire for knowledge.

35 Gibbes's narrators in the early novels often echo the pastoral tropes of Restoration comedy, such as the description of Clive as an "enamoured swain" (II. 62). Building on Spencer's discussion of the "Sons of Behn" noted earlier, *Francis Clive* refers to both Jonson and Behn with Hellena's cross-dressing in *The Rover* when Mrs. Clive cross-dresses as Pain (*Afterlife* 102–42).

1

The Life and Adventures of Mr. Francis Clive (1764): "A marriage, where love is wanting, is only a legal prostitution"

Foundational to the pattern of Gibbes's metanarrative mischief, *Francis Clive* destabilizes her third-person narrator's attempt to tell a traditional story of prodigality and return, of fallenness and redemption, and of young women navigating their way through a world of predatory men to be rewarded with marriage. Instead, stories within stories transform traditional plotlines to dizzying cyclicality, compounding the relentless predation of young women by powerful men who are defeated—or at least humbled—by storytelling women, often pariahs who scandalize the narrator. The spectrum of Gibbes's nefarious male characters ranges from overt predators to those whose avuncular overtures are more insidious, and ultimately to those embodiments of masculine heroism whom the narrator has promised both the reader and heroine as rescue from the perils that have formed the world of the novel. *Francis Clive* thus subverts the patriarchal assumptions of male domination behind the sentimental genre's marriage plot.[1] The trajectory of its pattern of sexual predation culminates at the novel's end with a pantomime, the novel's final denunciation of the dangerous power of the market for sentimentality. The pantomime needs no words: the layered audience of theatergoers and readers alike project their desires onto it.

The novel moves towards its ultimate subversion of sentimental fiction with this final pantomime, echoing and complicating the satire of masculine aggression in such seventeenth-century texts as Aphra Behn's play, *The Lucky Chance*, and early eighteenth-century fiction as Eliza Haywood's novella, *Fantomina*. Introducing a new level of metanarrative to her precursors' satire of their male precursors and contemporaries, Gibbes targets the hypocrisy of the reader of sentimental novels. She thus anticipates by more than a quarter century Wollstonecraft's attack on the genre as a source of women's miseducation.[2] Through her unreliable narrator, Gibbes exposes those readers of sentimental novels as masking their voyeurism with moral outrage at the attempted seduction of and violence towards young women by men in power. Gibbes specifically echoes Behn's *The Lucky Chance* regarding the double standard of marital infidelity when Francis Clive, Jr. refers to the "lucky chance" of his unplanned meeting with his cousin, also Francis Clive.[3] Gibbes does more than replicate Behn's satire, however. Gibbes's providential role as an author of fiction emerges obliquely, behind her characters and a narrator whose authority she perpetually erodes.

Francis Clive is Gibbes's earliest exploration of storytelling as manipulative fabrication. The novel mirrors the machinations of the characters' "elop[ing] with the marriage plot," the metanarrative phrase suggested by one of the novel's subplots in which the character Nancy Blissworth outsmarts her brother, the nefarious Captain Blissworth, who "tenders" his sister in marriage to Captain Seymour for his military advancement, an act tantamount to prostitution.[4] As Gibbes's moralistic narrator attempts to tell a tale of vulnerable young men pulled off the path of virtue by seductive women, Gibbes uses metanarrative wordplay and layers of plotting and scheming by her characters to derail her narrator's attempt to control the narrative. For instance, the narrator attempts to assert a benign level of erotic play with the term "frolic"; however, the term invariably bleeds into the realm of the disturbing, recurring throughout the novel to denote various levels of transgression, "frolic" thus becoming a euphemism for lying and, as the plot darkens, for rape.

Just as for his father at the opening of the novel, for Frank, Jr., the virtue/vice binary begins to blur as he comes to enjoy his own lies as stories to tell the prostitute, Penelope, herself a composite of self-created characters, from "Mrs. Pinkney" to "Mrs. Smith" to Mrs. Blissworth.[5] Gibbes creates a counterpoint between Frank, Jr.'s dissimulation and the chameleon shapeshifting of Penelope. Subverting the early promise of a virtuous son who would redeem his father's dissipation, Frank, Jr.'s prodigality jeopardizes his marriage through a sequence of elaborate ruses. When Frank, Jr. becomes entangled in Penelope's ploys, proving himself cowardly and self-deceiving, it is Charlotte, Frank, Jr.'s wife, who emerges with powerful authority. Disguising herself as a military man, she confronts Penelope, thus elevating the use of an assumed identity into an act of virtue. By the end of the novel, Charlotte appears to save the marriage plot while Penelope gets her comeuppance for murdering her husband, the same Blissworth who had attempted to barter his sister for military advancement earlier in the novel. As will be detailed later in this chapter, Gibbes ultimately reinforces the dissonance created by this multilayered counterpoint through the final pantomime.

Nominal replications and pseudonyms

Gibbes creates confusion in *Francis Clive* by giving the principal male characters the same names as other characters—most striking with the three Francis Clives as the protagonist, his father, and his cousin—as well as by coupling them with women of the same name: the wife and sister of the protagonist are both Charlotte Clive: the wife of the protagonist, née Charlotte Elliot, and his sister Charlotte who ultimately marries their cousin, Francis. Thus, there are two married couples named Francis and Charlotte Clive. Gibbes contrasts the repetitive names of the conventionally virtuous characters with the multiple aliases of the prostitute, Penelope, whose hijinks under the aliases Mrs. Pinkney, Mrs. Smith, and Mrs. Blissworth—her chameleon roles as various wives—intensify the antithetical pulls of the sentimental novel as she lures Frank, Jr., through layers of infidelity.

For women whose ideal trajectory is an arc ending in marriage, identity is thus formed and replicated through their relationships with men: father, brother, husband. By contrast, Penelope, as prostitute, assumes married identities to lure Frank off the path of the faithful husband until he is rescued by his quick-thinking wife who cross-dresses as a soldier. This wife, Charlotte, takes on the appropriate male pseudonym, Captain Pain, to create a temporary and liminal identity that eclipses her replicated married self to access the prostitute, her dark double.[6]

Despite the temptation to see Penelope as a caricature in the style of Restoration comedy and early eighteenth-century satire such as Haywood's self-replicating Fantomina, who assumes multiple roles of seductive women to continue luring Beauplaisir as he tires of each in succession, this early novel's use of female aliases—such as that of Charlotte, Frank, Jr.'s wife, saving him from the fate of Penelope by cross-dressing—looks forward to Gibbes's turn from satire to irony in her subsequent novels. In her 1778 *The American Fugitive*, for example, cross-dressing takes a grim turn when young women held captive in a convent disguise themselves in the clothes of boys who had died of a contagion spreading through the convent.

Even in this early novel, Gibbes grants Penelope a deeper layer of subjectivity beyond caricature through an albeit fleeting sketch of her background: at sixteen, Penelope "was carried off by her own consent from a country boarding-school by a lieutenant of marines. This gentleman brought her to London, and kept her six weeks only, then turned her adrift to want or prostitution" (I. 65). Penelope does not rise with virtuous heroism above her predators nor does she attain the martyrdom of the long-suffering—the traditional binary of female victims. Though ultimately punished for her crimes against the men whom she uses as they use her, Penelope is a survivor who quickly learns manipulation, paradoxically achieving masculine agency through her sexual power. The narrator's reference to Penelope's "masculine soul" may betray a condemnation of the strong woman; however, when viewed in the fuller perspective of the novel, the comment can be viewed in the pattern of Gibbes's wry allusions to the gender binary dominating masculinist literary worlds since Homer's *The Odyssey*. Thus,

Gibbes's irony can be heard behind the narrator's perpetuation of the female stereotype when Penelope is labeled the "syren" lodged in the same inn to which Frank's "evil genius" leads him, the narrator implicitly divorcing Frank from being the agent of his adultery (I. 65).

Generational cycles of fabrication

Behind the repetitive names in *Francis Clive*—a pattern that continues in Gibbes's later novels—is the generational cyclicality of an inescapable patriarchy. Gibbes frames *Francis Clive* with the story of the protagonist's father, Francis Clive, Sr., whom Gibbes dispatches quickly as he devolves from a "gentleman of genteel fortune," to an "old debauchee" when his wife becomes ill at the start of the novel (I. 4). He squanders the family estate and seduces young Hannah, nursemaid to his dying wife. Considering his son, Frank, Jr., a "spy," the senior Clive wants to get Frank, Jr. out of the way of his debauchery. He places his son "in a merchant's compting house in London where his attendance would be always required" rather than have him follow the intended trajectory from Eton, from which he has just graduated, to university (I. 5). Though young Frank is shocked by his father's degrading decision, he appears a virtuous young man dutifully obeying his father.

After Mrs. Clive dies, Hannah learns that Francis, Sr. has no intention of marrying her when she becomes pregnant. Both Hannah and the elder Clive decide that she should end the pregnancy with an abortifacient. Knowing the drug to be dangerous, Francis, Sr. risks Hannah's life to avoid the "publication of her shame" (I. 8). Hannah curses the "author of her misfortunes," the first of the novel's many metatextual references to Gibbes as the literal "author"; Gibbes is the providential hand behind the other possible authors of Hannah's misfortune: most obviously, Clive, who had seduced and impregnated her; the servant, John, who is implicated late in the novel for bribing the apothecary; the apothecary who takes the bribe for the drug; or perhaps Hannah herself, for accepting his advances, believing he would marry her (I. 8). Behind the actions of her characters, Gibbes suggests from the outset that she will not allow her readers to project the stereotypes of sentimental fiction onto her characters, Hannah admitting, "[M]y vanity has been the cause of my obliteration" (I. 8).

This early episode of Hannah's undoing and demise creates a prototype for the more complex plot developments of the novel's next generation, using wordplay specific to the sexual bartering of women. Thus, sent by Francis, Sr. to "procure the dreadful potion," John bribes the apothecary: "[U]pon making him an [*sic*] handsome tender," the apothecary "consented to prepare him in less than an hour a draught, that should answer the desired purpose" (I. 9). This is the first of many multilayered iterations of "tender," in this novel as well as among Gibbes's later novels: the euphemism of bribery as "tender" underscores the way negotiation works against its second meaning as "delicate"—the primary emotion of the sentimental novel that Gibbes subverts on multiple levels. The double meaning of "tender" suggests Gibbes's authorial irony as the apothecary, seduced by the bribe, makes the potion. The drug kills Hannah, an event that precipitates the downward spiral into depravity of the elder Francis Clive, as he drinks, gambles away his estate, and dies prematurely. This early episode gestures ahead to the junior Clive's repetition of his father's dissipation. Though Gibbes dispatches Francis, Sr. early in the novel, she returns to him in the final moments of the novel: the servant John reappears to connect Francis, Sr.'s cruelty toward Hannah with Penelope, executed for the murder of Blissworth, all indirectly implicating Frank, Jr. By its final moments, the novel splinters into myriad shorter stories that the scurrilous characters tell, wresting authority from the narrator.

At the outset, however, following the death of his father, Frank decides he will exploit the riches of India by joining the East India Company.[7] This source of colonial seduction recurs for several young men in Gibbes's fiction, especially significant here for Frank, who appears to have humbly accepted his demotion to compting house merchant. Frank aborts the plan to join the East India Company when Spranger, an unmarried acquaintance of his father, takes in young Frank as a godson. The narrator alludes to the prodigal son story, promising a redemptive role not to a victimized father, as in the traditional story, but to a father who has degraded himself and those around him. Gibbes subverts both the traditional prodigal son story and her narrator's authority by having this prodigal son fall into a more insidious variation of his father's dissipation.[8]

Spranger at first appears a welcome father figure for Frank but, despite his apparent good will, he makes ill-advised choices for his godson. Spranger's first act of misguided paternal care is to connect Frank to the Lord Lieutenant of Ireland, widower of Spranger's dead sister. The Irish lord responds to Spranger's request to hire Frank by disparaging Frank as a "merchant's clerk [who] would but ill suit with the politeness of a court"; Spranger leaps to Frank's defense, saying that Frank is "a gentleman both by birth and education, and all the mercantile rust he has contracted, is an integrity which ... would remain unshaken, even amidst the contagion of your boasted court politeness" (I. 11). The lord, however, instigates scandals of a predatory nature that Spranger himself appears to ignore in his misplaced "paternal ambition."[9] The manifold tragedies arising out of this alliance for both Frank and his family fuel the pattern of predations that ultimately subvert the novel's possibility of a comic resolution.

Spranger uses his paternal power to manipulate Frank by first introducing him to Charlotte Elliot, the young woman who will become Frank's wife, but then withholding Frank's agency in the courtship. Upon meeting Charlotte when the Elliot family comes to visit Spranger, Frank is struck by her "beauty and accomplishments." Fearing that he is outclassed by her, Frank attempts to "banish all remembrance of her," thereby distracting himself by visiting his sister, also named Charlotte. While with his sister, he receives a letter from Spranger arranging a meeting with Charlotte Elliot.[10] Gibbes deploys further ambiguities during the meeting Spranger sets up between Frank and the Elliots. Though the meeting appears amicable, the playful banter has an undercurrent of hostility: the Elliots refer to Spranger and Frank as "imposters" since they are not biological father and son (I. 20). More disturbing, Spranger, an "old man," refers to Charlotte, whom he is trying to set up with Frank, as "my wife" (I. 22). On the surface, Spranger appears to mean that Charlotte would be Spranger's choice for Frank's wife. However, occurring so soon in the novel after young Hannah's death resulting from Francis, Sr. having impregnated her, Spranger's ambiguity appears lecherous as he empowers himself to court Charlotte by proxy.[11] Gibbes underscores this dubiousness by having Frank worry that Spranger is interested in Charlotte for himself, Spranger assuring him, "As a good girl, and the daughter of my friend … no otherwise upon my honour; could you conceive me, at my time of day to be such a puppy, as to be ambling after a blooming young creature, who, with great propriety, might have been my grand-daughter" (I. 24). Nevertheless, he continues to flirt with Charlotte in ways that problematize his avuncular role, though he maintains his benevolence throughout the novel.

It becomes increasingly clear that the unmarried Spranger lives his erotic fantasy through Frank, even as he claims innocently paternal intentions. He addresses Charlotte as his wife once again: "As my dancing days are over, wife, if you will honour our son with your hand to-morrow, you will oblige me much, as I shall then be free from every jealous pang" (I. 33). At this early phase of the novel, Gibbes sets a precedent among various characters for disingenuousness about feelings or intentions. Spranger's enjoyment of the power either to "smoke the young man" or to scheme with the Elliots is more insidious than that of Francis, Sr. and other nefarious men to come, including Spranger's own brother-in-law, the Irish lord.

Gibbes triangulates the Francis Clives by introducing Frank's cousin, also named Frank. In a letter to Frank, Jr., Cousin Frank proposes to share with Frank, Jr. the inheritance Frank, Sr. has left Cousin Frank, who is concerned about Frank, Jr. and his sister, Charlotte, having been left with nothing. Later in Volume I, Frank, Jr.'s sister, Charlotte, is revealed to be in love with Cousin Frank, who here encloses with his letter another "of general credit"

(I. 36). When Frank, Jr. shows Spranger the letter, Spranger again offers misguided advice: "We have no need of his kind assistance," he reassures Frank, because the Irish lord would soon be returning from his trip to Bath and would take Frank, Jr. to Ireland, where Spranger suggests Frank's financial embarrassment will be resolved (I. 36). However, this plan of Spranger's is the catalyst to the disasters that propel the novel's plot.[12]

Behind his affable demeanor, Spranger appears to enjoy making Frank suffer, believing that "my former generosity, as you call it, must aggravate my present cruelty" (I. 40).[13] He continues plotting with the Elliots to have Frank and Charlotte married before Frank goes to Ireland. Assuring Frank that he shall "have fair play," in the courtship, then seeing Frank's dejection, Spranger says, "I assure you, your task shall be rendered as easy as possible" (I. 40). Though Frank is "obliged to appear satisfied with this assurance," the narrator refers to Spranger's strategizing as "his jest" that Spranger is "near carrying ... too far" (I. 40). Spranger's teasing "courtship" of Charlotte—referring to himself as "the old husband"—is part of his self-created fiction which puts both Frank and Charlotte in his power (I. 40). Spranger's courting by proxy miscarries, however. He tells Charlotte that he "shall have reason to wish [Frank] had never seen [her]," going further yet to tell her that "Frank does not deserve this neglect, for if ever an heart was truly devoted to any woman upon earth, his is to you," causing Charlotte to faint; when she recovers, Spranger insists that "their schemes should be kept no longer secret" (I. 41). Relieved to have come clean, he flatters himself to think he has "been the instrument of happiness to two worthy young creatures" (I. 42). In a moment of anticlimax characteristic of Gibbes's humor, Spranger eagerly returns to give Frank the good news that Charlotte reciprocates his affection but is disappointed to find Frank already happy since he has won the lottery for his sister, Charlotte (I. 43).

Spranger continues controlling the passive Frank's destiny by urging him to change course, telling him that "instead of sneaking off to the East-Indies," Frank should "set about making [his] fortune in Ireland" (I. 24). Spranger's insistence that Frank should make his fortune in Ireland rather than in India—trading one colony for another—parallels Frank's trading one father figure for another, from Frank, Sr. to Spranger, then to the Irish lord, whose malevolence and autocratic rule are the subject of much of Volume I (I. 24).[14] Spranger at first convinces Frank to marry Charlotte before going to Ireland as, he claims, it would be unseemly for an unmarried young woman to be in a strange country with "visitants of our sex, and without the least reflection upon her prudence" (I. 32). Yet Spranger changes his mind, now wanting Frank to wait to marry until obtaining his situation in Ireland. The lord is, at first, furious, saying, "Elliot can never be so infatuated as to bestow twelve thousand pounds, and such a lovely girl, upon a beggar" (I. 45). Gibbes has already shown two versions of patriarchal overstepping with Francis, Sr.'s indirect cause of Hannah's death and then Spranger's game of courting Charlotte by proxy. The lord strips Spranger's earlier antics with Charlotte of its euphemistic claim to benign play, the lord pursuing Charlotte with increasing sexual aggression. Realizing he will have a better chance if Charlotte has "the sanction of an easy husband," the lord resolves to "promote their union with as much warmth as he had before opposed it"; with the "smooth language of deceit," he apologizes to Spranger, assuring him that "Clive shall reap every advantage from my countenance and favour" (I. 48–49). The naive Spranger, who "knew but little of court promises and sincerity," accepts his apology (I. 49). Rather than waiting the three years that Spranger had believed appropriate for the courtship, the lord advocates that "the ceremony should be performed as soon as possible" (I. 52). Once in Ireland, the lord sexually assaults Charlotte, now Frank's wife.

The other Charlotte, Frank, Jr.'s sister, accompanies the two soon-to-be-newlyweds to Ireland. The two Charlottes are now objects of lust for the lord, who sees them as having contrasting attractions, "Miss Clive," Frank's sister, being lively, while "Miss Elliot stole upon you by degrees" (I. 53). In the first of a pattern in several of Gibbes's novels, a harrowing sea journey takes place, here endured by the four characters—the two Charlottes, Frank, and the lord—on their way to Ireland. From their ship, they witness the storm taking the lives of those aboard another ship, "not being so well manned, nor in such good repair," the narrator then describing the horrific scene from the perspective of the four as they contemplate the prospect of their own deaths: "Nothing was to be seen on board but distraction, no prospect around but inevitable destruction" (I. 54). While the newly wedded Mrs. Charlotte Clive speaks rationally about the lesson of the scene, namely, an "unanswerable argument that we ought always to be in readiness," Frank "perfectly raved, called himself the cause of her untimely fate, and declared perishing alone would have been happiness, to what he felt on her account" (I. 54). When his new wife answers that it is "the hand of providence, that has brought this to pass, and that hand is powerful enough to snatch us from the destruction, that now stares us in the face," Gibbes suggests her own providential role in deciding the fates of her characters, including those like the lord who, once out of harm's way and having manipulated the others to suit his needs, proclaims that "he had ever been of opinion that they should escape: no one presumed to question his Excellency's sagacity" (I. 55).

The lord's "base designs" begin once they are settled in Ireland, the "peer privately sneer[ing] at the intended wittal's eagerness to swallow the barbed hook he was preparing," he "behaved in such a manner, as not to give them the least suspicion" (I. 56). He offers a position in his court to Clive but insists that his wife, Charlotte, accept it in his place. Getting her alone, the lord lies to Charlotte, telling her that her husband has agreed to make her the "messenger of love," the lord continuing, "Did he not tell you, madam, how long I have sighed in secret for your favour ... [a]nd that he himself had consented to my happiness in lieu of extensive favours in my power to bestow?" (I. 58). Charlotte will have none of the lord's "consummate villainy," however, knowing that Frank would never have "consented to act the pander with his own wife," an assumption that takes on retrospective irony as the plot unfolds (I. 58). When Charlotte threatens to "quit this kingdom immediately," the lord becomes physically aggressive, "clap[ping] himself between her and the door" and saying that he has "gone too far to recede, nor shall you live to expose me" (I. 58). Charlotte is not swayed, saying, "I was not made to tremble at your lordship's menaces," and dares him to "murder the innocent," though she will not "shrink" (I. 59). Charlotte's reaction to the storm at sea and the shipwreck have prepared the reader for her heroism, as she tells the lord: "I that could undismayed behold the horrors of the deep, can see a pointed sword without a shock: but remember I have friends, though untitled, that will call you to a strict account" (I. 59). When seduction and then threats do not sway Charlotte, the lord tries a different strategy, telling her that he will give Frank a position if she does not mention his so-called "frolic," a euphemism for rape to be repeated by other empowered men in the novel (I. 59).

Following Charlotte's bold escape from the lord, Gibbes introduces the homosocial world of women that she will develop and complicate both in this novel and her later fiction.[15] Charlotte is relieved that Frank is not at home when she returns, not wanting to speak of her narrow escape from the lord. A debate between the two Charlottes about a woman's role in marriage ensues. Despite the differences between their personalities, the two Charlottes share an intimacy with each other that neither has with Frank, Jr., as brother or husband. His wife confides that Frank will "never receive a favour from the unworthy man," whom she paradoxically dubs "noble villain, our pretended patron" (I. 60). She shares this burden with her sister-in-law and with her mother, Mrs. Elliot, recounting the "horrid and unexpected adventure" in which "that very peer, who engaged himself, by all the ties of honour, to protect her, and promote her husband's interest" has "received the grossest insult and indignity imaginable" (I. 60). Charlotte explains that the lord "has offered an appointment of five hundred pounds a year, but his wife's virtue was to be the purchase," Charlotte understanding that the lord "expects this place will effectually silence me, but I am weary of this wicked, high, public life" (I. 61). The intimacies and mutual support of these female relationships become increasingly important in both the main plot, as Frank, Jr. comes to share his father's propensities for infidelity, and the subplot, involving Nancy Blissworth who finds comfort in female friendship when she escapes her brother's attempt to barter her for military advancement.

When Frank returns home, asking Charlotte how the meeting with the lord went, the narrator refers to her as "this tender wife"; the double meaning of "tender" as both delicate and, more problematic, offered in exchange—or nearly so, as Charlotte says in the letter to her mother, reveals Gibbes's irony behind the sentimentality of the narrator. From this point forward, Charlotte's role becomes increasingly authoritative, even as she is tested through the attempt at being bartered, or tendered. Though the lord acts out sexual aggression in its most sinister guise thus far in the novel, the grief uniting the women contrasts with the reaction of the men in their circle regarding the lord's transgression. Spranger, playing the part of the protective patriarch, reacts with rage at the lord. A significant detail to the source of Spranger's power over the lord is that the fortune Spranger wields is the legacy of his sister, deceased wife of the lord. Gibbes suggests Spranger's underlying likeness to the lord with Spranger's albeit less sinister "frolic" with Charlotte in pretending to be her "husband" when he courts her for Frank. Spranger refers to the inappropriateness of the lord's advanced age: "What! At this late hour, when time has begun to throw up furrows on his cheek, shall he have debauching his friend's daughter in his head"; enjoying the apparently benign power of his paternal role, therefore, Spranger decides that the lord shall "refund the forfeited moiety of [Spranger's] sister's fortune," and Spranger will give it to the Clives (I. 63).

When the lord receives the letter sent by Spranger's attorney demanding his late sister's money, the lord is "struck all of an [sic] heap, and concluding he was blown, cursed his perverse stars for admiring a little obstinate girl, whose education alone was the bar to his success" (I. 64). Gibbes anticipates Wollstonecraft's advocacy for women's education: the lord first refers to Charlotte in the patronizing terms of an "obstinate little girl," only to acknowledge that her "education" has allowed her to see through his various schemes.[16] The lord's attempts to diminish his rapacious attack on Charlotte fall flat: he writes to Spranger that "what had passed between Mrs. Clive and him was merely a frolic," again blaming her alleged misinterpretation of his euphemistic "frolic" as due to her "strict education and retired life" (I. 64).

The storytelling prostitute

The novel shifts from the early plot, in which the Irish lord extends the rapacious reach of Francis Clive, Sr., to the introduction of the prostitute's manipulation of Frank, Jr. Gibbes here marks a yet more pronounced split from her narrator, who apologizes for the clumsy transition with a new set of adventures involving a new cast of characters. By having the narrator call attention to this incoherence, Gibbes gestures to the paradoxical connection underlying the two storylines, thereby subverting the narrator's intention to tell a traditionally unified, linear story. Until this moment, Frank, Jr. has maintained a low profile, passively pawned by various father figures for their own exploits. Now, however, Gibbes as "providence" tests Frank's character in a sequence involving the prostitute, whose exposure of the dark flaws underlying Frank's apparent passivity is the subject of the remainder of the novel.

Demoted once again to "the merchant" now that he has left the employ of the lord, Frank meets a woman of "admirable personal accomplishments; but the utmost depravity of mind" (I. 65). The twenty-seven-year-old prostitute introduces herself as "Mrs. Pinkney," though this is only one of several names she assumes during the rest of the novel. The narrator gives Mrs. Pinkney's background to suggest that her "depravity began at sixteen" when "she was carried off by her own consent from a country boarding-school by a lieutenant of marines" who "kept her six weeks only, then turned her adrift to want or prostitution" (I. 65). That she had been a student at the time, never to return to her studies, underscores Gibbes's anticipation of Wollstonecraft's emphasis on education as the only means to elevate women beyond the poverty that turns some uneducated women to prostitution.[17] For the narrator, "Mrs. Pinkney" is a caricature of female vice, but through the larger perspective of Gibbes's female characters in this novel, where she is a foil to the two Charlottes, and in the fuller range of Gibbes's fiction, Mrs. Pinkney becomes more complex as a survivor in a man's world, predisposed to vice she learns from the predatory men of whom she is first victim, then with whom she consorts, and whom she ultimately victimizes.

Claiming that Mrs. Pinkney has a "masculine soul" for which love is "too soft a passion," the narrator comes into direct conflict with Gibbes's authorial position; that the narrator says that Mrs. Pinkney has "vengeance against the whole sex in general" suggests this distance between narrator and author (I. 65). Working against the narrator's limited gender binary, Gibbes presents the storytelling prostitute as self-fashioning in a world in which there is no possibility for her to survive according to its mores, represented by the narrator's scorn.[18] Though the narrator chastises Mrs. Pinkney, Gibbes grants her agency, a storyteller and actor in the tragicomedy this prostitute creates through her manifold identities at odds with the narrator's indignation.

At this early phase of Gibbes's career, her authorial voice can thus be extrapolated through various elements of her fiction. Through them, Gibbes undermines the patriarchal voice of her narrator who often takes the position of dominant male characters. Complicating the tradition of Behn and Haywood in satirizing the provincial mores behind the sentimental novel, Gibbes engages in a psychological depth traditionally associated with the Romantic period, the late pole of the long eighteenth century. When Penelope makes Frank her prey, Gibbes brings together the two worlds of the sentimental and the satirical to deepen the metafictional irony that becomes the hallmark of her writing. Mrs. Pinkney brings to the novel a new level of sophistication, seducing the reader along with Frank through her storytelling. Indeed, Penelope's improvised stories to ensnare Clive eclipse the machinations of Frank, Sr. and the Irish lord. Waiting at the inn to solicit potential johns arriving from an East India fleet, "Mrs. Pinkney" decides Frank is "worth the pains of entangling, being informed he was a man of considerable property" (I. 65). When she makes sure Frank can overhear her asking at the bar if anyone was going to London, he takes the bait, offering to accompany her. She pretends to be concerned about the impropriety of traveling with a stranger, Frank going beyond assuring her, offering to dine with her so that "he can approve himself worthy of her confidence" (I. 66). Gibbes's centrality in the long eighteenth century can thus be extrapolated through her hearkening back to her precursors in satire even as she anticipates the psychological awareness of perverse self-incrimination associated with Coleridge and then Poe. As noted earlier, Gibbes writes that Clive's "evil genius" brings him to the inn where the "syren," Mrs. Pinkney, is staying. From the narrator's insistence that Clive is a passive victim of this seductress out of Greek myth, Gibbes's psychological acuity moves her beyond the satire of her predecessors (I. 65).[19]

This sequence of episodes—the prostitute's ensnaring Frank following the lord's abuse of Charlotte—suggests that the double standard regarding sexual impropriety has darker strains, the lord entrapping Charlotte literally while Penelope preys on Frank's own weakness. Frank finds Penelope "extremely agreeable" though he doubts her story. He is thus not merely naive: he knows a "truly virtuous wife" would never "expose herself to so great an appearance of evil, as to entertain a young fellow tete-a-tete in an inn in the absence of her husband" (I. 66). However, he "humour[s] her ... until she herself should please unsolicited to throw off the mask she had assumed" (I. 66–67). Gibbes's use of the mask metaphor underscores the role Penelope assumes that Frank knows to be false. Thus, the narrator's reference to Frank as the "unsuspecting merchant," creates another disparity between narrator and authorial voice operating on two different psychological levels. While Frank is aware and playing his own game under his self-deception of innocence, he does not know that Penelope will not voluntarily expose her lie, the scheme becoming increasingly complex regarding the hermeneutics of human behavior.[20]

Simultaneously naive and complicit, Frank enjoys playing cards, drinking champagne, and singing "two or three lively songs" with Penelope, who contrasts with the virtuous Charlotte (I. 67). Penelope tells Frank of her marriage to the brutal "Captain Pinkney," whom she refers to as a "water savage" (I. 68). Whether or not this story is "true," based on the man who carried her off at sixteen, the reader does know that this could not be the same man she claims has just left for Bengal, the sole purpose of the story being to ensnare Frank. He consoles her "artfully" as he learns to play her game of manipulation, praising her "beauty and accomplishments" while assuring her that he will "be proud of becoming [her] banker" for the "trifling sum of forty pounds" that she claims Pinkney has taken from her (I. 69). Though she pretends to refuse taking advantage of Frank's "generosity and humanity," she resolves "to make the most of him" (I. 69).

Gibbes traces the psychological level of Frank's dissipation as he plays out a fantasy that he is rescuing Penelope, simultaneously hoping the two Charlottes never discover his adultery. Despite Frank's acquaintances in the town, he does not want to "expose himself" to them. When Penelope pretends illness, Frank plays along, though he "suspected she had some scheme, and was ... convinced her disorder was counterfeited" when she "surprisingly recovered" (I. 70). However, "the undaunted prostitute" says she would like to "engage a lodging in [Frank's] name" as a "sanction for her reputation," at which point Frank is "determined to shake her off as soon as possible" (I. 71). That he can even entertain the idea of allowing her to "make the least impression on his heart," however, links his patriarchal ties to those of the predatory men with whom the narrator has contrasted him earlier (I. 71). Despite deciding to cut his ties with her, he allows further entanglement, giving her money and promising to accommodate her with more. "Mrs. Pinkney's" deception continues as she uses Frank's name to book a room in a "bagnio," a term for a spa that also connotes a brothel (I. 71).[21] Penelope not only finds Frank's home address but Frank is "so indiscreet as to write his own name": she asks him to show her his handwriting, now having his signature with which she will blackmail him when he tries to cut his ties with her.

"The jade has eloped": refusing to be tendered

That moment arrives soon after, when Penelope, bored with Frank who is not "so generous in his presents, as she would have had him," finds a new john, though Frank is oblivious to her "new attachment for two months" (I. 73). He resolves again to cut his ties with her when he discovers the "whole intrigue," a reaction that underscores the double standard: the unfaithful husband is outraged that his lover has a new john while assuming his wife is a model of virtue (I. 74). Penelope's servant, Rachel, procures a "clever fellow" to "draw up a draught for five hundred pounds," a man who asks Frank's business partner, Mr. Sprat, to take the money out of the bank for which Frank had apparently signed the check (I. 74).[22] Penelope changes her lodging at the time Sprat confronts Frank with what he says must be a "fraudulent demand." Frank jeopardizes both himself and Cousin Frank, Frank, Jr. having told Penelope about him. Cousin Frank decides to go to Ireland to find him, thus leading to the next plot complication involving Frank, Jr.'s self-deception.

The new john, Colonel Blissworth, becomes Penelope's new husband and is involved in the plot complications for the rest of the novel. When she meets Blissworth on the ship to Ireland, he ogles her. The grammatical combination of passive voice and litotes reveals the nuanced irony of Gibbes behind the narrator, who notes that her "figure was not disregarded by the noble commander" (I. 76). When Blissworth presses Rachel, her servant, for information about Penelope, Rachel tells him that she is a "widow, in possession of a large fortune." Blissworth is pleased by "this intelligence," for he "began to flatter himself that he had now an opportunity cast in his way, of repairing his broken fortune" (I. 77). The mutual deceit thus continues its path to Penelope's murder of Blissworth and her subsequent execution.

Gibbes gestures towards her authorial irony here by having the narrator interrupt the story, begging the reader's pardon to "hope it will not be thought impertinent to give some account of this warrior" (I. 78). Not only is the era of chivalry long dead, as the ensuing story about Blissworth's past and current behavior shows but, by contrast to the chivalric ideal, Blissworth fits the novel's pattern of men using young women for profit. Quite unheroically, he had enlisted in the army at twenty to avoid marrying "a young woman he had seduced," a "twenty thousand pounder" (I. 78). Later, Gibbes compounds the lie Blissworth gives to the chivalric ideal when Mrs. Charlotte takes the role of the masculine hero, cross-dressing as a soldier to extricate her husband from his erotic and financial entanglements with Penelope.

Beyond Blissworth using Penelope as she uses him, he attempts to tender his own naive sister, Nancy, for his military advancement. Returning home, he discovers her "grown so fine a girl," he decides to "bring her to town" to "make her own fortune, [sic] and promote his" (I. 78). Blissworth thus offers his unwitting sister to his captain, Seymour, who tells his own story, later revealed to be a lie: having the "misfortune" to be "compelled about six years ago, to marry a disagreeable creature, but [with] an immense fortune," Seymour and his fictional wife were "heartily tired of each other in less than two months, and, at the expiration of half a year, agreed to separate upon some particular terms, and have not met since, nor perhaps ever shall, unless we should both go to the devil" (I. 79). Blissworth responds, "[Y]ou prove, sir, most incontestably, that a marriage, where love is wanting, is only a legal prostitution" (I. 79).

Though during the era marriage as legal prostitution was not an uncommon phrase as an attack on the oppression of women in marriage, Gibbes literalizes it: Blissworth finds it perfectly reasonable to offer his sister in marriage in exchange for his military advancement, thereby legalizing and, in his logic, legitimizing, what would otherwise be unqualified prostitution. He thus continues, "[I]f you do my sister all the justice in your power ... I don't see that there would be any great harm done" (I. 79–80). The captain, Seymour, promises Blissworth advancement and a "handsome settlement" for his sister, the marriage transaction thereby playing out as "legal prostitution," with Captain Seymour's story of his marriage a "base fiction" created to "extort the vile offer" of marriage to Nancy Blissworth (I. 79–80).

Blissworth's transaction—exchanging his sister for military advancement—thus subverts any pretense of a chivalric code of honor regarding either his relationship with his sister or his military ambition. When he discovers that Nancy finds Seymour attractive, Blissworth rushes to find "a vacancy in the army" that Seymour then procures for him. Blissworth's new commission is "an easy purchase," leading to his being "legally dubbed captain" even before he "breaks the matter to his sister," whom Blissworth prevails "upon ... to receive [Seymour] as a lover" (I. 81).

Blissworth typifies masculine objectification of women when he reassures Nancy that "the captain would be as well pleased with her silence, as any thing [sic] she could possibly say, and desired she would dress herself to the best advantage to receive him" (I. 81). His tactics to manipulate Seymour take to a new level the novel's pattern of characters scheming behind the backs of their dupes. The three meet: Blissworth as pander introducing his sister as prostitute to Seymour as john. Struck by the eighteen-year-old Nancy's naivete, Seymour offers to introduce her to some "ladies" in London so that she may be "able to converse with a gentleman without blushing" (I. 83). His attempts to groom Nancy as a prostitute are frustrated, however. Nancy refuses the wine with which he hopes to loosen her up, furious at both her brother and Seymour for their "gross error" in assuming she could be "an easy conquest of a poor, artless, inexperienced girl" (I. 85). Seymour accuses Blissworth of creating in him "false expectations" that Nancy is seducible, demanding that he make "amends" for "the wretchedness" Blissworth has brought upon him (I. 85). When Seymour refers to his "tender regard" for Nancy, Gibbes underscores the subversion of sensibility with the term's implicit secondary meaning of Nancy as an object of transaction.

Continuing the novel's pattern of "seduction" under the guise of courtship as a euphemism for rape, Blissworth takes this "tender" gambit to a disturbing new level by offering Seymour access to Nancy's apartment that evening (I. 86). When Seymour surprises Nancy in her room, she cries out, disconcerting Seymour, who promises to marry her the next morning "if she complied" (I. 87). Nancy's response reveals her courage: "[I]f your intentions were honourable, would you have been under the necessity of stealing at midnight like a thief into my chamber?" (I. 87). Yet Nancy claims that it is her brother rather than Seymour who disturbs her, instructing Seymour to tell Blissworth that she refuses to "sell" herself "to gratify his ambition" (I. 87). Seymour is "so awed by her resolution and true innocence that he had not the courage to offer the least violence"; once he is gone and she has locked her door, she sets out "to fix upon some scheme to avoid all future persecution from her great enemies" (I. 87).

From Nancy's point of view, then, Blissworth's transactional use of her to advance his career is a deeper level of offense than Seymour's would-be rape. Nevertheless, Gibbes underscores the false veneer of Seymour's courtly language to woo Nancy when he privately thinks of her as a "perverse toad of a sister" (I. 88). On a metanarrative level, Seymour is an instrument for Gibbes to subvert the sentimental since his marriage to Nancy later represses the doubleness underlying their happily-ever-after marriage, tinged as it would be by Blissworth's horrific end. In this earlier scene, though, Nancy realizes she has no recourse, no community in the unfamiliar city, thus "rack[ing] her imagination for a long time before she could fix upon any probable means of escaping" (I. 88). As is the case for her later novels, Gibbes suggests here that women must rely on each other for support and protection as men fail their antiquated vows of chivalry. Believing thus that "one female cannot be so abandoned, as not to deliver another from infamy and perdition," Nancy turns to the landlady, Mrs. Richardson, who agrees to accompany her to meet the stagecoach (I. 88).[23]

Seymour drops his pretense of gallantry when Nancy does not appear in the morning. Out of her presence, he gives full voice to his misogyny, telling Blissworth that "there was no perverse slut to brow beat them," while Blissworth, in turn, "pours forth invectives upon invectives against his sister" (I. 90). As Blissworth raises his voice so that "she should hear him," saying she "should never have another shilling from him," he sees her note and cries out, "[T]he jade has eloped" (I. 90). Blissworth dehumanizes his sister by reducing her to a beast of burden, a jade. He distills the misogynistic elements of the novel by using the term "elope," a general term in the eighteenth century meaning to run off, yet already having the connotation of marrying secretly. Blissworth's phrase, especially with the bestial word for his sister, suggests that she has cheated not just the two men but, on the metanarrative level that undercuts the sentimental genre, "eloping" by herself threatens to derail the marriage plot.[24]

Now finding Blissworth "distasteful," Seymour worries about the fate of Nancy. Seymour's newfound ability to *see more* suggests that Nancy may have perceived that, unlike her brother, Seymour is educable. He becomes so "engrossed" with her that he determines to "sell his commission" to avoid "the laugh of the world"; however, he receives a letter from Nancy announcing to Seymour that she has "regained [her] dear father's protection," going on to say that not only has she escaped but Seymour has been saved from the sin of "depriving a poor creature of her only possession," referring to her virginity (I. 92). Refashioning Seymour as her fellow victim rather than potential rapist, Nancy implies that the purpose of her letter is to remediate him for the good of other young women, forgiving him because her "brother's wickedness ... reduces [his] crime to nothing" (I. 92).

Touched by Nancy's display of "innate goodness," Seymour obtains the address of the senior Blissworth, "an honest, plain, industrious farmer" (I. 92). Taking the epistolary exchange to a new level of machinations, Seymour writes to their father, "offering his hand and fortune to Nancy" (I. 93). When Nancy reveals to her astonished father the full plot behind the letter, he says the only way he would accept Seymour's marriage proposal is that Nancy "should never be compelled to see her brother more" (I. 93). Seymour thus writes to the younger Blissworth, offering a "bank note for five hundred pounds," Seymour informing him that this is all Blissworth should expect from him, as "he had sold his own commission, and was retired with his lady with an intention to [become a] country squire," Seymour adding that he will break "all connexions [sic] with him, for reasons he might learn hereafter" (I. 93). Blissworth, "damn[ing]" his sister as a "minx," is so driven to be "dubbed Colonel Blissworth" that he is then duped when he becomes "the favourite of a great man ... on a new and uncertain establishment, without requiring any consideration," the desperate act reducing "his revenue" to "half pay" when the war ends, his only consolation being that the title alone "might perhaps recommend him ... to some woman of fortune" (I. 94). The irony plays out at the novel's end when the woman Blissworth marries is Penelope, the prostitute, who poisons him.[25]

Following the narrator's elaborate digression about Blissworth's attempt to sell his sister for military advancement, the plot returns to the meeting of Blissworth and Penelope, a coach ride providing a comical narrative opportunity to reveal their mutual scheming: the coach is involved in an accident, leaving Penelope's "forehead ... a little scarified," followed by a robbery testing Blissworth's ludicrous claim to being a "knight-errant," his "laurels ... blasted by the abrupt appearance of a couple of suspicious looking fellows" (I. 98). Robbing Blissworth, who pretends to sleep to avoid having to act, the highwaymen cannot "divest his little finger of its elegant ornament without some difficulty," at which point they consider "cutting it off," the women assuming that "the man must infallibly be dead," in which case they "could not reckon such an action inhuman"; "hastily open[ing] his eyes," Blissworth says he can take off the ring himself, riding off as the others have the "laugh ... against him for some time" (I. 100).[26]

Once this early scene shifts to Ireland, the plot of Blissworth and Penelope—the future Mrs. Blissworth—comes together with that of the Clives. Gibbes satirizes the marriage transaction as an elaborate game involving money and status, a theme recurring throughout the novel and continuing—albeit with darker strains—into Gibbes's later career. Penelope, as "Mrs. Pinkney" who is set on becoming "Mrs. Blissworth," observes him through these incidents during which she is "far from being displeased"; Blissworth now appears to her "fitter for the design she was forming against him," namely that, when they arrive at their destination, she asks him to take care of her money, the "golden bait," he in turn uses as a ploy to "attack" her "so vigorously, as to render the refunding unnecessary" (I. 100–01). The term "attack" belies the pretense of genteel courtship. However, when Penelope discovers that, though Blissworth comes from what he claims is a "genteel" family but is "neither the eldest son, nor the favourite," she attacks him through her own marriage plot (I. 102). Penelope no sooner becomes Mrs. Blissworth, marrying him in "utmost secrecy," than she announces that she is "wife of one Mr. Smith, an East India Captain" (I. 103).

"Your mirth is always ironical"

The narrator shifts back to the far less colorful Mr. and Mrs. Clive from the chameleon prostitute and her schemes to marry men with wealth. The contrast between the Clive and Blissworth marriages is striking. Whereas the prostitute assumes identities to dupe men into marriage, the ostensibly monogamous Clives are in the "happy possession of an easy fortune" (I. 103). Spranger forces his brother-in-law—the Irish lord who had schemed to rape Charlotte after her marriage to Frank—to refund Frank, who buys "a handsome estate" as well as "a chariot and an elegant table" (I. 103).

Charlotte's sister-in-law—Frank, Jr.'s sister, who is also Charlotte Clive—comes with the couple to Ireland. As opposed to her sister-in-law, Miss Charlotte's "mirth is always ironical" in the words of her brother, suggesting her character as the closest the novel comes to offering a persona for Gibbes, whose own authorial mirth may be described as "ironical" in contrast to the broad, satirical strokes of her forebears (I. 105).[27] "Whimsical" in rejecting the "many advantageous offers" of her admirers, Miss Charlotte reserves herself for her cousin Frank whom she says not only has the advantage of a strong "character," as described by her brother, but also that marriage to him would allow her to avoid "one of [her] grand objections to matrimony, the changing [of her] name" (I. 103). Her name's replication through Charlotte Elliot's marriage to Miss Charlotte's brother contrasts with the many married aliases of Penelope the prostitute. Having the same name with the difference of their titles, Mrs. and Miss, suggests that the two Charlottes become foils to each other in terms of the marriage debate that they play out at this phase of the novel.

Weaving together the incongruous marriages of the Blissworths, the Seymours, and the Clives, Gibbes creates several layers to subvert the marriage plot: Mrs. Blissworth, now "Mrs. Smith," plots to destroy Clive's marriage. However, Penelope's plot is suspended when Mrs. Charlotte is called home to England because of her father's illness. When Mr. Elliot recovers, however, the Clives decide to stay on "at least six months" because Charlotte is pregnant (I. 110). The Seymour plot connects with the Clives when Mrs. Elliot, Charlotte's mother, mentions that the Seymours are their new neighbors, having bought a house near theirs (I. 108). Pregnant at the same time as Charlotte, Nancy gives birth to a boy as does Charlotte, who names her baby Spranger—yet another name duplicated. Echoing his inappropriate wooing of Charlotte Elliot by proxy for Frank, Jr., Spranger as father-figure to Frank's sister, Charlotte, engages in apparently innocuous banter about her single state: "[I]t requires some philosophy, in even such an old fellow as I, not to be proposing myself," he tells Miss Charlotte (I. 108). Spranger's flirtation with the two Charlottes echoes the so-called "frolics" of men such as the Irish lord who use their power to abuse young women. Warning Spranger of the thin line between a so-called "frolic" and malevolence, Miss Charlotte has the wit to remind him that his proposal would be improper if he were serious: "[Y]ou would find yourself in an ugly scrape, sir, if you were to tender your person to me, for you are the only man I have ever yet seen that I could not refuse .... I should be tempted to exceed those bounds of decorum so essential and proper for the observation of our sex" (I. 108). Though the play on "tender" is ubiquitous in Gibbes's fiction, this is the first instance of a woman using the term with irony, appropriate since, when the male characters use it, they do not appear to understand the irony the author shares with the reader. Now, Charlotte uses the term to suggest the absurdity of Spranger offering himself to her as a suitor.

Miss Charlotte thus comes closest of the female characters to being a mouthpiece for Gibbes. By contrast to Nancy, who surrenders to the wiles of Seymour, Charlotte plays along with Spranger, diffusing his potential for more explicit misogyny. She understands that his teasing is an attempt at a vicarious courtship for Cousin Frank. The meeting of Spranger and Cousin

Frank, however, does not manifest until Volume II, as Gibbes underscores through a metanarrative observation that Spranger's "schemes [were] frustrated by … cross accidents" (I. 111). Those "accidents" are the very events of the Francis Clive/Charlotte Elliot marriage that complicate the world that Cousin Frank/Miss Charlotte Clive inhabit. Yet just as the narrator portrays Spranger as a benign, avuncular figure wishing to bequeath blessings and wealth upon the next generation, Spranger makes a disturbing comment about the Clives' baby resembling "both father and mother," adding "humorously" that the baby has "nothing of the peer about it, notwithstanding his good intentions" (I. 112). By reassuring them that the baby does not resemble the Irish lord, or "peer," Spranger uses the phrase "good intentions" for the lord's attempt to rape Charlotte. In another of the novel's double-edged "frolics," therefore, Spranger here takes on the sinister undertone of his rapacious brother-in-law.

Penelope, now Mrs. Blissworth, yet using the pseudonym Mrs. Smith, draws Frank, Jr. back into her own "frolic" with a letter simply signed "Penelope S," teasing him with a "surprise" should he have the "courage to venture to make a visit" to her lodging in Dublin. She asks him to introduce her to his friends in Dublin, "to give me a name": she means to be established there with a false referral, but Gibbes reminds the reader that we never do learn her true identity beyond her various aliases and marriages.[28] By the end of Penelope's brief note, the tone shifts from tantalizing to threatening: "In short, at your peril be it, if you fail either this appointment, or complying with my request; you can fear nothing, as my hand denotes me to be a petticoat challenger" (I. 115). Frank asks himself the seemingly rhetorical question, "[A]m I not master of my own actions?" as he mulls over the decision to "indulge [his] curiosity in visiting this fair incognito," aware that this is the "lure" of "a wanton" (I. 116). He fails to reason with himself as "a married man" who "ever shuddered at the bare thought of adultery," making the ludicrous claim in his meditations, "Yes, my heart shall sooner cease to beat than prove unfaithful to her" (I. 116). However, with his wife and sister detained, he yields "to the impulses of his curiosity," seeking "the dwelling of this sorceress" (I. 116). Frank's misogynistic label betrays his refusal to take accountability for his own actions of which he had claimed to be "master."[29]

As noted in this study's Introduction, one of Gibbes's strategies for destabilizing the narrator's authority is by anticipating and even complicating the free indirect discourse (FID) of later writers, as this moment illustrates. Gibbes's third-person narration gives voice to Frank's thoughts even as she uses metanarrative to make Penelope more than a seductress. Like Gibbes, Penelope is a storyteller who uses her sleight of hand to create her personae. She thus mirrors the fiction writer with elaborate ruses just as Gibbes confuses the reader with the replicating character names. Penelope, now "Mrs. Smith," gives Frank her fabricated autobiography as wife to an East India Captain currently at Madras at whose expense she plans "much innocent diversion at his surprize [sic]," Frank readily agreeing to this "humorous adventure" (I. 118).

At this point, Mrs. Smith recounts her scheme to her servant, Rachel, telling how she "dissembled fears ... innumerable" (I. 122). She refers to her heart as "so far masculine as to despise an easy conquest; I myself fell from an eminence, and ever since I became the prey of one man, have considered all the sex as prey for me" (I. 122).[30] Thus, she tells Rachel, though Frank "has not my seduction to answer for ... his manner of casting me off, upon a trifling detection before my designs upon him were half accomplished, has dug the pit for his beloved cousin," whose ruin "will wound him deeper, than any other stroke of fate or fortune" (I. 122). As she continues plotting against both Frank Clives, her addictive personality comes into sharper focus, her "spirits begin[ning] to droop" as she takes solace in her "friendly cordial that," she says, will "restore [her] to [her]self again" (I. 123).

Gibbes deepens the representation of Frank's anxious self-doubt. No sooner does he leave "Mrs. Smith" than he begins to have qualms about having "sought her out before he had communicated this curious letter to his wife and sister, that he might have had the sanction of their consent" (I. 123). He works himself up with these thoughts to the point that he determines "never to reveal it," like a child caught in a lie, then convincing himself that he, like a knight, is "bound in honour to shew her some civility on my cousin's account" (I. 123).[31]

By contrast to Gibbes's sly irony, the narrator offers a facile moral at the end of Volume I: the Clives enjoy their time in England with the baby, despite Frank being "so far advanced to the brink of the precipice as not to be able to recover himself, all which might have been avoided, by acting up to that laudable ingenuousness by which he obtained his friends, his fortune, and his wife" (I. 128). Gibbes undermines the didactic voice of the narrator who warns the "young mind" never to "lose sight of that excellent admonition in holy writ, by which we are forbid to do evil that good may come of it" (I. 128). Like Wollstonecraft's persona in *VRW*, the narrator urges the youth to "patiently submit the disposition of every event to that being, in whose hand are both the present, past and future, and by whom every seeming accidental contingencies, [sic] are regulated and appointed with the nicest order" (I. 128). Gibbes's authorial presence behind the moralizing narrator appears to relish fabricating the schemes and plotting that provide this early opportunity to hone her ironic edge. Gibbes herself is that providence who has created these "seeming accidental contingencies" (I. 128).

Benighted men; beknighted women

As Volume II continues Frank's elaborate rationalization about being manipulated by "Mrs. Smith," a new focus of the novel is the polemical relationship between the two Charlottes regarding marriage. The naming confusion becomes yet more pronounced as the two Charlotte Clives, romantically involved with the two Frank Clives, make for comic confusion on the surface of the novel and, on a deeper level, suggest the complexity of identity vis-à-vis familial relationships. Gibbes meanwhile intensifies the opposite naming problem with Penelope's identity based solely on the men she swindles sexually for financial gain, names that are interchangeable as though legalizing the union through marriage has little to do with the machinations that compose it.

Volume II thus opens with Miss Charlotte—Frank, Jr.'s sister—annoyed at her sister-in-law's "meek and forbearing" willingness to forgive her husband for staying away past dinnertime without notifying her, Mrs. Charlotte assuming "some matter of importance" must have kept him away (II. 4). While Mrs. Charlotte refers to Miss Charlotte's "strange notions" regarding husbands as "tyrant" and "lord of the creation," with women being "shackled" in marriage, and men "ever think[ing] us infants," Miss Charlotte worries about "the halcyon days in matrimony ... nip[ping] in the bud my hopes of dear contentment" (II. 4–5).[32]

Mrs. Charlotte is too prismatic a character to be reduced to a mere caricature of the subjugated wife. She claims Miss Charlotte is "much further read in romance than [she] imagined," referring to her "wild maidenly expectations," for "it is impossible for human nature to keep up to one particular pitch of good humour, as sickness, fatigue, or disappointment, will discompose our frail disposition." Mrs. Charlotte even blames "our wrong educations" for the fact that women are not 'treated as we ought beforehand" (II. 5–6). Miss Charlotte, however, understands more of romantic illusion than her sister-in-law gives her credit for, saying, "I begin to think that a young woman, without a lover, may very aptly (according to Don Quixote's simile of a knight-errant without a mistress) be compared to a tree without leaves" (II. 6). The parenthetical metaphor within the simile in which she gives Cervantes' reference reverses gender, as it is in Charlotte Lennox's 1752 novel, *The Female Quixote*. The debate ends when Frank, the belated and benighted knight errant, arrives, Mrs. Charlotte herself articulating her own double standard: "[T]hough I cannot consider his making the dinner wait for him as a fault, yet I should hold it an unpardonable one to make him wait for his dinner"; the double standard is immediately felt when Frank amuses them with "some tale to account for his exceeding the dinner hour," the narrator euphemistically turning the lie into an entertaining act of storytelling (II. 7).

Meanwhile, Penelope, the ostensible Mrs. Smith, falls deeper into alcoholism, staving off a guilty conscience with "the assistance of Bacchus," though she continues plotting for ways to relieve Frank of his virtue (II. 7). Though Gibbes reverses traditional gender roles, with Frank as the passive victim of the "masculine" criminal, Mrs. Smith, Gibbes shows Frank to be more complex than a mere passive victim to a vixen, for he perpetually takes himself in, such as when he attempts to reason that he has not "taken a criminal step, yet, as it is a clandestine one, it is improper, nor has my mind been perfectly at ease, since my commission of it .... But am I not likewise bound by the treble ties of honour, love, and justice, to make my wife acquainted with every transaction, which concealment alone would render mysterious?" (II. 8). It is ludicrous that he considers himself bound by a promise to be secretive about his affair with Mrs. Smith, endowing it with the sacred duty of a knight to rationalize his giving in to temptation. Mrs. Smith, however, increases the difficulty for him, leaving word that she wants him to see her in the evening, not during the day, so that he must embellish the previous lies. Penelope gets Frank drunk in what is the beginning of Frank's own downward spiral into alcoholism and increasingly erratic behavior. At this early phase, "one single deviation from candour and ingenuity was punished by years of remorse, and actual guilt was the consequence of a seeming trifling omission" (II. 12).

The morning after Frank first commits adultery, staying the night with Penelope, he vacillates between chastising himself and blaming "Mrs. Smith" in florid language: "[T]hou fiend ..., what atonement canst thou make for drawing down upon my miserable head this horrid guilt and calamity?" Frank berates himself for even worse behavior than that of the Irish lord who never got beyond his sexual designs on Frank's wife: "my lord __'s intended crime was not of half so deep a dye; he had no wife, nor friend to whom he owed such uncommon obligations, as I do this dear woman" (II. 16). Though Frank appears incapable of seeing the irony of this comparison regarding the lord's intended rape of his wife, he does project his father's guilt through the imagined eyes of Frank, Jr.'s own son, whom, he tells himself, will "curse [his] memory, when he hears [his]wickedness related!" (II. 16). Frank rationalizes his plunge into deeper betrayal immediately following these self-chastisements: deciding not to "reveal this shocking transaction" to his wife, he justifies his further betrayal of her by convincing himself it would be "worse than the crime itself to destroy her happiness," rationalizing that he "must add dissimulation to what [he has] already done, so impossible it is to commit a single vice" (II. 16). Adding another layer of retrospective irony to this moment, the novel ends with the accidental death of his young son, Spranger, Jr., Frank, Jr. believing his son is taken from him because of his infidelity (II. 126).

Though Mrs. Charlotte's apologetic attitude for her "impatience" to see her husband seems difficult to reconcile with her subsequent emergence as the cross-dressing heroine who will save him and their inheritance, it soon becomes apparent that she manipulates her husband, as Wollstonecraft later claims is the way the disempowered assert control. Yet again, she "beg[s] his pardon," telling him she will "ask no questions, whether business or company detained you" for, she claims, "you stand or fall by the judgment of your own heart alone" (II. 17). The effect of this "tender behaviour was at once a balm and a severe rebuke to his disordered mind; he recovered himself for her sake" (II. 17). Miss Charlotte, furious that her sister-in-law has indulged her brother with the "opiate" of forgiveness, says to herself that if Frank had been her husband, she "would have turned him inside out" (II. 19). Despite Mrs. Charlotte saying that Frank "has so much tenderness for [her] he would not have [her] dissatisfied," Miss Charlotte asks the question Gibbes may well be asking her reader: "[I]s not my brother yet old enough to chuse proper companions?" (II. 19). Yet Mrs. Charlotte appears not only to understand but to accept the double standard: "I am accountable to him for every Step I take, and acquaintance I commence; but it is reversing the medal to expect the same from him" (II. 19).

Penelope sets her traditionally masculine aggression against Frank's passivity. Discovering that Frank has not returned home to a furious wife, she writes him a letter threatening blackmail if he does not acquiesce to her ultimatum of either "dissembling" at home, or she, Penelope, will "appeal to [his] lady for that justice" (II. 21). She conspires with Rachel to "silence him at once, by convincing him how absolutely he is in my power, and then endeavour to reconcile him to it, to effect which will require some masterly strokes of my art" (II. 21). With playful banter that contrasts with Penelope's fury, Miss Charlotte, Frank's sister, attacks him for staying away from home for three days, to which he weakly says, "I make no defence [sic], but seriously cry *peccavi*" (II. 22, italics added). Mrs. Charlotte sees her sister-in-law's tirade as "satire," saying, "[Y]ou absolutely commit a breach of the peace in assaulting an unarmed man" (II. 22). By having Mrs. Charlotte charge Miss Charlotte with masculine aggression, Gibbes connects Miss Charlotte to Penelope, though her "assault" is out of protection for her, Frank's "saintly wife" (II. 22).

"Your peace is purchaseable"

When Frank receives Penelope's letter blackmailing him, he returns to her in impotent rage, cursing her as a "cruel and abandoned woman" (II. 24). She, however, the shrewder of the two, describes herself as "the mistress of

[his] fate," then chastises him as a "barbarous and ungrateful man" (II. 24). Despite his proclaimed "utmost horror" at her blackmail, Frank has indeed returned to her. His plea, "release me," shows how willing he is to be led. Mrs. Smith responds, "[Y]our peace is purchaseable; I cannot give you up, consent to visit me, which is not now a new crime, and you may rest assured you have no ill to fear from me .... [I]t is in vain to struggle with my fetters" (II. 25). Yet she follows with the opposite claim, namely, that it is his choice to be in this predicament: "[Y]ou have the power either to make [my fetters] iron or the soft reins of love" (II. 25).

Gibbes thus offers a more complex relationship among characters, identities, and the authorial voice than suggested by the narrator's facile label of vixen for the prostitute. At this stage, the source of Frank's ambivalence surfaces through a new metanarrative level in the novel, namely, his addiction to her storytelling. Thus, as she withholds her identity, taking on personae depending on her situation, Mrs. Smith emerges as a demonic underside of the authorial voice, one whose psychological acuity becomes providential for the characters as she chooses. When the narrator refers to her as "the syren," in a traditional masculinist reduction of the prostitute to a temptress, Gibbes reduces Frank to a passive character that the reader cannot respect when he says to Penelope, "I will be what you please," leading her to ask him for money. When he writes a "draught for fifty pounds," she is disgusted at the "scanty pittance" (II. 26). Despite loathing her and himself, Frank becomes habituated to his clandestine visits and the double life that parallel his addiction to alcohol, so that "it was not easy if three days elapsed without seeing her" (II. 27). Indeed, what appears to be the source of addiction is her "succession of diverting tales she found to amuse him with" (II. 27).

As the prostitute's pseudonyms proliferate, the protagonist's centrality disappears under the parallel proliferation of his name. Gibbes now more fully develops the role of Cousin Frank, the third Francis Clive. In another metanarrative moment, Cousin Frank notes that it is "a lucky chance" that he happens to be in Ireland, Gibbes using the title of Behn's satirical play about a man who prostitutes his wife to pay off his debts.[33] With this intensification of metanarrative, the reader is reminded that all such chances are creations of the author—in this case, giving Frank, Jr. the opportunity to design a scheme using his cousin to help him continue seeing Mrs. Smith (II. 28). Frank, Jr. euphemistically describes the plan as a "frolic," a term linking him to the Irish lord who referred to his attempt to rape Mrs. Charlotte as a "frolic" (I. 59).[34]

Admitting that it has been six weeks since he has been away from his family and out of communication with them, Frank, Jr. tells Cousin Frank, "I am not so good at either deceit or invention as to have imposed a false tale upon them" (II. 30). Yet create "a false tale" is precisely what he does by making it look like Cousin Frank is an acquaintance with whom he has been spending time. Though Cousin Frank disapproves, saying, "I don't love secrets between man and wife," Frank, Jr. continues instructing his cousin, "should I ever be obliged to be absent from home all night, I have been with you: this will preserve family peace" (II. 30–31).

A comedic scene of both double identity and mistaken identity ensues with the two Frank Clives and the two Charlotte Clives. Miss Charlotte teases Cousin Frank whom she takes to be the fictional "merchant" created by her brother. She chastises "the merchant" for not having visited sooner, asking about Cousin Frank whom he has said is a close friend. When Miss Charlotte asks about Cousin Frank's character, Gibbes uses dramatic irony to have him respond that "in his person he is allowed to be extremely like myself" and that he is "a much greater admirer of women of merit, than of his own sweet person," mentioning, slyly, that he is "quite weary of continuing a solitary Adam, and, for ought I know, is at this very instant in quest of that rib, for which he feels an uncommon vacancy nearest his heart" (33). The scene thus reads like a comic play, complete with staging directions, such as when Gibbes follows Miss Charlotte's teasing line, "I am quite out of conceit with my scheme now you are all become so officious: I will not be thrown at Frank's head neither, therefore madam, and gentlemen bowing humorously, you need not give yourselves any farther trouble"; Frank says of his sister, "Poor Charlotte (... tapping her cheek,), it shall have a husband before it is quite thirty, that it may not think itself forsaken" (II. 34). This metadramatic "friendly raillery" in which "all parties were pleased and pleasing" creates distance between the narrator and Gibbes. When Frank neuters his sister in the passage above, calling her "it" as though her refusal to marry makes her less of a woman, Gibbes underscores the cruelty underlying his claims to good fellowship. Cousin Frank tells Frank, Jr., "I begin to fear I am acting a very improper part" as he is drawn into his cousin's drama, while Frank, Jr. dismisses his cousin's "qualms" at the diversion: "Why Frank ..., I can remember the time when you would have jumped at a *frolic*, and were equal to laughing it off, without all these apprehensions" (II. 35, italics added). Gibbes exposes Frank, Jr.'s disingenuousness about such "frolics" through his spiral into deceit and repressed guilt.

Returning to the marriage debate that opens Volume II with the argument between the two Charlottes, now from the patriarchal view of Frank, Jr. to his cousin, Gibbes echoes her seventeenth-century forebears with intensifying irony when she has Frank, Jr. say to Cousin Frank,

> [U]nless you take pity on her virgin state, the poor girl must infallibly *lead apes in the other region* [ital added]: for what has so particularly charmed you, is

an antidote with most of our sex; who chuse to entrust the happiness of their lives, the keeping of their honour, and education of their children, to the half bred and half witted, from the terrible apprehension that a woman of sense should insist upon being treated like a rational being. (II. 36)

Gibbes's irony is transparent when Frank, Jr., the man who is scheming to keep his wife in the dark about his affair with a prostitute, echoes such seventeenth-century poets as Mary Astell, Margaret Cavendish, and Katherine Philips.[35]

In a plot sequence dizzying in its circuitousness, Mrs. Smith, beginning "to grow weary of a man, who she was thoroughly sensible had no other attachment to her than fear," decides to "fleece" the "close-fisted gallant" by demanding four thousand pounds as well as his wife's dowry of twelve thousand pounds (II. 37). Just as she goes over these plans with Rachel, Frank, Jr. appears at her door to announce, "in the strongest terms imaginable, that all his former objections were removed," now "sensible of his happiness in being the real object of so fine a woman's affections." When she brings out "the bottle and cards ... to dispel reflection," Frank becomes "soft and pliant as wax ... and childishly credulous" with the "excess of wine" (II. 39). As he prides himself on having manipulated her, she manipulates him by plying him with wine and, beginning to weep "in such terms as immediately penetrated her gentle natured gallant" (II. 39). She disingenuously expresses concern about being "an incumbrance to him," such that she would "patiently submit to the very worst of evils, as a prison might justly be called," the irony appearing retrospectively, Penelope going to prison and executed at the end of the novel, although here, her "gallant," Frank, assures her that "she should never go to prison whilst he had a shilling" (II. 39). Mrs. Smith takes advantage of Frank's offer, drawing up a draught of four thousand pounds. Frank, drunk, takes the draught, and "with sapient look and wig awry, endeavoured to examine the contents, but his sight was not sufficiently clear, and as he was not disposed to give himself too much trouble, he subscribed his name with tottering hand, but nevertheless legible enough to entitle Mrs. Smith most undoubtedly to the sum demanded" (II. 40).

When he receives a letter two days later, "requiring his immediate compliance with these several obligations, or that a prosecution should be the consequence," he confesses to Cousin Frank that he is "undone past redemption," yet makes him promise that he "will not visit [his] once happy house" until Frank contacts him (II. 41–42). The byzantine sequence reveals the psychology behind Frank, Jr.'s machinations: being "past redemption" means he is free from ethical responsibility to do right.

Mrs. Smith responds coolly to Frank's threat to sue her with a counter-threat of blackmail: if "legal action be your choice, you may begin your law-game to-morrow," she retorts, adding that he will become the topic of society's scandal-mongering and will "break the heart of your beloved ice-piece, your chaste Lucretia, and leave your child to reproach and beggary, which is all the success you can flatter yourself with from your fine suit," adding that even Spranger will discover his "double adultery," and that he has "incumbered [Spranger's] estate to reward his mistress" (II. 43). Though the narrator refers to Penelope-as-Mrs. Smith as "the audacious female" during her tirade, Gibbes's voice behind Mrs. Smith's ridicule of Mrs. Charlotte as an "ice-piece" suggests that Frank would not find Mrs. Smith as fascinating if his wife were less frigid.[36] Mrs. Smith gains the upper hand over the merely pathetic Frank, who has not played her game with her level of finesse (II. 43).

Throughout this sequence of episodes involving Penelope's duping of Frank, Gibbes subverts the narrator's abhorrence of Mrs. Smith and handwringing about the fate of the Clives through free indirect discourse. Penelope instead reduces Frank to one who, once the "check" of "narrow circumstances" that had "induced him to practice sobriety, chastity, and the utmost parsimony" is removed, finds he "can take his glass even to intoxication, debauch the wife of his relation's most intimate friend, and make her an appointment equal to the expectations she had formed of his generosity," yet when "the performance of his agreement is required ... with threatening words and stern aspect, [he] desires to be released from the obligation of those bonds he voluntarily executed, and says, that, truly, all the actions he has committed were in a drunken fit, and therefore of no force" (II. 44).

Even at this early phase of Gibbes's career she is too savvy a novelist merely to invert the roles of these two figures, however. Mrs. Smith's diatribe underscores the complexity of Frank, Jr.'s weakness but does not exonerate her own: she pays for her murderous rage with her life. At this point, however, Mrs. Smith plays the winning gambit, getting Frank to agree to live with her in England: "He resolved never to return to his family unless he was in a condition to repair his ruined fortune" (II. 44). When his "tenderness for his wife" returns, he asks Mrs. Smith "to furnish him with the means of raising his spirits. She instantly set a bottle and glass before him," and for the days ensuing before they set off for England, "Mr. Clive was never sober" (II. 44).

By having Frank mix up the two letters he writes before he leaves England, putting the letter for his wife in the envelope for Cousin Frank, and vice versa, Gibbes demonstrates her pioneering representation of the perverse.[37] Thus, when Cousin Frank opens the letter and sees it is addressed to Mrs. Charlotte with merely "idle excuses for his absence," he realizes that Frank, Jr. must have sent an unfiltered letter meant for Cousin Frank to Mrs. Charlotte. Cousin Frank is stymied by his promise to the misguided Frank, Jr. Though he knows he should warn Mrs. Charlotte about the letter meant for him, he does not, since he has sworn to Frank, Jr. that he would not visit them. Ludicrously, Cousin Frank remains a "prisoner in his own lodging," afraid that "if he went abroad, he might be seen by some of Mr. Clive's family" (II. 46).

While the two younger Francis Clives follow in the footsteps of the elder Francis Clive as they sink deeper into subterfuge, it takes Mrs. Charlotte, in the guise of a soldier, to rescue her husband. When Mrs. Charlotte reads the letter intended for Cousin Frank detailing his helplessness at the hands of the "most artful and abandoned of women," Gibbes further marginalizes the passive Frank, Jr., building towards a confrontation between Mrs. Charlotte and Mrs. Smith (II. 48). Gibbes's providential voice contrasts the didactic voice of the narrator, whose asides extol the virtues of a passive wife while demonizing the prostitute. Gibbes's narrative further resists the marriage plot through the appeal of Mrs. Smith as a deft constructor of plots, while the benighted Frank asks in his misdirected letter, now being read by his wife, "whether it is witchcraft or madness I know not, but I both abhor and admire the same object" (II. 49). Both horrified and mesmerized by the prostitute, Frank is willing to be led by her because her "witchcraft or madness" energizes him while his traditional "ice-piece" wife, he implicitly suggests, bores him (II. 43).

Once Mrs. Charlotte decides to disguise herself as a soldier, she emerges as the improbable hero, "a sad witness of my husband's conduct, and should some lucky chance put it in my power to save him from that worst of ills, despair, the constant attendant on guilt, I will cast off my disguise, and be again his wife" (II. 50).[38] Mrs. Charlotte's improvisational gift and intelligence come to the fore during this process of ratiocination, in which she observes her husband. (II. 50).

Gibbes creates symmetry in this episode with parallel relationships between Mrs. Smith's Rachel and Mrs. Charlotte's Swinbourn. Just as Rachel executes the plans of Mrs. Smith, so too does Swinbourn place herself in jeopardy for Mrs. Charlotte. Yet more than the villain being a foil to the heroine, the parallel duos suggest that Mrs. Charlotte is capable of machinations the reader has come to associate with Mrs. Smith, thus raising her beyond a mere "ice-piece." Behind the narrator's facile binary of good and evil, therefore, Gibbes suggests that Mrs. Charlotte's fidelity to her husband rests on a false sense of marital virtue. Charlotte blames Mrs. Smith, "the wicked creature of our sex," for having "deluded" Frank, seeing her husband as "the fittest prey for such an unhappy wretch" (II. 52). Oblivious to Frank's repeated refusal to take responsibility for his actions, Charlotte cannot see what Gibbes has shown the reader since the novel's opening: the pattern Frank perpetuates from his father as an abuser of women who refuses accountability, drinking to escape his problems.

Mrs. Charlotte's sole concerns are saving her marriage and her husband's reputation. Thus, as she and Swinbourn tail Mrs. Smith and Frank, returning from Ireland to London on the same ship, Miss Charlotte finds a letter from her sister-in-law, Mrs. Charlotte, who writes that "not a tittle may transpire" to Frank's "disadvantage; the future happiness of my life is hinged upon that single circumstance, therefore, I conjure you destroy it not," adding that she wants Miss Charlotte to tell their acquaintances that the Clives "were obliged to visit England for a month or two," to save them from any possibility of scandal, assuring Miss Charlotte, "[Y]ou may expect to see us return together" (II. 54). Warning Miss Charlotte not to "destroy" their "future happiness," the letter carries the metanarrative message that compromises the promised marriage plot: Mrs. Charlotte's mission is to save her husband from ruin.

By weaving the subplot of Cousin Frank and Miss Charlotte's courtship together with Mrs. Charlotte's rescue of her husband, Gibbes further complicates the foundational binaries of the sentimental novel, most importantly that of the virtuous wife and the prostitute. Miss Charlotte's rage against her brother's infidelity contrasts Mrs. Charlotte's attempt to rescue her husband. So concerned with saving her marriage, Mrs. Charlotte pretends to be a male suitor to woo the woman who has seduced her husband. While she thus creates a parodic love triangle, Miss Charlotte, by contrast to her sister-in-law, echoes Nancy Blissworth's rage against her own brother when she discovers that he has traded her for advancement in the army. Nancy is a parodic prolepsis of Miss Charlotte, who blames her brother when Mrs. Charlotte shares the letter Frank, Jr. inadvertently sent to Mrs. Charlotte. Miss Charlotte decides that none of this bodes well for Cousin Frank, and so she concludes, "[N]ever more shall I have a favourable thought of man, sure my steady brother has broke through the most solemn obligations upon earth, to act the villain, how greatly have I been deceived ... in the good opinion I was beginning to conceive of his sweet companion and help mate in iniquity," namely the "merchant" whom she does not know is Cousin Frank. Having thus convinced herself that the "merchant" has corrupted her brother, Miss Charlotte decides she will refuse any contact with this "merchant," who nevertheless shows up at her door, telling her he has "urgent business," whereupon Miss Charlotte accuses him of having "destroyed the best of women, and the best of brothers" (II. 55). Cousin Frank feels he must continue the ruse of being "the merchant" because of his promise to Frank, Jr., only responding, "[M]adam, you wrong me greatly" (II. 55).

Cousin Frank ultimately reveals himself to Miss Charlotte as "Frank Clive, whose friend only I pretended to be, and had not been arrived an hour, when your brother begged me to consent, in order as he said to create a little mirth, to suffer myself to be introduced in the manner I was; I little dreamt of the unhappy consequence" (II. 57). Though Miss Charlotte will not "acquit [him] of all blame, as perhaps [he] might have prevented this heavy evil by a contrary conduct," Cousin Frank, affected by her loyalty to her sister-in-law, tries "to sooth her with hopes of a better day," another metanarrative moment to remind the reader that all may not end well for the marriage plot (II. 57). Cousin Frank, a shrewd money manager, clears up Frank, Jr.'s financial mess quickly, going to Mrs. Smith's landlady and then the mortgager, paying off the debts, including interest, and taking the Clive estate "into his own hands" (II. 61).

Gibbes pursues the subversion of gender binaries more overtly as she pits Penelope's "masculine soul" against the feminized masculinity of "Colonel Pain," Charlotte Clive's pseudonym when she shifts to the climactic scene of Mrs. Charlotte's brilliant cross-dressing scheme to liberate her husband from the thrall of Mrs. Smith (I. 103). Mrs. Charlotte's character proves more complex than the traditionally virtuous and ultrafeminine wife, her earlier experience fending off the Irish lord having foreshadowed this new level of empowerment: Mrs. Charlotte assumes the disguise of a military man to save her husband from the ruin brought on by Penelope under the alias of Mrs. Smith. While Mrs. Swinbourn, Mrs. Charlotte's servant, obtains "the regimentals of an officer for her mistress's use, and a genteel livery for herself," Mrs. Charlotte's "agitation of mind" intensifies, unbelievably, for "the man of her heart" whom she is "grieved to think … must be fatigued with his journey, and perhaps his companion would not take seasonable tender care of him he might probably stand in need of" (II. 63). If the reader did not have Miss Charlotte's point of view earlier to counter that of her sister-in-law, one might be tempted to assume Gibbes is representing Mrs. Charlotte as the paragon of wifely duty. However, Mrs. Charlotte's concern that the prostitute may not be taking good enough care of her husband shows Gibbes's irony behind the narrator, culminating in the notion that her arms would be "open to receive him, with a generous oblivion of all the past" (II. 63). As the later episodes show, it will take more than the immediate rescue to ensure that he will not return to the patriarchal foibles that have characterized the men in the novel, beginning with his father.

The idea that a "marriage, where love is wanting, is only a legal prostitution" deepens at this stage of the novel, introduced in Volume I when Blissworth tendered his sister to Captain Seymour in exchange for military advancement (I. 79). Mrs. Charlotte's choice to cross-dress as a military man, ostensibly because of her concern that Penelope is not taking care of Mrs. Charlotte's husband, creates an odd twist on the sentimental notion of the passively virtuous wife. Mrs. Charlotte's servant, Mrs. Swinbourn, who also cross-dresses to become Mr. Robert, the valet to Mrs. Charlotte as

Captain Pain, discovers that Mrs. Smith is renting her room in a brothel, "notoriously known for a friendly house, and that her lodgings were open to the most abandoned of wretches" (II. 64). In cross-dressing as Captain Pain, Mrs. Charlotte has "a heavy heart in this masculine habit, which agreed but ill with either her delicate mind or person" (II. 64). Mrs. Swinbourn, as Mr. Robert, appears to woo Mrs. Rachel as a means of obtaining information about Mrs. Smith vis-à-vis Frank, Jr. Mrs. Swinbourn discovers that Penelope "is seldom of long continuance in her attachments, and this gentleman has to be sure the worst chance of any, for my mistress really lets him be here at present merely upon charity" (II. 66).

Discovering the double insult of having this prostitute seduce and then regard Frank as a "charity" case, Mrs. Charlotte is outraged by the news that her husband is undervalued by the prostitute, saying, "the dear man [is] kept upon charity," grieving for the "sufferings ... this noble generous heart [must] undergo from such treatment!" (II. 67). She is bewildered that he would "not fly to me in his adversity," saying, "with me he was ever secure of an asylum" (II. 68). Gibbes distinguishes here between the limitation of Mrs. Charlotte's chaste understanding of the heteronormative marriage contract and Frank's desire for more than "asylum" in his marriage to the "ice-piece," as Mrs. Smith refers to Mrs. Charlotte. The latter nevertheless rouses herself to heroic action as "wife and mother," saying she will "endeavour to rise superior to these great calamities .... And once more [become] Capt. Pain" (II. 68–69). In a remarkable twist, therefore, Mrs. Charlotte as Pain poses as a rival to her husband for the love of Mrs. Smith, who is nevertheless "perfectly tired of her old gallant, whose pockets were totally empty," Mrs. Smith telling Rachel she cannot marry Pain because she is "disposed of in a legal way to [C]olonel Blissworth" though it "need be no impediment to making a proper advantage of him without fetters" (II. 69).

Mrs. Charlotte proves to have a talent for improvisational acting, playing the part of the "gallant" theatrically, "bowing most obsequiously," flattering Mrs. Smith, and telling her he, Pain, has a fortune now that he has turned twenty-one (II. 70). On a deeper level, playing the rival lover allows her to express hostilities towards her husband she would never articulate as Mrs. Charlotte: "Shall a shabby dog, as I understand he is, pass unpunished for thus aspiring? No, he must, if a favoured rival support his pretensions with his sword: none but the brave, madam, deserve the fair" (II. 71). Charlotte has already proven herself to have more courage than her husband, rescuing him and ultimately their inheritance from Mrs. Smith. Gibbes engages with further name-play, Mrs. Smith saying that she finds "Pain" so "frank and generous in [his] professions" (II. 71): while Mrs. Charlotte is anything but "frank" in the scene, her honesty in contrast to Frank's lack thereof—even towards himself—cuts through the narrative.

The scene thus epitomizes Gibbes's foundation in and complication of Restoration comedy. When wife and lover are interrupted by Frank's unexpected return, Mrs. Charlotte loses her composure, Gibbes underscoring the scene's metatheatricality by likening the bravery of "Pain" to the "valor of Bobadil," a reference to the bragging, sword-fighting figure in Ben Jonson's 1598 comedy, *Every Man in his Humor*. The narrator adds parenthetically in what is no doubt meant to be a humorous understatement, "not with a tremendous voice" (II. 72). Gibbes thereby calls attention to Mrs. Charlotte/Pain's brief stint with androgyny in her complication of Jonson's caricature.[39]

The unheroic Frank proves himself bound to Mrs. Smith not by love but by slavery. Regarding his rivalry with "Pain," Frank tells Mrs. Smith, "[Y]ou have stripped me of my fortune, fame, nay, worse (sighing bitterly) my dearest wife, you cannot play the same game ... with that forward youth" who has no wife (II. 73). Mrs. Clive-as-Pain, however, not breaking character as the defiant lover, "lay[s] his hand upon his sword," excoriating Frank for "every disrespectful thing you utter relative to that lady" (II. 73). Most dramatic of these gender inversions, Frank becomes emotional, accusing Mrs. Smith of faithlessness, thus negating what he had just said about her having "stripped" him of everything including his wife. When Mrs. Smith, worrying that Captain Pain would be "disgusted by the insolence and familiarity of this cast-off," tells Frank to "begone," the narrator parenthetically adds that Mrs. Smith's eyes dart "masculine rage" (II. 73). The blurring of binaries during the cross-dressing scene, including Frank's cowering, Charlotte-as-Pain's gallantry, and Mrs. Smith's "masculine rage," allows the characters to express what the rigid gender binaries do not. When Mrs. Charlotte retreats from the scene, overwhelmed by emotion, the narrator refers to her as "this poor lady in masquerade" (II. 74).[40]

Tendering "whatever is purchaseable"

In his "horror and despair," Frank, Jr. wishes to "blot out the painful remembrance of [his] gentle, tender, faithful wife, [his] poor little innocent boy, and [his] much abused [*sic*] worthy Mr. Spranger" (II. 74). The reader is caught between the pathos of Frank's reaction and the knowledge that he is the cause of his family's suffering. Mrs. Charlotte no sooner returns to her own lodging, symbolic of her domestic identity, than she is "seized with a succession of fainting fits," the intensity of which emerges as a preeminent characteristic of late eighteenth-century female sensibility. Meanwhile, Rachel tells Swinbourn disguised as Robert, the pretended assistant to Captain Pain, the "secret" that Mrs. Smith is already married (II. 76). When

Captain Pain/Mrs. Charlotte sends a message to Mrs. Smith through Robert/Swinbourn not to do anything to Frank until Pain has had a chance to see her, Mrs. Smith is forced to extemporize: "[S]he therefore in an instant cast her snake's skin and resumed the syren, and going to [Frank's] bed-side, said she, 'now that my too just resentment has a little subsided, I am come to invite you to partake a chearing glass to the forgetfulness of all your guilt and woe'" (II. 78). Forgetfulness is precisely what Frank desires, not redemption for his past sins, and, though he says he will "bless [her] humanity" for "banishing the cruel reflections" that torture him, "his grief was still predominant; he wept abundantly," crying out for his wife and child as Mrs. Smith "did not fail plying him with this pleasant opiate, until she had so far conquered both reason and nature as to have laid him in a stupefied insensibility" (II. 78). Though the narrator refers to Mrs. Smith resuming the part of the "syren," Gibbes makes clear that Frank, in his self-pity and weakness, is author of his woes.

Through her "masquerade" as Pain, the seemingly demure Mrs. Charlotte trumps Mrs. Smith in her own game through a final, brilliant ruse. When Charlotte-as-Pain, knowing that Mrs. Smith is already married, plies her with fake jewels, saying, "my fortune is ample enough to procure whatever is purchaseable [sic]," Mrs. Smith "checks" her exultation due to "the recollection of her marriage, which she now considered as a terrible misfortune" (II. 79). Mrs. Smith claims that she is "affected with a sudden pain," Gibbes thereby bringing the comedic significance of Mrs. Charlotte's pseudonym, Pain, to the surface (II. 80). Mrs. Smith tells Charlotte/Pain that Frank has property in Ireland that she has charged in an annuity, upon which Charlotte/Pain demands that she "[relinquish] all claim to the estate of such a worthless ungrateful wretch, for a settlement of double that income" (II. 80–81). Equaling the deftness of Cousin Frank, who had come to Frank, Jr.'s financial rescue, so too does Mrs. Charlotte in the guise of Captain Pain save the Clive family finances.

This episode's reversal of gender binaries—assertion and passivity, financial savvy and domestic helplessness—culminates in a scene in the tavern where Pain and Mrs. Smith appear "as happy as a good entertainment could render designing hearts uncertain of success" (II. 82). The meta-theatricality of this moment—"a good entertainment"—reminds us that we are reading a novel rather than either watching a play or living the lives of the characters, moving the legacy of Behn beyond Restoration comedy and narrative satire into fiction that interweaves multiple layers of satire, irony, and subjectivity. Mrs. Charlotte's masquerade endows her with a "designing heart" equal to that of Mrs. Smith. Gaining a powerful agency through cross-dressing, Mrs. Charlotte is now able to speak to her husband as she cannot in her own person. When Mrs. Smith declares to "Pain" of Frank "that they should never see him more, "Pain" responds, "Hang him .... I'll answer for him he'll sneak here by and by" (II. 82). When Frank does appear, Pain takes control of the situation, asking what demands he would make of Mrs. Smith. When Frank answers, "Mad ones indeed ... for what can be expected from a bankrupt in virtue, fortune, and honour," Pain responds, sternly, "This stile but ill becomes you" (II. 83). Charlotte, the virtuous and honorable wife under her disguise, chastises her faithless and spineless husband (II. 83).

At the culmination of this scene, "Pain" tears up Frank's promissory note of four hundred pounds a year, putting both Frank, Jr. and Mrs. Smith under Pain's control. Gibbes here adds further irony to "tendering," or negotiating, as the basis of the marriage contract, Charlotte-as-Pain telling Mrs. Smith that her offer of riches depends upon Mrs. Smith "breaking off entirely with this wretch" (II. 84). In the guise of the imperialist Captain Pain, Mrs. Charlotte appeals to Mrs. Smith's greed by promising to reap the products of slavery and colonialism. With this elaborate transaction, Pain puts the final test to Frank, asking how he plans to "dispose of" himself, to which he answers, "I will immediately deposite [sic] all I have received in the hands of a friend, and never think of enjoying either rest or peace until I am reconciled to my injured wife"; when Pain asks if his happiness depends on that event and Frank assents, Charlotte reveals herself, "casting off her wig" (II. 85).

Charlotte has thus realized her gift for extemporized theatricality, telling her husband that her "scheme was unpremeditated, and executed as soon as formed" (II. 85). Her creative gift, Gibbes suggests, is unmarred by her compassion for her husband, for whom she cares in maternal terms rather than those of a traditional wife. Charlotte refers to him in an allusion to the prodigal son, saying, "[W]e'll kill the fatted calf, my prodigal convinced, reformed, restored, will give us joy unspeakable" (II. 86). At the opening of the novel, the elder Frank's casting off Frank, Jr. had set the tone for a tale that upends the traditional story of the prodigal son, as noted earlier in this chapter.[41] Now, by describing Frank's wandering from his marriage vows back to her, Charlotte adds another layer of irony to the comparison, suggesting a narrative end that replaces the marriage plot with the return of the son. Frank, Jr. responds with theatrics of his own, "swelling with revenge, envy and rage," hyperbolically contrasting Charlotte to Mrs. Smith: "[That wretch is a dishonour, you an ornament to your species" (II. 86). Frank diminishes Charlotte's powerful theater as Captain Pain. Performed to rescue him, the disguise has proven Charlotte far more than a mere "ornament," or object to make her husband's appearance more valuable.[42] By contrast, Charlotte expresses compassion even for Penelope, the "wicked author of the misery I have experienced," adding that she "shall receive infinite satisfaction from her sincere reformation" (II. 86). Charlotte's reference to Mrs. Smith as "wicked author" of her misery suggests Gibbes's metanarrative reference to Penelope's abuse of her authorial power in her tale of "pain" (II. 86).

Though Charlotte changes back into the women's clothing "suitable to her sex," declaring her husband "possessed [of] her unabated love," she not only "forbid[s] him ever repeating one tittle of the past" but requires that she "never have her newly recovered happiness interrupted by unnecessary painful recollections" (II. 87). Gibbes, however, has other plans for both Charlotte and Mrs. Smith, the latter executed at the end of the novel for her murder of Blissworth. Gibbes's providential role in Charlotte's story is appropriately more subtle. The Clives' son, Swinbourn, dies late in the novel, the result of Charlotte having left him with a caretaker who had neglected him. Though the Clives have another son later, Gibbes's message that one cannot bury the past becomes a tragic undercurrent throughout her career. At this point, however, Mrs. Charlotte believes that she has resolved her marital woes, writing to Miss Charlotte to "put a period to her unhappy suspense" (II. 88). The use of the punctuation metaphor suggests Mrs. Charlotte's metanarrative attempt to control the direction of the plot.

Just as Charlotte is Captain Pain no longer, Mrs. Blissworth is "Mrs. Smith no longer," hilariously missing the irony of her statement to Rachel about Pain and Robert: "[H]ow could we both ... be so egregiously imposed upon by the shallow artifice of a female and her ignorant maid [?]" a question more aptly pertaining to the two of them than to Charlotte and Swinbourn (II. 90). This protean prostitute, whose name the reader never fully knows, has survived in a world dominated by men through her masquerade as a range of seductive female characters to extort money from her johns, ranging from the young Pinkney, who abandoned her at sixteen, to Frank, Jr., whose "effeminacy" she finds pathetic. Penelope meets her match only in Charlotte, who is as bold as Mrs. Blissworth in controlling the "frolics" of those who would harm her or her family. Penelope realizes her 'happy days ... are at an end," ruing to Rachel the "two thousand pounds I shall bring this shabby, reduced, extravagant, weather-beaten colonel," adding that, should she ever be seen by this "trader," she "should be blown up, in spite of all [her] plots and arts" (II. 94). Her attempts to control her destiny have come to naught, and so "a single operation of chance shall destroy" all that she has done "which we could have no conception or apprehension of till actually come upon us" (II. 94). This "single operation of chance" connects the novel back to Behn's *Lucky Chance*. Mrs. Blissworth writes a "kind, submissive and dutiful letter to the colonel ... begging to see him" upon her return, while he, having spent all the money "she had entrusted him with and involved himself four hundred pounds in debt," did not "refuse a lady's request" (II. 94). The Blissworths are such "good oeconomists [sic] as to make the colonel's half-pay, pieced out with his lady's annuity, in conjunction with some lucky shakes of his elbow now and then, to support a tolerable appearance" (II. 95). Those "lucky shakes" suggest his gambling wins, though it is a fragile accord, arguments between them sending him "to the dice-box" and her "to her cordials" (II. 95).

Blissworth's "secret springs" of manipulation gush to the surface when he decides to request a reunion with Captain Seymour and his estranged sister, now Nancy Seymour, "to pardon a transgression which had been succeeded by many years of repentance and sincere mortification" (II. 96). Nancy, however, cannot forgive her brother "the evil he intended her," namely, to offer her sexually for his military advancement (II. 96). With Nancy "far advanced in her pregnancy," Seymour writes to Blissworth that they must "defer it to a later day than he could wish" (II. 97). Penelope-as-Mrs. Blissworth, though pleased with the prospect of the excursion, has become increasingly addicted to opiates, now having Rachel hooked on them as well.

Unmasking Miss Charlotte Clive's "proud, prudish heart"

The doubling of Franks and Charlottes intensifies when Frank, Jr. returns to his sister, Charlotte, and Cousin Frank, surprised to find that they have been courting in his absence: "Frank and Charlotte upon such friendly terms? (said Mr. Clive,) how comes this to pass?" (II. 98). In her most immediate attempt to bury the past, Mrs. Charlotte tells the young couple of her successful reunion with her husband, thus retelling the story of their adventures as a didactic tale to the younger Charlotte and Frank. However, Miss Charlotte needs no such lesson: her ambivalence about marriage is unambiguous as she describes "the natural instability and unfaithfulness of man's disposition, sacrificing her darling liberty, and bringing upon herself the weight and cares of conjugal prudence and parental tenderness" (II. 100). From Frank's intention "to make her a tender of his honest heart" to Charlotte's repudiation of "parental tenderness," Gibbes has the two meanings of "tender" subvert Cousin Frank's idealized proposal of marriage through Miss Charlotte's worries about the "weight and cares" marriage entails. This moment underscores the collision of the sentimental idea of marriage as destiny and the transactional idea of marriage as a business negotiation, suggested by Cousin Frank's "unexceptionable offer" that in turn can be traced throughout Gibbes's later novels representing the intersection of the two types of "tender."

When Mrs. Charlotte mentions the name Pinkney, Cousin Frank says, '[Y]ou have given me a clue by which I can unravel the whole mystery," warning that he risks the "condemnation of this company" by having "been the fatal, though innocent cause of this family's interrupted tranquillity" (II. 102). His admission of his "connexion [sic] with that creature," makes Miss Charlotte "highly displeased with him" as she whispers to herself, "there is no man commonly decent, no not one" (II. 102). Such a moment locates Gibbes as a pivotal figure between her Restoration-era forebears and those women engaging polemically with the "rights of woman" codified by Wollstonecraft. In the style of Behn, Gibbes both mocks Miss Charlotte's "sententious" disapproval through Mrs. Charlotte's perspective, yet Miss Charlotte can be seen as a harbinger of the voice of righteous indignation in *VRW*. Mrs. Charlotte hews to the gender binary that the novel itself has subverted, especially through Mrs. Charlotte's own cross-dressing heroism. She praises her sister-in-law as a "[g]ood girl" whose "silence has … some merit in it, as a female heart would be very unamiable, divested of lovely charity, and replete with masculine severity" (II. 102–03). When Miss Charlotte confesses that, though she loves Cousin Frank, she "abjure[s] marriage," Mrs. Charlotte dismisses her rejection of marriage as the corruption of "Platonism," explaining that "this is the man allotted for you; submit then to your destiny like a good child" (II. 103–04).

With the two Charlottes representing the ambivalence for women about their identity as wives, the conversation epitomizes a new stage in the evolution of gender during the long eighteenth century. Though inheriting such gender binaries as the prude and the prostitute from Restoration comedy, Gibbes represents through her fiction a more complex relationship among narrator and characters who articulate these binaries. Thus, as Mrs. Charlotte attempts to school Miss Charlotte regarding marriage, she tells Miss Charlotte, "[T]hat proud, prudish heart of yours shall submit to other concessions before I enter again upon my undertaking" (II. 105). Mrs. Charlotte continues, "but to me you shall be quite unmasked and ingenuous," Miss Charlotte "ventur[ing] to say to be sure she never had a dislike to him" (II. 105). Mrs. Charlotte's reference to unmasking Miss Charlotte figuratively follows her own literal unmasking before both her husband and Mrs. Smith earlier, one marking a triumph of her power to vindicate her husband. However, unmasking Miss Charlotte has already led Mrs. Charlotte to censure the young woman who now silences herself:

> "Then, sister …, since nothing less will satisfy you, know" (here she made a full stop) "Know what, interrogated Mrs. Clive, why that break?" "Know," resumed miss, "that I really feel a greater degree of approbation for the man in question than I ever thought my heart capable of; that if I could bring myself

to the resolution of renouncing my liberty, I should not hesitate to make him a present of it; that I believe him master of many excellent qualities, but I will not yet become a wife." "Notwithstanding the ill-nature you imputed to me in your wrath," returned Mrs. Charlotte, "I will now spare you, provided you consent to receive your cousin as the man you intend after a due probation to honor with your hand." (II. 105)

Miss Charlotte struggles, forced to finish the sentence by Mrs. Charlotte. She then cuts herself off, telling her sister-in-law what she wants to hear about renouncing her liberty.

Thus, no sooner does Miss Charlotte add the forceful, declarative statement: "I will not yet become a wife," than Mrs. Clive uses the opportunity to "tender" Miss Charlotte's liberty by referring to the marriage contract (II. 105). As she showed in her own forceful handling of Mrs. Smith, Mrs. Charlotte considers marriage a business transaction, reminding Miss Charlotte that Spranger "bespoke a share in that event" and that he "designs ... a handsome present" (II. 106). Proclaiming thereafter to her husband, "I am victorious," Mrs. Charlotte echoes her earlier militaristic diction after cross-dressing as a soldier in the apparently successful vanquishing of Mrs. Smith (II. 106).

Mrs. Charlotte has second thoughts about having been too easy on her sister-in-law. Grabbing her aggressively, militaristically "advancing" her to Cousin Frank, Mrs. Charlotte, even unmasked, has assimilated the role of Captain Pain, saying, "[R]eceive this lady as my gift, and judge of my sincere attachment to your happiness and interest, by the taking of this early opportunity to promote the one, and confirm the other," concluding that "we shall be the happiest family upon earth" (II. 107). Mrs. Charlotte transforms herself into the traditionally patriarchal figure, giving her sister-in-law to Cousin Frank as a "gift." Gibbes emphasizes this gender reversal when Cousin Frank "respectfully and silently received this inestimable present," Miss Charlotte remaining silent during "her sister's proceedings" (II. 107).

Marriage and hanging

With this scene of Mrs. Charlotte offering Miss Charlotte to Cousin Frank, Gibbes mimics the traditional marriage plot, suggesting perhaps that all will end well regarding the traditional comedic resolution through marriage. However, the novel is far from over, with its thorniest issues ahead. Having sold their estate in Ireland, the Clives return to the joyful Spranger who has been caring for the Clives' baby, his godson also named Spranger. The elder Spranger resumes his improvisational act as suitor to Miss Charlotte. He teases her by saying, "Was I not right ... to decline the encouragement you gave me at a certain time," implying that they had carried on a mutual flirtation, one that had served as a more benign precursor to the lechery of the men that inhabit the world of the novel thereafter. Now that the novel returns to Spranger's antics, however, they appear yet more disturbing. When Spranger says to Cousin Frank that the family has "long had this union in [their] eyes," he again teases, saying they worried that while he was in Germany "some pretty Hamburgher might have thrown us quite out," Cousin Frank's rejoinder exposing his underside. He claims, in ostensible play, that his heart "was in no danger from foreign attacks," after which he follows with a jingoistic criticism of "foreign ladies" who are "bred in such disagreeable extremes, either unrestrained to a degree of levity, or under such severe restrictions, that they are equally unsuitable companions for a British spirit" (II. 109). Spranger and Cousin Frank lay bare the nationalism that becomes central to the later novels, Spranger responding, "I do not love foreigners myself, and should have been sorry you had made some choice of one, as she could never have been so far naturalized as to become one of us" (II. 110). As seen through the retrospective lens of the later novels, from *The American Fugitive*, whose point of view is both female and transnational, to Zoriada's depiction of the xenophobia of provincial English villagers, this moment inaugurates a pattern in which Gibbes dissects the pretensions of such masculinist, Anglocentric views.[43]

Spranger concludes a sequence of glib aphorisms with the proverb, "marriage and hanging go by destiny" (II. 110). Linking marriage and hanging through destiny has multiple levels of irony for the novel, the "marriage and hanging" phrase literalized at the end of the novel when Mrs. Blissworth is executed for her murder of her husband. The witticisms conclude with Spranger and Miss Charlotte agreeing that there is a higher power that she refers to as an "over-ruling providence," Spranger following with the contradictory ideas in a single statement: "I love to bring things to a conclusion, there is nothing like taking time by the forelock" (II. 110). As the metatextual references continually remind the reader, Gibbes controls the characters through her authorial power as providential, while the characters who seek to take "time by the forelock" create the complications that give them a life of their own. Spranger's character is important to this early novel's satire of the marriage plot: never having married, he claims authority on marriage through his facile aphorisms though there is neither logic to them nor personal experience to support his ideas. It is Spranger, nevertheless, who precipitates the destiny that Gibbes has in store for his fellow characters in the final movement of the novel, insisting that he escort the group to Captain Seymour's, where they find "Mrs. Pinkney, alias Smith, alias Blissworth" (II. 111).

The Life and Adventures of Mr. Francis Clive 61

From storytelling to pantomime

The series of retellings of the novel's events from the perspectives of various characters, each of whom projects his or her interpretation onto the third-person narration, continues with Frank, Jr.'s second retelling of the events involving the Blissworths, the first having been his and Mrs. Charlotte's didactic version told to Miss Charlotte upon their return to England. The second is told to the Seymours as a morality tale in which Frank, Jr. appears to seek redemption through his narration. Seymour thanks Frank, Jr. for his "candid behaviour" in recounting the scandal of his involvement with Penelope, after which Seymour attempts, as do the Clives, to bury any "connexion [sic] with them" (II. 113). Suggesting that this morality tale, as Frank, Jr. has told it and to which the others agree, is far from such, the narrative takes a dark turn towards its culmination. Penelope, now Mrs. Blissworth, descends into alcoholism and deviousness that culminate in her decision to murder her husband.

The Clives' moral tale appears to have taken over the authority of the narrative, Mrs. Blissworth and Rachel reduced to unambiguous villains as they choose a "slow poison" that "would prey so imperceptibly upon his vitals, as to exempt [them] from every suspicion," the colonel thus "instantly sentenced to a living death" (II. 113–14). The narrator delves into the particulars of this slow and painful death, beginning with "violent disorders in his bowels," increasing so gradually that the two women become impatient and "impolitickly [sic] by one large potion, exposed themselves to that suspicion, they had ever before escaped" (II. 114). Penelope exposes herself to the law when she dismisses the physican's deducing her lies as "only speculative" (II. 115).[44] After Blissworth dies an agonizing death, both women are "examined before a magistrate and committed to Newgate" based on the physician's hermeneutical investigation exposing the depravity of Mrs. Blissworth (II. 116). Gibbes choreographs a final "providential" twist to connect the end of the novel to its beginning with the elder Francis Clive.

Cousin Frank goes to Newgate, hoping to "awaken these wretches to some sense of their guilt," his conversation overheard by a "poor fellow" in the next cell "who was to be executed the next morning for a rape" (II. 116). When he requests that Cousin Frank come to his cell, the inmate, John Brown, tells his story: he is none other than the servant of Francis Clive, Sr., retelling the story with the hindsight of paying the price for his master's transgressions as well as his own violence. Referring to Frank, Jr.'s mother who dies at the opening of the novel, the inmate tells Cousin Frank that he was servant with a worthy lady, and my master did not appear less deserving during her life; but after we lost her he became a very different man; he seduced a poor innocent creature under the solemn promise of marrying her, and did not undeceive her until she was in a condition which induced her for the sake of the poor infant to press him close with respect to his intentions. (II. 117)

He goes on to recount to Cousin Frank the young woman's discovery that her master never intended to "make her his wife," thus asking for an abortifacient that the master calls upon him to procure, a sequence that reminds the reader that she had died along with the baby (II. 118). As he recounts the degeneration of his master, he adds a new twist, however: while the master took to drinking, he, the servant, would "rob him of very considerable sums; he mortgaged his estate by my advice for partly the worth of it, of which money I stole twelve hundred pounds," going on to mix "laudanum in his punch," one dose having 'the desired effect, and he slept his last" (II. 119). The characters see the servant's confession of guilt as an exoneration of Francis, Sr. The servant says, "it was imagined he went off in a fit of intemperance" rather than having been murdered. The servant explains that he would have made his confession public but wanted to "save my young master from the disgrace of his father's crime" (II. 119).

The narrator offers a premature and facile moral after recounting the executions of Mrs. Blissworth, Rachel, and John Brown, stating, "Thus ended the lives of these wicked people," adding that "they reached the goal of vice at an early period," the former "just turned thirty, Rachel ten years older, and the poor footman thirty-one only" (II. 121). By having the narrator suggest that the scoundrels got their comeuppance, the distance widens further between the narrator and Gibbes, whose emphasis of the slippery line between good and evil works against the narrator throughout the novel. Spranger, in character, is afraid "his boy," Frank, Jr., "would be vastly hurt" by the news, suggesting that "it is a pity he should not possess his patrimony, notwithstanding he does not want it" (II. 121). Though Spranger is well-meaning in playing the father-figure, he describes Frank, Sr.'s "patrimony" in purely financial terms, participating in a legacy of paternalism whose misogyny, excess, and lying in the interest of control contribute to driving the plot's tragic outcomes, especially the most tragic event of all: the death of his namesake, Spranger, Jr.

As the novel heads to an apparently comic and sentimental closure with the wedding of Miss Charlotte and Cousin Frank, Spranger makes the disastrous decision to move the wedding from Elliot-Place to Spranger Hall. Following the wedding, Spranger brings Miss Charlotte into his study, insisting on "gilding" the matrimony with "a fatherly merit" (II. 123). Handing her a banknote for five thousand pounds, he cuts her off: "No thanks, said he, perceiving her about to speak" (II. 123). He explains that he is leaving his estate to the Clives, since the only relative he has is the Irish lord, the scoundrel who had abused Mrs. Charlotte and so "shall never have an [sic] half-penny of mine" (II. 124).[45] Spranger explains, sanctimoniously, his providential legacy to them: "[T]hough God was pleased to deprive your brother and you of one father, he was so gracious as to raise you up another" (II. 124). When Miss Charlotte thanks him and wonders at the "all-graciousness of providence," she asks for time alone to which Spranger responds, "No, no ..., we cannot allow you time for reflection" (II. 124). Callous to the deeper awareness of Miss Charlotte's ambivalence that she expresses as "divid[ing] her heart," Spranger replaces reflection with more glibly lecherous jokes: "I begin to think our conduct is censurable, a married lady should never retire with a quondam lover" (II. 124). Not only was she never his lover, but he enjoys the fantasy of an illicit union.[46]

When they go to Spranger's house, Francis, Jr. and Mrs. Charlotte leave Spranger, Jr. at home with a nursemaid who is distracted by one of the footmen who, seducing her, persuades her to "take four or five glasses" of wine, "more than she was accustomed to drink," the alcohol "affecting her head exceedingly"; as the nursemaid simultaneously holds Spranger and talks to the footman, "the lively infant [springs] out of her heedless arms," falling to the terrace below (II. 125–26). Young Spranger succumbs to his injuries after a long and agonizing death that echoes the drawn-out deaths first of the lover of Frank, Sr., and then of Blissworth. With the death of Spranger, Jr., Spranger's legacy fails, the baby's death counterbalancing the wedding's comic and sentimental resolution with the return of the repressed underside of the novel's darker strains.

The naming replication now takes on even greater significance for the novel's dismantling of patrimony. Spranger attempts to refashion the story of the elder Francis Clive's demise, bringing the grieving family together to tell them of his conversation at Newgate with Clive's servant, John Brown. However, Spranger prefaces his tale by attempting to invoke a superintendent power regarding the death of the baby: "Could we but perceive for what wise purpose this evil was brought upon us, we should infallibly cease to lament," offering cold comfort by suggesting young Spranger's death has prevented a possible life of misfortune: "[H]ad he fallen into guilty practices, either to come to an untimely end by the hands of the common executioner, or the treachery and malice of some of his vile accomplices, how would you all, under such circumstances, have wished he had died in his cradle?" (II. 129). Spranger is suggesting, in his characteristically tactless way, that the dead child is blessed in not having lived the prodigal lives of his father or grandfather. Yet Spranger adds that these "reflections" are only "prelude to a secret" (II. 129). Though the novel's narrator has given the events of Cousin Frank's depositing the sum of Francis Clive's estate earlier,

Spranger adds the new interpretation of Frank, Sr. as victim, eliding the elder Francis Clive's transgressions so that the news suggests he was pure victim of John Brown: "[Y]our father ... did not die a natural death, but was taken off at least by a penitent villain, who restored these sums, of which he had robbed him" (II. 130). Frank, Jr.'s reaction, "Great God ...! How wonderfully unsearchable are all thy ways" once again shows the metafictional play on Gibbes's authorship, who has choreographed not only these events themselves but also the characters' manipulation of those events in retelling them.

Though Frank, Jr. blames himself for his child's death, claiming that it was his own "criminal connexion, [sic] with an infamous woman" for which he has been punished "with the loss of [his] dear child …. [H]is innocent life was perhaps the forfeit of [his] transgression" (II. 131), the death of young Spranger is no more the end of the novel than the comedic marriage of Cousin Frank and Charlotte had been. Instead, the Clives go to Bristol to be healed, while Spranger "gallant[s] the ladies to a play," Colley Cibber's satirical *The Provoked Husband*, about a husband's affair, whose "reflections on conjugal felicity made poor Mr. Clive bite his lips but diverted the rest of the company extremely" (II. 133).[47]

Gibbes's use of metadrama to conclude the novel reveals the yet more nuanced irony that multiple layers of storytelling allow. Spranger's commentary on the play underscores its antiquated worldview: "Mr. Spranger extolled Lady Grace's conduct, and said, Sir Francis Wronghead was a queer dog, and that Manley's was a genteel and an amiable character" (II. 133–34). Even more interesting is Gibbes's decision to end the metadrama with a "Pantomime," a wordless drama that Spranger nevertheless narrates to his fellow theatergoers. Spranger sighs, reflecting that it "would have delighted his dear little Spranger," then concluding that the "present age abounded as much with old children as young" (II. 134). Criticizing the audience for their enjoyment of the "metamorphosis of Harlequin," Spranger bemoans the absence of the next generation to enjoy the drama, as the others in the party, silent as well, become audience to Spranger's opinions (II. 134).[48]

With this culminating moment of metadrama, Gibbes calls attention to the distance storytelling has come with the novel's more nuanced representation of character. In these final pages of the novel, Gibbes offers an alternative legacy, not only alluding to Restoration comedy but to the mock epic, *Don Quixote*. Though the description of Spranger "and his son Frank, like the Knight of La Mancha and the humble Squire," mocks the epic pretensions of the characters, it does so with compassion. Gibbes's authorial voice is the providential power that can heal her characters, even as the Clives go to Bath to heal.

The novel does not end without the illness and death of Spranger's brother-in-law, the evil Irish lord who had tried to rape Charlotte Clive early in the novel. That Gibbes juxtaposes "Mrs. Clive's health being perfectly restored" to this news suggests that it is the final catharsis for the novel that allows for "a second little Spranger" and, panning out further in time, to many years of health and felicity, when the elder Spranger is "taken off by a gentle stroke," leaving his fortune to the Clives. The narrator concludes the novel with the self-referential statement, "Thus have I conducted my hero through a variety of genuine scenes to the summit of human felicity, [*sic*] and were I to spin this work to a longer continuance, I must have recourse to fiction" (II. 136). Though the "hero" is apparently the eponymous Frank, Jr., Gibbes has problematized her narrator's moral directed at the "youth of both sexes, who may peruse this innocent Novel" to "hold fast their integrity, shun the flowery track of deceit, and remember, that a fair face must be illumined with the delightful glow of conscious innocence and virtue, to render it truly amiable" (II. 136). This facile closure hardly sustains the weight of the novel's metanarrative, providing a foundation for Gibbes's subsequent novels.

Notes

1 *Francis Clive* (as the novel will be abbreviated throughout this study) and *Lady Louisa Stroud and Caroline Stretton* are Gibbes's earliest known novels (1764).
2 VRW chapter XIII, section 2, decries the sentimental novel as responsible for so many young women's self-subjugation under the influence of "the reveries of the stupid novelists" (192). Later in that section of *VRW*, Wollstonecraft gives the example of the daughter of an acquaintance who "affected a simplicity bordering on folly; and with a simper would utter the most immodest remarks and questions, the full meaning of which she had learned whilst secluded from the world" (194). That Wollstonecraft was not the first to articulate the dangerous influence of sentimental novels on young women is further support for the connection between the two ends of the long eighteenth century. Charlotte Lennox's 1752 *The Female Quixote*, for instance, satirizes women's desire for romantic adventure through Arabella's "supposing Romances were real Pictures of Life" due to the "perfect Retirement she lived in" (4).
3 To help keep the characters straight when not clear from the context, I refer to the father and son as Frank, Sr. and Frank, Jr., and the cousin as Cousin Frank. The two Charlotte Clives will be distinguished in the context of the discussion as Miss Charlotte (sister of Frank, Jr.) and Mrs. Charlotte (wife of Frank, Jr.).
4 See Lisa O'Connell's *Literary Marriage Plots* for a fuller context. When Cousin Frank alludes to the "lucky chance" of their meeting, he becomes entangled in Frank's plot, now involving his own dissimulation.

5 The identity of the prostitute is fluid throughout the novel and will be indicated in this study in the context of her appearance as Penelope or any of the married names she assumes. See *Fantomina* by comparison, in which Haywood's nameless female protagonist assumes a range of characters to fool the man she has seduced and who has spurned her once he tires of her, only to become pregnant with his baby, so ending her own frolic. Gibbes not only develops the theme and devices of disguise but probes the darker underside of such frolic.

6 April London observes that "Francis would remain the gull of Mrs. Smith were it not for the actions of his long-suffering, but still devoted, wife. In a literalizing of Mrs. Smith's 'masculine soul' (I. 111)," Charlotte disguises herself as a soldier and "secure[s] her husband's reformation" (127).

7 This chapter will henceforth refer to the junior Clive as Frank unless discussed in relation to his father and cousin namesakes.

8 The Introduction to this study discusses the prodigal son motif in greater detail. See Barclay on the popularity of the "prodigal son" story during the Restoration period (316). Note Gibbes's complication of Behn's use of the story in the context of *Francis Clive*.

9 The phrase is the subtitle to Gibbes's 1786 *Elfrida*; the concept will thus be traced to this later novel in subsequent chapters.

10 This episode is the foundation for Gibbes's later, more complex conflict between the "tendering" of wives and tenderness of sensibility. See Spencer on Behn's bartered wife in *The Lucky Chance* (xvi ff).

11 Though the word "wife" could also mean "A woman considered without reference to marital status," Gibbes underscores Spranger's flirtatiousness (*OED*). www.oed.com/access.library.miami.edu/view/Entry/228941?redirectedFrom=wife#eid.

12 Wanting to share his "heart's ease" with his sister, Frank purchases a lottery ticket for her (I. 30–31). Gibbes uses the device of the lottery again in *The American Fugitive* (see Chapter 2).

13 Spranger appears to be paraphrasing Hamlet's "I must be cruel only to be kind." *Hamlet*, III. iv. 199. https://shakespeare.folger.edu/downloads/pdf/hamlet_PDF_FolgerShakespeare.pdf. Accessed May 17, 2021.

14 This early novel can thus be seen as a precursor to Gibbes's later Anglo-Indian novels that complicate the position of British colonialism in India, especially regarding from the subjectivity of the feminine.

15 See Chapter 2 regarding *The American Fugitive*, whose full title has two phrases, reversed in the two editions; the other half, *Friendship in a Nunnery*, is yet more telling of the homosocial complexity of the convent's microcosm. The topic recurs in *Zoriada*, *Hartly House*, and *Elfrida*, the subjects of this study's later chapters.

16 See the Introduction to this study regarding Wollstonecraft's admiring review of Gibbes as evidence that Wollstonecraft distinguishes the sentimental fiction she decries in *VRW* from Gibbes's female characters using their wits to extricate themselves from male aggression.

17 "A woman who has lost her honor, imagines that she cannot fall lower, and as for recovering her former station, it is impossible .... Losing thus every spur, and having no other means of support, prostitution becomes her only refuge" (*VRW* 77).

18 Making the provocative suggestion that Charlotte's later cross-dressing as Captain Pain connects her to the "masculine soul" of the prostitute, April London observes that Charlotte in military uniform not only vanquishes her rival and gets her husband out of the financial straits he has created but redeems the prostitute's androgynous subjectivity (London 127).

19 Frank, Jr.'s being led by his "evil genius" anticipates the Romantic complication of the classical binary of masculine disempowerment by a seductress (even seen in Percy Shelley's double-sided Preface to *Alastor* the poet's death blamed on the female temptress is none other than his own imagination.

20 Worth noting are this episode's similarities to and complications of Haywood's 1725 *Fantomina*, in which Beauplaisir is the dupe of Fantomina's multiple masks until her final undoing through her pregnancy.

21 www.oed.com/dictionary/elope_v?tab=meaning_and_use#5657539. Accessed September 15, 2024.

22 Rachel's name is doubly ironic through its biblical antecedents: Rachel is not only one of two wives of Jacob, but she is the prostitute's "Dorcas," a biblical character who sewed for the poor (I. 72).

23 Nancy's desperation is not new to women's literature, the desire for a "gynotopia" a point discussed as well in Chapter 2 of this study. As early as her 1405 allegory, *The Book of the City of Ladies*, Christine de Pizan writes that "women had not written books about themselves and were, therefore, represented unfairly over many centuries" (Blumenfeld-Kosinski 116). Reason comes to Christine in a dream to tell her, "[L]adies and all valiant women .... have been abandoned for so long, exposed like a field without a hedge, without finding a champion who would appear for their defense, notwithstanding the noble men who by order and right should defend them, but who through negligence and lack of interest have let them be mocked" (Blumenfeld-Kosinski 124). To extend Blumenfeld-Kosinksi's note on Christine's framing her allegory with the "reading of misogynistic authors recall[ing] Virginia Woolf's foray into the British Library in search of writings about women—which are all by men," moments such as this in *Francis Clive* are repeated often enough in Gibbes's oeuvre to add her voice to those of women crying out at a metanarrative level for a literary stronghold of women writers representing their subjectivity (Blumenfeld-Kosinski, 116 n. 1).

24 This statement gives fuller irony to the term "tender," surfacing again when the narrator refers to Blissworth as "the tender brother" who tells the Captain that Nancy has run off with the devil whom he "wishes had had her some time ago"; Seymour, however, is shocked by Blissworth's "brutality," saying, "A shew of tenderness would be worth the heart of so near a relation," as though his intention of raping her is pardonable in comparison to Blissworth's betrayal of his sister (I. 90).

25 Before returning to "Mrs. Pinkney," having updated the reader on Blissworth's background, the narrator steps out of the story to explain the lengthy digression: "[T]here are many Colonel Blissworths, who derive their origin, and owe their rise to as mean and unworthy foundation as he did …. Who bring this slur upon the profession and, when traced, are found to be neither better nor worse than our hero, who is indeed a scandal to the military cloth" (I. 94). This "scandal to the military cloth" is underscored retrospectively when Charlotte disguises herself as a colonel in Volume II to rescue her passive husband.

26 The contrast between this early ridiculing of Blissworth's cowardice and his painful and prolonged death at the hands of Penelope proleptically reverses Marx's statement about history in *The Eighteenth Brumaire of Louis Bonaparte* (1852): "Hegel remarks somewhere that all great world-historic facts and personages appear, so to speak, twice. He forgot to add: the first time as tragedy, the second time as farce." That revolution in the hands of a female writer reverses this pattern suggests the larger implications of the gendering of history. www.marxists.org/archive/marx/works/1852/18th-brumaire/ch01.htm. Accessed March 20, 2023.

27 As will be seen in the Conclusion to this study, Gibbes's "ironical" mirth first seen in the voice of Miss Charlotte anticipates Austen's nuanced irony in *Persuasion*'s representing the rights of woman.

28 This lack of a name is central to *Zoriada*, whose protagonist is only known by her eponymous pseudonym.

29 By ending Volume I with Frank describing the letter writer as "incognito," Gibbes may be referring to the final disguise of Fantomina as Incognita in Eliza Haywood's 1725 eponymous novella. In Haywood's satire on the sentimental novel, as noted in the Introduction to this study, the young aristocratic woman—never named—is more interested in what is going on in the "pit" of the theater: there, the aristocratic young men mingle with prostitutes while the privileged young ladies are consigned to the theater boxes aloft. By having the protagonist descend to the pit, Haywood comments on the double standard that allows men to do so with impunity; as clever as the female protagonist is in acting the part of multiple lovers as the object of her desire grows tired of them one by one, when she becomes pregnant, she is shamed by her mother and sent to a convent. Gibbes appears to extend Haywood's metafiction in *Francis Clive* by giving the female manipulator a more powerful role; on the surface she is the antagonist of Clive as protagonist, whereas Gibbes undermines the traditional roles to give her creative power over the passive and tormented Clive.

30 By looking at her in the larger context of Gibbes's career regarding female identity, Penelope can rather be seen as having learned survival at sixteen by playing the masculine role in society's gender binary. When Mrs. Charlotte cross-dresses to get Frank's inheritance back, she performs yet a different version of masculine entitlement, while Frank, having that entitlement by virtue of his gender despite his passivity, is pulled between the powerful women who abuse and rescue him. Thus, Penelope is one of a spectrum of women who finds power in nontraditional ways in Gibbes's novels, often because of masculine predation.

31 Gibbes's description of this psychological state predates Coleridge's psychoanalytic characterizations of the perverse. For a detailed study of Coleridge's challenges to the moral imperative in his writings on psychoanalysis and the nature of evil, see my *Rethinking the Romantic Era*.

32 The debate between the two sisters-in-law underscores how Gibbes bridges the satirical proto-feminism of her seventeenth-century forebears—including Behn, Amelia Lanyer, Margaret Cavendish, and Katherine Philips—and Wollstonecraft's late eighteenth-century polemic in *VRW*. See Frank's description of his sister's spinsterhood as "leading apes in hell" later in this chapter (II. 36), perhaps a reference to Philips's "A Married State" (www.poetrynook.com/poem/married-state). For Wollstonecraft on men treating women as infantile, see *VRW*, Chapter 2 in which men "try to secure the good conduct of women by attempting to keep them always in a state of childhood" (p. 22). See this chapter's earlier discussion of the distinction between Wollstonecraft's inversion of gender binaries and Gibbes's more nuanced dissection of these binaries. Gibbes gestures beyond Wollstonecraft in her challenge to the reason/sensibility binary to which Wollstonecraft hews by inverting it through Mrs. Clive's advice to her sister-in-law complicated by the context of Frank's infidelity.

33 II, 28. That Gibbes repeats the phrase when Mrs. Charlotte is hatching her plan to save her husband suggests that Gibbes is alluding to Behn's 1686 comedy, *The Lucky Chance*, another example of the reach of the "long eighteenth century."

34 The term is also used with erotic implications in Haywood's *Fantomina*.

35 Though Frank, Jr. adheres to the original meaning of "leading apes in hell," a Protestant warning to unmarried women that they will go to hell for not propagating, Gibbes adds a layer of historical irony, since Shakespeare used the phrase satirically in both *Taming of the Shrew* and *Much Ado About Nothing* to suggest an anti-religious attitude about woman's refusal to accept their subservient role in marriage. Inverting the original meaning of the proverb to suggest that being chained to a man is worse than "leading apes in hell," Katherine Philips ends her 1646 poem, "A Married State," that warns women about marriage as the most patriarchal abuse of women, "Therefore Madam, be advised by me / Turn, turn apostate to love's levity, / Suppress wild nature if she dare rebel. / There's no such thing as leading apes in hell."

36 According to the *OED*, "ice-piece" was defined as either a painting of a winter landscape or an actual block of ice, the latter probably closer to Penelope's meaning: "a lump or mass of ice. The closest example to this novel given in the *OED* is "1778 J. R. Forster *Observ. Voy. round World* ii. 93 As the ice-pieces are thrown one upon another, ice-mountains are formed by it." www.oed.com/access.library.miami.edu/view/Entry/90765?redirectedFrom=ice-piece#eid23 1299935. Accessed May 19, 2022.

37 See the Introduction to this study for Gibbes's anticipating the lineage from Coleridge's psychoanalytic interest in the "mobile without motive … [t]hrough [whose] promptings … we act," extending to Poe's "self-subverting impulse," and Freud's *parapraxis* (Coleridge and Poe qtd. in *Rethinking the Romantic Era*, 18).

38 See the earlier reference to the "lucky chance" that Cousin Frank is in Ireland, the phrase echoing Behn's 1686 comedy (II. 28).
39 Suggesting a meta-level of Gibbes's play on names in the novel, the reference to Ben Johnson as a forerunner of Restoration comedy is significant in relation to the influence by Behn on the "Daughters of Behn," a humorous name for the literary descendants of Behn as a parody of the "Sons of Behn," male Restoration playwrights influenced by Jonson. That Gibbes makes the reference here, specifically, suggests that Gibbes challenges the gender binary behind the masculinist—albeit satirical—depiction of virile heroism.
40 Gibbes's use of "masquerade"—as will be important for discussion of the end of the novel—functions similarly to the masquerade of Restoration comedy, including Behn's *The Rover*.
41 See also the Introduction's discussion of the gendering of the prodigal son story that connects Gibbes to Behn.
42 The praise is also made equivocal with the term "species," having multiple meanings during the eighteenth century, its adjective form from the singular, *specie*, "Of requital or repayment: In a similar fashion; with like treatment." Gibbes's play on the word reminds the reader that Frank has not been fully transformed, lest there be any doubt about it. *OED* (4.b). www.oed.com/access.library.miami.edu/view/Entry/185993?rskey=YrzLYk&result=1&isAdvanced=false#eid. Accessed June 20, 2021. This meaning was extant during Gibbes's life.
43 Chapter 2 focuses on this transitional novel while the subsequent chapters examine how female subjectivity in the later Anglo-Indian novels troubles British colonialism particularly in its subjugation of women. See Chapter 4 for discussion of *Zoriada*. Regarding the term "naturalized," the first reference to the term in the *OED* is late sixteenth century. www.oed.com/access.library.miami.edu/view/Entry/125343?rskey=Z70wgM&result=1&isAdvanced=false#eid. Accessed June 26, 2021.
44 Ever conniving, Mrs. Blissworth responds to the suspicious apothecary, Mr. Wilson, who wants to call in a physician, with the compliment that Mr. Wilson "was practical, the other only speculative," but being an honest man, the apothecary sends for Mr. Cartwright, the physician. Cartwright declares that Blissworth was poisoned and was "even then in the agonies of death," immediately suspecting her when she fakes a fainting spell and, suspecting as well that Mrs. Rachel is in on the scheme, claims that Mrs. Blissworth had already confessed and said that she is in on it, Mrs. Rachel thus admitting, "[M]y lady gave it him herself, I only bought it" (II. 115). See the discussion of this moment in Chapter 3 from the hindsight of *Zoriada*, regarding Withers and the hermeneutics of trying to deduce Zoriada's identity.
45 Gibbes has Spranger allude to Ben Jonson's 1598 comedy, saying he chooses to "deal [his fortune] out amongst those I esteem; every man in his humour, you know" (II. 124). This may be seen as Gibbes's critique of the old patriarchal perspective that has attempted to control and silence women, but which gave way to the female perspective through the legacy of Aphra Behn, one Gibbes continues to complicate in her subsequent novels.

46 The novel appears to be moving towards traditional comedic resolution with even Swinbourn, Mrs. Clive's servant who had masked as "Robert" to her "Pain" earlier, marrying "an humble swain, the son of a farmer" who "admired this woman with a disinterested heart, for he had never heard a tittle of her three hundred pounds" (II. 125). Once the Clives know about his interest, they purchase the farm he was about to rent, "settled upon the wife, and made him master of her three hundred pounds, with the interest due upon it, to stock his farm; he could hardly believe he was awake" (II. 125). However, no sooner does the novel appear to culminate with this double play of tenderness and tendering bringing about marriage at two different strata of society than it shifts to the greatest possible tragedy for the Clives, with the death of their two-year-old son, Spranger.

47 The 1728 play, subtitled "A Journey to London," is in the Restoration style, though written after the period. The metadrama underscores Gibbes's building upon Restoration comedy, as discussed in the Introduction to this study. Scholarship on the long eighteenth century that is founded on affect theory provides a significant perspective on this pivotal moment, as articulated by Marsden: "The affect of theater ... is, of necessity, connected to the collective response of a body of spectators who share in the same event at the same time and in the same space. It is reciprocal in a way that no other literary form is, as the spectators watch the performance and share their response with those around them, creating a synergy that impacts even the literary work itself" (Marsden 301). This application of affect theory to eighteenth-century drama becomes relevant again in *Elfrida*, as discussed in Chapter 4.

48 *Harlequinade* is a British comic theatrical genre, defined by the *OED* as "that part of a pantomime in which the harlequin and clown play the principal parts." It developed in England between the seventeenth and mid-nineteenth centuries, "originally a slapstick adaptation or variant of the Commedia dell'arte, which originated in Italy and reached its apogee there in the 16th and 17th centuries." See also Kate Novotny Owen's challenge to the traditional view of the structure of this genre that may have interesting implications for Gibbes's metatheatrical reference to Cibber.

2

The American Fugitive: or, *Friendship in a Nunnery* (1778, 1784): transnationalism between the Seven Years' War and the American Revolution

Had I been a man, I should surely have been a knight-errant.[1]

Like *Francis Clive* nearly a quarter-century earlier, Gibbes's *The American Fugitive* represents the machinations of lascivious men in power ultimately outsmarted by the young women they seek to oppress. A new dimension of this concern comes to the fore in *The American Fugitive*, however: the novel explores both the possibilities and limits of female community, suggested by the title's other half, *Friendship in a Nunnery*. Gibbes anticipates this new focus early in *Francis Clive* when Nancy Blissworth, despairing and alone, seeks the help of her landlady to extricate herself from her brother's attempt to sell her for his military advancement. Nancy's equivocal statement, "One female cannot be so abandoned, as not to deliver another from infamy and perdition," gestures ahead to the complicated network of sexuality, gender, and female friendship in Gibbes's evolving fiction (I. 88).

The structure of this novel injects even greater nuance into the sexual politics of the marriage plot than *Francis Clive*. As the double perspective of the title suggests, it resists the sentimental focus on a single protagonist. The new narrative structure of *The American Fugitive* reflects this development. While *Francis Clive* subverts the traditional trajectory towards marriage, connecting various plotlines through the tension between name repetitions among various characters and the exponential aliases of others, the epistolary *American Fugitive* informs its plot with a network of subjectivities that, in turn, offers a range of possibilities for its female characters within and even outside of marriage.

From America to France, Italy, and England, *The American Fugitive*'s new geographic reach informs the development of Gibbes's career with greater transnational possibility. *Francis Clive* anticipates this larger global perspective through its perilous journeys across the Irish Sea and its glimpses of the port where Penelope the prostitute awaits ships of commerce coming from the East with potential johns and where men abandon her for promise of wealth in the colonies. With *The American Fugitive*, Gibbes establishes more overtly her concern with the relationship between gender and British imperialism, a hallmark of the yet broader global reach of her Anglo-Indian novels beginning in 1786, less than a decade after this novel.

The two halves of this novel's full title, *The American Fugitive: or, Friendship in a Nunnery*, suggest the collision of two worlds. The first is an ambivalent, transatlantic colonialism, in which the eponymous American fugitive, Arabella, is caught through the political upheaval of her father's involvement with the Seven Years' War. The second is the microcosm of a French convent in which the lives of young women, of whom Arabella is one among several voices, intersect as they struggle to liberate themselves from the horrors of abuse within the convent's walls. This is not the first novel in which Gibbes takes on the dystopian world of a convent. Besides *Francis Clive*, Gibbes wrote *Lady Louisa Stroud and Caroline Stratton* in 1764, a more traditional, Augustan satire, distilled in Caroline's lamentation on nunneries. Punished by her uncle for having been involved with a young man, Caroline asks Louisa, facetiously, "How do I lament that England is unfurnished with those happy Institutions, Nunneries?" She herself answers satirically, "O how delightful, in a Fit of mortified Pride, and heart-felt Disgust, to fly for ever [sic] the ungrateful Face of Man, by throwing one's self into such a blissful Retreat!" (28). As she contemplates the "strange Lives" of the nuns, she concludes, "No emerging! I never yet heard of an emerging Clause, in favour of any she, whose Mind might change. On Reflection, I renounce my former Opinion. Hideous Places! What! Immured for Life? I die at the very Thoughts of such a Sacrifice" (28). Contrasting Louisa's flippancy towards the convent life over twenty-four years later, *The American Fugitive* signals a literal and proverbial sea change, the latter novel representing a spectrum of young nuns as victims of horrific abuse in the convent.

From the earliest phase of *The American Fugitive*, Arabella's letters represent a young woman's subjectivity during the Seven Years' War. Though Arabella's surname, Smith, suggests a working-class background, her genealogy challenges sociopolitical binaries in addition to the gender binaries that Gibbes subverts in *Francis Clive*.[2] Arabella's father had fought as a Loyalist to the Crown during the Seven Years' War, the family now on the lam. With the novel written two years after the end of the American Revolution, the title, *The American Fugitive*, is ambiguous in multiple ways that suggest Gibbes's interrogation of nationalism. The fourteen-year-old Arabella, whose father fought with the redcoats, is a fugitive from America, a land having shifted from colony to nation, the family now in exile. Yet as an American, Arabella represents a fugitive spirit regarded as "wild" by the other young women who nevertheless embrace her, hence the second half of the title, *Friendship in a Nunnery*. Though at first the other friends, principally Maria Gerrard and Nancy Freeman, condescend to Arabella's youthful emotionalism, they come to embrace her heterodoxy. Arabella remains a passionate renegade whose defiance towards the convent leaders opens the eyes of the religious Maria about their hypocrisy and cruelty. Though Arabella inspires Maria to escape the tyrannical sway of the convent, Maria remains pious, representing one of several choices the young women make once they escape the convent. As discussed later in this chapter, though Arabella's marriage to Lord D., who aids in the rescue of the young women, can be seen as a concession to the marriage plot, their union at the end of the novel is tempered by several contingencies: Arabella's continuing agency; Lord D.'s admiration of her; and, most important, the less traditional fates of the other women, whose backgrounds, ages, and choices regarding marriage represent a remarkable range of possibilities for women.

The historical context of the novel, written just after the American Revolution but before the French Revolution, is important not just regarding the "American Fugitive" but also the "Friendship in a Nunnery." Openly hostile to the French monarchy and the Catholic Church, the novel represents the impossibility of a utopian community of women within the walls of the convent.[3] The other half of the title, *Friendship in a Nunnery*, refers to the band of revolutionary young women who ultimately denounce their victimization by the Church. These friends plot their successful escape with the help of Lord D., who infiltrates the convent disguised as a priest. Targeting the abuses of the Catholic Church, *The American Fugitive* centralizes Gibbes's concern with the rights of women that *Francis Clive* presents most overtly through the debates on marriage between the two Charlotte Clives. The female letter writers in *The American Fugitive* include Nancy, Maria's close confidante, who remains in England throughout the novel, and who eventually corresponds with the American Arabella as well.[4] The camaraderie among the three young women suggests a community of mutual support, despite the occasional conflicts arising from their triangulated friendship. Gibbes contrasts the letter-writing friends with the other women of the convent who are either tragic victims to—or, in the case of the Superior, a tyrant complicit with—the male abusers of the convent. Complicating a simple binary between the convent directors and the homosocial community of the girls is Lord D., who not only disguises himself as a member of the clergy to aid in the escape of the renegades but joins their epistolary exchanges, exhibiting diplomacy and respect for the young women's different points of view.

The secular world proves as treacherous as the world inside the convent, as Maria's first letter to Nancy details. Describing herself as lacking traditional beauty, Maria writes that her mother shut her "only child in a convent" because she is "taller than girls of sixteen generally prove"; Maria wonders why her "[i]rregular features and a dowdy complexion," do not "atone" for her height in making her appear older than she is (2).[5] Maria refers to her "exportation" to the convent, a term that commodifies her in the context of her mother's suitor having paid Maria "certain attentions" when visiting their house. He had referred to Maria's mother—not Maria herself—as "a fine promising girl—a pretty sort of young woman," terms Maria considers epithets that "could not be very flattering to one who chose not to be deemed past her meridian" (I. 3). Maria scorns her mother for refusing to act her age, a rare perspective at this stage in literary history.[6]

Dominating the opening of the novel, Maria's voice is the sole subjectivity through the first nine letters. Gibbes shows the arc of Maria's shifting affinities before introducing the letters of both Nancy, in England, and Arabella, whose parents have placed her in the convent for political asylum after the family has fled America. The passion with which Maria addresses Nancy suggests Maria's homoerotic desire for her friend, innuendoes that grow more pointed as the novel develops. Nancy never reciprocates this intensity despite her sisterly devotion to Maria, who at the outset tries to convince Nancy to join her in the convent. Maria's expostulations are those one may expect to hear regarding a lover: "O Nancy, that it was but possible for us to spend our lives together! I cannot form an idea of higher felicity than strolling side by side through these beautiful gardens" (I. 12). In this early letter, Maria extols the Superior to the point of infatuation: "I almost deify" her, both "for person and mind" (I. 12). When the Superior is revealed later to be a tyrant, thanks to the intervention of Nancy's letters and Maria's complicated friendship with Arabella, who openly defies what she sees as the convent's superstitions, Maria must reckon with her submissiveness toward the Superior (I. 12).

Gibbes reveals her voice behind Maria's in her early letters' descriptions of the convent. Maria's diction anticipates the literal contagion that later spreads through the convent, exposing it as a bastion of abuse and complicity. In her early correspondence with Nancy, Maria describes the architecture of the convent as like the "ruins ... of Roman architecture" in which the "Attic story," appears innocuously "pretty," with cloisters, choir, and dormitory. Gardens, she gushes, are "laid out in a taste peculiar to their use; for whether it is contemplation or air, retirement or society, that is the motive for walking in them, the wish is gratified, and the satisfaction general and heart-felt" (I. 6). As revealed later, these spaces that lull Maria into trust for the convent hold horrors for the young women imprisoned there.

Maria's early description of the Superior lays the novel's foundation for exposing the repressiveness of consigning young women to convents as punishment for their sexual energy. Maria's description of the Superior as the "best-bred woman I ever met with, and in her day must have been a first-rate beauty," is tinged with irony for, she continues, the Superior's "lessons, therefore, on the vanity of personal charms, fall with inconceivable grace from her lips" (I. 6). Maria describes the class structure in the convent's microcosm, from those on the "high pension," who experience "no unpleasant round" of "reading, industry, exercise, and devotion," to those on the "low pension" excluded totally from the knowledge of what passes, and all intercourse with the interior parts of the convent" and "scratch up their learning as they can" (I. 7–8). Maria admires the "handsome nuns" whose "*whys* and *wherefores* which induced them to a recluse life" she finds entertaining (I. 8).[7] Gibbes delves into the roots of Maria's admiration of the Superior and other figures of female authority by having Maria compare them to her mother, the convent appealing as a place that promises more freedom than she had living under her mother's roof: "Instead of sharp lectures, or painful self-denials, which were frequently given me, and demanded from me, when under the parental roof, I here meet with nothing but commendation, sociality, and smiling countenances: nor do I believe I shall ever experience a change, contrary as your declared opinion is to that I entertain" (I. 11).

Though Gibbes soon complicates Maria's praise of the "unimpeachable" life and manners of the convent, at this early phase, she portrays Maria as seeing the world in stark binaries. Maria thus contrasts Nancy's English Protestantism to the French Catholicism to which she is becoming more and more attracted. She urges Nancy, "[M]ake a speedy and public renunciation of your error" (I. 14). While Maria later learns the priests use confession as a means of physically and emotionally abusing the young women in the convent, she claims at this early phase that Catholic confession makes it the superior branch of Christianity. Maria's subsequent "marriage" to Jesus parodies the sentimental marriage plot, though Maria later breaks her "wedding" vows within the convent. She reestablishes these vows at the end of the novel in her own terms, outside the convent. Unlike the other young women rescued from the convent, Maria decides to live a single life devoted to God.

Adonises and Niobes in America

As it develops the multiple subjectivities of its letter writers, the novel weaves together several strands of subversion against patriarchy into the homosocial world of the convent. The most radical voice is that of Arabella, at first indirectly relayed through Maria in her letters to Nancy. As noted earlier, Arabella's parents are themselves "fugitives, wanderers without home or habitations," having left Arabella at the convent for political asylum as they struggle to survive while fleeing America across the Atlantic. Though the humble, American Smith family contrasts the European aristocrats who make use of the convent for various purposes, including keeping their daughters out of sexual mischief or away from the parents' own sexual mischief, Gibbes complicates the implication of the Smith name. Arabella's father, a Loyalist to the Crown, had "served under General Wolf," the leader of the Red Coats in the Seven Years' War. Thus, Smith and his family are now the target of the American revolutionaries (I. 16). The political alliances are complicated, therefore, as suggested by the reference to "General Wolf": if Arabella is referring to James Wolfe, it would make her father British and fighting against the French, thereby explaining the political level of her hatred towards the French convent.[8] Maria tells Nancy that Arabella "professes the most loyal attachment to the Sovereign," Arabella "inveigh[ing] heavily against ministerial pride, and ministerial tyranny, which, she insists upon it, incited the crown to tax the Americans in a manner the most repugnant to their true interests …. Hence the opposition to the misrule of bad Ministers, which had been so fatally construed into disaffection for the King, and [sic] branded with the name of rebellion" (I. 16). As Maria suggests here, the danger for Arabella is the empowerment of corrupt individuals rather than government in the abstract. Maria's description idealizes Arabella and, through her, American democracy. When Maria expresses concern and support for her suffering, Arabella herself idealizes America, particularly for women: "Merit in my country never languishes in obscurity, or passes unrewarded," for, she says, people are rewarded for character rather than rank: "not what were their fathers [sic] fame and fortune, but what are their own principles and abilities; and every one [sic] is eager to support, encourage, and establish them accordingly" (I. 17). While Arabella speaks about American marriages in utopian terms, "not made up by bargain and sale; the wife pays no price for her husband, nor has the husband an idea of purchasing his wife," Gibbes presents a central subversion of the sentimental marriage plot. Not only does Maria refuse to marry when given the opportunity at the end of the novel, but Arabella herself settles in England, marrying the entitled Lord D., the novel's conclusion thus problematizing the sociopolitical categories her characters had earlier espoused (I. 18).[9]

In her opening letter to Nancy, Maria introduces Arabella, grief-stricken at being both fugitive and imprisoned in the convent of whose repressiveness Arabella is keenly aware. Yet despite the complexity of Arabella's political opinions and perceptiveness of the hypocrisy of the convent officials, Maria infantilizes Arabella with diminutive epithets such as "little enthusiast" and "little Niobe" because Arabella is perpetually in tears (I. 18). Maria's epithet of Niobe for Arabella cuts deeper than Maria suggests, however.

In one letter to Nancy, Maria imagines the "fairy land" of Arabella's America as an odd fantasy. Maria tells Nancy she would go there if Nancy were to come with her, even if "all the youths were Adonis's [sic] and all the maidens Niobe's [sic]," after which she adds, "for are we not already at too great a distance, and without the prospect, tho' the vast Atlantic rolls not between us, of being re-united? This recollection cools my transports" (I. 18). The language of Maria's "transports" at the idea of being reunited with Nancy is homoerotic, cooled, she says, by her odd fantasy of an American gender binary in which young American men epitomize masculine beauty, hence Adonises, and young American women are variants of Niobe, the mythological figure whose children have all been murdered and is hence perpetually crying, then turned to stone by Zeus.[10] The dark fate of the mythic Niobe suggests another means by which Gibbes problematizes the sentimentality of Arabella's marriage to the heroic Lord D., the novel's equivalent of an English Adonis, at the end of the novel.

As Maria's "Niobe" epithet for Arabella suggests, Gibbes complicates the novel's representation of the interplay of gender and nationalism through her letter writers' multiple perspectives. Maria recounts to Nancy her surprise at hearing Arabella's outspoken opinions regarding British colonialism. According to Maria, Arabella has argued with a boarder from Scotland over the difference between the Scots relationship to the British Crown and that of Americans, who defy the "ministers" of the King that, Arabella says, the Americans love. Maria then paraphrases Arabella who claims the Scots were traitors to the Crown, whereas "we, poor Americans, with English hearts in our bosoms, and English blood in our veins, were proclaimed rebels" (I. 21).[11] Arabella, bursting into tears, speaks with such great "sensibility" that she draws the Scottish boarder to her side. She does so by recontextualizing traditional femininity and thereby complicating conventional notions of gender. She compares her family's plight to that of the "Scotch fugitives" who, despite having "got into office ..., the navy and army saving them from famine and drudgery, and with sword in hand, as every bad woman is said to hunt down a betrayed innocent, advanced to scourge us into subjection" (I. 22). Beginning this sentence by questioning Scottish loyalty to England, Arabella proclaims American loyalty, but doing so in gendered terms that betray Arabella's personal stake in the argument. Because the simile of "bad women" hunting down a "betrayed innocent" has no clear connection to the sentence, it suggests that Arabella is repelled by the Scottish boarder who, Arabella suggests, represents the duplicity of the boarder's nation. If Arabella's nickname Niobe is a clue, however, she is not merely creating a duality between the Scot and herself, but rather suggests a more nuanced issue of identity as it interweaves gender and nationalism. As is America, Arabella herself is both the "bad woman" and the "betrayed innocent" since, in the Greek myth, the gods transform Niobe to stone out of both pity and punishment. Arabella articulates the ambivalence of America through the distinction between the treatment of Americans loyal to the Crown between the Seven Years' War and the American Revolution. The most tragic outcome, she claims, is that "the Americans were represented to the Sovereign as an ignorant, feeble race," the "bravery and resolution with which they fought under the English banner, during the last war ..., wholly forgotten" (I. 22).

Recounting Arabella's argument with the Scottish girl to Nancy, Maria suggests the deep roots of Arabella's ambivalence: "[F]orgetting at what price the victory must be purchased, [Arabella] sincerely wished her countrymen might be victorious" (I. 22). Maria explores American ambivalence further, telling Nancy that in Arabella's "cooler moments" she blames "East-India Gold" for the tea act, a theme Gibbes returns to in the Anglo-Indian novels (I. 22).[12] While Maria refuses to comment on Arabella's opinions, since she is neither "politician sufficient either to controvert or ascertain the truth of her assertion," Gibbes's own commentary underlying Maria's claim to being apolitical emerges: "but judging by the rules of reason and common sense, I should think it impossible such men could be entrusted with the care of the British empire, as are unable to distinguish between the value of a peppercorn and such a country as America" (I. 23). Gibbes here alludes to the importance of Scottish "common sense" philosophy on such founding figures in America as Thomas Jefferson.[13]

The microcosm of the convent thus represents both the intersection of the sociopolitical and religious issues dominating the lives of the young women as well as the way these issues are filtered through the young women's relationships with their parents, different though each of these relationships is from the others. While Arabella's parents are ambivalent as both victims and supporters of British colonialism, Maria's mother announces in a letter to her daughter that her inheritance will depend upon her marrying, with her mother's "approbation" or a "handsome support" if Maria stays in the convent, her mother having "pledged herself at the altar to make the happiness of her husband the sole object of her attention" (I. 24). Later it becomes clear that this marriage will not be the last for Maria's mother. Maria herself goes through multiple changes in her attitude towards the convent so that, by the novel's end, she rejects marriage. She chooses instead to live comfortably with Arabella's parents, thanks to Gibbes having Arabella win the lottery late in the novel. This *deus ex machina* appears less a sign of narrative weakness than a metanarrative device by which Gibbes slyly mocks the hopefulness of her readers for a tidy plot resolution.

At this early stage of the novel, however, by having Maria share with Arabella her mother's letter, Gibbes explores matriarchal ties constrained by patriarchal institutions, a topic that Wollstonecraft would broach indirectly fifteen years later, in her 1792 *Vindication of the Rights of Woman*.[14] When she reads the letter from Maria's mother, Arabella proclaims, "We have no such mothers ... in America," Arabella weeping over her "lost family" (25). Gibbes underscores the contrast between Arabella's ambivalence about America's independence as she weeps for her lost family, and Maria's dry-eyed mother, who has gotten her daughter out of the way of her erotic dalliances.[15] Yet Gibbes offers another maternal figure, Mrs. Ashley, an inmate of the convent. Though piously fatalistic at this early stage of the novel, Mrs. Ashley contrasts not only the failed, repressive, or victimized mothers in the novel but, most important, she stands as a foil to the Mother Superior whom Maria mistakes for a genuine mentor of the highest order. As Maria recounts her conversation with Arabella to Nancy, Mrs. Ashley interrupts the melancholy exchange with her worldly experience: "Calamity is the common inheritance of existence, and teaches us a lesson prosperity never so much as hints at; namely, that it is not in this world we are to fix our everlasting abode; but that youth, beauty, honours, as well as age, disease and misery, alike lead on to the grave, where all things can alone be equally and permanently adjusted" (I. 26). Though Maria has promised Mrs. Ashley to "submit ... to providence, whose designs are most excellent," the young women—and Mrs. Ashley herself—take matters into their own hands by escaping the convent and choosing paths that reflect their individual desires (26).

Even as the renegades in the convent move towards discovering their agency among the range of choices available to them by the novel's end, Maria's homoerotic desire for Nancy remains closeted. She alludes to it obliquely in a letter amounting to a sequence of non sequiturs.[16] Maria's passion for Nancy momentarily surfaces when she recounts Arabella's disbelief that Maria's anxiety as she awaits "a letter from England" is not from a man but "a female friend alone I am anxious to hear from"; however, Arabella then claims, "[N]o man on earth will ever be so dear to her as I am" (1778 ed., 53).[17] The logic is askew: one might think Arabella is competing with the as-yet-unnamed female friend but, shifting genders, Arabella suggests she will value no man as much as she does Maria. Adding yet another layer of seeming non sequiturs to this letter, Maria shifts in the subsequent paragraph of this letter to Nancy to talk about reading Boileau's satires which, she says, should find a middle ground between impudence and modesty. Maria's reference to neoclassical satire, however, creates a deeper metatextual moment, a device Gibbes had introduced in *Francis Clive* and develops both here and then, in yet more nuanced ways, in the Anglo-Indian novels. Here, Gibbes calls attention to her authorial voice often subverting those of the letter writers.

Eros, religion, and the blurred line between abuse and seduction

Gibbes underscores the complexity of Maria's deeply divided allegiances as the young women become more overtly aware of the abuses in the convent. When arguing with Nancy, Maria must confront the naivete of her own claim that "confession must be a blessed relief to the oppressed mind …, the voice of religion speak[ing] me into resignation" (1778 ed., 53–54). Maria's friends ultimately awaken her from the church's indoctrination following Maria's taking orders, forcing her to retract her defensive assurance to Nancy, "I am in no danger of becoming an apostate from the religion of my forefathers" (1778, 54). However, in the same letter, Maria warns Nancy that what she has to say next will "frighten" her, warning Gibbes's reader as well of the darker strains to come in this novel. From this point on, *The American Fugitive* draws closer even than *Francis Clive* to the overt concern characterizing Gibbes's late fiction with patriarchal abuses that link gender to the sociopolitical.

Maria thus confides to Nancy that the convent has attempted to indoctrinate Arabella, Maria telling her that Arabella has been "tampered with," though she "always flies out at a rate which is by no means pleasing to her "tempters" (1784, 29). Though on one level Maria is referring to the convent's desire to convert Arabella, the juxtaposition of "tampered" with "tempters" and "flies out" suggests a tension between a primal level of abuse and a more sophisticated level of seduction, complicating the binary implicit in the passive "tampered with" and the active "flies out"; these multiple levels of agency become entwined in the letters shared among the correspondents as the plot unfolds. As Maria tells Nancy, Arabella understands the multilayered nature of the convent's stratagems, Maria recounting that Arabella has warned her, "*silken nets* are spread for me, in which she fears my passions will be entangled, though my reason and conscience should make ever such powerful resistance" (I. 29). As Maria thus describes to Nancy Arabella's shrewd understanding of the convent's sexual manipulation of the young women, Maria expresses her repressed homoeroticism in sublimated, religious language, embracing the convent's "perfections": "fastings, self-examinations" that bring back "the wandering heart" (I. 33). Maria describes a "beautiful young creature" having taken orders "with rapture," suggesting the sexual sublimation of religious iconography.[18] Maria objectifies the religious enthusiasm of the novitiates from the perspective of "men and angels" (I. 33). Noticing Maria's fascination with the ways of the convent, Arabella warns her to be rational: "Is it possible … that your good sense can be so taken in!" (I. 34). Arabella uses disease as a metaphor for the contaminating effect of the convent that, she says, creates "a slow poison, and the mind is *lost* before we are sensible it is *infected*," the contagion metaphor literalized later in the novel when a deadly infection spreads through the convent (I. 35).[19]

The sequence of letters that opens the novel, from Maria's paraphrasing and editorializing Arabella's views followed by Arabella's own letters, demonstrates Gibbes's new level of sophistication as she experiments with multiple narrative perspectives. At this stage, Arabella's anti-Catholicism only makes the convent more attractive to Maria, who tries to pre-empt Arabella from writing to Nancy whom Maria warns, "the Americans ... bring up their children in an absolute abhorrence of the Catholic religion, and, in the wildness of their zeal, condemn its purities, because it has, perhaps, some errors" (I. 36). The atrocities that unfold in the convent later underscore Maria's ignorance as she criticizes Arabella for her "zeal" and as she attempts to convert Nancy to Catholicism. In a lengthy diatribe against the beginning of Protestantism, Maria denounces Henry VIII who had "no pope to regulate his conduct," thereby reducing the relationship between the two branches of Christianity to the Pope as embodiment of morality and the Protestant King who betrays his wife when he sees "the beautiful Anna Bullen [sic]," Maria ending the letter with a prayer that Nancy "may become a *true* Christian" (I. 37).

Arabella's voice in her first letter to Nancy contrasts not only Maria's paraphrasing of Arabella's intellectual "zeal" but Maria's own religious zeal. Referring to her "favourite quotation," a passage from Pope's "Essay on Man," Arabella introduces herself to Nancy as rational, endowed with an Enlightenment education that makes her capable of demystifying religious superstition (I. 40).[20] The strength of Arabella's intellect in this letter to Nancy belies Maria's infantilizing of Arabella as "little Niobe." Arabella is not only a fugitive from her homeland but from the gender binary that she sees divided between classically educated men of reason and the "worthless women, worn out in the public eye, or broke down by disease, [who] retire here on small annuities, and close a life of licentiousness by a mockery of penitence" (I. 41). Urging Nancy to "rouse [her] friend from the lethargy her good sense has fallen into," Arabella's voice merges with Gibbes through metafiction. Arabella urges Nancy to convince Maria "that all she beholds is a farce, a stage trick, and that when the curtain is once drawn aside she will shudder at her condition" (I. 42).

At this early stage of the novel, Gibbes suggests another potential layer of significance for the epithet, "little Niobe." Arabella's fate has the potential to be tragic, her fugitive status and the repression of her voice of resistance by the convent having the power to turn her to stone, metaphorically. However, as will be discussed later in the chapter, Arabella evolves as both autonomous and heroic, defying external forms of oppression. That Gibbes has Arabella function as one of a network of female subjectivities with different outcomes tempers Arabella's union with Lord D. at the end of the novel, simultaneously fulfilling and problematizing the marriage plot. Gibbes thus sets the novel on a trajectory that paradoxically fulfills the sentimental desires of the reader while dismantling them.

Gibbes therefore opens the novel by framing the plot with a triangle created by the two correspondents from the convent, Maria and Arabella, vying to warn Nancy about each other's attempt to lure her. Following Maria's plea for Nancy to come to the convent, Arabella writes to warn her not to come for, even "if you become not a [C]atholic, you will cease to be a [P]rotestant, and have your mind rendered a mere chaos in religion" (I. 48). Arabella interprets Maria's shunning of her "as a proof of the pernicious tenets she has imbibed," Arabella defying the Superior and the holy Fathers: "[T]hey are welcome to anathematize me, expel me, torture me ... rather than make me a proselyte" (I. 48). Arabella then turns her anger towards the political situation in America, hoping Nancy can give her news regarding England's assault on America and, specifically, about her fugitive parents.

As the epistolary relationship among the three young women thus unfolds, Maria warns Nancy that Arabella is devious, adding that "the whole convent" hopes she will soon be called to England since "souls have actually been undone" by her "little tricks" (I. 54). By this point in the competing letters, Maria is won over by the unfounded gossip of the other women in the convent. Despite her claims to piety, Maria is still strategizing with Nancy to get her to the convent. Maria's early letters to Nancy struggle to repress her homoerotic desire even though she says she is resolved to "bid a final adieu to the world" despite her love for Nancy, their "hearts so perfectly in unison ... from our very cradle to this period" (I. 51). Maria follows the urging of the priest to "convert [her] love of [Nancy] into a love of [her] soul only" (I. 52). She describes Nancy's "image" in confession as an obstacle to her union with God, presenting the binary between Nancy and the Catholic God in erotic terms, saying, "I will be the bride of Him that made me what I am" (I. 53).

When Maria tells Nancy that, even though the nun's habit only adds to Maria's own "plainness," it would suit Nancy: "the very things which are most unbecoming to me, would abundantly increase the loveliness of your person" (I. 53). Nancy's response to this transformed Maria is both frank and curt in her warning against the Catholic Church: "However the secret may be hid from yourself, it is apparent to me that the religion you have embraced *contracts*, not, *enlarges*, the heart, and teaches its votaries to sacrifice every finer feeling on the altar of superstition" (I. 55). She demands Maria answer the question of what Arabella has done to "forfeit [Maria's] good opinion" for, as "Niobe," she is "an alien to [Maria's] affections, and weep[s] ... the loss of [Maria's] friendly brow and agreeable conversation" (56). Nancy shrewdly addresses the convent's censors and spies, "who are to peruse this letter," advising them, "[D]rop your labours in the cause of piety, where I am the object;—for a [P]rotestant I have lived, and a [P]rotestant I will die" (I. 57).

Maria continues writing to Nancy in the self-contradictory language of her ambivalent erotic desire for her, Maria telling her that she must say goodbye forever, while admitting, "I not only pity and forgive you, but languish for our re-union" (I. 60). The erotic diction of "languishing" underscores Maria's setting her union with Nancy against the sublimated union with God. Speaking to Nancy's sexual attractiveness and brilliance, Maria foreswears her own identification with the female gender: "Your person is lovely, your understanding superior to most of your sex" (I. 60). She warns Nancy about the impermanence of marriage as "a human, a political, a divine institution ... but, as there is a sufficient number of persons in the world to fulfill this duty, I cannot bear to think heaven should be robbed of such a prize as your virgin affection," adding, "What husband can love you better than I do?" (I. 61). Though Maria does not acknowledge how her passion for the convent sublimates her homoeroticism, she offers Nancy an apartment in the convent, suggesting that the distance between England and France is a small price compared to "an East-India voyage"—a glimpse ahead, perhaps, to the global sweep of the later novels. She promises, bitterly, that if Nancy agrees to the offer, Arabella, whom Maria refers to enviously as Nancy's "new favourite" will be able to be with her wherever she goes, "sleep with you; eat with you: and you know her obstinacy too well not to be sensible she will much rather harden then [sic] soften your heart" (I. 62).

Arabella's subjectivity deepens as her letters to Nancy show her maturation from the weeping Niobe to a sharp analyst of the multilayered dynamics within the convent. Despite her criticism of Maria's religious zeal, Arabella chastises Nancy's "silent contempt" of Maria, continuing to hope that Maria will have misgivings once the "flutter of her probation is over, and the irrevocable vow has passed her lips" (I. 62). Arabella's anticipation of Maria's change of heart is precisely what happens later, confirming Arabella's prescience beyond the ken of her elders. She tells Nancy that the convent is trying to seduce her with riches, offering her a "diamond crucifix" if she "would relax [her] *obduracy*" (I. 63). Linking the two halves of the novel's title, the sixteen-year-old Arabella increasingly represents an idealized America in her resistance to the Church: "Liberty of conscience is the birth-right of every individual, and I will not ... set it up for sale for all their gems" (I. 63). Even as she embraces the sisterhood among the inmates of the convent, Arabella distinguishes herself as the only one among them as a fugitive from political oppression. Meanwhile, she responds with excitement to Nancy's news of King George's "accommodation," asserting Americans' loyalty "above all his British subjects," as she blames "rapacious, or at best cruelly misjudging ministers" for their plight (I. 64). Arabella continues her correspondence with Nancy not only with anti-Catholic but anti-French rhetoric. Arabella echoes the earlier metaphor of infection when she refers to "French vices [that spread] infection throughout all ranks of the community," the metaphor literalized later in the novel by the contagion in the convent that allows their escape (I. 68).

With the novel's multiple subjectivities and lack of a narrator, Arabella's voice becomes a mouthpiece, albeit a flawed one, for Gibbes's authorial voice. For instance, when Arabella says that she is excluded from the chapel on "the *day of days*, lest my distress should be found contagious, and ruffle the new convert," not only is the italicized phrase an indication of verbal irony on Arabella's part but the double-edged significance of contagion here plays out through Gibbes's metanarrative stratagem (I. 69). That the convent worries that Arabella will contaminate Maria is ironic from the perspective of the literal contagion that spreads through the convent later. Gibbes reminds the reader that the providential will aiding her characters in their escape from the convent is that of the author, not the God that the convent believes punishes young women for disobedience.

The reader thus sees the spectacle of Maria's initiation into the order through Arabella's eyes, Gibbes's use of metanarrative here looking ahead to its more complex role in the later novels. Arabella compares Maria's dress to a "robe-coat ... such as your tragedy of queens strut their little hour in on the stage," after which she is led to "the altar to finish the *raree-show*" (I. 69). Gibbes's metanarrative usage of the term *raree-show* is suggestive on many levels. According to the *Oxford English Dictionary*, such a spectacle was a "set of pictures or a puppet show exhibited in a portable box for public entertainment; a peep show."[21] From Arabella's/Gibbes's perspective, Maria is indeed used as a puppet by the convent, Arabella thus demystifying the ritual. The "peep show" element, however, is yet to come in the novel, with the priests' sexual predations both in the nuns' cloisters and during confession. Arabella ends the letter by returning to the subject of her parents, comparing them to "the poor Jews of old" who were "despoiled of their possessions, and driven out from their native land" (I. 71–72).[22] Arabella later wins the lottery, sharing its spoils with her parents in England, falls in love with Lord D., and happily takes on the new persona of Lady D., never looking back to America. With such an outcome, the reader is reminded that the authorial voice paradoxically speaks through and is ultimately independent from her characters, including Arabella, the character with the greatest potential to act for her yet, for whom "there are certain subjects that unhinge [her] reason" (I. 72). The metatheatrical "*raree show*" is ultimately a foil to the young women who emancipate themselves from the convent as agents of their destinies.

Nation building and the female revolt against patriarchy: "lopped off from the parent stock"

The metanarrative connecting Gibbes to Arabella at this early stage of the novel surfaces most directly with Arabella describing the tragic spectacle of Maria's initiation. She tells Nancy that, to the priests, "it is a glorious sight" for "an English lady, bred up in Protestantism, and in the bloom of life, not only to embrace their faith, but be wedded to her Saviour from deliberate choice, self-dictated election, and unbiassed [sic] conduct" (I. 73). Maria's "wedding" vow to Christ stands as an important early iteration of Gibbes's subversion of the marriage plot. In the case of this novel's larger cast of young women, Gibbes further departs from the centralized focus of the development of a single heroine with a trajectory towards marriage to the hero, instead playing the various characters off each other. Maria's choice to "marry" her "Saviour" is thus set against the later choice for Arabella to marry her own savior, Lord D., while Nancy marries the man assigned her by Maria, leaving the marginal figure of the elder Mrs. Ashly to live with Arabella's parents (I. 73).

Reacting with intense emotion to Maria's "wedding," Arabella tells Nancy, "The moment I perceived her approach, my sight failed me, I fainted, and was conveyed to my own apartment with as little bustle as possible" (I. 73). Despite this apparent weakening of her claim to rationality, Arabella's recording of the events has power: she follows the description of the ceremony with the observation that another "English girl, of small fortune, captivated with the splendor of the show and the applauses bestowed on our lost friend, has ... solicited to be put on her noviciate [sic]" (I. 74). Concluding that the "artful people" of the convent "poison every mind they can come at," Arabella thus analyzes the ceremony's purpose to entice more innocents through the trappings of their religion (I. 74). Gibbes here gestures ahead to the complication of the reason/sensibility binary. Arabella's apology to the staid Nancy for her "wildnesses" anticipates the fascination with madness as a rebellion against Enlightenment reason associated with Romanticism (I. 76).[23]

Nancy extends the metaphor of Arabella's wildness by connecting Nancy's own lack of independence in her father's house to her concerns about pre-revolutionary America: "I cannot, I own to you, conceive it a reasonable demand, that so large a limb of the British empire should be lopped off from the parent stock—Independence was not what the Americans looked up to, when they started aside from our friendship; for, instead of the aggrieved, they would have then been … the aggressors," the revolutionaries as rebellious children of the monarchy as well as fledglings who "grew up under our wing" (I. 78). When she concludes that "wicked men ever poison the minds of the good," she appears, on the metanarrative level, to be infected by the contagion of Arabella's diction regarding the convent (I. 78). Yet her notion of the good—those who are revolting against the monarchy—being poisoned in America contrasts the situation in the convent, in which the superiors are the ones poisoning the young.[24]

Gibbes thus gives the reader a glimpse of revolutionary possibility through Arabella as a wild, young American woman defying the patriarchal power of the convent. Gibbes both echoes and complicates *Francis Clive*'s satire of chivalry when Arabella tell Nancy, "I have a turn … for chivalry, and, had I been a man, I should surely have been a knight-errant," a significant turn from Charlotte Clive's cross-dressing as a military hero to rescue her husband and their finances from the conniving prostitute by whom he has become enthralled (I. 85). Though Charlotte returns to her women's clothes and her role as Mrs. Clive, and though Arabella succumbs to the heteronormative role of the sentimental heroine—marrying the entitled Lord D. who has rescued the young women, her defiance becomes more nuanced as the novel develops. Arabella finds an outlet through verbal irony in her letters to Nancy, announcing, "A day of fasting and outrageous humiliation is at hand, for the martyrdom of one of their legendary saints …. As to austerities, except in appearances, they are not … imposed, but rods are conveyed into every separate cell, as a hint how they may voluntarily please the God of love and mercy" (I. 86). Arabella underscores the dissonance between any possibility of romance and the growing awareness of the horrors of the convent. Thus, after telling Nancy that Maria declares herself "undone …. Deceived, abused …, beyond all remedy," Arabella remarks that

> romances are only witty and sarcastic parables; for the giant's den, the monster's cavern, the distressed damsels … pictured therein, are taken originally from, and are even at this day found, in convents.—The magicians that lie in wait for the innocent and unwary at the doors of the fatal castles, are they not the likenesses of these lady-abbesses, who, with smooth and dissembling speech, allure them into the gripe of their lords? (87–88)

Gibbes may here be alluding to Spenser's anti-Catholic allegory in the *Faerie Queen*, appearing to extend Spenser's indictment of Catholicism. However, Gibbes challenges the *Faerie Queen*'s misogyny through the complexity and realism of her characters. Complicating the possible reference to Spenser, Gibbes juxtaposes Shakespeare with this reference to "romances."

Shakespeare, Arabella says, never experienced "such an hour as I now experience [since] his imagination ... was of nature and the passions" (88). This metanarrative moment reminds the reader that Gibbes's characters arise out of her own imaginative rendering of psychological realism. Extending Shakespeare, Gibbes represents a comprehensive human nature that includes the female psyche.[25]

The dual references to Spenser and Shakespeare create tension that the novel realizes with the clandestine arrangement of Arabella as the go-between for Maria and Nancy. From the allegorical romance of Spenser to the psychological realism of Shakespeare, these metanarrative references together create an important shift both within the novel and in Gibbes's career regarding the authorial voice, now doubly mediated when Gibbes embeds Arabella's epistolary response to Nancy's letter contained within Maria's letter. Gibbes thus disperses the authorial voice by having Arabella send Maria's letter in her own voice rather than paraphrase it. Writing of the sexual predations of priests, with "licentious passions in their hearts," Maria now acknowledges the fears of "Little Niobe" as "prophetic" (I. 89). Maria herself appears unscathed by the sexual abuse of some of the other nuns because of her "want of personal charms ... the only protection a convent knows from the overtures of diabolical libertinism" (I. 89).

Maria writes that she now realizes the "act of confession" which she had "thought must be balm to the afflicted heart ... is only practiced as a cover for assignation" (I. 90). When she says that her confessions are "always short," as she is "enjoined to ... break down every hold of carnality (under which profane terms our friendship is alluded to)," Maria comes closest to an explicit admission of her homoerotic love for Nancy (I. 90). She then tells of a young nun who, dying in her cell, had told Maria—in a dark parody of confession—that she was urged to take poison "conveyed to me by the author of all my calamities .... I have been betrayed, every way betrayed, and die, that the reputation of the convent may live" (I. 91). As she is dying in Maria's arms, the nun says,

> I have written ... my life, at stolen periods, and wished to send it into the world as a warning voice; but it has been carried away from my cell by the infernal hero of it; and indeed, could I have put it into your hands, it was too imperfect for the press, and too dangerous to be kept by you within these walls: and what could it have told you more than you behold, that the wretch, thus untimely sunk to the grave. (I. 92)

Lest the reader, whom Nancy here represents, miss the tacit message of Maria's letter, Arabella says, "Intrigue, I was convinced, dwelt within a convent; but murder, gracious Providence! Who could have thought of murder?" (I. 94). The priest's forcing this young nun to drink what may have been an abortifacient both recalls and complicates the opening of *Francis Clive*, in which the elder Clive, having impregnated his dying wife's nurse, has her take an abortifacient from which she dies.

With Arabella's secondhand account of Maria's new perception of the horrors around her, Gibbes creates a yet more mediated narrative that splinters into stories within stories. Maria catalogues the nuns' ruined lives at the hands of the priests, from a "beautiful nun" who is persecuted for refusing the advances of the priest to another young woman, sent by her family to the convent when she formed "a tender intimacy with a youth" with "no provision to hope for" (I. 95). Maria implies that this young woman performed sexual favors for the priest ("at what price I leave you to imagine") to "contrive a means of escaping to [the youth's] arms" (I. 96). However, she is duped by the priest, caught, and brought back to the convent (I. 97). Yet another had "eloped at fifteen with her dancing-master," her brother pursuing them, murdered the lover and "dragged her in all the horrors of despair" to the convent (I. 97). Maria now functions as a moral touchstone for these young women regarding the sins of the priests, describing in her letter yet another young beauty cruelly used, forced to marry a man twice her age and then falling in love with a young man. Maria says this young woman "confessed to me," telling Maria, "I was buried most inhumanly alive" (I. 98, 100). Maria ends this catalog of horrors in the convent by acknowledging that she "threw [her]self into the pit from whence there is no temporal resurrection" (I. 100).

The metafictional level of Arabella's commentary on Maria's letters to Nancy becomes most pointed through Gibbes's wry humor behind Arabella's naive analysis of Maria's letter. Arabella concludes that Maria's letter "proves her ... happier than usual: but, if these priests are the libertines she describes them, I fear she has very little chance for escaping their attacks; for, though no beauty, she is one of your first-rate agreeables, which is often more attaching, if not equally attractive with the utmost symmetry of features" (I. 101). In spite of Gibbes's authorial irony behind Arabella's sexual naivete, however, Arabella claims to "exult in seeing the mask torn from the face of hypocrisy, and would most gladly lend a helping hand towards making the shame indeliable [sic]," (I. 101). Gibbes emphasizes the innocence of Arabella's "wild" American spirit, irrepressible in resisting patriarchal oppression.

Despite her earlier claim that she would be a knight errant if she had been born a man, Arabella is heroic precisely as a young woman who has stayed in the convent to help the victims of abuse. Such heroism extends beyond even the later rescue by two men endowed with patriarchal authority, Lord D. and Venols. Because of their status, both men are at less risk than Arabella, who claims she would "head a little army in [Maria's] cause, and either rescue her or perish in the attempt," adding, "I am a very heroine, not in word, but deed, where my friend's honor or reputation is at stake" (I. 102). That Arabella signs the letter not with "little Niobe" or even her name, but "A little fugitive" underscores the tension Gibbes creates between her naivete and her heroism (I. 102).

As the convent's treachery affects Maria more directly as the plot unfolds, her subjectivity deepens. In a letter to Nancy, Maria describes a priest's attempt to seduce her, her reaction one of shocked naivete and a depth of understanding that connects the evil to Shakespeare's *Othello*. When the priest first makes what she calls his "*tender* overture," she says, "[M]y beads fell from my hands, my *Pater Noster* was suspended on my tongue, and I looked instantly for his cloven foot" (I. 103).[26] Referring to the belated observation of Othello who, looking down at Iago's feet, realizes that evil comes in human form, Maria reveals how far she has come since her opening letters. She is now aware of the psychological depth of the priest's evil. Within the Catholic Church, Gibbes here suggests, the devil is not the mythologized figure of Bible but the Church's own abuse of its power.

Despite her deepening concern about the horrors surrounding her, however, Maria lacks the heroism of Arabella. Having been abandoned by her mother and persecuted within the convent, Maria feels doomed to die there. She thus tells Nancy, "I therefore absolve you from every tie of secrecy: if it should become necessary, speak out …. Before that period arrives … I shall be no more" (I. 107). However, of Nancy she says, "For you other scenes than those of vice and horror are prepared …. Live the honor of our sex and admiration of the men, and shew [sic] what an accomplished woman should be and what reverence she is intitled [sic] to, and will always receive from liberal and distinguishing minds" (I. 108). At the novel's end, Nancy marries Venols, the man who had wanted to marry Maria.

"We will elope together": breaching gender binaries

Gibbes complicates the binary of the evil convent and victimized young women with the arrival of Lord D. and Louisa, whom Maria describes to Nancy as a "beautiful" young nun. Louisa might well have been a protagonist in a traditional, sentimental novel, yet after she is rescued by Lord D., she reveals herself to be spoiled and manipulative. Even before the reader discovers her true nature, however, Lord D.'s infiltration of the convent to rescue Louisa upends the heteronormative idealization of the sentimental tradition. To the amusement of Arabella, Lord D. disguises himself in a nun's habit. As Arabella notes, he is an odd chivalric hero: an "enterprising young spark, disguised in a female dress" who not only enters the convent but "visits [the]

Superior, into the very parlour," breaching the *sanctum sanctorum* of this homosocial world. Arabella notes that his features "favoured his designs: for he is within the middle size, slim and genteel" (I. 116). Just as Arabella wishes to be a knight so she can rescue the female victims of the convent, Lord D. is feminized not only to aid in his design but, suggesting a sensibility later associated with the Romantic period, Lord D.'s androgynous appearance anticipates a new masculine ideal emerging at the end of the long eighteenth century.[27]

Gibbes subverts the marriage plot on multiple levels when Arabella, describing Lord D.'s intended rescue of the three young women, says, "[W]e will all elope together—I mean, Maria, Louisa, and myself" (I. 117). Extant during Gibbes's time, "elope" could denote a wife leaving her husband with a paramour.[28] This meaning is significant on multiple levels, not the least of which is its implication for Maria leaving her "marriage" to the Church to embrace the secular world. From Arabella's point of view, the three women are defying the homosocial world of the convent to navigate their own destinies. Though at this stage Arabella admits that "my Lord's abilities may exceed mine," Gibbes bases Arabella's marriage to Lord D. at the close of the novel on a mutual recognition of each other's power. This episode thus introduces the skeleton of a heteronormative love triangle among Arabella, Louisa, and Lord D. that complicates the homosocial triangle among Arabella, Maria, and Nancy.[29] Confiding to Nancy her concern that Arabella's "young heart is surely captivated, though she knows it not, by my Lord," Maria refers to Arabella's love as a "disease" (II. 141). While Arabella becomes Lady D. at the end of the novel, Maria only realizes belatedly that the convent bears literal and figurative "disease."

This pivotal moment in which the young women decide to escape adds yet another layer of subversion, not only of the sentimental novel but of the oldest of western romances, *The Odyssey*.[30] Maria compares the planned escape from the convent to Homer's Penelope, whose "honest artifice" she likens to the young women "contriv[ing] to undo what [they] have done in the day." By comparing the young women to Penelope, weaving and unweaving her shroud to fend off her unwanted suitors, Maria evokes the image of an albeit clever woman awaiting rescue by her husband. Gibbes thus challenges this most canonical of texts by contrasting Penelope, biding her time until her husband's rescue, to this community of women who must leave the place of oppression as agents of their own rescue. Through these three young women, then, Gibbes explores different perspectives of liberation from the predations of patriarchy, from Maria's ambivalent "marriage" to the Church despite the convent's hypocrisy, to Louisa's self-centered rejection of the homosocial community of renegades, and to Arabella, whose ultimate marriage to Lord D. appears to balance her "wild" American challenge to old-world traditionalism.

Gibbes represents an intricate and ambivalent relationship between English and American women through Maria's view of Arabella. Maria praises "our Niobe," Arabella, whose attributes she sees as particularly those of American women, "blessed with a mind of the noblest cast, and, if characteristic of her country, the females there are as great as any roman *she's* [*sic*] the world ever produced" (I. 126). Referring to the Boston tea party that had sparked the American Revolution two years before the novel's first printing, Maria only sees such "nobility" as a "spirit with which the American ladies (believing themselves aggrieved) resolved to renounce tea-drinking" (I. 127). Contrasting Arabella's ambivalent perspective of the relationship between America and the Crown, coming from an American family that denounced the Revolution, Maria's dismissive attitude reflects England's inability to understand the plight of the colonists regarding the American Revolution.[31] Gibbes intensifies the contrast between Arabella and Maria by shifting to Arabella's worry about their fate if Lord D. were discovered: "Our sweet nuns will be burned alive, and the Bastile [*sic*] hide his miserable head for ever" (I. 127–28). It is a haunting image that, perhaps, can only come from a character who herself is fugitive from the ravages of war, anticipating the liberation of the Bastille's prisoners that would occur less than a decade after this novel's first edition.

Nevertheless, it becomes increasingly apparent that the convent is the equivalent of the Bastille for the women who are its prisoners. Gibbes injects her authorial presence when Arabella tells Nancy of "Providence" putting her in the path of "the young father," Lord D., now disguised not as a nun but as a priest, in the convent's garden (I. 128). As "Providence," the authorial Gibbes emphasizes the significance of this moment in erotic terms by having the first meeting between Arabella and Lord D. take place in a garden hearkening back to Eden, for he tells her "I am not what I seem, but, instead of a priest, the most tender and faithful of lovers—You have a friend" (I. 129). The statement is ambiguous, though at this stage Arabella understands him to be "the bold adventurer" who is Louisa's lover and friend to Arabella and Maria (I. 129). Gibbes provides a radical revision of Genesis: neither Arabella nor the reader knows that Lord D. will be her "bridegroom" rather than Louisa's. While Arabella may not be seduced by Lord D., Gibbes slyly suggests that it is the sentimental desire for the romantic hero to be both rescuer and "bridegroom" that seduces the young women, another anticipation of Wollstonecraft's warning against the damaging effect of the sentimental novel on the minds of young women.[32]

While nationalism and the homosocial world of the convent complicate each other when Lord D. enters the convent at the end of Volume I, Volume II begins with the two halves of the title reflecting on each other yet more overtly.[33] Maria further feminizes Lord D. even as she idealizes him in her description to Nancy: "Light as fairy footsteps did this man of men trip along the cloisters, insomuch that the first notice we had of his arrival was a gentle tap at the door of Louisa's cell, which discomposed us both, but from different motives; she fearing, I hoping every thing [sic] from this rencounter" (II. 132). Louisa's fears seem exaggerated based on Maria's feminizing of Lord D., who "[o]n opening the door ..., bowed, blushed, and entered: the awkwardness of true passion tied up his tongue" (II. 132). Whether Maria is aware of them, multiple ironies are at play when Lord D. says, "I considered no price too great to purchase her esteem," despite being rejected by Louisa's relations who "tore her from the world" (II. 132). Lord D. himself will evolve beyond the commodification of courtship in "purchas[ing] her esteem" when he realizes Louisa's pettiness, shifting his attraction to the passionate and principled Arabella.

Louisa's manipulation of Lord D. appears the more cold-hearted with Gibbes's elaboration of Lord D.'s ordeals getting to the convent, including his elaborate initiation into a brotherhood in Rome and his winning the Pope's "countenance and favour" that allows Lord D. to become Louisa's confessor. Louisa's response to her rescuer is lukewarm in its formality, as she tells him, "with downcast eyes," that she is "indebted to him for the trouble he had been at on her account" (II. 135). By contrast to this tepid rendition of a love plot, Maria uses the traditional language of marriage to describe to Nancy the "knot of honest dissimulation" among the "eloping" young women through which they will be "tied fast" (II. 136). Lord D.'s growing attraction to Arabella complicates the facile idealization of his hero's rescue of Louisa. It is in the garden once again that Arabella meets the disguised Lord D. "by accident" and in which he notes, "You are not unlike my Louisa in person as well as mind"; Arabella feels her "cheek glow with pleasure" as he continues: "I should therefore have loved you, my young friend, for the resemblance, if I had had no other motive" (II. 137).[34] Gibbes creates a deeper challenge for her romantic hero when this seductive comment, heightened by the Edenic setting, suggests to Arabella that Lord D. is a "dissembler" (II. 137).

Romeo and Juliet, *Othello*, and Gibbes's subversion of the sentimental

Just as Gibbes distinguishes her male hero from those of sentimental fiction, she contrasts the planned escape to other tales of women fleeing convents, hearkening back to *Lady Louisa Stroud and Caroline Stratton*. In such a metanarrative moment, Arabella thus tells Nancy, "I have heard of convent-adventures, and convent-scenes ... but supposed them imaginary draughts, and proofs alone of the ingenuity of authors" (II. 138).

As Arabella continues, the reader can sense Gibbes's sophistication behind the sentimental cliché: "But these fictions are realized in my Lord's person; with this difference, that intrigue is the object with the several pretended friars for visiting the sisterhood" (II. 138). Instead of creating yet another "convent-adventure," Gibbes layers the planned escape with deeper metatextual levels by having Maria worry that the plot will surely fail, as did that of Friar Laurence in *Romeo and Juliet* (II. 140). Maria tells Nancy that Lord D.'s friend, Venols, to whom she refers as her "confessor," is the "only man I ever beheld that I could love—but he is here come too late—my vow is irrevocable, let my situation be what it may, for I seek to fly from vice, not from God" (II. 142). Despite what Maria sees as Venols's ideal attributes as a suitor, her marriage to God makes it conveniently impossible for her to consider an erotic attachment to Venols. Maria thus offers Venols to Nancy. Venols, she writes to Nancy, is "a man worthy of ... your best approbation," as the end of the novel realizes. Maria concludes this letter with another hint at the novel's end, letting Nancy know that Mrs. Ashley has "had a legacy left her, which will enable her to ... live her own choice" (II. 143). That money enables women to "live [their] choice" becomes an important component in allowing the inmates of the convent to extricate themselves from their "Bastille."

Though Gibbes raises the interesting possibility that Lord D.'s disguise as a confessor to the young women problematizes his heroism, it is only seen through Arabella's sly observation that the other members of the "sisterhood" are "too sensible of his perfections, [*sic*] and are ... far from behaving towards him like holy vestals" (145). Arabella refers to Louisa, prematurely, as "Lady D."; however, with a teasing reminder of Gibbes's providential role, Arabella adds, "unless some evil accident intervenes" (II. 146). Offending Arabella, Maria frets over Arabella's apparent infatuation with Lord D. Nancy assures Arabella that what appeared to Arabella as a slight by Maria was rather "a mother's tenderness ... in compassion to your youth, inexperience, and quick sensibility," Maria wishing to "caution [her] against too lively an affection for any man" (II. 146). Eager to "give all the colour to [Arabella's] future life: yet lessen not [her] good opinion of his Lordship," Nancy says, "[Y]ou are not yet sixteen, to think of becoming a wife, take my word for it you have attained the full age of tender, of permanent susceptibility, from which I thus seek to secure you" (II. 148). By the end of the novel, it becomes clear that chronological age is not a mark of Arabella's maturity, as she has evolved through her part in the dangerous and heroic escape to embrace her union with Lord D. as a marriage of equals.

At this earlier stage, however, Maria does not entirely repress her own erotic yearnings. Maria mentions that Venols and Lord D. do not sleep in the convent with the "holy virgins," but rather "have a sweet little romantic lodge at the extremity of the garden, from whence, free as air, by private key, the favour of the night, and the privilege of their function, they can visit" (II. 149). Having noted the "romantic lodge" of the two men at the edge of the garden, Maria eroticizes Lord D. and Venols—down to their "private keys," believing that they are there to tempt Maria to betray her vow of marriage to God. She admits that she may be projecting her fantasy that she could "pass [her] days, [her] life, with the engaging Venols" when she expresses to Nancy her concern about Arabella's infatuation with Lord D. (II. 149). Like her concern about her own temptation to fall, Maria projects onto Arabella the plight of a sentimental heroine, worrying that without Mrs. Ashley playing the part of the absent chaperone of the sentimental tradition, Arabella "has now no companion to her taste, or other confident [sic] to divide her hopes or fears with but this handsome Lord, who must be a dangerous friend to so young a heart" (II. 151). This moment complicates Lord D.'s fulfillment of the role of hero, Maria speculating here that he could instead be the rogue who will be responsible for her ruin. Though Gibbes provides no third-person narrator to correct the faulty hermeneutics of the young women, she does give the reader a psychoanalytic layering in such a moment that we may see in Maria's projected concern an ambivalence between desire and fear. Lord D. thus appears morally ambiguous until the end of the novel.[35]

As the suspense of the escape builds, with obstacles to the plan arising because of the insulation of the convent and the tightly guarded French ports, Gibbes intensifies the novel's subversion of the sentimental formula. Injecting what Arabella had referred to as the young women's "elopement" with an awareness of the potential for tragedy, Gibbes turns to *Romeo and Juliet* as the novel approaches the escape from the convent. The exit strategy echoes the ploy of Juliet's potion meant to make her appear dead so that she can elope with Romeo. Maria announces that the Lady Abbess is apparently ill and has fallen in love with Venols, the only "confessor" she will see. Maria notes later that she and Venols both suspect the Lady Abbess's "illness is all a sham," though she regards "[t]his favouritism" as "a feather in all our caps" (II. 151). Maria follows this detail with the plan to give the young women an "opiate" that, she assures Nancy, "has been tried on two or three animals, which have lain to all appearance dead for several hours" in Lord D.'s lodge, the animals reviving "without any visible pang or inconvenience" (II. 152). To the ploy upon which the *Romeo and Juliet* tragedy turns, Gibbes adds the scientific disclaimer that the opiate has been tested on animals first and deemed safe.

Unlike the potion in *Romeo and Juliet*, the opiate is thus not used for the elopement of a pair of lovers but for the rescue of three female convent inmates facilitated by two young men. Gibbes further complicates the Shakespearean allusion in this escape strategy by conflating *Romeo and Juliet* with *Othello*. Telling Nancy of the plan, Maria says that the opiate will be administered "when *out-of-door* things are in a proper train" (II. 151). Iago uses the phrase italicized by Gibbes in his misogynistic claim to his wife: "You are pictures out of door, / bells in your parlors, wildcats in your kitchens, / saints in your injuries, devils being offended, players / in your huswifery, and huswives in your beds" (*Othello*, II. i. 122–25).[36] If Iago's phrase implies that women outside the home hide their animality behind a façade of virtue, Maria creates a paradox by saying that the escape by means of the potion will occur when "out-of-door things" are in a "proper train" (II. 151). By conflating the two Shakespearean tragedies, Gibbes transforms "*out-of-door things*" from Iago's accusation of woman's false behavior outside the home to the young women's escape from the repressive confines of the convent to live according to their own agency, yet in order to do so, they must pretend to be dead.[37] Maria worries that the plan will go awry as it does in *Romeo and Juliet*, raising suspicions about "the sudden death of two young women only a few hours before in perfect health" (II. 152).

As this tension precipitates at this stage of the plot, the two halves of the title—Arabella as American fugitive and her friendship in the convent with Maria—come together with her refusal to play the part of the sentimental heroine during the escape. Arabella writes to Nancy of her own concern, having "expressed [her] terrors, and in the strongest terms conjured Lord D. not to be accessory to such a scheme" (II. 157). Arabella realizes that her infatuation with Lord D. has idealized him, whereas she now sees him as "only … a man who, with the best intentions possible, is on the point of committing a fatal action" (II. 157). Indeed, she tells Lord D., "You know, Sir, I may be confided in—recollect, I am an American and have been bred up to despise bugbears—no one can assist her in an hour of need so effectually as myself" (II. 158). In a postscript, she tells Nancy that Louisa and Maria "drew lots" to see who would go first, and Maria, "our dear friend[,] will be the victim" (II. 158).

Nancy's role thus far has been as sympathetic auditor and liaison for both Maria and Arabella. Now that Mrs. Ashley has left the convent and arrived in England, Nancy's character comes into focus, first in her praise to Maria about Mrs. Ashley. Nancy's father expresses "surprise and admiration" when meeting Mrs. Ashley, leading Nancy to hope that Mrs. Ashley and her father will marry. This anticipation of such a comedic marriage plot, however, is not the way Gibbes chooses to resolve the plot, leaving the idealized Mrs. Ashley both true to the memory of her dead husband and content in her independence (II. 158). In a subsequent letter, when Nancy's father proposes to Mrs. Ashley, she is careful not to wound his pride: "The husband I have buried, was the first and only man I ever considered in the light of a lover" (II. 184). His response is one of respect: "Her way of thinking ... is singular, but it is amiable" (II. 185). Nancy's letter then turns to her father's ability to rise above his own patriarchal ambitions: when he tells her that he has not only found out a husband" for her but has "pledged his honour to the young fellow's father to bestow me on no other," Nancy says, "I open[ed] my heart to him," stating that "a single life was most pleasing" to her. She tells Maria that her father responded, without irony, "God forbid I should make my girl miserable by any busy step of mine! You are and shall be mistress of your own person," assuring her that she "shall have no reason to repent confiding in him" (II. 159). Maria comments that she had never realized how "liberalminded" Nancy's father was, perhaps Gibbes playing on the family name, "Freeman." If so, Gibbes may have chosen the name to convey that he values his daughter's freedom, the name potentially representing a legacy of liberation from patriarchal imposition.

Nancy reports to Maria that Mrs. Gerrard, Maria's mother, has undergone a tragedy that has made her realize and regret her cruelty in sending Maria to the convent. Mrs. Gerrard blames her behavior on Deering, her husband at the time whom she refers to as a "specious ... gambler" whom she had believed to be "an angel," and so "threw her fortune as well as happiness on his mercy" (II. 160). After Deering "gambled away his fortune," he "shot himself dead at her feet" (II. 161–62). He is a variant in the pattern of gambling-addicted husbands responsible for the financial and emotional ruin that pervade Gibbes's novels, beginning with *Francis Clive* (II. 161–62). Maria's mother goes to Nancy for help, Nancy interrupting her narrative to say, "Judge, if you can, what I felt on learning the dreadful catastrophe she had been witness of and the barbarity of the wretch who owed her all to your family" (II. 162). The catastrophe Nancy refers to is Deering's suicide literally at the feet of Maria's mother. However, the term "catastrophe" is a metatextual signal from Gibbes that the novel swerves to the comedic not despite but because of the tragedy. Not only does Nancy find lodging for Maria's mother and her children fathered by Deering, but his relatives offer support, one "great aunt to the deceased" even paying for the "education of the little girl," her daughter with Deering. Maria's response to this news of her stepsister is typically compassionate: "No convent, Nancy, shall ensnare her; for I will be her sister, friend, protector" (II. 179).

Throughout this period of the attempted escape, Gibbes reminds the reader that the fate of the young women still hangs in the balance. Nancy's letter ends with another metatextual signal, here in her observation that Maria's letters "properly arranged, will be an agreeable present to the public, if your adventures have a happy conclusion; otherwise I shall keep them to weep over" (II. 166). Tragedy is averted in the convent when, in the next letter, Arabella tells Nancy that the *Romeo and Juliet* plot never came about because the "bottle which contained the precious liquid was burst and the contents spilt" (II. 167). Arabella is overjoyed when Lord D. delivers the news that, as Gibbes's providential voice can be heard behind Lord D., "Heaven has thus been graciously pleased, my dear Madam, to interfere, and save our beloved Maria from destruction" (II. 168).

Gibbes slyly asserts her providential authority once again when Arabella, assuming that fortune is smiling on her, ends the letter by asking Nancy to buy her a lottery ticket for twelve pounds, the amount of her savings.[38] Nancy informs Arabella that she has won the "British Lottery," asking Arabella whether she herself will deliver the news to her parents "at a time when the calamities of war have deprived them of their usual resources" (II. 183). Arabella's response is to assure Nancy that it is for the "end of [her parents'] sorrows, their poverty, their persecutions" (II. 187). She thus encloses a letter to her parents for Nancy to deliver along with the money in which she commits "the necessary fraud of calling the ticket theirs"; she refers to herself as their "poor little girl, late a fugitive ... now, by the immediate interposition of Providence, raised to such an eminence, as to be the minister of glad-tidings to your worthy hearts" (II. 188). Despite Arabella's means of leaving the convent, she will not do so until Maria is rescued. Arabella refers to her "wildness" as she had earlier (I. 76). She now adds, "I fancy I am set down by all that see me for a lunatic," explaining to Nancy, "They say, indeed, there is 'a pleasure in madness which none but madmen know,' and I begin to be of the same opinion" (II. 190–91). The impulsiveness to which she has been prone throughout the novel is now channeled from sorrow into joy that she "cannot desire to subdue" (II. 191). By the novel's conclusion, Arabella wins more than the lottery, though marriage to Lord D. is not the source of wealth and security Arabella is able share among her friends. Gibbes's providential role thus empowers Arabella to disburse wealth to her family and friends since, married to Lord D., she will not need it.

Meanwhile, however, while they are still inmates of the convent, the young women must struggle against those who hold sway over them. Maria describes the "confessionary" ordered by the "household deputy" whose "holy function" is no "more than a cloak for his licentiousness" (II. 174). While he tells the less attractive Maria to "resume your veil, and retire," he projects his erotic desire onto to Louisa, to whom he asks, "[H]ow many hearts have you seduced?" (II. 175). Gibbes here anticipates Wollstonecraft's articulation of the specific form of misogyny in which men blame women for their own sexual desire.[39] Indeed, when Louisa offers to "put her veil on" during her confession, the priest "violently protest[s], reprimanding her for "omitting her attendance at many ceremonies"; he tells her to "set a mark on her veil," saying that he would "consider her case, and see her again in a few days" (II. 176). In her second "interview with the amorous priest," Maria tells Nancy, "[H]e dared to salute her with a *holy* kiss" (II. 178). By contrast, Maria tells Nancy of her admiration for Lord D. who, as Louisa's lover, has either given up or waived "title, fortune, pleasure, liberty … for the sole delight of seeing, and the hope of serving, his beloved" (II. 180). As soon as Louisa is free, she haughtily rejects Lord D. once she no longer needs him.[40]

The subconscious as *deus ex machina*: Arabella's trepanning, delirium, and unwitting confession of love to Lord D.

Even though Arabella now has enough money to rejoin her parents in England, the Lady Abbess and her deputy bar her from leaving the convent, claiming she has not "profited by father [sic] Stephen's conversation" about conversion (II. 201). The reprimand is important on two counts: first, this "father" is none other than the disguised Lord D. who is arranging the escape of the young women of the convent; second, the term "profit" takes on the double meaning of financial value more important than the claimed religious conversion (II. 203). With Lord D. having infiltrated the convent, another layer of this microcosm is exposed, this time glimpsing ahead at Gibbes's evolving concern with the relationship between colonialism and the sentimental tradition. Arabella refers to the convent's attempt to force her into "taking the veil" as their desire to "trepan" her, a term Gibbes uses later in the Anglo-Indian novels to denote kidnapping for slave labor in the colonies (II. 202).[41] The term here suggests that the convent is not only a microcosm of patriarchy but more specifically a colony in which women are enslaved by Rome's papal authoritarianism which, in turn, reduces "profit" to economic exploitation. Nevertheless, Arabella refers to Lord D.'s chivalric promise of rescue as "an antidote," for he will "prove himself as warm a champion in my cause as in the cause of the other distressed damsels" (II. 203). The archaic phrase "damsels" suggests Gibbes's irony. However, though Arabella can be considered a mouthpiece for Gibbes's subversion of romance, she is falling in love with Lord D., telling him that she "was surprised at his ill-timed gallantry in saluting me after the manner of the sisterhood, when he knew the whole of my behaviour to be a joke" (II. 204). Before she and Lord D. can be united at the end of the novel, Arabella needs to overcome this bitterness at believing she does not conform to the sentimental tradition.

Lord D., too, must evolve before he can be joined with Arabella, whose attempt to laugh in the face of her potentially inescapable imprisonment coincides with Lord D.'s awareness of Louisa's change in attitude towards him. Lord D.'s voice appears directly for the first time through his letter to Nancy, whom he informs that Arabella is "confined to her bed by a fever" (II. 207). Assuring Nancy that "no mock vows have passed [his] lips" as Father Stephen, he explains that he "*purchased* every necessary dispensation," the italicized "purchased" connecting his "dispensations" to the "profiting" of the young women by his conversion (II. 207). He worries that, with her "suspension of her reason" because of her fever, Arabella might inadvertently betray their stratagem. When he thus tells the Superior he will watch over Arabella during the night "in order to take advantage of her mind," the Superior happily agrees that Lord D.'s attempts may convert Arabella subconsciously. We learn by the end of the novel, however, that in her "delirium" that night, with Lord D. watching over her, Arabella unconsciously utters her love for him, ultimately leading to their union (II. 207).

At this pivotal point in the plot, Gibbes deepens the novel's roots in the sentimental tradition while deploying its sociopolitical message through Arabella's delirium. In the exposure of Arabella's subconscious desires, Gibbes takes her beyond the binary of reason and "wildness" with which the other characters have labeled Arabella's peculiarly American freedom from the mores of Anglo-European society. Lord D. tells Nancy that, though Arabella did indeed mention "such things as would have ruined all our schemes," yet "there was so much matter of fact, of good sense, in all her wildnesses and incoherences" (II. 208). Gibbes here suggests that, for all the efforts of Arabella's friends to tame her, Arabella paradoxically remains clear-headed in her wildness, thereby disproving the binary of reason and irrationality.[42] Though Lord D. keeps secret Arabella's declaration of love for him uttered from her subconscious, he makes explicit that, when Arabella wakes up, he tells her "everything she had uttered, except the article she anxiously wished, I dare say, should be concealed" (II. 208). That Lord D. refers to Arabella's delirium as her "wanderings" suggests a parallel between her fugitive status as an American and her emotional complexity. Such wanderings in turn suggest the pattern of female prodigality that Gibbes develops in her later novels, connecting women's geographic wandering with their challenge to the gender norms of their time, such breaking of convention labeling them as irrational.

In her letter back to Lord D., Nancy responds explicitly to Lord D.'s implicit concerns about church and nationalism, saying that Arabella is indeed an American fugitive, cast out of the former colony for siding with the King, but rejected, as Nancy imagines, by the British, while the French monarchy, just before its fall a year after the first edition of the novel, would never accept the "outrage" of her leaving the convent. She speculates that, if Arabella's parents knew of "the deep-laid artifices, the internal designings, [sic] of religious houses, to let her remain there, though on the noblest motives," it would be "fatal" if the Smiths were to "fetch home their entrapped child" (II. 211). Nancy then addresses the larger political landscape at play: "But surely, the French King will never countenance such an outrage!—Yet who could call him to account for it?—The Americans cannot at this crisis, and the English *dare* not, however loyal a subject her father might be proved" (II. 211). This epistolary exchange thus serves a yet more important purpose than liberating Lord D. from his sentimental preoccupations with the apparently undeserving Louisa. It reminds the reader of the potential tragic consequences for all, including Maria, whose "anguish will probably hurt her health," Nancy blaming herself as she projects that she "shall destroy those [she] love[s]" (II. 211). Marveling at Lord D.'s "perseverance in a business that promises so little," Nancy helps clarify why Gibbes exempts Lord D. from the indictment of British aristocracy that is a hallmark of Gibbes's fiction, from the Irish lord in *Francis Clive* to Ellison in *Elfrida* (II. 211).[43] She wonders that he can "wear out" his days "in a convent and disappoint the hopes of" his uncle, "who looks up to [him] as the last prop of [his] illustrious house? Our father has now been dead above two years, and you have never done more in all that time than visit your friends and country for a few days" (II. 212). Nancy's perspective on Lord D. offers clarity about his liberation from the trappings of entitlement, turning the focus from Arabella's marrying into nobility towards Lord D.'s marrying for love rather than carrying on his forebears' patriarchal assumptions.

At this critical turn in the novel, Nancy lets Lord D. know of the arrival in England of Arabella's parents, making excuses to them for Arabella's absence by saying she would be arriving with Maria. Nancy writes to Lord D. that "Mr. Smith said he should rejoice in an opportunity of dividing his fortune with some man of merit, that would ensure his poor girl a protector when he should be no more—but I am of opinion an object worthy such a prize as her hand, will not easily be met with" (II. 213). Gibbes reminds the reader of the potential for an alternative ending in which Arabella would remain fugitive since, in a world dominated by patriarchy, no one can truly be her "protector." Instead, however, Gibbes frees Arabella from the rigidness of either alternative, giving her money—albeit won in a lottery—to disburse among her friends. Gibbes thus offers an alternative to the traditional punishment of a prodigal woman.[44]

As counterpoint to the double-edged "elopement" of the young women's escape, Nancy asks Lord D. to relay to Maria that her mother will be married a third time, to a Methodist parson.[45] Nancy asks Lord D. to tell Maria to "give up every expectation of finding a mother … and to resolve to keep the secret of her elopement, and let this strange woman enjoy the annuity she cannot claim without danger" (II. 214). Once again, Gibbes uses the term "elopement" to complicate the young women's escape from the convent, Maria divorcing herself from the Church while her mother marries so many times that she makes a mockery of her wedding vows.

While she awaits a response from Lord D., Nancy receives a letter from Arabella confiding her concern that Lord D. has changed since Arabella's fever. Noting the garden as the site of meeting with him during her recovery, she worries that she has disclosed more than she intended during her delirium, for "he professes more esteem for me, but is not so lively or so free in his conversation as before my illness" (II. 215). Arabella tells Nancy that the source of her imprisonment in the convent is that the Superior believes Venols loves Arabella. Lord D. says that he can use this misconception to their advantage by enlisting Venols to act as though he wants Arabella removed from the convent by the Superior. The ploy is successful, the Superior telling Arabella she is "at liberty to go where [she] pleased" (II. 221). Arabella is once again fugitive, Lord D. telling her, "[T]o-morrow morning throws you back on the rough ocean of life, and may you escape every threatening shipwreck!" (II. 222). Her next letter tells Nancy of her escape to Dover.

Maria lets Nancy know that, upon Venols's return to the convent, he declares Maria "the woman of his choice," but, she tells Nancy, you "shall teach him a new lesson" (II. 226–27). Just as Maria hands off her suitor to Nancy, she bitterly reacts to the news of her mother's third marriage. Though the juxtaposition reveals the underpinnings of Maria's antipathy towards marriage, Maria's experience in the convent teaches her that women's victimization at the hands of men empowered to abuse them extends beyond marriage. She records the sudden and horrifying murder of a child, the product of the rape of a nun, later identified as Frances, by a priest. Maria sees Frances "tearing her hair and wringing her hands over it in the agonies of grief and despair," the other nuns "cross[ing] themselves [while they,] as if afraid of infection, stood at a distance" (II. 228). Maria underscores the convergence of the literal infection spreading through the convent and its moral contamination when she adds next sentence about the assistant who "withdrew to report the affair to the sick Superior" (II. 228). Frances explains to Maria—the only one who stays with her, the mother—that a "cruel visitor" happened upon her as she performed "some maternal offices," the man, whom she refers to as "my child's murderer," offering to "bury my shame and it together," which she refuses (II. 228–29). Frances bitterly articulates the double standard, in which she must pay with her life for her rape by a man who would go unpunished, for "they wish not to know the father, though they will cut off the mother with an unrelenting hand"; Frances tells Maria she will be "excommunicated, anathematized, and then executed," saying, "This, my sister, this is the justice, the charity of the religion we profess! The seducer, the spoiler, walks at large, while the poor helpless undone one is set up for a mark of infamy ... to strengthen the authority, and enforce the voice that bids *destroy*!" (II. 229).

To add further pathos to the hypocrisy of the Church behind this tragic story, Gibbes has Frances tell Maria that she herself was born out of wedlock and thus thought "that the only way to secure herself from danger and guilt ... was to devote herself to her God" (II. 230). The cruelty of the convent is yet more extreme, making a spectacle of her execution, a ceremony in which she will "be brought up a public spectacle to the chapel in the morning, and at noon be conducted to the fatal stake," that Maria says are the "remains of the Roman barbarity" (II. 230–31). On the day of her execution, Frances says, "I will rush into the flames to avoid" the murderer (II. 233).[46] Maria's transformation appears complete through this grim episode. From her naivete at the beginning of the novel when she had embraced the sequestered life of the convent to her heroism in befriending the tragic figure of Frances, Maria states to Louisa that there is "[n]o life but social life," thereby deciding to leave the convent for a secular community in the world (II. 232).

Though Maria rues the fact that this is "not the age for miracles," Gibbes as "Providence [...] has not forgotten to be gracious" (II. 235): "Father Stephen," the alias of the disguised Lord D., chosen to preside over the execution, exchanges Frances's cell with that of a nun who died of infection, her dead body substituting for Frances whom Lord D. claims took her own life so she would not be executed. Gibbes provides a graphic description of Lord D. carrying out the plan: he "stabbed the miserable corpse in the side [and] Lord D. buried her, together with the poor infant, without the convent walls" (II. 238).

Dead boys and cross-dressing nuns: escape from the convent and gender norms

Providing comic relief in this dark, final stretch of the escape from the convent is a rare moment of overt satire for this novel: the hypocritical nuns, discovering that the immolation has been cancelled, are "much disappointed ... to find that suicide had prevented the legal tragedy" (238). As more nuns die of the contagion, the only "Fathers" who dare to visit Louisa and Maria are Lord D. and Venols. When one of the convent boys who "assist in many of the church ceremonies" gets sick, Lord D. prepares for Maria to trade places with him if he is to die (II. 240). Grimly echoing Charlotte's cross-dressing to save her husband in *Francis Clive*, Maria—who had changed her clothes from secular life to that of a nun—now transforms herself into a boy to escape back to secular life, as she will later make explicit in one of her final letters to Nancy.

When Maria becomes ill, however, Lord D. considers changing the order of escape to allow Maria to be rescued before Louisa. The first overt sign of Louisa's selfishness arises when she expresses her bitterness: "Happy Maria! Said she—I hope at least, you will be happy, whatever fate attends me" (II. 240). Anticipating Wollstonecraft's disparaging women's use of emotional manipulation, Louisa "we[eps] abundantly" when Lord D. reminds her that she herself "insisted upon drawing lots" (II. 241).[47] Maria offers for Louisa to take her place, but Lord D. insists on Maria going first because of her illness. Lord D.'s chivalry appears to be more than the cliché of the knight errant. He values the sisterhood that has developed among the reprobate women, fighting to save them all in a declaration that sparks an even more extreme tantrum from Louisa: "'Let me stay!' cried Louisa, bursting into tears.—'Let me remain in this hateful house forever!'" (II. 242). Maria's own heroism comes to the fore when she tries to calm the petulant Louisa: "We shall both of us be delivered …. I can steal to you at midnight, receive the corpse, if the poor boy dies, and equip you for your change of situation" (II. 243). Nancy informs Maria, still imprisoned in the convent since Louisa has gone in her place, that Lord D. reciprocates Arabella's love for him. Gibbes speaks with proleptic irony through Nancy about the trajectory of the novel: "[W]hat if I should take upon me to affirm that Lord D. loves our Niobe—you would … think me insane" (II. 247). Nancy encloses Lord D.'s letter so that Maria can see that "he loves Louisa's person, but [sic] adores Miss Smith's mind; and he shall have her mind, body, fortune, and ten thousand thanks into the bargain, if he *does* perfectly recover the use of his reason, and [sic] can prefer a permanent to a temporary treasure" (II. 248).

Maria must at least temporarily change her sex to be liberated from both the convent and her own self-sacrificing tendency. Her moral quandary intensifies when, still imprisoned in the convent, Maria tells Nancy her life will be saved if another boy dies and she can take his place: "[F]or how can I wish the death of an innocent, perhaps an amiable youth—Yet there is not another chance for me on earth for escaping these walls" (II. 249). Maria's rationale that "it is the will of Heaven, and he would have fallen a victim to this disease, though I had never been born" gives way to her assertion of her free will to embrace life: "We are, it seems, to remain a short time on the spot, after I have changed my sex, as my Lord cannot throw up [his] office until some one [sic] is found willing to accept it; and to fly would create suspicion" (II. 250). "The spot" is a curious phrase for the place where she is: it speaks to the novel's play with identity based on national, religious, and gender identity. Having placed the dead boy in Maria's room, Lord

D. and Maria, disguised as the boy, go to Rome under the pretext of having "Te-Deums sung on the recovery of two thirds of the sick" (II. 251).

As much as the novel focuses on the convent's hypocrisy, the plight of the young women also represents France as a nation ripe for revolution. Gibbes underscores France's insulated nationalism through Lord D.'s difficulties getting to the convent and anticipation of those they will have in escaping: "[S]uch is the internal policy of the French nation, that no passengers whatever can obtain, unquestioned, egress or ingress with the several towns: who then could flatter himself with bearing off a prize of such a critical nature as [a] devotee, undiscovered and undetected?" (II. 133). By suggesting France has reduced the young women to "a prize" being hoarded, Gibbes reflects the radicalism that leads to the French Revolution only five years following the second edition of this novel.

Through the French Venols, Gibbes adds another layer to the novel's complicated transnationalism. Maria, continuing her matchmaking of Venols and Nancy, describes Venols as "a man of extraordinary merit, though small fortune, and of English extraction, and a protestant [*sic*], though born in France" (II. 252). When Maria says, "What I therefore called love must become friendship," it only gradually becomes clear that the love she is speaking of is that which she harbors for Nancy (II. 253). If this had been a traditional sentimental novel, the reader would assume Maria was speaking of a love for Venols as her romantic hero. Yet the only love she has expressed is for Nancy. Thus, her escape from the horrors of the convent will not resolve her innermost conflict regarding the heteronormative prescription she must follow once she returns to secular life, though she adds, "I protest to you I will never be his, or any man's living, but the pure glowings of amity abstracted, devote myself wholly to my divine deliverer." Maria tells Nancy that she looks forward to "all the pleasure" she will have "in the sweet society of [her] female friends" (II. 253). However, she then addresses how she will live without a husband and without the patriarchal religious structure promised by the convent: "I will be the happy pentioner [*sic*] of my beloved Niobe and my Nancy, nor will I ever ask a superior provision from heaven" (254). Maria's story culminates with Nancy and Arabella allowing her to live without patriarchal demands through their own financial stability.

Before that culmination, however, Gibbes details Maria's route more elaborately than she had Arabella's, suggesting that Maria undergoes a transformation as she moves from the convent to the secular world. On her first stop in Turin, Italy, Maria writes to Nancy that she is happy to "get out of the French King's dominions," thanking "Providence" for delivering her from the convent, explaining that she "resumes her female dress" (II. 255–56). This letter ends on a superficially playful note with deeper undertones regarding Maria's refusal to have her story written by a man: Lord D. "insists upon" Maria "laying down [her] pen, on pain of having [Nancy] informed how untractable [*sic*]" she is (II. 256). When Maria adds to Nancy, "ungovernable I suppose he means" Maria suggests that, for all his heroism, Lord D. acts the part of the patriarch, silencing her; thus, she concludes that she must "live to my own choice" once she is "safely landed in Britain" (II. 256). Maria tells Nancy that she would have preferred going straight to London but must go with this "generous nobleman in his visit to his fair mistress," once again addressing Nancy with the tone of eros: "We shall soon meet, never more to part," she tells Nancy, adding, "Lord D. is the kindest, best of men; but I fear, will not be all you wish him" (II. 257). Maria anticipates that, despite being back in women's garb, Nancy will find her appearance "*en etrangere*," assuring her that her "mind is English and wholly yours—and yours—and yours" (II. 257). This repetition delivers the intensity of a lover. Though Maria's French garb is "strange" she implies that all the changes of clothes disguise her deeply buried sexual identity.

In recounting to Nancy her arrival at the home of Louisa's aunt, Maria notes that Louisa receives Maria's embrace coldly. Louisa scolds Lord D., saying, "You are come then at last, Sir!" (II. 258). Maria, however, is struck by the "most pleasing and venerable lady, Louisa's aunt," who becomes another of the novel's positive female mentors despite her inability to influence Louisa's peevishness (II. 258). Mrs. Finnette, Louisa's aunt, distinguishes between lovers and friends, saying, "Lovers ... may have quarrels; but friends must rejoice in every worthy step their friends take, though at the price of some little self-denial. I have too good an opinion of Louisa, to suppose she can consider any man in the light of a lover" (II. 259). Mrs. Finnette here articulates a principle that underlies the novel regarding the importance of friendship even between the sexes over erotic relationships, though Mrs. Finnette woefully misinterprets her niece's motives. Mrs. Finnette is a proto-Wollstonecraftian mentor trying though failing to educate Louisa: "[I]f she thinks she can escape from God—I shall regret we ever met, as we must, on such a contingence, part to meet no more" (II. 259). Louisa's response is in character: "[B]ursting into tears," she "hastily left the room" (II. 259). When Maria is alone with Louisa, the latter says she "detested my Lord ... for his fickle turn of mind," blaming Maria for his delay. Lord D. then approaches and defends both himself and Maria to Louisa saying she has wronged them both, declaring, "[S]ince I find it impossible to obtain the honour of your hand, Miss Smith is too deservedly and too highly the object of my esteem to be forgot by me; nor shall it be my fault if her noble-mindedness does not make me amends for the loss of your *beauty*" (II. 260). Rejecting Louisa here, despite her beauty, and claiming Arabella as his worthy choice, Lord D. sounds haughty, problematic for the apparent romantic hero. Yet his ability to grow in subjectivity especially at this late phase of the novel underscores Gibbes's voice emerging behind Maria's at the end of the letter: acknowledging the anticlimax of the visit, Maria says, "and thus, my Nancy, did our romance terminate" (II. 261). By referring to the adventure as "our romance," she returns the notion of "romance" from the erotic union of sentimental heroine and her lover back to quest romance, in this case, the escape of the young women and their rescuers from the patriarchal abode of religious, political, and social oppression.

Gibbes gives the penultimate voice of the novel to Lord D., whose letter to Nancy is that of an ideal man worthy of Wollstonecraft: "Louisa is still as beautiful as ever; but beauty of person alone is too slender a foundation for a man of even common understanding to venture to build his happiness upon" (II. 262). Gibbes's anticipation of Wollstonecraft through Lord D. is even more pronounced when he then describes his admiration for Arabella, whose "greatness of mind ... taught me to revere her" (II. 262). He had never realized he loved her, he tells Nancy, until, in the "violence of her fever, unconscious of what she did, she sweetly whispered her love of me" (II. 262). This subconscious passion suggests Gibbes's sophistication beyond VRW's polemical strategy of reversing the gender binary to assert men sexualize women for their own advantage.[48] Gibbes underscores that Lord D. loves Arabella for beauty, intelligence, and passion or, in Arabella's case, her American wildness. In her earlier fevered delirium, Arabella thinks she speaks to Nancy when she tells Lord D. the intensity of her love, Lord D. saying that he "listened with astonishment, with admiration—so young a creature, capable of conquering herself on principles of honour and delicacy!" (II. 263).

Lord D. thus asks Nancy to make "a proper tender" of his "affections" (II. 264). Gibbes plays once again on "tender," connecting sensibility and negotiation.[49] In an earlier letter, Maria, suspecting Louisa's ingratitude towards her rescuers, writes to Nancy that Lord D., "in return for his months and months of assiduity, must have a tender interest in her heart" (II. 253). Taken together, the two uses of the term regarding Lord D. intensify his prototypical role as the hero manqué that the later novels explore more explicitly. Despite Lord D.'s considerable wealth and therefore Arabella's not needing the money she won in the lottery, he says that Mr. Smith, Arabella's father, should "compliment his daughter with five thousand pounds for her separate use; that this amiable girl may have it in her power to make our Maria independent without my assistance and as she is resolved never to marry, I hope to reconcile her good sense and good-nature to accepting an annuity from her little friend" (II. 264). In an act that shows the potential of the British aristocracy to embrace change, Lord D. offers his voice in the financial negotiations that accompany marriage and the sentimental novel's resolution. Arabella's lottery win suggests that her financial endowment could have been that of anyone regardless of social class or gender. Thus, when Lord D. closes the letter by saying that Arabella's "sensibility is intitled [sic] to" "every desired purpose" of his heart, Gibbes appears to play on the double meaning of entitlement as both Arabella's deserving happiness and the title she will obtain through marriage.[50]

That this novel has complicated a traditional narrative voice is demonstrated most aptly when Gibbes gives the final letter to Maria who, writing to Venols, does more than stand in as a narrator *cum* gossip. Gossip she does, recounting the wedding preparations for Lord D. and Arabella. Maria adds that Louisa has "gone off with a young ensign in a marching regiment," and that Maria herself will live "occasionally with you all," a phrase that would suggest Maria will stay with Nancy and Venols sometimes, her "established home" being with the Arabella's parents. Mrs. Ashley will live with Lord D. and Arabella—now referred to as Lady D. In another odd twist to the conventional sentimental ending, Maria adds, "My dear Nancy has owned you are the man of her choice, and Mr. Freeman declares he shall be proud of his son-in-law" (II. 266). Maria informs Venols that Nancy has accepted his proposal of marriage with the blessings of Nancy's father. Emphasizing the negotiated transaction behind the term "tender" becomes a hallmark of Gibbes's irony throughout her career. By including the character of Venols, Gibbes creates a complex arrangement regarding the powerful emotional bond between Maria and Nancy. In another example of the novel's subversion of the marriage plot, therefore, Nancy's marriage to Venols legitimizes a continued, if closeted, bond between Maria and Nancy.

Gibbes does not end the novel without a culmination of the novel's integration of its marriage plot and transatlantic politics. Maria tells Venols that Louisa has run off with a "red-coat" who "unlocked her heart of all its secrets …, jockied [sic] his Lordship out of his chance, by the mere dint of representing him a lukewarm, a contemptible lover, for outstaying her on any occasion, and exposing her to the attacks of a whole army of new admirers" (II. 267). The soldier, Maria explains, had discovered Louisa when she, whom Maria refers to as "the fugitive devotee," is in Calais during her "passage from France"; behind the soldier's criticism of Lord D. for "exposing her to the attacks of a whole army" of new admirers is the disparagement of Louisa for allowing herself to be the object of negotiation among these men.

Even Louisa is not exempt from the abundant goodwill that ends the novel, despite her aunt, Mrs. Finnette, having "cast her off" (II. 268). Forgiving Louisa's reprehensible behavior, Maria writes, Louisa "shall never want a decent pecuniary support," by which Maria suggests Arabella's and Lord D.'s mutual wealth being shared among all, even those who wronged them.

Maria offers a benediction to Venols for a happy marriage, with an underlying projection of her own love for Nancy as "the only woman, believe me (nor do I hesitate to affirm it,) that can, that does deserve you" (II. 268). The novel's final letter is, appropriately, from Maria to Mrs. Ashley, the young women's role model who herself had experienced the horrors of the convent. Maria describes the weddings of Lord and Lady D. and of "Venols and his wife (late my sweet Ann Freeman)" as celebrations of both "social felicity" and "rational scenes," a balance that Wollstonecraft would no doubt admire (II. 269).

Notes

1 I. 85. Unless indicated otherwise, all references are in the text and refer to the 1778 two-volume edition except for the title, whose two phrases are reversed as chosen here, *The American Fugitive* preceding *Friendship in a Nunnery*. The 1784 edition contains significantly more errata than the earlier edition.
2 See the comparison of Austen's and Gibbes's character names in the Conclusion to this study, regarding commonality between Gibbes's use of the name and Austen's giving Anne Elliot's old school friend, the widowed "Mrs. Smith," the name in *Persuasion*; the name of Austen's Mrs. Smith suggests lowered status from that of her birth name, "Miss Hamilton," perhaps as a foil to Anne's choice of Wentworth, whose name suggests that, rather than inherit his wealth, he "went" to get his "worth."
3 Scholarship has applied the term "gynotopia," an idealized world of women, to texts written as early as Christine de Pizan's fifteenth-century allegory, *The Book of the City of Ladies*, a dream vision in which Justice demands that she create a protected space for women since "the noble men who by order and right should defend them, but who through negligence and lack of interest have let them be mocked" (124).
4 Nancy signs some of her letters Anne or Ann.
5 Along with other mid- to late-eighteenth-century heroines who challenge the sentimental stereotype, Gibbes gives Maria subjectivity through her letters, anticipating Charlotte Brontë's revolutionary first-person narration by Jane Eyre. However, Gibbes appears yet more radical than Brontë, representing through multiple subjectivities not only the homosocial relationships among the central characters but Maria's homoerotic desire for Nancy. Gibbes underscores her anti-sentimental stance by having Maria choose not to marry at the end of the novel, a choice remarkably radical in contrast to Brontë's deference to the marriage plot.
6 Maria's criticism of her mother looks ahead to women later in the long eighteenth century who write on the positive consequences of aging. Three works in polemical prose, drama, and poetry respectively illustrate the common concern: Wollstonecraft's *VRW*, Joanna Baillie's Albini in *Count Basil*, and

Charlotte Smith's "Thirty-Eight" all describe the prospect of gaining reason when a woman abandons the emphasis on youth and beauty, instead celebrating her cultivation of reason as she grows older.

7 This passage gestures ahead to *Hartly House*, whose authorial voice subverts that of its sole letter writer, Sophia Goldborne, equally naive in her early letters as she makes her way through Anglo-India as represented by Hartly House.

8 "By late June 1759, Wolfe's entire convoy had passed up the St. Lawrence River and had reached the island of Orleans, which lay opposite Quebec along the river. The army of the French defender of Quebec, the marquis de Montcalm, was strongly entrenched on the high cliffs along the river frontage. Unable to lure Montcalm out from the safety of his defenses, Wolfe on July 31 ordered an assault on the Beauport shore east of the city, which proved to be a costly failure" (Britannica). See James Farago's fascinating analysis of Benjamin West's 1770 painting, "The Death of General Wolfe," in which he points out that, "[i]n 1770, neither the United States nor Canada had yet been established. But West's painting—the first by an American artist to gain international renown—stands at the origin of a New World narrative that would stubbornly endure in both countries for centuries." Through Arabella, Gibbes adds a radically different perspective, from the hindsight of the American Revolution in 1778, contrasting the chorus of propaganda deifying Wolfe following his death. Regarding the recent shift in emphasis on the Seven Years' War in the trajectory of the revolutionary period, see Hamish Scott, discussed as well the Introduction to this study.

9 As discussed later in this chapter, Nancy marries Venols, as though given a hand-me-down from Maria, who chooses to live a single life with the Smiths, Arabella's parents, while the older Mrs. Ashley rejects an offer of marriage to live with Lord and Lady D. A larger historical irony is that the trajectory of Austen's Mrs. Smith in *Persuasion* contrasts that of Gibbes's Arabella Smith: as discussed in this study's Conclusion, Austen's Mrs. Smith had been born into an aristocratic family and loses everything upon the imperialistic involvement in the West Indies of her lower-class husband, Charles Smith.

10 "Niobe." *Encyclopedia Britannica*, May 15, 2020. www.britannica.com/topic/Niobe-Greek-mythology. Accessed April 13, 2021.

11 See Dziennik on the history of the complex relationship among Scotland, England, and America, in which he details the Scottish ambivalence towards the colonies' revolt against the Crown. "Scotland and the American Revolution." *Journal of the American Revolution*. October 14, 2013. https://allthingsliberty.com/2013/10/scotland-american-revolution/. Accessed April 13, 2021.

12 See the following chapters for Gibbes's increasing concern with the topic of British imperialism in the East.

13 Dziennik notes that "Scottish philosophy did have a role in developing common sense moral codes and the belief that society could be improved by evaluating cause and effect. It was under Aberdeen's-own William Small that Thomas Jefferson received his undergraduate education at the College of William and Mary. In some respects, American independence was one of the towering

achievements of the applied enlightenment. One the other hand, Scottish philosophers were only one small group among many influences on American revolutionaries" (8).
14 For Wollstonecraft, mothers are perpetrators of women's oppression because they pass down their own ignorance to their daughters, as witnessed throughout *VRW*: "[W]omen of sensibility are the most unfit for [the task of managing children during their childhood], because they will infallibly, carried away by their feelings, spoil a child's temper" (73). See the earlier note on Gibbes's anticipation of women writers including Baillie and Charlotte Smith who pay homage to the development of reason as a woman ages.
15 This emphasis on daughters' relationship to parents, specifically mothers, stands in contrast to *Francis Clive*'s main plot, based upon the theme of the prodigal son. Though Clive is rescued by his cross-dressing wife, the emphasis is on the distinction between the tone of authorial irony and the narrator's insistence on his remediation.
16 Gibbes uses the device to great effect in *Hartly House*, her other epistolary novel, to glean her authorial presence through her protagonist's epistolary voice.
17 As noted in the title of this chapter [section], pages 27 and 28 are missing from the 1784 edition; the 1778 edition substitutions are noted as such above.
18 See Nobus on the historical connection between eros and religious enthusiasm, especially regarding Lacan's reading of Bernini's "The Ecstasy of Saint Teresa."
19 The theme of contagion recurs in *Elfrida* through the smallpox epidemic claiming the lives of the entitled Ellisons who falsely believe they can protect themselves by going to the exclusive Bath.
20 In this way as well, Gibbes anticipates Wollstonecraft in espousing Enlightenment views of reason for women's education.
21 www.oed.com/access.library.miami.edu/view/Entry/158253?redirectedFrom =raree+show#eid. Accessed April 20, 2021.
22 Arabella's comparison of her parents to the wandering Jews looks ahead to the Romantic trope of the persona as outcast in general and Ahasuerus specifically (see Percy Shelley's *Queen Mab*, for instance). Such a moment, linked to Arabella's "wildness," situates Gibbes as pivotal in the long eighteenth century as she looks ahead to canonical Romanticism.
23 Arabella later describes her "wild manner" in telling Lord D. that, even though she had won the lottery, she would not leave the convent until her "continuance therein ceased to be serviceable" to her friends" despite "being set down by all that see [her] for a lunatic" (I. 190–91). For more on canonical Romanticism and madness, see James Whitehead. That Arabella is paradoxically rational and emotional anticipates the recently recovered poetry of Charlotte Smith and Mary Hays, both of whom exhibit what Isobel Armstrong refers to as women poets' turning affect to "analytical account" and using it "to think with" (15).
24 The entitlement that Arabella opts for suggests the more overt message Gibbes establishes in the later novel, *Elfrida*, in which indigenous America is subjected to the abuse by the privileged Ellison. Here, Nancy introduces another theme

that evolves in the latter novel, namely the tragic consequences of Elfrida's marrying a "dissipated and unprincipled" man whom she "entrusts with her whole fortune."
25 See Roche on the symbolism of Duessa in *FQ* (1080, n. 13). The reference to Shakespeare, by further extension, anticipates the association of Shakespeare with psychological complexity, first in Coleridge's prose and then in Keats's notion of Shakespeare's comprehensive "negative capability."
26 "I look down towards his feet; but that's a fable.— / If that thou be'st a devil, I cannot kill thee" (V. ii. 336–37).
27 See Ross on the new masculinity of the Romantic period. This feminization of the hero is more overt than the softening of Wilmot's sensibility in *Elfrida*; as discussed in Chapter 4, Wilmot finds inspiration in Goethe's *Werther*, anticipating the fascination of Frankenstein's creature with *Werther*.
28 www.oed.com/dictionary/elope_v?tab=meaning_and_use#5657539. Accessed September 15, 2024.
29 This earlier novel's subplot exploring the relationship between eros and nationalism may be a blueprint for Gibbes's far more complex love triangle in *Elfrida*, discussed in Chapter 4, that in turn anticipates Austen's love triangle in *Persuasion*, discussed in this study's Conclusion.
30 Compare Gibbes's ironic allusion to *The Odyssey* in *Francis Clive* with the prostitute, Penelope, discussed in Chapter 1.
31 See Gibbes's reference to Arabella's father fighting on the side of General Wolfe discussed earlier in this chapter.
32 See the Introduction to this study for discussion of *VRW*, Chapter XIII.
33 In the 1778 edition, Letter XXX begins Volume II, keeping the original pagination, though the earlier edition does not divide the novel into two volumes.
34 See the earlier discussion of the first garden scene on p. 128 of the novel.
35 See the discussion in Chapter 4 of Gibbes further complicating the romantic hero of *Elfrida*, Wilmot, through the life-long love triangle with Ellison and Wilmot. Ellison is on one level a foil to Wilmot but, more deeply, his character contaminates that of Wilmot; in this earlier novel, by contrast, Lord D. redeems himself of any ambiguity by the end of the novel as tidily as Maria's offering of Venols to Nancy appears to satisfy the needs of the two young women for a happy ending in a heteronormative world.
36 See Chapter 4 on Gibbes's reference to these lines in *Elfrida*. As noted there, the phrase took on figurative meaning suggested in the sixteenth century and lasting into the eighteenth century, as seen in the *OED*'s citations. www.oed.com/view/Entry/56820?rskey=RkSunj&result=1&isAdvanced=false#eid126392681. Accessed September 15, 2024. P4. *out (†forth) of door* (also *doors*): out of the house; in the open air, abroad; hence *figurative* out of place, lost, abroad, irrelevant, worthless (*obsolete*).
37 The double standard of men's freedom to travel the globe while women are confined to the domestic sphere is central to the plot of *Elfrida*, the subject of Chapter 4.

38 The lottery is another theme that recurs in Gibbes's novels, seen in Chapter 1 when Frank, Jr. buys a lottery ticket for his sister. Gibbes does not hide or apologize for her repeated use of this *deus ex machina*, however, which in each case brings the entitlement of patrimony into relief.
39 In Chapter 5 of *VRW* Wollstonecraft attacks Rousseau for projecting his sexuality onto women, stating that "all Rousseau's errors in reasoning arose from sensibility .... When he should have reasoned he became impassioned, and reflection inflamed his imagination instead of enlightening his understanding" (97). Mary Poovey first observed Wollstonecraft's gender reversal: "The root of the wrongs of women, according to Wollstonecraft, is the general acceptance of the idea that women are *essentially* sexual beings .... Wollstonecraft's response to [Rousseau's] sexual characterization of women is simply to reverse the charge: not *women*, she argues, but *men* are dominated by their sexual desires; *men*'s insatiable appetites are the root of both economic inequality and social injustice. Arguments about women's 'natural' inferiority, then, are only men's rationalizations for the superior social position they have unjustifiably seized, and their talk of 'natural' female wantonness is merely a cover for the sexual appetite that men both fear and relish in themselves" (reprinted in *VRW*, ed. Lynch, 345).
40 Louisa also anticipates Wollstonecraft's *VRW* as the embodiment of female manipulation resulting from patriarchal emphasis on female beauty.
41 See *OED* and discussion of *Zoriada* and *Elfrida*, Chapters 3 and 4.
42 Gibbes's paradoxical representation of Arabella's delirium anticipates the complicating of subjectivity associated with Romanticism. See my study, *Rethinking Romanticism*, regarding the watershed period for a new psychology that defies the hierarchy of mental faculties entrenched in Enlightenment thought.
43 For specific discussions of these works vis-à-vis Gibbes on class and patriarchy, see Chapter 1 for *Francis Clive* and Chapter 5 for *Elfrida*.
44 As noted earlier, Haywood satirizes this rejection of the prodigal female protagonist in *Fantomina*, whose sexual escapades catch up with her when she gets pregnant and her mother confines her in a convent.
45 Such instances as this story of Maria's mother and that of the prostitute, Penelope, in *Francis Clive* not only demonstrate Gibbes's indictment of women whose identity is formed by her lover but transmutes the satire of Haywood's *Fantomina*, in which the nameless protagonist perpetually remakes herself to keep her lover erotically interested in her. See the Introduction to this study for more on Haywood's place in the long eighteenth century.
46 Her reaction to being burned at the stake is the opposite of the intended purpose of *sati*, the Indian ritual of widow immolation that Gibbes explores through Sophia Goldborne's horrified account in *Hartly House, Calcutta*; see Chapter 3 for the fuller discussion of the ritual.
47 "Women are ... so much degraded by mistaken notions of female excellence, that I do not mean to add a paradox when I assert that this artificial weakness produces a propensity to tyrannize, and gives birth to cunning, the natural

opponent of strength, which leads them to play off those contemptible infantine airs that undermine esteem even whilst they excite desire" (*VRW*, 14).
48 See the Introduction's discussion of Wollstonecraft's complexity beyond *VRW* regarding her career beginning and ending with fiction and including a positive review of Gibbes.
49 See Chapter 1's discussion of the recurrence of the term in *Clive*; this study's Conclusion discusses the triple meanings of tender common to *Elfrida* and Austen's *Persuasion*.
50 As noted in the Conclusion to this study, the meaning of "entitlement" was shifting away from solely signifying a legal right to an estate. Lord D.'s usage suggests Arabella is both "worthy" and will literally become "entitled" when she marries him. See the *OED* for the 1817 example of this meaning: www.oed.com/search/advanced/Entries?textTermText0=entitle&textTermOpt0=Etymology&dateOfUseFirstUse=false&page=1&sortOption=Frequency. Accessed March 9, 2024.

3

Transnationalism in the Anglo-Indian novels: *Zoriada, or, Village Annals* (1786) and *Hartly House, Calcutta: A Novel of the Days of Warren Hastings* (1789)

Gibbes's central concern with Anglo-India in her two novels of the late 1780s marks a significant shift from her earlier fiction. Yet the evolution of the expansive worlds of mutually entangled cultures in these later novels can be traced from *Francis Clive* through *The American Fugitive*.[1] Gibbes's characteristic use of incongruity, metanarrative, nuanced irony, and wordplay finds a new direction in the Anglo-Indian novels as does her pattern of upending the sentimental tradition through female prodigality. The movement of women away from the domestic sphere in these later novels widens to the transnational voyages of female protagonists in a colonial world defined by patriarchal repressiveness. However, this focus on colonialism from the subjectivity of a woman at the center of sociopolitical crisis can be traced to *Frances Clive*. As Chapter 1 of this study details, Mrs. Charlotte crosses the Irish Sea, first as victim of the entitled Irish lord, then as rescuer of her husband from the chameleon prostitute, Penelope, who crosses the same Irish Sea to ply her trade. Gibbes expands and complicates female prodigality in *The American Fugitive*, as seen in Chapter 2, with the trajectory of a range of female subjectivities beyond national boundaries. Arabella, the eponymous fugitive, has travelled from America to France and then, along with the other young women of the French convent, endures a harrowing escape by sea from France and the convent's abuses and contagion.

These earlier novels thus prepare the way for the global consciousness of Gibbes's Anglo-Indian protagonists.[2] In their respective novels, Zoriada and Sophia contrast with these precursors, not only because of the expanded geography they must navigate, but because they have more at stake in the sociopolitical jeopardy they face as aliens to their surroundings. In these ways, both novels subvert another popular eighteenth-century genre, the British oriental tale that takes its readers to exotic locales through the traditional subjectivity of an Englishman traveling to the east.[3] The heroines of these two novels, one Indian and one English, view from radically different subjectivities the racial, cultural, and ideological clashes between the patriarchal imposition of colonialism and the indigenous people. Their contrast with each other begins with their opposing trajectories: the eponymous Zoriada is an Indian Muslim woman in England, Sophia Goldbourne, of *Hartly House*, an English woman in India who becomes steeped in Hindu culture and religion.[4] These two protagonists come into each other's worlds from their own increasingly polarized national identities.

As Gibbes complicates cultural and national identities in these novels, so too does she deepen her previous interrogation of gender binaries. By contrasting the tenderness of the romantic male heroes with the rapacious men surrounding them in these later novels, Gibbes anticipates the shift in masculinity traditionally ascribed to the canonical Romantic poets. Lord D. of *The American Fugitive*, whose masculine sensibility earns him the love and admiration of Arabella, anticipates that of Edmund Mims in *Zoriada* and the Brahmin priest—and ultimately the British Doyly—in *Hartly House*.[5] The pattern of this new masculinity in Gibbes's fiction suggests her increasing concern with balancing the powerful subjectivity of her new heroines with likeminded men, nevertheless set against those who persecute these women.

Part I

Zoriada, or, Village Annals (1786): *reinventing the oriental tale*

By placing the subjectivity of a young Indian woman at the center of *Zoriada, or, Village Annals*, the novel earns an important place among literary treatments of globalism's impact on the relationship among gender, culture, race, and socioeconomics during the long eighteenth century. As she had in her earlier novels, Gibbes takes aim at the sentimental tradition. This tripledecker novel upends the genre through incongruity, a strategy characteristic of Gibbes's fiction throughout her career. In this novel, incongruity manifests through reversing both gender and narrative trajectory, with Zoriada having traveled west while the traditional British oriental tale's male protagonist journeys east.

Onto the growing problem of British imperialism during the long eighteenth century, *Zoriada* overlays another concern that Gibbes has traced since her earliest fiction: the systemic binaries at the heart of Enlightenment hermeneutics. Gibbes now adds the complex layering of race and culture to her earlier representation of the debasing and othering of women by Anglo-European patriarchy. Gibbes sets *Zoriada* in a rural English village among whose provincial inhabitants the young Indian woman appears. Repeatedly attempting to discover the identity of the stranger, known only through her pseudonym, Zoriada, villagers and reader alike arm themselves with tools of rational investigation available to all social strata. The villagers represent a spectrum of hermeneutical strategies ranging from an unschooled caretaker's gossip reliant on a culture of objectification, to a rapacious man's aggression in trying to determine whether Zoriada is witch or angel, to a physician's flawed scientific method in seeking the source of her suffering in order to heal her. The novel thus marks a significant turn in the evolution of Gibbes's concerns regarding Enlightenment binaries associated with gender and socioeconomics, seen in *Francis Clive* and complicated with the interplay of religious oppression and nationalism in the *American Fugitive*. Now superimposing these concerns onto racial and cultural binaries, Gibbes creates a yet more radical vision of global nondualism from the perspective of a non-western woman.

Leveling the investigative urges of the villagers, from the unschooled to the highly educated, Gibbes both participates in and complicates the late eighteenth-century revolt against the Enlightenment's celebration of deductive reasoning. Even more than Gibbes's earlier novels, *Zoriada* anticipates Wollstonecraft's 1792 *Vindication of the Rights of Woman*. Though *VRW* is considered the first detailed analysis of the masculinist system of women's education in England, by deconstructing the gendered sensibility/reason binary, Gibbes moves beyond *VRW*'s inversion of masculine reason/female sensibility.[6] Underlying the hermeneutical empiricism of the late Enlightenment is the assumption that identity is knowable through binaries including east/west, subject/object, masculine/feminine, and highbrow/illiterate. Gibbes departs from tradition not only by withholding her protagonist's identity but, yet more radically, by withholding her subjectivity. The distinction between identity and subjectivity is a new one in the late eighteenth century. Traditional notions of identity formed through ancestry, culture, and relationships were beginning to be distinguished from the deeper explorations of selfhood emerging through the ontological and epistemic breakthroughs that came to be associated with the revolt against western materialism.[7]

Through Zoriada's emerging subjectivity, Gibbes simultaneously transforms both the traditionally objectified, exotic female of the oriental tale and the generic heroine of the sentimental novel's marriage plot.[8] Though the novel's end resolves questions of her identity, Zoriada's subjectivity remains her own to withhold, defined by neither her ancestry nor her role in the novel's interconnected threads. By refusing to endow her third-person narrator with omniscience, and by having Zoriada refuse the villagers' probing demands for her identity, Gibbes ends the novel with villagers and reader no closer to Zoriada's subjectivity though perhaps too distracted by the busy plot to realize the novel's distinction between identity revealed and subjectivity withheld.

The novel's challenge to narrative commonplaces founded on both the sentimental tradition and on the systemic binaries underlying the genre begins with the novel's title. Its either/or construction, *Zoriada, or, Village Annals*, announces the collision of two spheres traditionally separated through geography, culture, and epistemology. In terms of subject/object duality, the title appears to give the reader a choice of which lens to use for viewing the events of the novel: Zoriada's subjectivity or the village "annals," a term implying a discursive history composed of the villagers' collected stories. However, the novel itself deconstructs the simplicity of the title's apparent choice on both sides of the comma's divide: to the left of the comma is *Zoriada*; that this is merely the pseudonym of the stranger, as the reader will discover, suggests that her subjectivity has greater authority than the novel's third-person narrator to whom this unnamed protagonist denies full entrance to her story. To the right of the comma, the villagers' stories are a collection of misguided and sometimes nefarious assumptions, hardly the codified history the term "annals" suggests.

Like the title of the earlier *American Fugitive: or, Friendship in a Nunnery*, discussed in Chapter 2, the two sides of the title unspool through the novel's double trajectory. Underneath its convoluted and unlikely plot that spans generations and zigzags across the Atlantic, however, this novel steadily resists the objectification of her nameless protagonist by characters who project identity onto her. They thereby view her with a potent ambivalence of attraction and repulsion. By the novel's end, these assumptions meet their ultimate challenge when many of the villagers discover their own stories are bound inextricably with hers. Zoriada is not only revealed to be of mixed English and Indian parentage but, to the surprise of the characters and reader, Gibbes belatedly integrates Zoriada's bloodlines and culture with those of the villagers. Gibbes defers until the end of the novel the revelation that Zoriada's mother was a Muslim married to the betrayed brother of Crosby, one of the villagers introduced early in the novel. The man Zoriada chooses to marry at the end of the novel, Edmund Mims, is the son of the Anglo-Indian sea-captain who had rescued Zoriada after her family was murdered and their home in India burned. Captain Mims, in turn, is the son of the village doctor, Withers, and his wife.

The "village annals" that prove to be interconnected through Zoriada are stories within stories including betrayals, families torn apart, and lost children. They form a prismatic lens to view the political, religious, social, and gender issues at stake in the characters' projection of identity onto Zoriada. This sophisticated plot structure, sustained over the novel's three volumes, is paradoxical. It simultaneously embraces and evades the hermeneutical process of reading. Gibbes achieves this narrative deconstruction through repeated gestures to the novel's metanarrative commentary. In the quest to find meaning in the text, the reader is complicit in the villagers' projecting identity onto Zoriada. She is an empty center in a novel whose multiple subplots, filled with violence, intrigue, and a complicated network of relationships, appear designed to overwhelm the reader.

Gibbes deepens the novel's metatextual irony through repeated references to the Arabic language. She pairs her ineffable heroine with an equally ineffable Arabic manuscript—called *Zoriada*. One of the villagers, the rapacious Parson Swinborne, steals the manuscript from Zoriada's room, hoping to deduce her identity from it. The reader implicitly colludes with the voyeuristic Swinborne, peering over his shoulder as he scrutinizes the objects in her room. That the manuscript remains untranslated to the end of the novel, however, defies the villagers' and reader's desire to do no less than include it in a monolithic western history that the phrase "village annals" suggests. The protagonist's chosen pseudonym, Zoriada, is Arabic, its long literary history underscoring Gibbes's complication of western imperialism. Commonly translated as "enchanting," or "dawn," Zoriada is the name of a saint who converted from Islam in twelfth-century Spain that Gibbes probably knew from *Don Quixote* as the Muslim woman Cervantes associates with the Virgin Mary.[9] The significance of the name vis-à-vis both figures of conversion from Islam to Christianity emerges gradually in the novel. Gibbes presents a contrasting erosion of Christian hegemony that culminates in the final revelation of Zoriada's mixed Christian and Muslim parentage.[10] Remaining a cypher until the novel's end, Zoriada and her manuscript embody a nondualism that eludes western binaries and, ultimately, the failure of western hermeneutics to crack the code of subjectivity.[11]

Despite the villagers operating from sharply divided social classes, then, their dualistic approach to solving the mystery of Zoriada's identity is the common denominator that contrasts with Zoriada's own resistance to the collective binaries they project upon her. From the novel's opening, Gibbes upends narrative commonplaces of the eighteenth-century novel founded on systemic binaries. A double objectification introduces Zoriada in Volume I through the conversation between the old physician, Dr. Withers, and Mrs. Leland, the housekeeper where Zoriada is staying. Mrs. Leland has called the doctor to attend the newly arrived "dying young lady" (I. 1). Mrs. Leland is "bathed in tears" over what she assumes to be the imminent death of this young woman who, she says, is done in by "close study of learning."[12]

At this early point we are given no narrative authority to debunk Mrs. Leland's speculation and gossip. To Mrs. Leland's frustration, Mrs. Quinbrook, the captain's friend who had put the young woman in Mrs. Leland's care, has no information about her. That Mrs. Quinbrook only tells her that Captain Mims brought the stranger from India leads

Mrs. Leland to suspect Mims "was dying in love with her" though "so much older than herself," misinformation remaining uncorrected until the end of the novel when, along with the villagers, the reader discovers Mims to be the father of Edmund, the man Zoriada chooses to marry (I. 22). In fact, Gibbes uses Mrs. Leland's lowbrow gossip as a foil not to highbrow snobbery as one might expect in traditional eighteenth-century satire, but rather as a foil to the failure of Dr. Withers's scientific approach to deducing both the identity and malady of the stranger. Expert in empirical reasoning, his name resonates with irony: the Age of Enlightenment "withers" by the late eighteenth century.

More than a mere caricature of the man of science, however, Dr. Withers has the greatest potential of any of the villagers to grant Zoriada her subjectivity. Withers asks Mrs. Leland to let the stranger tell "her story in her own words," suggesting his sophistication in knowing what he does not know. Yet trained in deductive reasoning, Dr. Withers fails to place into the western paradigm not only the stranger herself but the "striking tokens" in her room. These objects defy facile categorization within the systemic binaries forming the basis for his diagnosis. Singly and together, Zoriada's possessions appear incongruous to Withers, though they speak to a common pattern that defies western logic. For instance, some objects in the room are associated with sound. One, a lute, is a musical instrument evolved from a common ancestor to both eastern and western music. Another object is a "repeater," an intricate part in an eighteenth-century timepiece chiming the hour. Taken together they suggest the stranger's cultural fluidity and paradoxical interest in sound, both musical and mechanical. The most enigmatic and binary-defying object Withers finds in her room is called an "armillary sphere." This astronomical model connects Zoriada to an east/west nondualism, for it was simultaneously created in ancient Greece and China, later adopted in both the Islamic world and medieval Europe (I. 3).[13] Unable to deduce her identity through these signifiers, Withers turns to her art but neither describes nor therefore interprets it. He concludes that the drawings are "the labors (it was evident) of her pencil," the parenthetical aside a limp attempt at rational deduction (I. 3). Withers determines, nevertheless, that she is a "superior order of beings"—superior, it would seem, not only to the quaint Mrs. Leland but even to himself and to Enlightenment epistemology (I. 3).

Withers easily determines that the young woman is not dying, as Mrs. Leland had feared, but has merely swooned. However, the cause of her deep misery is inaccessible to him. He warns Zoriada that her constitution is too delicate to bear "violent shocks," though the emerging details of Zoriada's melodramatic story prove him wrong. Zoriada has undergone and will continue from this point forward to undergo shock after shock (I. 8).

At this early stage of her story, she assures Dr. Withers, "I am accustomed ... to such temporary suspensions of sense and motion, yet apprehend no fatal consequence" (I. 8). Zoriada is thus no Della Cruscan sentimental heroine that Wollstonecraft would deplore as "in a perpetual state of childhood, unable to stand alone" (*VRW* 12). When the barbarity that Zoriada had overcome in India and then in this provincial English village comes to light, the reader marvels at her power in controlling her narrative.

Attempting to convince Zoriada that her swoon should not be taken lightly, Dr. Withers compares her body to "a human machine" whose "springs ... cannot be so suddenly let down without sustaining great injury" (I. 8). When Zoriada rejects his scientific account of the body, saying, "I am no friend to medicines," Dr. Withers responds that the pulse is the "little pendulum of life," a phrase that Gibbes may have gotten from Galileo's "pendulum clock" to regulate the pulse (I. 8–9).[14] If so, the allusion is particularly important, since Dr. Withers attributes the metaphor to "an English writer" rather than Galileo, the figure established as the creator of the scientific method (I. 9). By invoking the "pendulum clock" metaphor, Dr. Withers imposes on Zoriada his ontological materialism as he attempts to find a logical connection between her and the objects in her room.

Gibbes neither caricatures nor idealizes Dr. Withers, instead humanizing him through his concern for Zoriada. He attempts to restore her health through the Romantic prescription of walks through "artless" nature, all elements of which "appear'd conscious of their peculiarly happy condition" (I. 34–35).[15] Though she feels "insensibly harmonised" when Dr. Withers attempts to "regulate her feelings" by showing her his temple of Resignation, Zoriada bursts into tears, saying her mind is incapable of learning resignation (I. 35, 45). However well intentioned, Withers makes matters worse for the grieving Zoriada by offering as a parable of resignation how he and Mrs. Withers have coped with their own tragedy, the early losses of their young son and infant daughter. Having just warned Zoriada that she is too delicate to bear violent shocks, Withers tells of the accidental death of his baby daughter thirty-eight years before due, indirectly, to his assumption that a cold bath would "confirm the promise of a good constitution, [*sic*] and brace the tender nerves of our little girl" (I. 43–44). He explains that a woman who had been left alone to bathe the baby for the first time wrapped her too tightly in a blanket following the cold bath, suffocating her. Perhaps defensively, Withers says he had ordered the bath "in the fullness of human wisdom" (I. 44). Although he attributes his daughter's death to the woman's carelessness, blaming himself only for having left the baby in her care, he implicates himself through the unnecessary prescription of the cold bath, the indirect cause of her death. As a man of science, Withers is misguided in the decisions he has made, both those leading up to his baby's death and, here, his well-intentioned but counterproductive treatment of Zoriada.

The weeping Zoriada's response underscores Withers' lack of emotional sensitivity in his misguided attempt to heal her. By having Zoriada tell him, ambiguously, "[A]n invisible power has brought me here, and all I can do shall be done," Gibbes draws metanarrative attention to the novelist's "invisible power" in choreographing the interwoven destinies of her characters (I. 47). Gibbes achieves this providential power most dramatically through one of the most unlikely of the novel's many plot twists: Withers tells Zoriada not only of the daughter who died in infancy over thirty years before, but of a son who wandered off as a young child during the crisis with his sister's death. Gibbes reveals late in the novel that Withers's son is Mims, the sea captain who rescued Zoriada and who turns out to be father of Edmund, the man Zoriada will marry by the novel's end. The far-fetched coincidences are not narrative weaknesses, but a means for Gibbes to represent global interconnectedness.

In the aptly titled chapter, "The Scrutiny," the novel returns to Zoriada's room through a contrasting though equally failed "scrutiny" to that of Dr. Withers. Through the malevolent Parson Swinborne, Gibbes portrays a more sinister manifestation of western hermeneutics as both absurd and unethical. Swinborne breaks into Zoriada's room, arming himself with a magnifying glass that hangs "pendent in the true coxcomb style, by a black ribband from his neck" (I. 112). Swinborne vainly examines what he ridicules as Zoriada's strange "gimcracks" and "globuses." This term, globuses, a variant of "globe," perhaps refers to the model Withers had identified as her "armillary sphere." Yet Swinborne's reference to "*globuses*" instead reduces the sacred relics of this globe-traveling but reserved stranger to a Latin term that hints at the misogynistically conceived condition, "*globus hystericus*," that refers to anxiety paralyzing a woman's voice (I. 109). Gibbes exposes the fallacy of this phallocentric term by not only distinguishing Zoriada's grief from hysteria, but by making Zoriada's silence a form of autonomy in her refusal to capitulate to the villagers' demands for her story.

Baffled by what he perceives as Zoriada's lack of vanity, Swinborne assumes she is "either the most insensible, or the most artful of females" (I. 93). By contrast to Swinborne, Mrs. Leland is determined to prove Zoriada's innocence. Mrs. Leland articulates the binary of female stereotypes as the only two options for a woman: "See ... who is wrong and who is right, I for believing her an angel, or you for taking her for a --" (I. 93, 110). Her incomplete sentence suggests the term is taboo, for the choice is not angel/devil but the misogynistic angel/whore. By creating a heroine who transcends the traditional binary, Gibbes is at the forefront of the nascent women's rights movement of the late eighteenth century.

Swinborne's violation thus takes Dr. Withers's well-meaning if invasive scientific scrutiny of Zoriada's body-as-machine to a predatory level. Unlike Withers, who had not known what to make of the art in Zoriada's room except to assert that it was her creation, Swinborne is determined to discover Zoriada's identity by interpreting her drawings. One appears to him to represent the "black hole of Calcutta," including "a prison with the dead and dying, lying before it" which he later assumes proves her being party to the "scene of carnage" (I. 112, 115). Another is "a house, with one side in flames, and on the other a slaughter of helpless individuals." He then adds, "... blood, blood, a dismal scene" (I. 113).[16] Swinborne's allusion to *Othello* says more about Swinborne's projection of faulty "optics" onto the drawing than it does about Zoriada: contrary to Swinborne's assumption that the drawings verify her guilt, late in the novel we learn that they depict her having escaped when her family was murdered and their home was burned. This belated revelation of the brutal victimization of Zoriada and her family that she represents as well in her painting of the girl with the urn, contrasts with Swinborne's projection of his own capacity, like that of Iago, to bring about the downfall of an innocent. Swinborne's descriptions of the symbols up to that point are of a devouring feminine principle: the "black hole" of Calcutta; the prison; the house in flames. That the reader is no cannier than Swinborne underscores both the providential role of Gibbes and her withholding of Zoriada's subjectivity. Not until Volume III is the meaning of Zoriada's painting of the girl with an urn revealed. Zoriada has brought her family's ashes with her to England, her desire to keep their remains with her putting her at odds with the burial practices of the village.

Zoriada's identity nevertheless eludes the aggressive hermeneutics of characters and reader. In this pivotal scene, Swinborne's investigation of Zoriada's possessions is but prelude to his discovery of the most mysterious object in the room: a "small manuscript, in the Oriental language, intitled [sic] *Zoriada*" (I. 114). Finding it impenetrable, Swinborne plots to have the manuscript translated, convinced that it holds the key to Zoriada's enigmatic drawings that he already assumes, incorrectly, point to "her being a party in [its] scene of carnage" (I. 114, 115). Swinborne's objectification of Zoriada is thus a grotesque parody of the hegemonic, masculinist dualism at the heart of Enlightenment epistemology. That the title of the manuscript is the same as the first half of the novel's title is a reminder that the reader participates in the villagers' aggressively misguided "scrutiny" of Gibbes's heroine.

Yet Gibbes portrays the villagers through multiple tonalities, from satire to irony, here balancing Swinborne's caricatured swindling with the more nuanced flaws of Lord Drew, whom Swinborne has enlisted to steal the manuscript. Unlike Swinborne, Drew has the potential to make ethical choices and thereby becomes a potential suitor to Zoriada. Gibbes creates in Drew a character who, not only wishing to earn privilege but hoping his ancestors had earned their entitlement, hearkens to the late eighteenth-century shift towards social mobility: "[I]t was the fame of well doing, and well-meriting, that he must conceive ennobled his forefathers" (I. 139). Nevertheless, "fashion" rather than "natural depravity," has turned Drew into a "libertine," for he "had not the firmness either to shun or detect vice" (I. 142). His failure in the hermeneutics of detecting Swinborne's vice complicates his growing love for Zoriada. That Drew becomes concerned about reputation, referring to it as "the world's dread laugh" at the "man of such daring, as to marry a stranger in the land" resonates later: Edmund Mims, forming the third point in this love triangle, was born in India, contrasting Drew who wishes "he had been born on the banks of the Ganges" so that he could ask "her hand with confidence," unhindered by social mores from which Swinborne ironically leads Drew astray (I. 147). As he plays into Swinborne's plot, Drew has him go to London to seek out Mrs. Quinbrook, beginning a motif of romance as business that becomes increasingly complicated in Volumes II and III. Agreeing to gain information about Zoriada so that Drew can marry her, Swinborne baldly states, "I accept the terms of purchase" (I. 152).

Swinborne's aim in the business of manipulating the marriage between Drew and Zoriada is no less than "a grand source of knowledge," to bring about "the downfall of the loveliest girl on earth" (I. 184). His plot works against both Gibbes's providential plan and the emerging power of Zoriada's subjectivity: Swinborne "conjure[s]" Drew to write to him by every post, Gibbes ironically echoing Swinborne's own projection of evil onto Zoriada. By this point in the novel, the invasion of Zoriada's room suggests a double projection in which the objects that are studied to understand her come to inform her with a body viewed as a shell. Swinborne's stalking of Zoriada takes an increasingly dark turn through the ironic connection between his insistence on detecting Zoriada's witchcraft and the nadir of his actual evil (I. 152, 153). Plotting the kidnap and rape of Zoriada, Swinborne tells a fellow conspirator of his plan to abduct her to the home of a deaf man and "almost blind woman," both of whom drink. Thus, Swinborne tells him, "We may, without danger of detection, do whatever we please." His choice of the hermeneutical word "detection" increases the ironic divide between the elusive Zoriada and the predatory Swinborne (I. 186). The manuscript, the novel's symbol of metanarrative hermeneutics, goes unresolved, however, still untranslated as the novel ends. The reader is left to speculate upon what is knowable through the limited paradigm of western epistemology.

Even as Gibbes leaves no ambiguity about her outrage over the abuses perpetrated by the empire of "Barbarous England," the multiple points of view in Volume II vis-à-vis colonial abuses further problematize the binary of empire and colony. The entitled though morally educable Drew recognizes, for instance, that "civilized Great Britain does have cruelty she likens to destruction of her family in India" (II. 13ff, 17). Thus, though India is the locus of carnage that Zoriada has fled, Gibbes never specifies whether the perpetrators of the violence against Zoriada's family were indigenous Indians or colonists, the novel ultimately revealing the mixed bloodlines that deconstruct the empire/colony binary. Far from being the haven to which Captain Mims appears to have spirited Zoriada, the English village is filled with peril, as Swinborne's sequence of abuses represents with increasing aggression, from his symbolic violation of her room and projection of superstition onto the objects there to his attempted kidnap and rape of Zoriada.

As this aggression intensifies, however, Zoriada's voice emerges, countering the villagers' desire for knowledge through hermeneutical investigation as a means of hegemonic control. Superimposing references to Genesis onto the villagers' craving for knowledge, Gibbes simultaneously represents through Zoriada's relationship to knowledge a counternarrative to the Judeo-Christian story of the desire for forbidden knowledge as original sin. Gibbes makes the connection among Enlightenment hermeneutics, gender, and colonialism yet more pointed, for instance, when Drew, leaving the village for "the great city," invokes *Paradise Lost* XI. With her characteristic irony, Gibbes gives Drew Eve's words when, departing "with the same lingering pace our first parents are described to have quitted the primitive spot of human existence ..., [he] seem'd to exclaim[:] 'And must I leave thee, paradise / For ever leave thee!'" (II. 36–37). Eve speaks the first line in this passage from *Paradise Lost* when Michael tells the fallen couple that they must leave Eden. Drew must depart the paradise that the village has become because of Zoriada's presence: she has imbued it with innocence that transcends the biblical binary of pre- and postlapsarian Eden. Swinborne's *modus operandi* is "insinuating," lexically connecting him to the serpent in Eden. Gibbes deepens the implications of the desire for knowledge about Zoriada on the part of the villagers, for whom it is axiomatic that "Curiosity was nevertheless the sin in paradise" (I. 84). The villagers are thus implicated in Miltonic terms, their agrarian paradise deconstructed as a postlapsarian world, where knowledge is a means to appropriation through intrigue, spying, and coercion, paradoxically distinguished from the Zoriada's innocence.

The postlapsarian world is one of negotiation, as Gibbes shows by returning to the business motif introduced earlier through the plotting of Drew and Swinborne.[17] Now even Dr. Withers appears influenced by Swinborne's manipulation. He recommends that Drew "make an immediate journey to London" to "promote your tender interests," namely, "the true claims of this lovely stranger that has stole [sic] all our hearts" (II. 33). Gibbes's irony here emerges through the word "stole": taking the tired Petrarchan trope of the male subject having his heart stolen by the female object, Gibbes reverses the gendered association, Swinborne having literally stolen Zoriada's manuscript (II. 42). Just as the plotting to win Zoriada's hand in marriage intensifies in Volume II, so too does the attempt to coopt Zoriada's story.

In his desire to make her attractive to Drew, Captain Mims tells Drew Zoriada's story before Zoriada herself can recount it to Drew. Mims's story is a graphic, first-hand account describing the aftermath of the massacre of Zoriada's family and destruction of her home in India. In Mims's account, a wounded man approaches him for help, telling Mims he was servant to a family that has just been butchered, though "whether from motives of malice or plunder cannot be ascertained"; he tells Mims of "treasures ... buried deep in the earth ... with an Arabic inscription" to guide him (II. 47). The man says that the "eldest child of the family must have escaped," urging Mims to "seek her, preserve her" so that he can die in peace (II. 48). Mims then tells Drew of the brutal murder scene he discovers: "Tracks of blood were our clue to the house, where seventeen persons lay butchered, and though dead, were not cold, and even defaced as they were, and their cloaths [sic] drenched in gore, we could distinguish that two of them were ladies, a young and an old gentleman, three children, and the rest attendants" (II. 49).

By contrast to Mims's detailed description of the violent scene of murder, Zoriada, as the only one of its victims besides the servant to have escaped, cannot describe it from such a graphically objectified perspective. Instead, she nostalgically describes her lost home and family as "this garden" that had "smiled" (II. 53). Gibbes has Zoriada transform the garden imagery from the earlier perspective of the villagers' quest for knowledge as original sin. Here, Zoriada instead portrays the garden of her Indian home as communal in its state of innocence: "affection and friendship glowed in every heart; the conversation, how delightful!" (II. 53). The innocence of Zoriada's garden thus transcends the prelapsarian/postlapsarian binary of Genesis not only because it was communal but, as we come to learn, it was racially and culturally mixed.

The fate of the urn containing the remains of Zoriada's family parallels the villagers' attempts to appropriate Zoriada's subjectivity. Mims promises Zoriada to give her family a "funeral pile erected for them after the Eastern manner," after which he would "collect their ashes into an urn, to be deposited in some suitable sepulchre in England" (II. 54). Mims, however, confides to Drew that "this idea of burning the house, [sic] and its unfortunate inhabitants suggested itself to me as the most effectual means to detach her mind from India; where, if she continued under my protection, she could not long reside, and it had in a great degree the desired effect" (II. 55). Mims assumes that he can achieve catharsis for Zoriada through immolation of her Indian past, even as he tells the story following the villagers' earlier impressions of Zoriada as an embodiment of pathos.

Following Mims's story, Drew marvels at the "mystery and *inexplicability*" of Zoriada, Gibbes's italicized term stressing both the inability of the captain to tell the story or the suitor to apprehend her story from the elder man's perspective (II. 60). The immolation of the dead and the burial of the remains become literally and metaphorically complicated when Volume II returns to Zoriada's initial request to Mrs. Quinbrook to protect not only her but her "whole family ... contained in this precious urn, which shall be deposited in my own chamber" (II. 67). Despite Mims having promised Zoriada to respect Indian burial rites, he chastises her for ignoring his "judgment and decision: that I have held that urn sacred, I need only refer you to my conduct for a testimony, but when I proposed bringing it over, I little imagined you would have violated, you must allow me to call it the rights of the dead, or robbed the sepulchre of its proper deposit" (II. 68). Only now does the reader learn Zoriada's wish was to keep the urn with her family's remains in the room that Swinborne desecrated. That Zoriada would have included the urn in her chamber, her own created microcosm, until she is ready to bury the urn, contrasts with Mims who "decides" it should be in a sepulchre; "taking advantage of her silence," Mims cruelly "conveyed the melancholy memento out of her sight" (II. 69).

The literal burial of the urn takes on metaphorical significance when, contrary to the captain's own desire for Drew to win Zoriada, Mrs. Quinbrook, rooting for Edmund, Mims's son, decides to "bury ... deep in her own bosom" her "design ... until an opportunity should mature them, and prepare a way for their happy prosecution" (II. 72–73). That design is to "counterplot" the business-transaction deal between Mims and Drew that, Mrs. Quinbrook is convinced, will "manoeuvre the young lady out of her heart" (II. 72). The "opportunity" to "mature" her designs has metanarrative implications, reminding the reader that Gibbes is behind Mrs. Quinbrook, maturing the plot and wresting control of it from the machinations of Swinborne, Drew, and the captain (II. 73). Burial takes multiple levels of signification: the exhuming of Zoriada's treasures and the burial of her family's remains. By having Mrs. Quinbrook keep her motives hidden or "buried" suggests the doubleness of the novel's conflicting burials: of treasure—here, knowledge—to be exhumed for the right time but potentially repressed or threatened. A third connotation of burial is added in this phase of the imagery's development: the agricultural suggestion of planting the seed until it is ripe. Yet this connotation is compromised linguistically as well, since the designs will have "a way for their happy prosecution," a term signifying fruition as well as the litigation of a crime (II. 73). Drawn into the hermeneutics of the novel and wishing for the happy ending from Mrs. Quinbrook's point of view, the reader is thus implicated in the crime against Zoriada who, behind all this espionage, silently waits for her own opportunity to assert her subjectivity. She knows nothing of either party's machinations as they plan their competing "nuptial festival[s]" (II. 76).

Gibbes creates a counterbalance between burial and the exhuming of knowledge when the novel hints at the truth of the biological relationships among the villagers and Zoriada. Here, Captain Mims identifies as his parents the couple who raised him after he ran away from his biological parents, the Witherses, following the death of his sister. Mims tells Zoriada and the Witherses that he had to "bury" both parents—Anglo-Indians—in Calcutta, where he was raised. Mrs. Withers senses her "lost child's accents" in Captain Mims's story. Simultaneously, Crosby beholds the "living image of [his] lamented brother" in Zoriada, these plot twists returning in Volume III when Mims is revealed to be the lost son of the Witherses, adopted by Anglo-Indians, and Zoriada is revealed to be the daughter of Cosby's Anglo-Indian brother (II. 82, 83). Mrs. Withers, not yet knowing Captain Mims is her son, is convinced that Edmund Mims, her grandson, is her lost son. Not realizing she is a generation off in her hermeneutical reasoning, Mrs. Withers says, "His age does not agree with the period of our misfortunes; and yet his features, his features, are our child's!" (II. 119). Mrs. Withers's inability to verify her observation leads to "dreams that tortured her; she insisted upon it there was some concealment about the young fellow," forcing Edmund to reveal his identity to Zoriada (II. 137).

As noted at the opening of this chapter, Gibbes frames the revelation of Edmund as the romantic hero by giving him a traditionally feminine sensibility as he takes in the mysterious beauty of the monastery: "Mims was no stranger to all its intricacies, the rock, the grotto, the cave" (II. 137). He leads Zoriada through the cave's "subterraneous passage," bringing her "into full light at the foot of the declivity, where a prospect of the seas was enchanting, and the cave of his former residence and asylum, beyond description, antique and striking" (II. 137–38). The complexity of this narrative voice anticipates Austen's free indirect discourse in *Persuasion*.[18] The shift here in the third-person narration from Mims to Zoriada suggests a leveling of their power dynamic. Thus, when he asks if she hates him, Zoriada's response is to assure him, "I am above the little customs of my sex" underscoring her agency and his acquiescence: "Rise sir," she says (II. 139–40). Zoriada then adds, "Accept my hand to assist you to rise" (II. 140). She says, to herself, "He deserves my hand," observing her heart "had decided in his favour, before I knew his claim to it" (II. 140). Beyond the complicated selfhood that the pseudonymous Zoriada represents, even to herself, here her heart represents an intuitive knowledge transcending the ineffectual hermeneutics of the villagers. They nevertheless appear capable of embracing the intuitive, as when Mrs. Withers knows that Edmund is her relation even though the complexities of the events do not yet make sense to her.

Volume II closes the framing imagery of Genesis, now from the point of view of Drew. He has just discovered Mims is courting Zoriada: with "deceitful calm," Drew returns to "behold Zoriada in the garden, chatting, with apparent delight with his rival"; the narrator continues through Drew's point of view, "The Devil, when he beheld the first pair in Paradise, had not more envious or more torturing sensations" (II. 145). As the model of a new Romantic masculinity, Edmund contrasts with Drew.[19] Edmund has earned his worthiness in the eyes of the woman who chooses him because his "understanding [is] cultivated to [her] taste"; even his lower social class makes him more desirable, as Zoriada tells Drew: though Mims is his "inferior" in "the world's estimate," his "spirit is gentle, his manners engaging, his understanding cultivated to my taste, and need I speak the consequence, thus, my Lord, you find me a woman of my word; and it now remains for you to prove yourself a man of honor" (II. 148). Equally significant in the context of Edmund's attributes is that Zoriada identifies with him as "an East Indian by birth," regardless of his English ancestry. Through Zoriada's attraction to Mims, Gibbes anticipates Sophia's love of the Brahmin in *Hartly House*, the Brahmin's gentle masculinity contrasting the rapacious East India servants (II. 146).[20] Gibbes nevertheless complicates Drew as a foil to Mims by giving a multiplicity of conflicting perspectives on him: while Zoriada does not "read" Drew's behavior towards her as dissimulation, thinking he is "subscribing to her wishes," the Witherses "could read in the sullen brow of Lord Drew, sentiments inimical to general tranquility" (II. 150). Mrs. Quinbrook, despite wanting Edmund to win Zoriada, sees Drew as "very distant and reserved" (II. 151). This contrast between the conflicting views of Drew and Mims, idealized precisely because he is identified with Zoriada as sympathetic and East Indian, culminates when Drew challenges Edmund to a duel. Edmund is "petrified," a reaction that highlights the new Romantic masculinity, sentimental rather than virile (II. 154).

While the two men fight over Zoriada, Drew objectifying her as an embodiment of the exotic East when he refers to her as "the beautiful East-Indian," Zoriada, by contrast, deconstructs this objectification with language pointing to the hypocrisy of British judgment of indigenous East Indians as barbaric. She reasons to herself that Drew seeks a "human sacrifice as the duel's desired end" (II. 154, 155). Volume II thus ends with Zoriada interceding successfully on behalf of Edmund, whose identity she reveals as the son of her rescuer, Captain Mims. Despite having been corrupted by fashion to the point of engaging in the barbarity of duel, however, Drew has a "natural goodness of ... heart" that had repeatedly suggested to him the violence and injustice of his proceedings (II. 156). In this way Zoriada is able to reason with him.[21] In the context of the violent underpinnings of the novel, Gibbes's darker condemnation of the abuses of the powerful can be discerned underlying Mrs. Leland's comical remark on the difference between a gentleman and a low-born man: for the gentleman, "nothing but cutting one another's throats can content them" as opposed to "the good people of low degree" who "can box away their anger" (III. 3).

Volume III builds towards a paradoxical conclusion by intensifying the conflict between the reader's desire for a happy resolution to the marriage plot and the multiple perspectives of the characters that undermine such a prospect.[22] Thus, while Zoriada expresses her pity for Drew regarding his rashness, Gibbes uses metafiction through Mrs. Leland's reference to the artificiality of a tidy ending: Mrs. Leland remarks that "no stage play can out do Madam Zoriada's behavior, and yet my mind had its mis-givings [sic], for a second time, for as certain, as I once believed, overlearning had killed her, so certain, did I this day think it had driven her beside herself" (III. 8). Gibbes yokes seemingly incongruous reactions to the duel by following Mrs. Leland's remark with Withers referring to the duel as a "transaction," thereby picking up the business motif in describing marriage. Withers condemns Drew: "I hate an assassin ... however dignified" (III. 9). Yet Withers blames women for duels, saying that if "no one woman" were found "capable of smiling upon the successful murderer" it would put an end to duels (III. 10).[23]

Gibbes balances Withers's masculinist comment through the servant, Martha, who rages against the "barbarous" Lord Drew, underscoring the novel's indictment of class inequities and the hypocrisy of the aristocracy (III. 34). Her diatribe undercuts any sentimentality about Zoriada as heroine, since Martha's main concern is losing her "place" as servant. Coming even before her concern for Zoriada, Martha lets Drew know with unabashed honesty that the source of her anger is this threat to her livelihood: "[N]ow you have killed her, and turned me out of my place. I must not tell you of it, because you are a lord; but I say, noble is, that noble does; and if a prince, nay a king, was to act the part of a villain, I would twit him with it to his face, though he hanged me for it" (III. 35). Through Martha, Gibbes reverses the gender binary of rational men and seductive women, Martha reducing Drew to a "conjuror" who "bewitched us all," his castle, she imagines, "full of unhappy women" (III. 36). Crosby, who walks in on her upbraiding Drew, reveals his own liminality between the two extremes they represent when he notes that Martha is "one of the best but most uncultivated of hearts" (III. 39).

The novel complicates Zoriada's assertion of her subjectivity yet more strongly with this emerging focus on the relationship between gender and social class. It is in this context of class that Zoriada proposes to Crosby that he marry her to Edmund and that they elope: "I shall be one and twenty next week, Edmund is already three and twenty .... The superiority of my fortune, it seems, creates a delicacy between us; could Mims reverse our conditions, I know he would not cease soliciting me until I bestowed my hand upon him" (III. 64–65). Yet it is not merely a matter of the reversal of their stations that is at stake in her hints about the nature of the "fruits brought with [her] from India" (III. 67). When Crosby urges her to tell him her story, she says he must wait until Edmund is there, for "the story is too melancholy to be told more than once" (III. 67). In a novel whose details of dead and missing children and parents accrue with each character's story, the metatextual statement puts the reader in a double bind regarding wanting to know the truth of Zoriada yet finding repeatedly a heart-numbing regularity with which tragedy unfolds at every level.

Zoriada's voice reaches its full strength in her letter to Edmund Mims proposing their elopement. Zoriada asserts her authority by appropriating the language of business: "No transaction was ever more privately, or silently effected" (III. 71). Meanwhile, Captain Mims discovers that Mrs. Quinbrook has betrayed him by allowing Mims to see Zoriada and plots to send Edmund to India, by tricking him to go aboard a ship to have dinner with a "brother captain" (III. 82). That Gibbes not only sends her Indian heroine to England but has her romantic hero, an English national, sent to India to be trepanned, or kidnapped as a slave, deconstructs yet another binary along with those of culture, social class, and colonialism: active male/passive female.[24]

While Edmund is thus trepanned, Captain Mims reveals that he is the Withers's son after news arrives explaining how he came under the care of his adoptive parents, Stephen and Jane James, who had found Withers's son thirty-eight years before. When Mims then announces that he has just shipped the Withers's grandson, Edmund, off to India, Drew decides to rescue his rival, underscoring that he has a conscience under his narcissism, a product of his education. Drew betrays his ambivalence when he claims, "it will be an act worthy of humanity," a statement diminished immediately after when Drew adds, "and give lustre to my character" (III. 95). Gibbes represents the cruelty of Captain Mims towards Edmund, whom he is sending away at the peril of Edmund's new wife, by having Captain Mims quote Colley Cibber's 1699 revision of Shakespeare's *Richard III*: "They will bend, indeed, indeed, but he must strain, that cracks them" (III. 115–16). In *Richard III*, Gloucester gives these lines in an aside when he appears before Lady Anne.

Though the novel ends with Zoriada's union with Edmund Mims in what may appear to be the happily-ever-after of the traditional marriage plot, several factors undercut the sentimental formula. First, Zoriada's final actions emerge as authoritatively as do her words. Thus, when she discovers that she is the rightful heir to the English farm associated with the village, she announces that she will give her inheritance to the farm dwellers "who shall hold it rent-free." Zoriada asserts that "No one has the power" to resist her "grateful resolutions," for, she says, "I am of age, I am a wife; but my husband's heart is in unison with my own, and he will promote every good work, I am inclined to engage in" (III. 128).

The second factor in undercutting sentimentality is that tragedy and comedy are held in equipoise at the novel's end, the union of Zoriada and Mims tinged with the "solemn ceremony" of interring the ashes of Zoriada's family, "a whole household."[25] The inscription on the urn eulogizes the "unfortunate family who fell victims to the barbarous rapine of a set of ruffians on the banks of the Ganges." The family is reduced to one half of a binary by identifying its "English extraction"—implying the other half, the "barbarous rapine," is indigenous (III. 138). Yet the novel itself has deconstructed such a claim to "English extraction"; the word "rapine" calls to mind Swinborne's rapaciousness, bringing together the threat of his sexual violation of Zoriada with his stealing the Arabic manuscript, *Zoriada*, and the novel's larger perspective of the English rapine of India.

The third factor that undercuts the sentimentality of the marriage plot at the end of the novel is Zoriada belatedly telling for the first time her own story of her mixed bloodlines. When Lord Drew produces the manuscript stolen by Swinborne, Zoriada responds, "When I have a little overcome ... these tumults, I will endeavor to put the story into an English dress, for the general entertainment" (III. 149). That it would be premature for her to translate her manuscript into English at the end of the novel suggests that the translation would run counter to the English hegemony of the urn's inscription. In her most nuanced deference to the authority of her protagonist, then, Gibbes grants Zoriada the creative act.

Gibbes thus saves for the novel's final chapter Zoriada's narration of her story in her own voice. Zoriada describes herself as "half blood," a category underscoring her paradoxical position as both subject and object (III. 159). Zoriada's selfhood stands at the nexus of the waning binary system extolled during the Enlightenment and the nascent exploration of nondual epistemology associated with Romanticism. Zoriada reveals that her father was an Anglo-Indian gentleman, employed by the East India Company. He was imprisoned due to the earlier transgression of his brother, Crosby—now, therefore, identified as her uncle; her father was freed from prison by a Muslim whose daughter he would marry, producing Zoriada. Crosby, now revealed to be Zoriada's uncle, realizes that she is "the offspring of a brother I have undone" (III. 160–61). The novel thus culminates with a vision of a feminized India sharing her riches both east and west with the downtrodden of England.

Zoriada's triumph over western hegemony manifests through her refusal to surrender her subjectivity to the villagers and even the reader. *Zoriada*, the manuscript, as a textual symbol of eastern epistemology, has also overcome the villagers' attempted cultural appropriation. Through her layering of her heroine's subjectivity and the metatextuality of Zoriada's story, Gibbes signals the late eighteenth-century ambivalence underlying the revolt against Enlightenment thought. The novel gestures ahead to modern and even postmodern representation of unknowability by distinguishing between the creation of selfhood through one's story and the self that resists the laws of time and space upon which narratives are constructed. Despite her providential design and adherence to the sentimental formula of the marriage plot, Gibbes gives Zoriada the agency to choose the man she will marry. Perhaps more indicative of the autonomy Gibbes grants Zoriada in her quest for knowledge, Gibbes allows her to keep the manuscript untranslated to the end and her name undisclosed. Gibbes thus grants her heroine authority beyond even Gibbes's own authorship.

Part II

Subjectivity and miscegenation in Hartly House, Calcutta: A Novel of the Days of Warren Hastings *(1789)*

Hartly House is Gibbes's best-known novel, thanks to the pioneering work of Michael Franklin both in making the novel accessible through his superbly annotated edition and his critical analysis of the novel. The novel is a culmination in Gibbes's trajectory of an evolving female subjectivity intersecting with a world transformed during the period from the Seven Years' War (1756–63) to the global reach of British imperialism. *Hartly House* thus emerges from Gibbes's exploration of the upheavals with which she began her career in the 1760s, a perspective that underscores the ambivalence behind the novel's subtitle, *A Novel of the Days of Warren Hastings*.

Readers until the late twentieth century assumed that *Hartly House, Calcutta* was either an actual memoir of a sixteen-year-old British girl named Sophia Goldborne, describing her experiences in India, or the fiction of an anonymous man with first-hand knowledge of India, the distorted hermeneutics of previous scholars who assumed that Anglo-Indian texts were either travel narratives by women or authoritative texts of male

Orientalists.[26] Nevertheless, the historical confusion over the novel's authorship is understandable, given the doubleness of a narrative voice paradoxically naive and authoritative.[27] The novel represents late eighteenth-century Anglo-India as a welter of political uncertainty through irregularities often dismissed as making for "uneven progress through the book" (Clough viii). The novel underscores the instability of this early phase of Anglo-India through its recurrent references to Warren Hastings, governor-general of Bengal, from his visits to Hartly House to his forced departure and the subsequent arrival of his replacement, Charles Cornwallis. The 1908 edition's added subtitle, *A Novel of the Days of Warren Hastings*, suggests the historical perspective gained over a century later regarding Hastings's importance to the narrative. For Edmund Burke, who led the charge against him, Hastings embodied the East India Company's abuse of power during this early period of British colonialism in India, before the government itself took control. Many in England were sympathetic to Hastings during the trial, extolling him not only as a shrewd administrator who used the ancient Indian legal system to rule but also as patron of the Asiatic Society.

The novel connects this destabilized political context to the irregularities reflected in the equally destabilized sexual and racial mores of early Anglo-India. Gibbes plays out this dynamic through the mutual attraction between Sophia and the young Brahmin who teaches her Vedic philosophy, even as the novel appears to follow a conventionally sentimental trajectory, Sophia courted by a variety of East India Company men and ultimately marrying one of them. The sudden death of the Brahmin, whose mutual attraction to Sophia threatens both the marriage plot and British mores, allows the novel to return to its sentimental conclusion, leaving Sophia en route to England to marry her East India Company fiancé. More than a foil to the retinue of Sophia's martial and imperialist East India Company suitors, however, the Brahmin embodies masculinity as gentle, idealistic, and companionable to the feminine, while British masculinity in the novel becomes not only less attractive but, undercutting the sentimental ending, more rapacious as Sophia describes her horror in learning of a British soldier's rape of an Indian girl.[28]

The novel connects these volatile sociopolitical, racial, and sexual elements through the epistemological dissonance between the western subject–object dualism that informs Sophia's response to her early experience of India and the Vedic nondualism that she absorbs through the Brahmin. Gibbes's familiarity with the contemporaneous Sanskrit scholarship of the Orientalists who formed the Asiatic Society of Bengal, under the patronage of Hastings, emerges thus not only through the Brahmin's overt lessons in the Vedic roots of Hinduism but, more subtly, through its influence on Sophia's most fundamental understanding of selfhood.[29]

Informing the instability of Gibbes's British India is the double role of the Orientalists as scholars of ancient Indian literature and participants in British colonialism. The grand British home, Hartly House, symbolizes the paradox of early Anglo-India in which the Brahmin has access to Hartly House to teach Sanskrit to the British. The dichotomy of Indian as primitive and British as civilized would be codified fewer than fifty years later with the Anglicist period of British rule in India, in which Macaulay's "Minute on Indian Education" proclaimed an end to studying and disseminating the Sanskrit language and texts that Macaulay deemed "not merely as useless, but as positively noxious," essentially eradicating Orientalism (730).[30]

At the core of the novel, then, Gibbes associates the uncertain political identity of early British India with the fascination of the British with Vedic philosophy. Against the western dualism of the otherness of the east, Gibbes sets the Vedic nondualism of these ancient texts that more than influences Sophia—it transforms her.[31] Sophia's premature declaration at the opening of Letter IX, "I adore the customs of the East," is naive in its assumption of having a safe epistemological and emotional distance that the novel gradually erodes, uncovering an east that threatens the defensive structure of western dualism (34). As a female subjectivity whose foundation Gibbes lays in her earlier fiction, Sophia's character evolves as her understanding of Indian culture and epistemology deepens.

The novel holds Sophia's excitement over her new knowledge of Indian nondualism in tension with her inadvertent projection of British materialism through a larger pattern of non sequiturs sometimes evident through Sophia rhapsodizing about India through a pattern of poetic quotation. The tendency irritated Mary Wollstonecraft, whose 1789 review characterizes the novel as "stretched out by introducing quotations from our English poets— a little too often perhaps," an idiosyncrasy that continues to be the object of critical scorn (qtd. in *HHC* xxi). Though Sophia's snippets of British poetry, from Shakespeare to Thomson, appear to be random narrative interruptions reflecting her inflated sense of "the height and depth of [her] intellectual endowments," Gibbes's authorial voice emerges as gesturing to the quotations as more than *bon mots* for Arabella's pleasure, but rather signals about Sophia's shifting subjectivity (35).

At the heart of the long eighteenth century, then, Gibbes transforms the wit of her Restoration forebears into a sophisticated pattern of ironic juxtapositions to represent Sophia's growing ambivalence about Anglo-India. The narrative pattern of Sophia's seemingly incongruous thought sequences suggests Gibbes's engagement with the associational psychology of David Hartley and other eighteenth-century British philosophers who drew on Lockean philosophy to claim that "one thought is often suggested to the mind by another"; the notion that the "connexion [sic] which is formed in the mind between the words of a language and the ideas they denote" was a catalyst to the relationship between poetry and consciousness emerging at this point, the center of the long eighteenth century (Dugald Stewart, qtd. in Duthrie Appendix 5.i, 408).[32] In one such moment, Sophia suggests a connection between India's climate and her own emotion when she quotes Thomson's "All-conquering heat! O intermit thy wrath / And on my throbbing temples potent thus / Beam not so fierce"; "the poet's words," Sophia continues, "at this moment spontaneously flow from my pen" (14). Sophia here anticipates Wordsworth's "all good poetry is the spontaneous overflow of powerful feelings" (448). Though the playful suggestion of literally channeling Thomson's poetic spirit deflects the didacticism that was to characterize Wordsworth's poetics, Gibbes deploys associational psychology on the metanarrative level by having Sophia "wander wide from [her] intended subject"; following the Thomson quotation is Sophia's speculation about the possibilities for a young woman surrounded by the "fine fellows ... the East India Company's servants!" (15). Gibbes both anticipates and proleptically complicates the canonical lineage of male poets culminating in Wordsworth's "Preface" to *The Lyrical Ballads*.[33]

As Gibbes represents the intersection of the political and the epistemological through Sophia's subjectivity, she links both to the third prong in the novel's development, gender and sexuality. The appearance of the Brahmin in Hartly House, noted earlier as a microcosm of British colonialism, ushers in a masculine sensibility that counters the rapacious British men laying claim to India. Subverting the bildungsroman formula, Gibbes traces Sophia's coming of age as a trajectory of intensifying ambivalence. The Sophia that emerges as the plot unfolds is increasingly more complex than the rather flighty Sophia of her early letters to Arabella. Sophia's development takes her beyond both her British suitors and the negative female role models who either capitulate to these men or are victimized by them. As Sophia falls in love with the young Brahmin and, in turn, with Vedic nondualism, she comes to see her identity, in which self merges with other, as formed by India. The Greek name, Sophia, as "spiritual wisdom," has both ironic and serious valences at different stages of her development. Sophia cannot remain in this state of nondualism, for both narrative and epistemological reasons. Her full name's juxtaposition of "Sophia" with "Gold-borne" is the most ironic of the novel's juxtapositions, Gibbes's wry commentary on the lack of wisdom in Britain bearing Indian wealth—material and cultural—back to England. In this way, the novel stands as a warning about British imperialism in India at the inception of what was to become its long and complex history. Sophia internalizes India as she returns to England, projecting the now-dead Brahmin's gentle manhood onto her British fiancé, Doyly.

Progressing through three phases corresponding to its three volumes, the novel is driven by a teleology traceable linguistically. At central moments, Sophia echoes and complicates her first breathless declaration that she has become "orientalised at all points," Gibbes creating a diachronic shift from the noun, Orient, to her apparent coinage of the verb, "orientalise" (8).[34] In the first phase, Sophia's early letters reveal a life of insulated privilege so that to declare that she has become "orientalised" is seen as naive when it is retrospectively tinged with pathos and, finally, compromise. Her view of native Indians during this early stage is that of both colonist with "Gentoo" servants, and megalomaniac tourist, amused by what she perceives as a native culture of oddities. She proclaims breezily to Arabella that "to taste the beauties of the poet's pencil ... you must visit Bengal," sounding more like the writer of a travel brochure than one whose being "orientalised" is later disorienting in its challenge to her identity as a British woman (28, 8). At this early phase, Gibbes's acerbic anti-imperialism can be gleaned from Sophia's random and undigested observations. In one such case, she abruptly shifts from a description of Mogul "haughtiness" that styles itself "Governor of the Universe, the Ornament of the Earth ... on the assumption of the imperial diadem," to a banal discussion of the East India Company's housing rentals (29). The non sequitur elliptically incriminates the entitlement of middle-class company men acting the part of aristocracy in India.

The catalyst to the novel's second phase is Sophia's meeting the Brahmin who, she remarks, "walks in & out of Hartly House at pleasure," a phenomenon that would be unheard of fewer than fifty years later, as noted earlier (51). The implicit ironies of the novel's earlier phase surface as Sophia finds herself drawn to the philosophy and culture that the Brahmin imparts as well as to the Brahmin himself. A more complex subjectivity now connects Sophia to India both emotionally and intellectually, imbuing her tendency to poeticize, particularly via her references to Thomson, with a deeper significance beyond the early impression of merely displaying her erudition.

Though the Brahmin's "orientalizing" of Sophia threatens to transgress both erotic and epistemological boundaries, the final phase of Sophia's development recoups the safe distance of the opening section with a return to the marriage plot: her engagement to the aptly named Doyly creates a homespun image simultaneously pointing to the sentimental novel's return to English domesticity while underscoring Doyly's regrettable lack of the Brahmin's exotic appeal.[35] Such a denouement both capitulates to and subverts the sentimental formula, poised on a delicate balance between satire and tragedy not possible in Sophia's earlier letters.

Gibbes's Anglo-Indian novels deepen this intersection of the sociopolitical and epistemological with gender and race. As Gibbes reveals by the end of *Zoriada*, the exotic stranger appearing in an English village, and whom the English villagers see as other, turns out to be related to them and whose marriage to one of them promises a future that defies racial binaries. In *Hartly House*, Gibbes complicates what it means for a young English woman to become "Asiatic" in the late eighteenth century. While Sophia refers with ostensible playfulness to herself and the other British in India as "we Asiatics" and to Arabella as "you English," suggesting that to become "orientalised" involves losing racial identity, Gibbes peppers the early letters with references to miscegenation, significant from the hindsight of Sophia's falling in love with the Brahmin in the novel's second phase (86, 49). The most pointed early reference to miscegenation follows Sophia's initial claim that the "European world faded" before her eyes and she became "orientalised at all points": among a party of admiring British gentlemen Sophia describes herself in "the language of Southerne's *Oroonoko*" (8). In Southerne's rendering of Aphra Behn's *Oroonoko*, the African princess Imoinda is transmuted into a white European while Oroonoko remains a black African prince. Gibbes's interracial reference signals that there is more to being "orientalised" than Sophia may wish to acknowledge at this early stage, especially considering that the choice of Southerne would run counter to the acceptable coupling of British men with Indian women.

Gibbes thus simultaneously exposes and masks the subject of intermarriage through Sophia's playful innuendoes at this stage of the novel. In one such case, Sophia proposes that Arabella come to India and marry a nabob with a "copper complexion" (40). Gibbes deflects attention from the racial implications when Sophia claims, "I should rejoice to see you a Nabobess, that you may surpass me as much in rank" (40). While Sophia suggests that the Nabob's class outweighs his racial difference, she implies that Arabella would never marry for money, concluding with a quotation by Young that, Sophia claims, voices Arabella's disposition: "Can wealth give happiness?" (40). Arabella, being "sentimental," will probably refuse—not because of race, but because love outweighs class, as the second line of the Young quotation affirms: "What gay distress, what splendid misery!" (40). This hint of a potential narrative in which love transcends marrying for social advantage calls into question the novel's end in which Gibbes ultimately averts Sophia's potential to marry for love rather than for the financial stability, if not aristocracy, of the middle-class Doyly.

The racial tension builds novelistically through a sequence of apparently random observations, beginning with Sophia's admiring description of a military party in mythically idealized terms and culminating in a yet more embedded sequence of references to Shakespeare's *Othello*:

> The party to-day was brilliant—all that pomp and splendor could do, was done, to conceal the ravages of burning suns; and never were military gentlemen

more animated, more obsequious, or camp more delightful; but Mars in the East ... has more gallantry than hostility about him. (46)

Earlier readers tended to dismiss such moments of Sophia's hyperbole as either the girlish giddiness of a sixteen-year-old or, as in the case of Wollstonecraft's review noted earlier, Gibbes's annoying overuse of literary quotations. However, when Gibbes follows this hyperbolic praise of the "pomp and splendor" by having Sophia refer, with apparent incongruity, to *Othello* in the context of the military presence among the wedding guests, the novel's deconstruction of the racial and cultural oppression behind Britain's imposition of military force reaches a pivotal stage in the evolution of Sophia's non sequiturs:

> You can have no notion of the nonchalance ... with which I conducted myself through the day; but you will recollect that women who are accustomed to live with a multitude of men, acquire a modest assurance (let me call it) private education cannot bestow.—Friendship and respect are the sentiments reciprocally professed, and chearfulness [*sic*] and joy the universal objects: therefore, those who can do the kindest, or say the pleasantest things, are unquestionably the most esteemed companions; for Othello's liberal-mindedness seems to prevail throughout (at least) all my agreeable connections. (47)

Sophia then misquotes Act III, scene 3 of *Othello*. In Shakespeare's version, the passage is the culmination of Othello's dialogue with Iago who, plotting Othello's ruin, has just made the speech beginning, "O, beware, my lord, of jealousy! / It is the green-ey'd monster" (165–66). Shakespeare's Othello, as opposed to Gibbes's, responds to Iago,

> 'Tis not to make me jealous [*sic*]
> To say my wife is fair, feeds well,
> loves company,
> Is free of speech, sings, plays, and
> dances well;
> Where virtue is, these are more
> virtuous.
> Nor from mine own weak
> merits will I draw
> The smallest fear or doubt of
> her revolt,
> For she had eyes, and chose me. (183–89)

By having Sophia preface her recitation with the acknowledgment, "I am not correct in my quotation," Gibbes calls attention to Sophia's subsequent misprision and elision: "'Tis not to make me jealous, to say my wife is fair, loves company, sings, dances well, &c &c; for, where virtue is, these are most virtuous" (47). In Shakespeare's play, the speech precedes Othello's murder of Desdemona. In Gibbes's novel, Sophia's misprision comes between her description of the wedding of an East India Company man and Sophia's meeting of the young Brahmin with whom she will fall in love.

While the *Othello* reference can be dismissed as another of Sophia's attempts to display her erudition, there are enough strategically placed references that signal Gibbes's underlying design of providing and then manipulating the critical moment of what her contemporaries would know as the most famous literary precedent of an interracial marriage, in which the white wife is victim to the violence of a racially other husband. Sophia's preceding claim, that "Othello's liberal-mindedness seems to prevail throughout (at least) all my agreeable connections," underscores Gibbes's authorial voice behind Sophia's misprision: the quotation is far from an expression of liberal-mindedness in the context of *Othello*, in which Othello's suspicion takes hold, leading to his murder of Desdemona (47).

The odd context in which Sophia makes the reference is problematized further by two lines that she omits from the passage. First, by eliding Shakespeare's line, "fear or doubt of her revolt," in which Othello equates an unfaithful wife with a traitor or rebel, Gibbes demilitarizes Othello's marital/martial metaphor, thus creating a contrast to the British military men at the wedding that Sophia is attending. Gibbes's manipulation of the racial and sexual dynamics of Shakespeare's play, having begun with Sophia's describing Othello as liberal-minded, is apparent as well in the second omitted line, "she had eyes, and chose me." Suggesting that Othello's insecurity stems from his appearance, Gibbes censors Othello's weak rationalization that Desdemona would not betray him because she chose him with full knowledge of his racial otherness. By repressing the line, Gibbes anticipates Sophia's discomfort with the implied active choice behind what will transpire following this moment, love for the Brahmin, whom she meets shortly after. That Gibbes puts Sophia in the potential role of Desdemona takes on growing irony, for the Brahmin is the antithesis of the increasingly violent British men, while Sophia, in turn no mere victim, makes choices that are informed by her increasing awareness of the erotic dynamics that surround her. By calling attention to the elisions, with Sophia's reference to her memory lapse and then the "&c, &c" of the two missing lines, Gibbes signals not only Sophia's discomfort but her own choice to avert one potentially tragic outcome—namely, the death of a white woman at the hands of her non-white husband—in favor of a different outcome that nevertheless remains latent in the last third of the novel—namely, Gibbes's own choice to dispatch the Brahmin before he and Sophia can even consider consummating their love, thereby allowing the Brahmin to remain gently and companionably heroic.[36]

Compounding the racial implications of the digression that "spontaneously flows" from Sophia's pen from the military wedding party to the

Othello reference, Sophia compares the effects of the sun on the skin of the British and Indians:

> [T]he early maturity of the natives leading down to early decay; insomuch, that you would be shocked to behold a woman of thirty; for her appearance ... is equal, in infirmity and wrinkles, to the oldest looking woman in England at three score. Both sexes marry young, have families, decline, depart, and are remembered only in their offspring—Not so the Europeans, even at Calcutta—having received their birth in the happy zone of your residence, Arabella, their nerves are much stronger strung; their youth, moreover, is passed under the same healthful meridian; which enables them to endure the Eastern sun for ten or twelve years of their mid-life with tolerable satisfaction; and their days are lengthened into old age by their return to Britain. (48)

Buried in what might simply be dismissed as a young woman's preoccupation with appearance and aging is a logical leap that connects mortality and race. That indigenous Indians look older than their years is causally related to being remembered "only in their offspring," while the English attain longevity as their "days are lengthened into old age by their return to Britain." This deepening layer of anxiety about racial identity displaces the novel's subverted marriage plot. Marriage to Doyly will be her ticket to England and a legacy equated with prolonged life, in contrast to the potential consequence of marriage to the Brahmin, namely Sophia's early death in a symbolic if not literal act of *sati*, the ritual of widow suicide suggested by the return of Sophia's repressed fear of losing her British identity.

Her anxiety rises to the surface as the most banal of her observations, particularly regarding weddings, become laden with subtext. Letter XVI opens with Sophia's description of the "very joyous" weddings among the English in India. However, she quickly adds, "It is a festival I have not, however, the smallest desire to treat my friends with; for, even was my choice fixed, and every obstacle obviated, I should have unconquerable objections to making so public an exhibition of myself on so solemn a change of condition" (67). Making this claim in British India as well as in the context of Sophia's attraction to the Brahmin belies her ostensible subject of East India Company weddings. Gibbes thus subverts the sentimental marriage plot in which the heroine's coming of age in society leads to her final union with the hero. As becomes more explicit later in the novel, a "public exhibition of myself on so solemn a change of condition" in the context of India suggests not only marriage, but *sati*, the phrase thus conflating the rituals of marriage and death (67).

A yet more satirical juxtaposition illustrates Sophia's increasingly polarized ambivalence. Having expounded on "the wonders of a dessert," namely, "ices, Arabella ... ices" (69), she proceeds incongruously to marvel at Thomson's description of a serpent. How, she wonders, could one who had "never been in India," have "so admirably described an animal that, to be known in all its terrors, must be seen" (70). She then quotes Thomson: "Lo! the green serpent, from its dark abode / Which e'en Imagination fears to tread … Seeks the refreshing fount" (70). As Franklin observes, the "green serpent" suggests Sophia's jealousy "concerning her father's affections," for she is about to meet Mrs. D— whom, she suspects, her father is courting (*HHC* 190). Yet the serpent also recalls Sophia's previous references to *Othello* coinciding with her own marriage prospects, a connection underscored in the subsequent letter describing the visit to Mrs. D—.

When Sophia describes her interactions with the East India Company men, she uses theatrical allusions. By contrast, with the Brahmin her subjectivity is direct. Thus, discovering that Mrs. D— has a son, Sophia confides, "I am more than half afraid there is some plot in this sudden acquaintance and friendship," and with that, Gibbes simultaneously provides and alters the repressed line from the earlier passage from *Othello*. Echoing Shakespeare's "she had eyes, and chose me," Sophia writes, "Let the man have eyes to chuse me, on whom I am ever prevailed upon to bestow my hand, that I may not suppose the question is coolly canvassed whether I shall be accepted by him" (72). Sophia reverses the gender relationship in *Othello* so that she would be object of the man's choice, as opposed to Othello's implication that Desdemona chose him with the knowledge of his racial otherness. Sophia's chilly formality here is a thin mask for the offense she takes at the second-hand proposal, which Gibbes underscores by adding an allusion to the racial dynamic of *Othello*: "Jerry Blackacre (for so my mind would perversely call this unknown young man) never once, however, made his appearance; nor did Mamma glance the way I apprehended" (72). As Franklin notes, the reference to Jerry Blackacre, "son of the litigious and petulant Widow Blackacre" from William Wycherley's *The Plain-Dealer*, is an insult to mother as well as son (*HHC* 188). The immediate reason for Sophia's huffiness is the umbrage she takes at having been insulted, particularly since the son never emerges. Yet Sophia's aside, in the parenthetically stated "for so my mind would perversely call" Mrs. D—'s son, is further testimony to Gibbes's interest in associational psychology. By having Sophia dismiss as perverse her insult in referring to the young man as Jerry Blackacre, Gibbes points to the epithet's deeper implications, namely, Sophia's preoccupation with complexion, particularly vis-à-vis her marriage prospects (70). As another link in the chain of racial images, it builds most directly and problematically to Sophia's idealizing the Brahmin as "a Moor of such great dignity" (72).

By this point, the connection between the Brahmin and Othello underscores the complexity of Sophia's ambivalence in terms of race, sexuality, and empire. The reference to the Brahmin as Moor comes just after Sophia has described British lawyers returning from India "rolling in wealth" (74). Here, she uses the Moor epithet to introduce the Brahmin's lesson on the Indian caste system which, she says, is divided into "five tribes" (74).[37] That she follows Dow's 1770 *History of Hindostan* by including the untouchables, or outcastes, as a fifth caste is a significant departure from what surely would have been the Brahmin's teaching of the *Vedas*'s system of four castes that does not include the outcastes as a caste.[38]

Gibbes's inclusion of a fifth caste, via Dow, reflects the underlying cultural anxiety of the British about participating in the creation of a new caste of Anglo-Indians.[39] Gibbes's text demonstrates that the subject of miscegenation was fraught with fear and uncertainty in eighteenth-century British culture. By 1750, the Anglo-Indians exceeded the British in India. The British government, comparing the Anglo-Indians to the Haitian mulattos, feared revolution by the Anglo-Indians far more than by either Hindus or Moslems.[40] Not only does Gibbes thus explore the nascent taboo of miscegenation by reversing the accepted coupling of white male and indigenous female. Adopting Dow's claim to a five-caste society, Gibbes simultaneously mirrors and subverts the undercurrent of cultural anxiety about the Anglo-Indian community itself. In another non sequitur, Gibbes has Sophia follow her summary of the Brahmin's lesson on the caste system with a recounting of the British Mrs. D—'s tragic story of having been sold at twelve into marriage to a tyrant (73). As Franklin notes, "It is significant that the patriarchal despotism and arranged child marriage are wholly Occidental" (*HHC* 193). Though a seemingly different subject from the Brahmin's lesson, the selling of the English child bride underscores the havoc played by British masculine aggression not only in India but in its own society.

Doyly, with his "sensibility so oriental" is the closest Sophia can come to union with the Brahmin (93). Yet in one of the novel's most bizarre non sequiturs, Sophia begins Letter XXIII with the girlish worry that Doyly "breathes not a syllable" about the "state of his affections, or the colour of his wishes"—a striking allusion to the now-prevalent theme of complexion. She proceeds directly from "I will, Arabella, think ... no more of him" to a graphic description of corpses in the Ganges, so that the oddly phrased "breathes not a syllable" takes on morbid implications made odder yet in a parenthetical aside, in which Gibbes gives the metatextual allusion to the incongruity: "You have heard of alligators (a pretty contrast for the gentle Doyly!) and their depredations—but it seems, unless you throw yourself in their way, in their natural element, the human species have nothing to fear from them, whilst living" (102). Sophia proceeds with a horrifying description of the laying down of the dead, parenthetically adding, "(or, what is more shocking, their dying friends) at low-water mark, that the flowing tide of the sacred Ganges may bury [them]" (102). She elaborates on the grotesque vision of alligators feeding on the dead or, worse, not quite dead, down to the "mangled limbs and headless trunks, which are daily seen by all who pass that way"; she then speculates on the "impurities [that] must impregnate the air, to augment [the Ganges'] native putridity at certain periods, and endanger the lives of the inhabitants of this place" (99). The "sacred" Ganges is reduced to an embodiment of "native putridity" made pestilent by the corpses it holds, in a narrative tension underscoring the ambivalence that emerges with the splintering of narrator and authorial voice.

Sophia follows this gruesome description of violent death with an incongruously idealized portrait of the bodies that are burned in the ritual of *sati*, "those wives, who, with a degree of heroism that ... would do honour to the female world, make an affectionate and voluntary sacrifice of themselves upon the funeral pile of their departed husbands"; she continues with the enthusiasm of a society page journalist, gushing about the way the wives prepare themselves for their immolation: "No bride ever decked herself out with more alacrity or elegance, than the women about to give this last great proof of their conjugal attachment" (103). Franklin suggests that this "largely positive opinion of the abhorrent gynophobic practice" reveals Sophia's desire to impress Arabella, "anxious to stress ... female courage and devotion rather than to appear the apologist reveals her Orientalist credentials" (197). However, placing the comment in the context of its surrounding observations filters Gibbes's voice behind Sophia's.

The sequence—concern about Doyly's affection, alligators devouring bodies in the Ganges, and heroic wives performing *sati*—occurs between Sophia's meeting the Brahmin and his death. In the letter that follows, complicating the sequence further, Sophia comes closest to avowing her love for the Brahmin. She refers to him as "my" Brahmin in a passage replete with the language of sensibility traditionally reserved for the heroine's intended: "For love, this young priest affirms, refines the sentiment, softens the sensibility"; the Brahmin goes so far, in the presence of Mrs. Hartly, to say to Sophia, "you are the loveliest of women" (108). Sophia tells Arabella, "I was astonished—Mrs. Hartly was silent and the Bramin retired, with more emotion than quite accorded with his corrected temper, as if he felt he had said too much. Wretch that I am, Arabella! This confession, which I shall ever remember with pain, did I ... ardently aspire after" (108). Sophia follows her own confession by meditating on the unnaturalness of a life of celibacy, as though what she believes to be the Brahmin's monastic vows were the obstacle to their union rather than the racial and cultural divide that would make any thought of such a union impossible.

Underscoring her centrality to the long eighteenth century, Gibbes is prescient in anticipating the pivotal nature of this period of change and ambivalence in the history of British India. The climactic end to Volume II is an elaborate description of Hastings's forced departure immediately following the narrative sequence of Doyly's departure, the Brahmin's near-declaration of his love for Sophia and Sophia's confessing to Arabella her love for the Brahmin. Making these associations explicit, Sophia writes, "Doyly's departure has only been a prelude to the loss of our Governor, and every creature is plunged into disconsolation" as they show "their heart-felt respect" (108). The departure of Doyly, the would-be hero of a more formulaic sentimental novel, is merely a "prelude" to the governor's departure. Sophia exudes passion about Hastings's departure that eludes her when describing Doyly. Gibbes's subversiveness comes closest to the surface when she has Sophia speculate on a replacement for the peerless Hastings: "A more uniform good man, or so competent a judge of the advantages of the people, he will not leave behind him; nor possibly can a successor be transmitted, of equal information and abilities" (109). Indeed, when Sophia brushes aside the political implications of one who has mastered "the Persian language, that key to the knowledge of all that ought to constitute the British conduct in India, or can truly advance the British interests," she seems to realize that she has come dangerously close to betraying the "British interests" in her claim to having become "Asiatic" (109).

Novelistically, therefore, the Brahmin must die. Though Gibbes may be exploring British ambivalence, Sophia herself is hardly a revolutionary, caught in her own illusion that the east–west duality can be transcended. Gibbes nevertheless does not allow Sophia's relationship with the Brahmin simply to evaporate. After his death, Sophia muses on how his remains will be disposed of, gesturing back to the earlier letter describing the Indian death rituals: "No funeral pile will, I hope, consume [his remains] to ashes—Yet wherefore that wish?—for then will they be secure from every possibility of insult" (139). In an internalized Hindu ritual, Sophia vows to "raise a pagoda to his memory in [her] heart," linking her to those Indian widows preparing for *sati* (139). However, she immediately complicates this eastern vision of mourning with what she regards as a western sentimental tradition. Requesting a lock of the Brahmin's hair, "a mental talisman ... against all the irregularities to which we Christians are subject," Sophia worries that such a ritual would be "incompatible with the Gentoo customs" (139). Indicating the distance she has traveled in the psychic landscape of east and west, Sophia's phrase, "we Christians," is a significant shift from the earlier, playful binary, "we Asiatics" and "you British." In fact, she tempers her ardent avowal of her devotion to the Brahmin by telling Arabella that Doyly, now in England, will surely feel for Sophia if Arabella tells him of the Brahmin's death.

In the trajectory of Gibbes's fiction, Sophia's love for the Brahmin is a pivotal representation of nonbinary dynamics in race, religion, social class, and gender.[41] Gibbes heightens her complication of the sentimental novel by exploring the potential for a tragic outcome beyond the death of the Brahmin. Sophia abruptly shifts from the Brahmin's death to imagining Doyly dying at sea: "Doyly may, nevertheless, even whilst I am writing his name, have reached the confines of eternity, and found the ocean as merciless, as the cruel disease to which our favourite has fallen a victim" (140). Such an outcome would doubly subvert the marriage plot. Instead, Gibbes submerges the novel's disturbances of tradition to allow the sentimental ending, though not without Sophia's tepid response to what should be the climactic news of Doyly's fortune and the prospect of their marriage. Referring to her *deus ex machina*, Gibbes gives Sophia the wryly metatextual remark, "a pretty plot, this!" (150). The implications of such a resolution extend to the macrocosmic happily-ever-after promised by Cornwallis, who simultaneously arrives "to assume the reins of government," promising to eradicate the corruption of the Hastings regime, and thus ushering in the believed utopian outcome of colonial India (149).

Lest the reader mistake what appears a tidy ending as Gibbes's support for the new British colonialism, she concludes the novel with a haunting end frame to the hospitality of Hartly House that had welcomed the Brahmin early in the novel. The novel's subversion of the marriage plot culminates with Sophia, "all indignation, terror, compassion, and agitation," telling Arabella of a British officer's rape of an old man's daughter and subsequent murder of the father (163). Gibbes invokes *Othello* once again, signaling the tragic consequences of imperialism that the novel refuses to repress: "There are monsters, Arabella, in human shapes, and the Eastern world is … the scene of tragedies that dishonour mankind" (162).[42] For Sophia, there are multiple layers to this violation: though it dishonors "mankind" in general, it degrades any honor represented earlier by Hartly House in its "the laws of hospitality," for the old man had trusted the soldier by inviting him into his house and, rather than carry her off, he "accomplish[ed] his work of darkness under the paternal roof!" (163). The vulnerability of the Indian's home to British aggression stands in contrast to the welcoming into Hartly House of the Brahmin who bestows enlightenment on its British inhabitants.

This culmination of rage at British masculine aggression and Sophia's subsequent dark thoughts about her own fate provide a final ironic juxtaposition. Just before the brief concluding letter announcing their arrival at Portsmouth, as she writes, "[S]hould we all be buried in the deep," Arabella should be consoled that "Providence has a right to dispose of us at will; and that, however unable mortals are to penetrate Heaven's design, every seeming misfortune is a disguised blessing" (164). Behind Sophia's recurrence to violent death, Gibbes—the novelist as "Providence"—must dispose of the Brahmin and, possibly, of Doyly, wielding the novelist's power to use misfortune to resolve her characters' ambivalence.

Gibbes's plot resolution, therefore, subverts even as it capitulates to the demand for a racially and socially normative sentimental ending. She neither chooses the unrealistic escape of her interracial lovers into a world that can transcend even Hartly House, nor does she simply have her heroine forget him and embrace her life with the "inarticulate paragon," Doyly (Clough ix). Sophia, instead, molds the pliant Doyly into an ersatz Brahmin, her marriage to Doyly the closest she can come to union with her Brahmin:

> Doyly shall figure away as my Bramin and so well have I instructed him in every humane tenet of that humane religion, that he will not hurt a butterfly, nor can he dispatch even a troublesome musketto without a correspondent pang, [concluding that Doyly is] the universal admirer of all Nature's productions. (151)

Gibbes here compensates for the potentially facile choice of the British colonist over the native Indian by virtually superimposing the Brahmin onto Doyly, whose sensibility could not harm a mosquito.

The marriage plot and the new empire of British India prevail over "the smallest fear or doubt of her revolt," in the words of Shakespeare's Othello (if not Sophia's). As opposed to Sophia, who elides Othello's reference to her revolt, Gibbes gives the reader ample, though oblique, opportunity to speculate about the alternative fates of her characters beyond the point that Sophia dares consider, including the glimpse of Sophia as Hindu widow heroically offering herself to the funeral pyre of her beloved and the imagined death of Doyly at sea echoing the intended purification of the bodies in the Ganges horribly disfigured by alligators and spreading disease to the living. Amid the late Enlightenment departure from the traditionally martial masculine ideal, Gibbes's British India finds an uneasy balance between horror at its predatory nature and devotion to the Orientalism of the Hastings administration.

***

Together, *Zoriada* and *Hartly House* represent Gibbes's engagement with growing global concerns during this pivotal moment in British colonialism. Despite the shift this phase of Gibbes's career represents, one can trace the genetic code that links these new protagonists to Gibbes's previous female characters, from the two Charlotte Clives and the young American fugitive, Arabella. Gibbes portrays the cruelty and complexity of Anglo-India through the two contrasting perspectives of Zoriada, who controls her narrative beyond the ability even of the narrator to inform the reader of her identity, and Sophia, who claims to have become "Orientalised" when she sets foot on Indian soil, yet whose sense of what this means deepens in the course of her experiences in India and her travel between England and India.

Though Gibbes appears to succumb to the marriage plot in each case, she does so ambivalently, leaving her reader with the bitter taste of the predations of patriarchy that reach their nadir in the Anglo-Indian novels. Zoriada endures abuse in both India and England as she is not only demonized and eroticized by provincial English villagers but tells the horrific story of her family's massacre and her own escape from colonial India. By contrast, Gibbes transforms Sophia Goldborne from a young Englishwoman who suggests the heroine of a traditional sentimental novel at the outset of *Hartly House*, intending to marry an East India Company man upon arriving in India to her embracing Indian culture and philosophy inspired by the young Brahmin, and finally to witnessing the predations inflicted on the indigenous Indians by the English.

Contemporaneous with *Zoriada* is *Elfrida*, the subject of Chapter 4. In *Elfrida*, Gibbes most directly dismantles the formula of the sentimental novel with an Englishwoman's prodigality set against that of the two men with whom she forms a love triangle. Gibbes returns to her characteristic proto-feminism and indictment of British imperialism by having Elfrida finding her agency in a world controlled by fathers, husbands, and patriarchal laws.

Notes

1 As Franklin notes of Gibbes's personal connection to Anglo-India, her petition to the Royal Literary Fund for financial support describes her "distress of losing an only son at Calcutta"; speculation is that he was her eldest son, Anthony, "an East India Company writer" who died in 1786 (xiv). Anglo-India (n) or Anglo-Indian (adj, n) has multiple meanings, some of which are employed in this chapter and whose meaning should be clear in context. See Merriam Webster for a breakdown of these meanings: www.merriam-webster.com/dictionary/Anglo-Indian. Accessed July 26, 2022.

2 Though *Zoriada* was previously attributed to Anne Hughes, Gibbes claimed the novel in 1786. As noted above, Gibbes's authorship is supported by her characteristic style among her books written between 1764 and 1790, seen in elements such as ironic juxtapositions; ubiquitous allusions to the English poetic tradition, with references from Shakespeare, particularly *Othello*, Milton's *Paradise Lost*, and Thomas Gray; and its metafictional sophistication. *Zoriada* includes a nod to Sophia, the protagonist of *Hartly House*, who, like the secondary character of the same name in *Zoriada*, writes letters to her friend, Arabella (III. 98).

3 For a recent discussion of the oriental tale genre, see Ros Ballaster, "Fakiry: The Oriental Tale," at http://writersinspire.org/content/fakiry-oriental-tale. Licensed as Creative Commons BY-NC-SA (2.0 UK).
4 The manuscript uses the spelling *Zoriada* rather than the traditional *Zoraida*. Whether or not the transposition of vowels is an idiosyncratic choice or an error, the essay follows this and other irregular spellings in the manuscript, bracketed for clarification when necessary. Phebe Gibbes, *Zoriada, or, Village Annals* (London: T. Axtell, Royal Exchange. 1786); *ECCO*. All references to this source are in the text.
5 Masculine tenderness, as discussed in Chapter 4, becomes more complicated with the development of Wilmot in *Elfrida*. While Gibbes sets him against the cruel misogyny of Ellison, Wilmot is more ambivalent in his masculine identity than Gibbes's other romantic heroes. Wilmot is seduced by the imperial trade of the East India Company and sometimes mirrors even as he opposes Ellison.
6 See the Introduction to this study for discussion of Gibbes's prescience of the "woman question" traditionally associated with the later eighteenth and nineteenth centuries.
7 A case in point is Coleridge's development from his early poetics founded on Associationism, the final phase of Enlightenment philosophy, to his outright rejection of it as he embraced German transcendental philosophy. For two perspectives on Coleridge's ambivalence towards Enlightenment materialist philosophy, see Berkeley and my earlier monograph, *Rethinking Romanticism*.
8 See Part II of this chapter for Gibbes's challenge to the genre in *Hartly House* through the "orientalizing" of her English protagonist, Sophia Goldborne discussed as well in my book, *British Women Writers and the Asiatic Society of Bengal, 1785–1835: Re-Orienting Anglo-India* (New York: Ashgate, 2014). As noted previously in this study, for a detailed discussion of the sentimental genre, see Janet Todd, *Sensibility: An Introduction* (New York: Methuen, 1986).
9 Note that Gibbes takes her engagement with Cervantes's text deeper than Charlotte Lennox's satirical *Female Quixote* discussed in the earlier chapters.
10 See Christina Lee, "The Legend of the Christian Arab Madonna in Cervantes' Don Quijote," *Revista Canadiense de Estudios Hispánicos* 32, no. 1 (Autumn 2007): 105–21. www.jstor.org/stable/27764178?seq=2#page_scan_tab_contents.
11 I use "nondualism" as an epistemological term in other publications as well as throughout this study to describe an element central to the revolutionary period, namely its often-ambivalent relationship western binary systems and the pull towards the nonbinary represented by eastern thought as discovered during this period. See below for *HHC*'s representation of Sophia's deepening awareness of her claim to becoming "orientalized" as glimpsing and ultimately embracing the nondual.
12 Through Mrs. Leland, Gibbes appears to satirize both Della Cruscan emotionalism and the common eighteenth-century superstition that women subject themselves to untimely deaths through intellectual pursuits (I. 1–2). Mary Tighe's early death, for example, was attributed to her desire for literary fame.

In a letter, Felicia Hemans quoted Tighe's mother saying, "Oh! my Mary, my Mary! The pride of literature has destroyed you!" (qtd. in Clarke 50–51).

13 www.ancient-origins.net/artifacts-ancient-technology/armillary-spheres-following-celestial-objects-ancient-world-004025. Accessed September 15, 2024. For a fascinating lesson using an actual armillary sphere, see Chris Parkin's demonstration for the Museum of the History of Science. www.youtube.com/watch?v=AaWuJHQL-bQ. Accessed September 15, 2024.

14 See Adrian Johnstone, "Galileo and the Pendulum Clock." www.cs.rhul.ac.uk/~adrian/timekeeping/galileo/. Accessed July 29, 2022. For general information on the scientific method, see https://plato.stanford.edu/entries/scientific-method/. Accessed July 29, 2022.

15 See the discussion of the Romantic label vis-à-vis gender in the Introduction to this study.

16 The allusion to Iago may be further evidence of the connection of *Zoriada* to the early novels, to *Hartly House*, and to *Elfrida*. Gibbes's ubiquitous references to *Othello* throughout her career prove not mere ornamentation. As suggested earlier in this study, they signal Gibbes's deepening psychological representation of evil, particular in male abuse of women.

17 The etymology of "negotiate," without *otium*, the peace of retirement from public life, adds further irony to the plotting that undermines the bucolic setting of the novel. See the *OED* entry: www.oed.com/access.library.miami.edu/view/Entry/125878?redirectedFrom=negotiate#eid. Accessed September 15, 2024.

18 See the Conclusion to this study for the discussion of *Elfrida*'s commonalities with *Persuasion*, particularly in Gibbes's anticipation of Austen's use of FID.

19 See the earlier note in this chapter on the capitalized term, Romantic. The subject of Romantic masculinity involves the shift from earlier definitions of manliness connected to martial virility to the traditional feminine quality of emotion that came to characterize Romantic poetry. For his pioneering discussion of shifting definitions of masculinity during the period, see Marlon Ross, "Romantic Quest and Conquest," in *Romanticism and Feminism*, ed. Anne Mellor (Bloomington: Indiana University Press, 1988).

20 See the second section of this chapter for the development of this discussion.

21 Given Gibbes's propensity for wordplay, it may not be overreading to suggest a play on his name: though he "drew" his sword, he has the wherewithal to withdraw it.

22 Volume III appears unedited in comparison with the markups and corrections in Volumes I and II. Because the chapters appear mismarked at a certain point, I give both the printed chapter number and what is probably itended based on the sequence from the beginning of Volume III.

23 See Chapter 1 of this study for discussion of Charlotte Clive's cross-dressing duel.

24 The novel thus indicts the treatment of both the colonized and the British underclass by the East India Company with its tradition of "trepanning" or selling Europeans to the colonies as slaves.

25 Such a tension between tragedy and comedy points to the distance that Gibbes has brought the genre through narrative from Behn's tragicomic play, *The Widow Ranter*, discussed in the Introduction to this study.
26 Through the 1980s, in fact, readers offered various suggestions about Sophia as author, including historical travel writer and disguised man. See Clough and Basham respectively. E.M. Forster assumed Sophia Goldborne to be a contemporary of the travel writer, Eliza Fay. In his introduction to Fay's *Letters from India* he quotes *Hartly House*, opining that as a travel writer, "Miss Sophia Goldborn [was] her rival in narrative style" (21).
27 Michael Franklin regards *Hartly House* as the culmination of Gibbes's prolific literary career. (*HHC* xi). All references to this edition are in the text. When citing Franklin's introduction, the abbreviation *HHC* is given.
28 The attractiveness of the gentle Brahmin runs counter to the contemporary stereotypes of Indian men as effeminate. See Rajan's essay, "Feminizing the Feminine," for a nuanced discussion of women whose subjective writing on India predates the British male perception of a passively feminine India. See also Ross on the canonical Romantic poets' "attempt to bring the 'feminine' vulnerability of emotion into the realm of 'masculine' power" (37). Considering yet another dimension of masculinity in the novel, namely, Sophia's avowed desire to be a Nabobess, Franklin notes that the novel perpetuates "the Orientalist stereotyping of feminized Hindoo and virile Muslim" (*Romantic Representations* 4). By contrast, the premise of this book, that Gibbes often uses Sophia to challenge rather than perpetuate such stereotypes, applies in this case as well, first, through Sophia's playful teasing of Arabella and, second, through setting Hindu and Muslim against British and European vis-à-vis race. Germane to Gibbes's treatment of British masculinity is Nicole Reynolds's study of the novel's comparison between English and Indian women, particularly the "nautch girls," as commodities (168ff).
29 The popularity of the novel is indicative of just how much Orientalism was celebrated not only as the first systematic study of ancient India, but as evidence of a common Indo-European linguistic history. See Franklin's synopsis of the novel's historical context of British India, particularly in its contextualization of the novel vis-à-vis Orientalist publications (*HHC* xxiii–xxviii).
30 See the introduction to my monograph, *British Women Writers and the Asiatic Society of Bengal* for more on this Anglicist suppression of Orientalist scholarship in Anglo-India.
31 See the above discussion of *Zoriada* as embodying nondualism. The introduction to *British Women Writers and the Asiatic Society of Bengal* gives a detailed discussion on the Sanskrit *advaita* vis-à-vis this book's use of the term "nondualism" to convey a dynamic rather than static principle of oneness that more accurately represents the dissolution of subject-object duality than the term "monism."
32 See Duthrie on Hartley's influence on Joanna Baillie (31). Hartley is a well-established source for the early philosophical poetry of Coleridge and then Wordsworth.

33 In the 1800 Preface, Wordsworth repeats the statement a second time, adding "recollected in tranquility," a phrase that underscores the associational influence with its claim for the mind's discursive interpretation of the earlier spontaneous overflow of feeling (460).

34 Franklin notes that Gibbes's use of the term "orientalised" antedates the first *OED* citation by over twenty years (*HHC* 166).

35 Franklin suggests that the name may be based on Sir John D'Oyly, an East India Company administrator and friend of Hastings (*HHC* 195). Gibbes may also be playing on doily as "a woollen stuff, 'at once cheap and genteel,' introduced for summer wear in the latter part of the 17th c." (*OED*). The Brahmin's gentle masculinity, it suggests, would be merely effete, colorless, and bourgeois without the Brahmin's exotic allure. An observation originally made as a criticism of Gibbes can equally be enlisted to distinguish author and protagonist: while Sophia does not "differentiate between her train of admirers," Doyly himself is "an inarticulate paragon" who "wins her father's consent, a fortune and her hand, in that order" (Clough viii, ix).

36 See Kelsall's discussion of the contemporary importance of *Othello* as "one of the fundamental texts of British Orientalism" (255). See also my discussion in the previous chapters of this study regarding Gibbes's earlier novels' use of *Othello* at moments of psychological complexity when representing evil.

37 The *OED* traces the etymology of *caste* to Latin, *castor -a* meaning "pure, unpolluted" through the Portuguese *casta*, or race. The etymological link to *chaste* is especially significant regarding the implication of miscegenation since it conflates racial and sexual purity through unadulterated "stock or breed." The link between sexual and racial purity further complicates Sophia's reference to *Othello* since the issue of his wife's chastity is fraught with the implications of the racial intermixture of their own union. See below for Sophia's further concern with the racial binary.

38 See Franklin's note on Dow's "five tribes" (*HHC* 189).

39 See chapter 1 of my monograph, *Eighteenth-Century British Women Writers and the Asiatic Society of Bengal*, for discussion of Charles Wilkins's non-translation of the phrase *Varna Shankar*, or mixed caste, as suggestive of his anxiety about British participation in the creation of the Anglo-Indian subcaste.

40 See Anderson for the history of the Anglo-Indian community, originating in the seventeenth century, in which the East India Company coerced its employees to marry and convert Hindu women rather than marry the Catholic Portuguese and French then living in India (12). For detailed discussions of the Anglo-Indian community, see Anthony, Ballhatchet, and Sharpe.

41 Franklin cites Nussbaum on the challenge to the western gender binary: "Indian men are the feminized binary against which Englishwomen can experiment with unorthodox femininity" (qtd. in Franklin xxxi). The black/white binary appears again with Sophia's description of the racially segregated island of Madras off Africa's west coast, under possession of the East India Company.

Franklin notes that Gibbes "appears unaware that Calcutta was similarly segregated" (204).

42 In the play's final scene, Othello alludes to the mythical cloven hooves of the devil when he realizes that he has been duped by Iago: "I look down towards his feet; but that's a fable.—If that thou be'st a devil, I cannot kill thee" (V. ii. 336–37).

4

Elfrida; or Paternal Ambition (1786): "fled from Arcadia, she could not fly from the apprehended disease"

As seen in Chapter 3, the expanding world of Gibbes's fiction culminates in the 1780s, as global revolutions intensify the relationship among gender, sexuality, and sociopolitical upheavals. Though Gibbes wrote *Elfrida* and *Zoriada* in the same year, the two novels take radically different perspectives on the tension between provincial insularity and global expansion. Unlike both *Zoriada* and *Hartly House*, *Elfrida* represents British colonialism without the perspective of the colonized. Instead, it traces patriarchy across three generations marking the shift from provincialism to nation building and colonialism through the subjectivity of a woman whose coming of age resembles no protagonist before her. Elfrida's rival lovers, Ellison and Wilmot, crisscross the East and West Indies and America, both men engaging in war and colonialism for self-promotion. Elfrida's world, from childhood to young adulthood, is circumscribed by patriarchal authority, first that of her father, Overbury, whose "paternal ambition" creates misery that has repercussions for generations; then Ellison, her husband; and, less overtly, her lover, Wilmot, whom Elfrida marries when it is believed that Ellison was killed fighting in America. While Ellison's aristocratic birth makes his patriarchal presumption overt, Wilmot's humbler origin and compassion mask but ultimately overcome his seduction by colonial power.

Though readers of sentimental novels would not have been surprised by *Elfrida*'s use of the familiar plot device of the love triangle, contemporaries criticized Gibbes's choice to begin the rivalry of Ellison and Wilmot for Elfrida during the early childhood of the three.[1] For later readers armed with the theoretical tools to recognize the novel's metanarrative deepening of the busy surface plot from its inception, Gibbes's choice to begin the triangle in childhood can be seen to represent the exploitation of women marking the trajectory of their lives from early childhood on. The development of the triangle from childhood to adulthood is thus foundational to a novel that is not limited to tracing Elfrida's own development, but one that expands outward to three generations as it dissects patterns of masculine oppression and women's struggle to assert their own agency.

Amid the posturing of her two suitors for control of the marriage plot, Elfrida's emerging subjectivity is pivotal on many levels. Elfrida emerges at the center of a lineage of women named "Ella"—Elfrida's birthname being Ella—that represents an alternative to generations of women during the long eighteenth century whose surnames become a confusion of paternal and married names.[2] This alternate female legacy stretches from her mother, Ella, to Elfrida's adopted daughter, Ella, who continues a female legacy unbound by ancestral entitlement. The third-generation Ella adopted by Elfrida is the rejected offspring of the extramarital affair of Ellison, Elfrida's husband, with a woman whom he later rejects, disavowing their relationship as the young woman lies dying of smallpox.[3]

This novel's subversion of the sentimental can be seen through its iteration of the pattern of naming confusion in many of Gibbes's novels. Like the name Zoriada, Elfrida is not the birthname of the protagonist, as noted above. Unlike Zoriada, however, Elfrida does not choose her renaming; this protagonist's renaming at the start of the novel is the catalyst to an ambivalent matriarchal lineage with which Elfrida comes to terms in the novel. The emerging matriarchal legacy resists the patriarchal connection between bloodlines and the economic exploitation of women. Instead, these women discover a subjectivity distinct from female identity defined through their roles as mother, daughter, and wife. Gibbes's multi-generational Ellas wreak havoc with patriarchal inheritance represented through generations of men named "Charles" or "Henry"; these female characters scramble the bloodline of patrimony as well by calling attention to their chosen lineage by contrast to "Ellison," for instance, whose name, with the "son" suffix, suggests the inherited masculine title that he uses to subjugate and abuse the Ella lineage.[4] Like the challenge to both the characters in and readers of *Zoriada* in their attempts to discover Zoriada's identity, keeping the "Ella" characters in *Elfrida* straight is the first of many layers of hermeneutical irony informing this novel.

Gibbes uses authorial irony towards her readers not only through the pattern of character name confusions, but through her creation of a metanarrative, providential connection between her characters and readers. However, while *Zoriada* leaves the reader in the dark, forced along with the provincial characters to piece together Zoriada's identity, *Elfrida* gives clues to the reader that reveal Gibbes's presence behind the characters' cluelessness. Gibbes thus plays on the hermeneutics of reading through the patriarchal name, "Cluwyd," first brought to the surface in a chapter appropriately entitled "A Discovery" (29).

Such purposeful confusion across generations suggests the need for Elfrida to liberate herself from the cycle of patriarchal oppression and to create a new social order founded on female agency. Gibbes creates confusion through repetition not only of names but also of plots, and even words with multiple meanings. Thus, for instance, in the first of the three generations, the cousins of Elfrida's mother, the Miss Cluwyds, attempt to make the senior Ella, Elfrida's mother, ashamed of her "tender" feelings for Lieutenant Overbury, who falls in love with her when he visits the Cluwyd patriarch at The Grange. The word "tender" appears repeatedly here and with increasing irony throughout the novel to suggest the double meaning of the term that refers not only to sensibility but also to economic negotiation. Overbury's desire to "tender" his daughter for the sake of his own lineage is the foundation of the novel's means of tracing the conflict between the sentimental novel's marriage plot and the economic exploitation of women.[5]

"Their alienation of their child"

The novel's opening scenes of domestic harmony in the Overbury family are laden with forecasts of dissonance. Lieutenant Overbury, his wife, Ella, and their young daughter, Ella—to become Elfrida—appear to live an idyllic though humble life, the lieutenant an adoring husband of the wife he objectifies as saintly. However ideal this domestic circle appears before external forces threaten it, humming under the surface is its own internal conflict that will take the novel's three volumes to unspool. Overbury's name suggests his class-based self-division. He is soon revealed to be "buried" by those who tower over him. Despite his feats of military heroism, Overbury is enchanted by wealth that perpetually eludes him. As a soldier, he is outclassed by his wife's family, the Cluwyds, whose name, noted earlier, provides a metanarrative "clue" regarding the hermeneutical emphasis of the novel, Gibbes even gesturing to the pun by having the patriarchal Cluwyd's wife call him "Clue" (I. 112).

In one of the novel's many instances of scrambling generational linearity regarding marriage and property, Ella, Sr. is cheated out of her inheritance by her jealous stepmother, a much younger woman than her father, Cluwyd, this new wife only three years older than Ella, his daughter. This stepmother of the elder Ella thinks of her as an "over-grown girl" whom, the stepmother fears, has "influence over her husband," Ella, Sr.'s father (I. 114). She thus casts the Overburys "from his house and heart," Mrs. Cluwyd referring to the Overburys as "you young people," despite being in their generation (I. 114). Not till Volume III, long after this second wife has fled with a lover, does the eighty-year-old Cluwyd reconcile with and embrace the three generations gathering round him.

This patriarch's embrace of the new lineage that culminates in Volume III presents a striking contrast to the polarized world that opens the novel.

Elfrida; or Paternal Ambition 157

In an early chapter entitled "Paternal Folly," Gibbes traces the origin of the "paternal ambition" that Overbury projects onto his daughter, namely his descent from the paradoxically broken lineage of a Royalist whose estate was taken at the Civil War, one of "the many sufferers in Charles the Second's cause, who were unrequited at the restoration; but, being a royalist upon principle, his great grandfather brought up his son in the same political faith with himself, and pointed out the army as his natural and sole inheritance" (I.17). At several points in the novel, Overbury's own military commission is compromised. From the start, "the father of our heroine was compelled to retire upon lieutenant's half pay" (I. 18). From his perspective—the focus of the third-person narration in this early phase—Overbury's only recourse is allowing his wife's cousins, Bell and Christiana Cluwyd, to take the daughter of the Overburys, whom the Cluwyds will rename as Elfrida, to make her an heiress under their one condition that the Overburys cut all ties with their daughter. Playing on the word "alienation" that becomes central to the economic exploitation of women in marriage, Gibbes has Mrs. Overbury, Ella, Sr., refer to her husband's "alienation of their child" in describing the Cluwyds' "splendor and privileges of wealth" having "so dazzling an effect, as to induce him to part with his only child" (I. 17). As their daughter's names multiply in the novel, she is alienated existentially as well as economically.[6] With his "soul formed to taste and to diffuse happiness, he became the votary, and author of misery" that continues till the end of the novel (I. 18).

When the novel's subtitle, *Paternal Ambition*, is echoed midway through Volume I, the connection between patriarchy and naming surfaces. Miss Cluwyd, who renames the young Ella "Elfrida" because she considers it more aristocratic, is convinced that

> paternal ambition would fix him hers, and their little girl become their no less natural than common heir; she therefore, congratulated herself again and again, that her conduct had been such ... that none could suspect her of other motives, than such as it would do her honor to acknowledge, a family pride, to enrich a near relation, and a family tenderness for the infant Ella. (I. 139)

The Cluwyd cousins thus target the Overburys' young daughter, Ella, as a valuable commodity by whom to regain power over her parents. The name of one of the cousins, Bell, suggests a play on the twin seductions of the popular novel, war and beauty, brought to the surface when the two sisters argue over educating the young Ella/Elfrida; for the other cousin, Christiana, "sons of war ... are ever more devoted to the alternate sovereignty of Bellona and Venus," whereupon "Miss Bell" complains that her sister is "too flowery" for Ella's "fancy" has "run away with her reason" because of the "nonsense of love" (I. 24). That the Cluwyd cousins rebrand

Ella with the name of the first queen of England, Elfrida, who murdered King Edward in 978 is characteristic of Gibbes's irony throughout her writings:

> Elfrida (or Ælfthryth) ... was of royal descent on her mother's side, but not born to queen .... Elfrida was renowned for her beauty. Her attractiveness was so famed that, in her youth, she attracted the attention of Edgar, the new king of England. According to later accounts, he sent his friend, Ethelwold, to visit her to determine whether she was worthy of him. The young nobleman fell in love, informing the king that Elfrida "was misshapen, ugly, and dark," before seeking permission to wed her himself.[7]

By alluding to the first queen of England whose royalty traces back to her maternal lineage, Gibbes suggests that, by renaming Ella, Jr., the Cluwyd cousins are trying to wrest back the Cluwyd lineage their cousin Ella squandered by marrying Overbury. However, the cousins represent a parody of the matriarchal lineage of the generations of Ellas, whose passivity each Ella needs to overcome over the three volumes.

Seeking to control the family inheritance, the Cluwyd cousins, described wryly as "sage and busy gentlewomen," realize their best course of action is steering Ella, Sr. away from Overbury who, they claim, is dangerous because "whatever [he] was *out of doors* ... as their favourite Shakespear [sic] phrased it, was infinitely attractive"; the sisters echo the phrase when they warn Ella that their "doors as well as ... hearts were continually barred close against every soft temptation in the shape of a red coat" (I. 21–22). The reference to the British army's uniform links the cousins' plot to Iago's in a convoluted cross-gendering of the masculinist tradition out of which Shakespeare's tragedy emerges. The context of these two phrases resonates with several layers of irony, including the gender reversal of these female cousins seeking to wreak havoc with the marriage plot. In *Othello*, the phrase "out of doors" is spoken by Othello's ensign, Iago, who brings about his general's ruin out of revenge for having been passed over for promotion: "Come on, come on. You are pictures out of door, bells in your parlors, wildcats in your kitchens, saints in your injuries, devils being offended, players in your huswifery [sic], and huswives [sic] in your beds" (II. i. 122–25).[8] To underscore what appears the dark undertone of the Iago quotation, the cousins repeat the word "reputation," Iago's theme.[9] Bell—whose name echoes Iago's "bells in your parlors"—says to Ella, Sr., "[W]e came to yourself, to win you, to conjure you, to be the guardian of your own reputation and happiness"; Christiana adds, "I repeat your *reputation*; for, unless this young man marries you, when the neighborhood has talked itself into the firm expectation of that event, *slander*, Miss Ella, will dare shew her head, and nods and winks to convey a meaning too terrible to mention" (I. 26–27). In these cross-gendering references, Gibbes bring together the archetypal stepsisters of Cinderella with the sinister destructiveness of Iago through the Cluwyd cousins (I. 22).

Hermeneutically, then, Gibbes offers the reader a range of clues by which to solve Elfrida's problem, suggested by Christiana Cluwyd's mysterious reference to "the family secret" of which, she says, Overbury is "master" (I. 35). As it turns out, there is no explicitly revealed secret, though the cousins hint at having orchestrated Ella, Sr.'s marriage to Overbury to bring "shame ... disgrace ... upon their house ... which had been celebrated time immemorial, for the rigid prudence of its females" (I. 23). Long after the Cluwyd sisters have been dispatched from the plot, their secret contaminates the family. Thus, when the cousins make Overbury promise never to see his daughter again, the injunction is repeated by Overbury himself in the next generation when he demands that the romantic hero, Wilmot, stay away from his then eighteen-year-old daughter, Elfrida (I. 32). The "secret" is not only that of the Cluwyd sisters, but of Gibbes as she teases the reader, whose desire to know keeps the plot pressing forward through the multiplying iterations of names and patterns of behavior in the dense fabric that makes up its three volumes.[10]

Having begun the novel with the early marriage of Ella, Sr. and Overbury, the plot moves not forward with Elfrida's childhood but back to her mother, Ella, Sr., née Cluwyd, when she meets and falls in love with Lieutenant Overbury. Though all the ingredients are present for the sentimental in this earlier-generation love story, Gibbes complicates them by adding a darker layer to Overbury's military heroism that will reverberate throughout the novel. While the young Overbury is visiting Cluwyd, a valet in the Cluwyd house plots to have the family killed and young Ella Cluwyd abducted in the family's "pleasure boat." Overbury foils the valet and his accomplices, a heroic act echoed later in Volume I by Wilmot when he rescues the second-generation Ella, now Elfrida, from the very pleasure boat from which her mother had narrowly escaped.

Overbury's rescue of Ella could have been the culmination of a traditional love story, but as the beginning of a new matriarchal line of Ellas and the introduction of female characters who support them, the incident lays the foundation for the novel's deconstruction of the gender binary Overbury's rescue of Ella appears to represent. At the trial of the valet and accomplices, for instance, Ella Cluwyd is unable to "give her evidence, her tender spirits were so agitated that she fainted, and was scarcely articulate in her account of her danger and deliverance" (I. 124). Though this detail suggests that the court is clearly no place for women, Gibbes contrasts Ella's inability to testify with Hannah, Ella's caretaker, who has no problem speaking, albeit as "the great entertainment of the court" when she bestows hyperbolic praise on Overbury, concluding, "I hope to see them all hanged, and this without one dread of their ghosts haunting me" (I. 124–25).[11] Gibbes spares no description for the intention of the would-be murderers, "one of the most daring designs that was ever planned, for the number of innocent persons marked down for slaughter, was thirteen besides the young lady, who was destined to survive them for the worst of purposes" (I. 126).

With her characteristic authorial irony, Gibbes draws a connection between economic negotiation and sentimentality from the start of the novel, as the pun on "tender" noted above suggests. The Cluwyd patriarch is nagged by his jealous wife to pay off his daughter to leave the paternal estate with Overbury. Cluwyd is "strongly prompted ... to have pressed them, as his beloved children to his heart," yet he urges them to follow his wife's inclinations by "leaving his house immediately" to "save his credit with" his wife (I. 128). The banknote Cluwyd gives Ella is the first in a series of negotiations that entangles sensibility and economy. Ella Cluwyd and Overbury thus become romantic "wanderers from their late paternal and hospitable mansion" to a humble cottage. The servant, Hannah, comments on the cruelty of the wealthy Cluwyd in the colorful language that becomes Hannah's hallmark as a storyteller, rivalling the novel's narrator. Here, Hannah herself procures the Overburys' new quarters, she says, "since Mr. Cluwyd can be so hard-natured, as to turn out to the wide world his only child, and the Captain Overbury that saved him from being murdered" (I. 130).

The fall of Ella, Sr. from the aristocratic entitlement of her Cluwyd ancestry to Hannah's working-class cottage is the first of many ways the term "tender" holds in tension the language of negotiation and sensibility. Thus, the Overburys' early marriage appears a "union of affection of tender solicitude for each other's happiness ... which neither time, chance, or circumstances, could destroy" (I. 134). Immediately following this idyllic sentiment, however, the narrator destroys the illusion of romantic idealism with the young couple's bickering over money: "Mr. Overbury would not comply with his wife's request, to devote the five hundred pounds to his military advancement" and, more somberly, their having "buried several children" (I. 134, 135). Thus, Gibbes brings Volume I back to the opening scene with the narrator's explanation of Overbury's allowing the Cluwyd sisters to take his daughter: "No wonder, then, that with apprehensions so strong, and feelings so tender, he should eagerly embrace the first *family* offer for improving his Ella's fortune" (I. 135).

As she shifts to the second generation with her protagonist's yet more complex story, Gibbes introduces the contrasting lineages of the two rivals for Elfrida, Wilmot and Ellison, through their fathers. The elder Wilmot, the rector of the parish, is father of Edmund, the young man whom Elfrida loves and who has inherited his father's humility and compassion; by contrast, Mr. Ellison is lord of next manor, "an odd compound of pride and sentiment" from whom his son, Frederic, inherits a "cruel kindness" already manifesting at age nine as "ill-natured and "actively mischievous" (I. 142, 143). These early moments in the love triangle lay the foundation for the dynamic among the three for the rest of the novel: Ellison, who is aware of "his consequence" holds himself "intitled" [*sic*] to "dance the first" minuet with Elfrida, "whilst Wilmot, with humility and often down-cast eyes, would wait his turn" (I. 145).

However, the young, outspoken Elfrida is strikingly different from the repressed adult she becomes and with which she must reckon later, through the crisis of her inadvertent bigamy. As a child, she lacks patience, wishing that Ellison's wealthy father "would send [him] to some of the great London schools, that they might not be troubled by him" (I. 145). The adult Elfrida, by contrast, becomes docile as the patriarchal powers act more aggressively upon her during the later episodes. In this early episode, however, she confides in Wilmot about her parents and, most important, urges Wilmot, "Call me Ella" since that was her name "as a happy child; Elfrida is a fine lady and makes a great shew" (I. 147). She understands that "Elfrida" defines her by the entitlement of her mother's cousin, a hierarchy upended from the beginning with the oxymoronic name of Overbury. As father to Ella, Overbury desires her to have the privileges of wealth, but he becomes buried under that persistent desire at each critical juncture of the novel: insisting that she marry Ellison, he rejects Wilmot until late in Volume I.

As young Wilmot and Ella become confidantes, Ella expresses her rejection of identity based on entitlement: "I ought to have been poor, for I should like it, and should say to myself, now this is right, that a child should be what heaven has made its parents" (I. 148). Though Gibbes's metanarrative role as providence will test Elfrida's childlike fatalism as the plot unfolds, even from the novel's beginning, Elfrida prefers poverty. This trait culminates in Volume III when Elfrida rejects marriage to make her own living. As will be seen later in this chapter, although the novel is still constrained by the marriage plot in ending with her re-marriage to Wilmot, Gibbes repeatedly shows Ella happiest when she is alone, creating.

The conflict between Wilmot and Overbury emerges when Elfrida, now a teenager, confides to Wilmot her sadness at being separated from her parents, Wilmot thus deciding to contact Overbury about his daughter's unhappiness. However, Overbury refuses to acknowledge Elfrida's unhappiness over "what they had done to make her fortune" (I. 151). Against the cruelty produced by Overbury's "paternal ambition," Gibbes injects a metanarrative moment that anticipates Wollstonecraft's later warning in *VRW* about the corrupting influence of sentimental novels on young women. Gibbes shows the hypocrisy of Christiana Cluwyd, the elder Ella's cousin whose manipulation carries into the next generation with her attempt to groom

Elfrida as a young, marriageable aristocrat. In the midst of a conversation with Ellison, Sr., regarding the co-education of young Elfrida, his own son, Ellison, Jr., and Wilmot, Christiana says, "[A]n evil, of all others the most to be dreaded for a girl, *reading romances*, will be guarded against; books, my good Sir, that give such false pictures of life, as turn the heads of female children" (I. 153). Mr. Ellison commends her, saying "Elfrida's mind, under her formation, would be as pure as her person was lovely, and she would shew the world what a woman of honor and elegance ought to be" (I. 154). However, though Christiana enjoys this praise, the narrator adds that, though Miss Cluwyd "so highly disapproved of novel-reading in the young, she seemed to consider that amusement as the natural food of the mind, for ladies of a certain age; her closet was accordingly furnished with every production of the eventful kind ... down to the last publication of her day" (I. 154). Proleptic of Wollstonecraft's warning, the titillation for which Miss Cluwyd enjoys novels is yet more insidious in the ways she attempts to plot Elfrida's life, beginning with her re-naming, to follow the trajectory of the sentimental novels she herself enjoys reading. Christiana is thus a doppelganger to Gibbes, who plots her own characters at odds with the prescription of sentimental fiction that she deconstructs even as she ultimately gives her reader the desired marriage of heroine and hero.[12]

Besides Gibbes's metafictional presence subverting moments of sentimentality, this novel's love triangle works against the traditional marriage plot with Wilmot's anticipation of the male sensibility often attributed to the canonical Romantic poets.[13] Gibbes sets the "mild, the liberal-minded Wilmot," full of the sensibility to which Ella responds, against the wealthy, cruel Ellison, who is "fond of tormenting," Ellison demonstrating his desire for Ella's attention through "ill-natured strokes" that include stalking Ella and Wilmot (I. 160). This polarization between Wilmot and Ellison surfaces most dramatically when Wilmot decides to tell Elfrida all he knows about her parents, including the valet's planned murders of the Cluwyd family from which Overbury had saved them. Wilmot takes Elfrida to the very "pleasure-boat" that was the planned site of abduction of the elder Ella. When young Elfrida decides impulsively to get into the boat, Ellison surprises them, untying the rope. Wilmot then jumps into the boat, prepared to die with her, a contrast to the military heroism of Overbury a generation earlier (I. 161). As the boat is about to sink, Hannah's husband rescues Wilmot and Elfrida, echoing Hannah's rescue of the elder Ella and Overbury when she finds the cottage for them after Ella's father casts them out.

Wilmot is quick to forgive Ellison, making Elfrida concerned about Ellison's potential to corrupt Wilmot: "I can think it possible for one bad boy to corrupt another; but Ellison's mischief is all his own; if he would have taken lessons from you, he would have been as good as you" (I. 173).

As the love triangle develops into their adult entanglement, Elfrida's concern appears to be well founded: Wilmot's behavior comes dangerously close to mirroring Ellison's. Gibbes ends the dramatic episode of the rescue of Wilmot and Elfrida from the foundering pleasure-boat with Hannah's point of view. Having told them of her and her husband's struggles, Hannah "believed every thing [sic] was ordered for the best, and would never more repine at what seemed cross accidents; for why? They often occasioned the most comfortable endings" (I. 176). This remark signals Gibbes's sly metanarrative presence behind Hannah, creating the "cross accidents" that form the trajectory of the novel's plot as a whole and of this moment, in which the "pleasure-boat" takes on the metaphorical significance of wealth, potentially fatal to both Ellas.

Elfrida's awakening: unspooling the marriage plot

Through this metanarrative bridge, Gibbes ushers in a more overt level of hermeneutics with a chapter entitled "An Hint [sic]," beginning with Ellison's father bringing his son to apologize to Wilmot and Elfrida for the pleasure-boat debacle (I. 177). No sooner does the younger Ellison ask her forgiveness than he "relapse[s] into his old practices of teizing [sic]," to which Elfrida responds, "You bad, bad gentleman ... how richly do you deserve to be punished!" (I. 179–80). Behind Elfrida's referring to Ellison as a "bad, bad gentleman" then adding the double meaning of his "richly" deserving punishment, Gibbes underscores the immorality of Ellison's entitlement.[14] At this early phase of her life, Elfrida speaks her mind to Ellison with no compunction, saying, "[T]hough *my* Wilmot knows I can only fear you, he never spoke of you, in your absence, but with good humor and respect, except when you had like to have drowned me, Sir" (I. 180).

While this early chapter gestures ahead to the unchanging character of Ellison, by contrast, it shows a dramatic change in Elfrida from this moment on: "[F]or the first time in her life, from the dictates of her own mind, [she] felt the painful necessity of dissembling" (I. 182). Elfrida now feels she must hide her rage at Ellison, who tells her that they should "kiss and forgive each other" (I. 183). Elfrida's response is that "though I am not yet twelve years old, I will be a child no more, nor will I play again with any boy" (I. 183). Ellison walks away, saying, "[W]e shall see how long you will be suffered to give yourself airs," a threat leading to the narrator's disturbing description of Elfrida's reaction: "Never was mind more deranged than that of the innocent Elfrida" (183–84). Through Elfrida's realization, Gibbes reflects the physical and emotional toll on women's silencing, a curse that reverberate through the rest of the novel.[15]

Rather than spend time openly with Wilmot, the young Elfrida "applied herself ... with redoubled diligence ... to her harpsichord and her pencil," forming two early habits that acquire importance to the adult Elfrida who, shamed by her bigamy, chooses to pursue her art. By contrast, when Ellison's mother here sees Elfrida's painting of a bouquet and hears her play the harpsichord, she decides Elfrida will give Ellison pleasure through them. Elfrida, however, asks herself, "is it for Master Ellison's entertainment, that I have had my little talents cultivated? Impossible; I dare not look that way; no, no, there will be happy times, when I shall still have it in my power to please a certain person, worth fifty Master Ellison's" (I. 186). The reader would assume from familiarity with the sentimental novel's marriage plot that the "certain person" Elfrida refers to being "worth fifty" Ellisons is Wilmot. However, this moment of the child Elfrida's revelation underscores what the adult Elfrida will take the three volumes to understand: that she must ultimately create for herself.

Hannah becomes an increasingly important confidante for both Wilmot—in advancing the marriage plot, and Elfrida—in advancing Gibbes's subversion of the marriage plot. For Elfrida, Hannah provides a perspective uncorrupted by the entitlement Wollstonecraft disparages in *VRW*, though Hannah herself draws a clear line between the privilege of the Ellas and her own humble status.[16] Elfrida's conversations with Hannah begin at this turning point, when she must give up her childhood play with Wilmot. Elfrida challenges Hannah's binary thinking regarding the idle rich and the working poor, saying that "there are idle poor as well as idle rich" (I. 190). Yet Elfrida is nevertheless "struck forcibly" by Hannah's logic when the latter responds that while wealthy women take fashionable exercise yet would never do "household work" to keep them from "falling into lethargies, and whimsies" (I. 190). Elfrida describes the difference between the health of her "soul" when she is with Hannah as opposed to being with the Cluwyd sisters at "Arcadia House," a name rife with Gibbes's characteristic irony (I. 191). Elfrida shares the revelations of these conversations with Wilmot: "Hannah ... teaches me more than all my masters; she teaches me to distinguish between the arts and the true conduct of the world; for it is pride, Wilmot ... that puts people upon hindering me from speaking what I think" (I. 192). Ella's awakening includes her awareness of what her future will entail: "Wilmot, when I am a woman, I will not be acquainted with those strange people that can call deceit virtue, and truth vice" (I. 193). Yet looking back from the events that transpire in the later episodes, the reader knows that she will be forced to confront such "strange people" as she continues her evolution.

From the chapter, "An Hint," to one called "A Parting," Gibbes suggests how to read against the grain of the sentimental novel. One might speculate that, if Ella's newfound wisdom induces Wilmot's "Parting" from "Arcadia," then Gibbes is presenting her authorial cross-purposes for the novel, namely, to move both towards the union of Elfrida and Wilmot and to work against it until Elfrida can fully embrace her subjectivity. Being provided an education reserved for the aristocracy, Wilmot thus makes plans to go to Eton, while Elfrida is forced to stay behind in the company of Ellison. She urges Wilmot to visit her parents since he is now near London. Like Elfrida's father, Wilmot wants her to have wealth rather than love, as he confides to Hannah: "Miss Ella is much too open, and too young to be trusted with a knowledge of my wishes" (I. 202).[17] Through Elfrida's awakening subjectivity, Wilmot's surreptitious confederacy with Hannah is questionable, though they ostensibly conspire out of concern for Elfrida. Wilmot rightly articulates Elfrida's idealism when he tells Hannah that "fortune … will never make Miss Ella Overbury happy; a cottage and a competency, [sic] are best suited to her nature; the life I read of in the poets, for she is all humility and sweetness" (I. 203). However, he eclipses her subjectivity even at such a moment, urging Hannah to write to him: "I shall never see her more," he says dramatically, setting in motion a chain of epistles. When Hannah responds, "I am but a poor pen-woman" (I. 203), Gibbes prepares the reader for Hannah's ironically colorful letters in the upcoming episodes, an unexpected channel for Gibbes's authorial voice as the plot develops.

Wilmot's response to Hannah's letter announcing that Elfrida will marry Ellison is that Hannah "prophane not my Ella's name, by joining it with his" (I. 204). By referring to her as Ella rather than Elfrida, Wilmot demonstrates his respect for her place in the matriarchal lineage. Before Wilmot leaves for Eton, Ellison goes to Bath with his parents, an opportunity for Wilmot to say goodbye privately to Elfrida. She tells Wilmot that Ellison has threatened to spy on her while he is in Bath, behavior that is repeated into his adulthood. Ellison's double standard regarding infidelity manifests most overtly later, when he fathers two children outside his marriage to Elfrida but is enraged at his own paranoid fantasy of her betrayal. Yet Wilmot, who appreciates Elfrida's "uncorrupted nature" and "undesigning innocence," is perhaps more insidious than Ellison in his objectification of Ella, whom Wilmot describes as "dangerously beautiful" for, he muses, "her winning artlessness will destroy my peace of mind for ever [sic]" (I. 210).

Contamination in Arcadia

The irony of the name "Arcadia" surfaces most dramatically as the locus of smallpox. Elfrida, now fifteen, contracts the disease there, while the entitled Ellisons attempt to flee contamination by going to the exclusive

Bath. However, along with Miss Cluwyd, they are "enemies to inoculation, because not practiced by the *ancients*," thereby contracting the disease (I. 214). Amid this outbreak, Ellison returns to Arcadia to declare his love for Elfrida. Given the context of rampant disease, Gibbes doubles her metanarrative irony as the narrator blames Ellison's sentimentality on "novel-reading, which opening a kind of new world upon his knowledge, he pursued with such avidity, that he set up half the night, indulging his newborn taste in literature, which the accidental meeting with a novel ... had given birth to" (I. 220–21).

Though their wealth buys the Ellisons retreat to the pampered world of Bath, therefore, it cannot protect them from disease. Ellison not only gets sick despite Elfrida's warning but, unlike Elfrida who is free of any blemish from the disease, his face is "pitted," smallpox representing the contamination that inflicts the wealthy (I. 229). Thus, "though Mrs. Ellison fled from Arcadia, she could not fly from the apprehended disease; she was taken ill a few hours after her arrival at Bath, [*sic*] and expired the eleventh day" (I. 228). Through the smallpox outbreak, Gibbes ties patriarchy's insulated power to contamination: having lost his wife to smallpox, the elder Ellison marries Miss Cluwyd, thereby joining their estates. Gibbes plays on the word "tender" once again to underscore the relationship between sentimentality and marriage as business negotiation, following the statement, "Mr. Ellison ... pressed her hand with ardor" as "proof positive of his tender intentions," in the next paragraph with the calculated transaction behind his profession of love: "He made a tender of himself in form, and was in form accepted ..." (I. 231).

Pleased by the power Ellison has gained through this union, Overbury refuses to grant Wilmot a visit when he comes to London. Hannah's letter introducing Wilmot to Elfrida's parents awakens "fears in [Overbury's] breast" that she will marry Wilmot, "the very evil he dreaded" (I. 218, 219). Ever the model of repressed wifely virtue, Elfrida's mother responds to Wilmot with characteristically ineffectual piety and compassion: "[T]hank[ing] him, with tears in her eyes, for what he had done for her child, [she] told him she would pray for him" (I. 217). Yet the elder Ella steps out of her subservient role to disobey her husband. Meeting Wilmot, she rebels against Overbury for the first time, adding that Wilmot's "merit evidently entitles" him to be happy (I. 232). That Elfrida's mother had chosen love over inheritance as a young woman by marrying the humble but heroic Overbury has important consequences in its generational echo. Overbury becomes the impediment to his daughter's union with Wilmot because Overbury wants Elfrida to live the life her mother has rejected on his account. Thus, when Wilmot presents the portrait of Elfrida to her mother, she promises "to consider it as the deposit of friendship, and friendly confidence, to conceal it from her husband," a tendering of love and friendship that counterbalances that of the Ellison/Cluwyd negotiation (I. 234). Later, however, the plan backfires when Overbury finds the portrait, his paternalism once again running counter to his own early courtship of Ella, Sr. Thus, the secretiveness that began with the Cluwyd sisters' "family secret" at the beginning of the novel contaminates the generations of Ellas who must engage in subterfuge rather than assertion (I. 39).

As this double tendering ensues between Ella Overbury and Wilmot and between Lieutenant Overbury and Ellison, Elfrida appears to have consciously decided to repress her spirit of childhood rebellion against patriarchal strictures. When he returns to Arcadia, therefore, Wilmot finds Elfrida changed—not marred by smallpox but now manifesting "an appearance of womanhood that awed him, and Ellison [wearing] all the marks of a favored lover" (I. 234). Elfrida's reaction to Wilmot's friendship with her mother is visceral: "Elfrida vibrated from head to foot"; her response underscores her repressed rebellion: "[T]he maternal blessing! ... sacred sound and sacred commission" (I. 235). Yet Wilmot is formal towards Elfrida when they meet; when he calls her "Miss Overbury," she calls him "cruel Wilmot," Elfrida wishing to return to childhood; however, the "days of innocence and peace," as Wilmot refers to them, not only are "never more to return" but were never truly ideal, the patriarchal demand always shadowing her (I. 236).

The effects of the novel's two levels of contamination, the literal smallpox outbreak and the "family secret" of the manipulative Cluwyd cousins, intersect with the marriage of Christiana Cluwyd now becoming the new Mrs. Ellison after the death of Ellison's mother from smallpox. As stepmother to Ellison, Christiana Cluwyd advises Wilmot to take orders, hoping to get him out of the way for Elfrida to marry Ellison. However, when Christiana promises Wilmot the rectory so that he can succeed his own father, Wilmot says he does not want to pursue a profession in the Church. Echoing his new stepmother, Ellison tells Wilmot the Church is "best adapted to your meek and gentle nature" (I. 240). At the metanarrative level, Gibbes has Wilmot engage both Ellison and Christiana Cluwyd to claim a new masculine ideal. Asking the new Mrs. Ellison if she has read *The Sorrows of Werther*, Wilmot proceeds to compare the "opposites" in Goethe's novel, thereby suggesting a parallel between the pair of characters in the novel and himself and Ellison. Gibbes transforms the masculine ideal from one who exhibits martial prowess, *virtú*, to one who has the capacity to feel for others. However, Werther's suicide, Wilmot is quick to point out, "fortifies [his own] soul against it" by showing him the "barbarity of the individual, who, rather than bear his own discontents ... would rush into eternity" (I. 243).[18] The significance of Wilmot's reading of Werther unspools during the next two volumes. Gibbes complicates not only the male figures but Elfrida herself who, recounting the incident to Hannah, remarks that "the great misfortune in Ellison's case is, that some innocent and deserving person will, perhaps, be condemned to suffer with him; how tenderly should I pity the woman, I had reason to think was born to become his wife" (I. 245). Looking back from the hindsight of Elfrida's evolution through her relationships to the two adult rivals, her providential language in referring to a woman born to become his wife as pitiful is both true and yet more complicated: she becomes both Ellison's wife and Wilmot's wife; later, when she has to confront the legal and moral implications of her bigamy, she retreats into that pathetic woman only to emerge with a self-affirming agency and legacy.

Overbury's paternal ambition deepens into ambivalence by the end of the first volume. Contrasting his earlier overweening desire to have the wealthy Cluwyds take his daughter, Overbury's tyranny over his wife is now sparked by the "confusion in his breast, that he knew not how to support" (I. 245). When he discovers his wife "weeping over the miniature of Elfrida" he sees it as a "treasonable act" against his tyrannical authority. Contrasting the thickheadedness of Overbury's claim that Wilmot "will be the bane of all our hopes," Ella Overbury sees the parallels between her daughter's love for Wilmot and her own early love for Overbury; she refers to Wilmot as having "a worthy mind, and we owe him even our Ella's life" for having saved Elfrida from Ellison in her daughter's iteration of the deadly "pleasure-boat" (I. 246).

Despite his ambivalence, Overbury locks up Ella's miniature, a substitute for his desire to control the woman it depicts. This ludicrous act precedes Overbury's elaborate negotiations with Mrs. Ellison née Cluwyd to keep Elfrida, now almost eighteen, away from Wilmot. Elfrida is informed by Mrs. Ellison that "with the sanction … of parental authority," Elfrida will marry Ellison (I. 254). Not knowing her father is behind the scheme, Elfrida writes to her parents, but "avarice and ambition, under the deceiving forms of tenderness and true regard for his child's happiness, hardened [her father's heart] to cruelty" (I. 256). Overbury tells Wilmot that his daughter only thinks of him with sisterly affection, adding, "You are far gone … in romance, but you will please to [sic] recollect, that it is long since I have been disenchanted"; he then tells his own story of wooing the elder Ella at the expense of her "large fortune" (I. 260–61). Gibbes's metanarrative layering becomes yet more dense with the male characters attempting to control Elfrida's story: Overbury usurps the plot development of Wilmot's "romance": "[Y]ou, Mr. Wilmot, are the only impediment, from our child's false notions of the rights of friendship, to perfecting the scene, and the curtain must drop, that for ever [sic] obscures our hopes" (I. 261).

Gibbes thus ends Volume I with the male characters vying for control of the narrative. Overbury's "paternal ambition" attempts to "[perfect] the scene" of traditional romance by convincing Wilmot to leave England and go to India. Wilmot lets Elfrida know that "he was preparing for India, to improve his fortune," rather than merely to retreat as the loser of the battle for Elfrida. However, both Overbury's and Wilmot's claims are followed by Elfrida's realization that Wilmot will "sacrifice" the "delights of friendship ... on the altar of ambition" in his quest for riches in India, Wilmot's motive not unlike her father's in having cast her out as a child and now forcing her to marry Ellison. Attempting to wrest control over her own narrative, Elfrida is determined to make her parents see "the insufficiency of wealth to support such a heart" as hers (I. 264).

"In the kingdom ... of my mind, I shall be free"

While Gibbes thus frames Volume I with Overbury's paternal ambition driving the plot from Elfrida's adoption by the Cluwyd cousins to her engagement to Ellison that ends Volume I, Volume II begins with Wilmot's letter to Hannah regarding his decision to go to India and ends with Hannah's lengthy letter to Wilmot—which he never receives, as will be discussed later—telling him to return since Ellison is, presumably, dead. The separate friendships between Elfrida and Hannah and between Wilmot and Hannah become central to a deepening psychological level as the plot unfolds. Undercutting Elfrida's and Wilmot's platitudes, Hannah is free from the strictures that the two lovers' upbringing has entailed. As she gives voice to the subconscious that the lovers repress, Hannah exacerbates the conflicts to come. When Elfrida reacts with horror at Hannah's suggestion that Elfrida and Wilmot elope, Hannah provides the alternative, taboo voice: "[B]ut then to wed the man one hates—," she begins, suggesting a perspective liberated from Elfrida's fear of transgressing the moral code of her upbringing in Arcadia (II. 2). Yet once Hannah voices such repressed ideas, she evokes in Elfrida an increasingly righteous anger at Ellison for his emotional abuse of both Wilmot and Elfrida herself.

Gibbes deepens the metaphorical layering of Volume I's smallpox outbreak when Elfrida tells Hannah, "I must content myself with lingering out my days, the victim of a slow, consuming and a secret disease" (II. 6). Susceptible to Ellison's emotional disease, Elfrida agrees against her "heart's inclination" to the Ellison family's pressing her to marry him, even as Elfrida compares Ellison's love to the murderous plot against her mother's family by the valet, who would have "violated the person of [her] dear mother, and [sic] rioted in the blood of [her] grandfather" (II. 9). Gibbes brings the double meaning of "tender" and "alienation" to the surface again when Elfrida bitterly tells Ellison that, despite the "venom" of his "sarcasms," he will have "Elfrida's hand, by her passive alienation of her rights, as an individual, to do your pleasure," Ellison responding, sarcastically, to the "tender interview" given by their "indulgent relations" (II. 11). The tendering of Elfrida to join the Cluwyds to the Ellisons depends upon Elfrida's alienation on both existential and economic levels.

Gibbes again anticipates Wollstonecraft when Elfrida articulates a rational strength in defending Wilmot to Ellison: "Wilmot ... deserves, and ever shall enjoy my friendship, my esteem, my gratitude; nor will I marry even you, Sir, let the consequence be what it may, if you again strike at the object of those rational, just, and honest susceptibilities" (II. 12). Yet Gibbes suggests that such lofty speech is not enough to resolve the problem of women's oppression when the paternal will is dominant: "I would not marry him," she says to Ellison of Wilmot, "were he blessed, as you are, with fortune, with all this declared approbation, without the full and perfect consent of my father and mother" (II. 12). When Ellison responds that he cannot live without her, Elfrida's speech regains her childhood defiance: "Suppose I was to tell you I could not exist *with* you," she says, gaining momentum as she continues: "My mind, you know, is my own; and though my conduct must be such, out of respect to myself, as cannot dishonor you; in my kingdom, the kingdom of my mind, I shall be free" (II. 14). The underlying tragedy is that Elfrida exists in a patriarchal world that will not allow her the freedom she experiences in her mind.[19] Not heeding Elfrida's words, therefore, Ellison says, "[Y]ou *shall* be mine" (II. 14). The statement complicates even as it predates Wollstonecraft's condemnation of the influence of sentimental novels on women, Ellison using the sentimental novels that made him fall in love with Elfrida to couch his aggression, saying that he cannot show "himself capable of so unknightly an act, as knowingly to take a fair lady's hand by violence, an act so contrary to all the rules of chivalry as to endanger his reputation at all points" (II. 15). Gibbes thus subverts the marriage plot with the tragic disjunction between Elfrida's vision and her inability to act on it, only able to sigh despite her "disinclination to become his wife" (II. 16).

Elfrida is thus bleakly fatalistic, avoiding "every mention of the preparations, as she called them, for sacrifice, except the execution of the marriage-articles, when Ellison, with the importance of an approved lover, supported her and guided her hand, or her name would not have been legible" (II. 17). This tableau has legal and cultural significance, for Elfrida appears physically powerless. Despite her resistance to signing the documents that will bind her name to Ellison's, it is indeed an act of violation if not violence through which he literally manipulates her into signing of the papers. Thus, "stupefied with grief" following the signing of the marriage papers, Elfrida cannot bear to see herself in the mirror; objectified as Ellison's bride, she "suffer[s] herself to be adorned, only taking care to seat herself far out of the view of her dressing-glass" (II. 18). Gibbes undercuts Elfrida's tragic realization that Ellison has the legal "right to regulate [her] actions" with Elfrida's apparently bathetic[20] statement, "When do we set off for Bath?" (II. 20). The apathetic question suggests her "alienation" on multiple levels, not least of which is her alienation from herself. Though Elfrida, now part of the Ellison family, has access to the exclusive Bath, she sees it as a further retreat from her own self.[21]

The patriarchal oppression behind the love triangle intensifies when Elfrida discovers that Wilmot has agreed to her father's admonishment that he leave England. Elfrida wonders at Wilmot's willingness to obey her father's injunction: "O why did he not ... leave my father and mother to exert the authority over me, and make miserable without uniting with them, in this only instance of unkindness, against my everlasting peace[?]" (II. 22–23). This moment is an important awakening of Elfrida's understanding that, as heroic as Wilmot has been portrayed—along with her own father's early rescue of the Cluwyds from the valet—none of the men will rescue Elfrida from what is ultimately the power of patriarchy that they themselves perpetuate. The portrait of Elfrida re-emerges to symbolize this failure of patriarchy to protect Elfrida, Wilmot demanding the painting from the elder Ella when he discovers that Elfrida's wedding to Ellison is fixed. Ella, Sr. responds by telling Wilmot, "Alas, my noble minded [sic] young friend I am now going to lose your esteem ...; my husband surprized [sic] me contemplating the features of my beloved child; he has got possession of [it]," Overbury telling her that "it would be dishonorable to her character, for it to be in any body's possession but his own" (II. 24). Ella's doting on the image of Elfrida, her daughter taken from her long before, evokes pathos rendered yet more tragic when her husband claims patriarchal "possession" of even their daughter's image.

As hyperbolic as is Ella Overbury's reaction to losing possession of her daughter's portrait to her husband, Wilmot's response appears not only equally overblown but callous: he "smote his forehead," blaming Mrs. Overbury: "you have done me an irreparable injury, you have, unintentionally, destroyed me" (II. 25). Yet both Overburys forgive him his accusations: returning to discover how distraught Wilmot is, Overbury reconciles with him and, when Wilmot subsequently develops a "high fever," Mrs. Overbury rushes to his aid, urging him, "compose your mind, or, if it will relieve you, make my breast the repository of your sorrows .... For henceforth I will consider you as my own child" (II. 30). Nevertheless, the Overburys welcome Ellison and Elfrida to London. When Elfrida is reunited with her parents for the first time, she asks her mother whether it was worth losing the years of their mother-daughter relationship in which she would have been "rich in content" rather than gaining "fine accomplishments"; Elfrida then tries to let her mother know her desperation: "I am thrown out of my track, and nature has sustained a force, by making me a fine lady" (II. 32). Though Ella, Sr. empathizes with her daughter, she lets Elfrida know she feels powerless against Overbury's will: "Life of my life ... if it had depended upon my choice we had never been separated"; Overbury himself, however, experiences twinges of regret. For the first time "reviving some recollections of the smarting heart under tender disappointments ... he sighed and trembled for his Elfrida" (II. 33). The repetition of the word "tender" recurs to Overbury's using Elfrida as a transaction with the Cluwyds at the start of the novel, thereby throwing into question any tender sentiment he feels towards her.

Though the Overburys both embrace Wilmot as their own child, the differences between their responses to seeing their daughter again contrast each other, underscoring Gibbes's representation of the larger differences between the paternal and maternal relationships to their daughter. Overbury again represses the twinge of doubt he had had a moment before, saying, "I do believe Ellison will deserve her," whereas his wife uses her hermeneutical skill to deduce Ellison's hypocrisy: "I do not take upon me to be an infallible translator of looks, but if I am not greatly deceived, Ellison is one of those who are subject to sudden and violent changes of humor, and can hate tomorrow what he doated [sic] upon to day" (II. 34). Overbury meets his wife's canny assessment of Ellison, both as Ellison has behaved previously and as he will become a cruel and unpredictable husband to their daughter, with chastisement for her "alarming and ungenerous picture ... [o]f a young fellow you have seen but for a few hours," followed by his blaming Elfrida for any problem in their union (II. 34). As Ella, Sr. had anticipated, London's seductions are too powerful for Ellison to resist.[22] That his dissipated "intimacy" with a "man of fashion" draws Ellison "often from home," however, is welcomed by Elfrida (II. 35).

Though Gibbes's portrayal of Ellison's dissipation is unambiguous, the reader must tease out the more insidious problems of Wilmot, the romantic hero. Thus, after Wilmot has gotten the permission of both his uncle and his father to go to India, his mission is "the recovery of immense wealth, buried and scattered in various parts of the scene of warfare and carnage in the Eastern world, which promised to lead to great advantage" (II. 36). This brief description of his motive for going to India, to make a fortune that will put him on more equal footing with Ellison, is indeed ambiguous: whose wealth is he recovering, or is the term euphemistic? Is Wilmot merely one of many young British men seeking advancement through appropriation of eastern wealth? By Volume III, Wilmot concludes that he is not a businessman, and abandons such plundering, if that is what it is—for Gibbes is careful to say that the treasures are scattered through previous carnage, suggesting some ambiguity regarding Wilmot's heroism. Even Ellison attacks Wilmot's character when he finds the Overburys want Wilmot to be able to say goodbye to Elfrida before he leaves for India: "We shall have him return a Nabob upon us ... many young fellows who go out adventurers, as I presume is the case with our young friend, have returned rolling in wealth" (II. 39–40). Because Gibbes chooses not to have her narrator give a decisive view on Wilmot's motivation, Ellison's barb raises as much doubt about Wilmot as it does about Ellison's own hypocrisy. Gibbes's authorial voice is thus able to use Ellison's sarcasm to cast doubt on Wilmot: "I wish him the treasures of the East, to make him amends for his loss of the bright gem my better destiny has made me master of; he knows its value and would ... exchange both Indies for it"; foreshadowing the events to follow, Ellison adds, "but who can tell what may be in the chapter of probabilities for him; my mortality may give him an opportunity in his *nabobship*, to become a candidate for the hand I have robbed him of" (II. 40). Gibbes uses this metanarrative marker of Ellison's reflections on a later "chapter" when Wilmot does give up the quest for wealth in both the East and West Indies, thus reuniting with Elfrida. Whether he fully redeems his former propensity towards imperial conquest is the subject of that late chapter in Volume III.

In London with Ellison, Elfrida appears depressed, "unconcerned for the future, and uninterested by the present," while Ellison, "free from the restraint" of the Overburys and of his deceased parents, gives free reign to "the passion he contracted for gaming" (II. 55). Months later, Ellison reveals to Elfrida that he is "undone," his "connexions [sic] broken," adding "unless you could consent—," to which Elfrida responds, "Name your wishes" (II. 58). Emboldened, he tells her that he wishes her to disinherit herself, adding that he has "encumbered" his estate, but the "sale of one part would redeem the other"; her response, however, is simple and direct: "Sell it then" (II. 59). Ellison, "frantic with surprize [sic] and joy," takes her to court "to alienate her dower" to "enable him to do as he pleased with his whole estate" (II. 60). The recurrence of "alienate" adds yet greater significance to the situation, as it first appears when Overbury offers his daughter as a child to the Cluwyd cousins. The double meanings of alienate and tender become increasingly complex as Elfrida, once again alienated from the world of the Ellisons and ultimately herself, is reduced to monetary value.

When the Cluwyds rent Arcadia to a baronet and his haughty wife, Lady Stephens, Gibbes anticipates Wollstonecraft's attack on upper-class women in *VRW*. Elfrida remarks that, as an aristocrat, Lady Stephens does not remember that she is "a rational being" (II. 63). When Lady

Stephens offers to teach Elfrida to be a lady, Elfrida grasps a different lesson after perusing her books, noting the reason for the "fetters and chains upon the manners and expressions of the individual": "If male and female intercourse is merely ... licentiousness and deceit ... then indeed was it good policy to keep them at a distance"; however, Elfrida concludes, "this is not nature, as Wilmot's heart and mind can bear testimony," but rather "the wicked art of a false and unfortunate education" (II. 64). While this moment gestures to Gibbes as a pivotal figure between such works as *The Female Quixote*, Charlotte Lennox's satire of sentimentality, and Wollstonecraft's argument about aristocratic women's participation in their own subjugation, Elfrida's pious rejection of the superficiality of Lady Stephens is a facile binary that the novel itself rejects. Gibbes shows Elfrida to have been a passionate child who then represses her sensibility as a woman. Elfrida concludes here with the language of contamination that, though "it is too late for me ... to fear the infection, I will nevertheless shun it ...; the best security of a woman is, always, retreat" (II. 65). In the literal smallpox episode of Volume I, Elfrida is both victim and spreader of contagion, with the elder Ellisons having vainly sought refuge in Bath and Ellison contracting smallpox from Elfrida when returning early to propose to her. Gibbes juxtaposes Elfrida's waxing polemical on the insidiousness of aristocratic women and Lady Stephens attempting to seduce Ellison. He defends Elfrida's virtuousness with an equivocal simile, namely, that being around Elfrida is like finding oneself in "Elysium"; Mrs. Stephens takes the allusion to imply Elfrida's sexual repression, saying, "[T]he old ferry-boat was never better freighted, or the Elysian fields better peopled by any of Charon's labors" (II. 67). She concludes by offering to take Ellison to town without Elfrida.[23]

History, contamination, and anti-romance: subverting Romantic heroism

Gibbes follows Mrs. Stephens and Ellison's flirtatious mocking of Elfrida's sexual repression with Elfrida and Mrs. Overbury's discovery of Hannah with two orphans whom they later find are the offspring of Ellison's tryst with a poverty-stricken young woman who has died of starvation. Ellison, at this point, appears not to know the children are his; when they are brought to him, he says that he does not like children. Indeed, he envies them the affection his wife and mother-in-law, Mrs. Overbury, heap on them, Ellison "smiling maliciously" as he says, "[T]hey are like Wilmot" (II. 75). Ellison, having both sired the children and abandoned the mother, cruelly dismisses them as "beggars' brats, and the offspring, perhaps of infamy" (II. 76).

Gibbes thus brings Ellison's earlier language of "romance" when wooing Elfrida into direct conflict with the realism of his abuse of women and children through the "history" of his two children fathered outside his marriage to Elfrida. According to Hannah as she recounts the story to the Overburys, the young woman has told Wilmot that she had been living for four years "in this hovel" when her mother had died of smallpox, "just when the father of these children ... married and forsook me" (II. 85). Gibbes details the timeline of these events to suggest that the young mother's exposure to smallpox may have been spread to Ellison, who infected Elfrida, rather than vice versa. Regardless of whether he was infected by Elfrida or the young woman, however, the critical point is that Ellison is the nexus of contamination.

Predating Wollstonecraft's diatribe against novels, this "history" as anti-romance is remarkable for its empathic portrayal of the abandoned mother.[24] Gibbes works against the sentimental novel by connecting the young mother's victimization by Ellison to Elfrida's victimization first by her father and then by Ellison. By contrast to the nameless young woman giving up her children by necessity to Wilmot, Overbury had turned Elfrida over to the Cluwyd cousins because he wanted her to have the wealth that ultimately made her Ellison's wife. Telling the story to Hannah's husband, Richard, Wilmot identifies Ellison as the father and asks that, if he does not return from India, Richard should deliver a letter to Mrs. Overbury to have the children "intrusted [sic]" to her who has learned that "this horrid creature ... is the husband of my gentle, my pure, my benevolent-hearted child" (II. 94). Though Mrs. Overbury had intended to keep the "history" secret from her husband, she finally tells him, knowing "he would keep [it] secret upon Elfrida's account" (II. 101). Thus, Elfrida's mother, Ella, has herself shifted from her passivity at the opening of the novel in allowing her husband to give up her daughter, to becoming the guardian of Ellison's illegitimate son and daughter, who becomes the third-generation Ella.

Though Overbury now allegorizes the marriage between Elfrida and Ellison as that between "an angel and a fiend," his flattening of the relationship does not accord with the nuance that Gibbes adds not only to these characters but to the plot whose patterns echo across generations. By sending Wilmot to India, Gibbes adds further depth to her challenge to the binaries underlying the sentimental tradition. Reminiscent of the feminized Doyly, the East India Company man whom Sophia marries at the end of *Hartly House*, Wilmot's transformation is suggestive rather than overt. Gibbes only gives a paragraph to Wilmot's "commission" in India: after a "most favorable voyage" to Bombay and then to Bengal, we are only told that he is "most happy in the execution of his commissions, at least in the prospect of their future and speedy accomplishment, and, loaded with presents and rewards, for his diligent and upright conduct, returned to England, what he called a rich man" (II. 105).

Gibbes further complicates Wilmot's subjectivity through metanarrative; upon his seeing Elfrida for the first time upon his return to England, Wilmot discovers Elfrida, now Mrs. Ellison, at the theatre in Covent Garden, watching "the Tragedy of the Gamester," a 1637 play by James Shirley about gambling. The reader sees Elfrida, presumably from Wilmot's point of view, as she "felt the conclusion, a natural termination of the existence of a man precipitated from the elevation of hope, into the depths of disappointment; a transition that must fall with tenfold weight upon the heart with no resources in itself, and [sic] resting wholly upon the exterior of happiness" (II. 106). Yet only the reader—rather than either Wilmot or even Elfrida—can appreciate the irony behind the juxtaposition of the two descriptions: Wilmot rushing back to London with riches for Elfrida, and then Elfrida watching a play about a man addicted to gambling, whose life is shattered when he has no recourse because the "exterior of happiness" is gone. Point of view is thus complex in and critical to this scene in Covent Garden: Gibbes begins with the omniscient narration of Elfrida watching the "The Gamester," then, in another paragraph, gives Wilmot's perspective of Elfrida watching the play: "Wilmot passed the evening in anxiously tracing the turns in Elfrida's countenance, who was too much taken up with the performance, to look for faces which she might know in the pit; and more particularly as her connexions [sic] were all of that rank, which made it very unlikely she could have a friend there" (II. 106–07). Symbolically in the pit despite his newfound wealth, Wilmot realizes Elfrida's rank would never cause her to look for anyone in the pit. Thus, Wilmot cannot fathom the depth of Elfrida's response to the play because he is contemplating his own desire to compete with Ellison for her admiration. Happy to discover that "she did not appear to be much delighted with her company," namely, "people of fashion," Wilmot follows her to "discover her place of residence; then walked home more than usually disconsolate" (II. 107). Though Gibbes shows Wilmot's awakening desire for patriarchal power, he will have to shed it to be with Elfrida by the end of the novel. Only with a changed romantic hero does Gibbes concede the marriage plot.

Gibbes brings the metalevel of "The Gamester" to the surface immediately after the Covent Garden episode. At this turning point in Volume II—the center of the novel—a fight over a woman erupts in a coffee-house. Wilmot discovers that the woman at the center of the fight is Elfrida and that one of the men is, of course, Ellison, who says he "will die in defence [sic] of her spotless honor" when the other man demands Ellison tender her sexually to repay Ellison's gambling debt. The absurdity of Ellison's claims to chivalry reaches a climax when he kills the man, exclaiming belatedly, the "measure of my misery is now complete" (II. 109).

Not recognizing Wilmot who has attempted unsuccessfully to stop the fight, Ellison urges that Wilmot "break my destruction tenderly upon my Elfrida, save her from insult, and ... deliver her into the arms of her family," to which Wilmot responds, "[Y]ou have fought in a worthy cause ...; for, had I died by your hands, on a similar occasion, I would have died celebrating your honest prowess" (II. 110). Wilmot here appears either disingenuous or naive, as Ellison has "tendered" his wife against his gambling debt. Gibbes's play on "tender" again brings to the surface the subversion of "tender" feelings celebrated in sentimental fiction by patriarchy's hypocritical negotiating with women's sexuality. The bargaining continues when Ellison tells Wilmot he will flee from England as "a volunteer in America, [sic] and die fighting for my king and country" (II. 112). Having returned from India with riches, Wilmot now has the means to help Ellison and, with their power dynamic reversed, urges Ellison to take a generous sum of money that Ellison, in turn, asks Wilmot to take to Elfrida. Gibbes underscores this shift in the power when the narrator says that Ellison does not recognize Wilmot because of the "manly appearance a voyage to the East had given him" (II. 112).

Unlike Ellison, however, Elfrida recognizes Wilmot immediately, adjusting her initial gushing gratitude ("a second time my deliverer") by "correcting herself" with the propriety of a married woman to her benefactor: "[D]ispose of me ... as your benevolence dictates" (II. 113). However, her response shifts instantly from sentimentality to the realism of needing to repress such emotion with the propriety expected of a married woman. When she sees the blood on Wilmot's clothes, Elfrida's first assumption is that they have fought over her: "[H]as the friend of my infancy imbrued his hands in my husband's blood?" (II. 114). With language of chivalry so overblown that it would be difficult not to hear irony—either his own or that of Gibbes behind him—Wilmot tells Elfrida that Ellison "nobly fought to chastise a titled villain" who "plundered him of his fortune" and who had "a most diabolical purpose to Mrs. Overbury's Elfrida" (II. 115). Whether Wilmot is attempting to save face for Ellison or, more likely, that he is ridiculing Ellison, Wilmot's sympathetic portrayal of Ellison as victim of a "diabolical" man suggests Ellison has been passively "plundered" of his fortune by this "titled villain." In fact, Ellison's gaming has been the primary cause of the tragic situation that has compromised Elfrida and will continue to jeopardize her safety as the plot develops.

By contrast to the chivalric portrait of Ellison that Wilmot had described to Elfrida, Wilmot tells Overbury that Ellison's "vice of gaming" has "robbed him of his last shilling, together with this house, and all that belongs to it" (II. 117). With Overbury's reaction to the news of Ellison's crimes and flight to America, Overbury's "paternal ambition" begins to lose its foothold. Though the old patriarchy may be eroding, however, Wilmot represents its newer and more insidious form. There is no clearer example of this misogyny than his use of "seduction" as a euphemism for rape. Visiting Hannah, Wilmot urges her to "keep his secret respecting the children" and to clear "Ellison's character of all but the sin of seduction," referring to his having fathered the two illegitimate children that Wilmot is raising (II. 121). Enraptured at Wilmot's return, Hannah teaches Ellison's illegitimate children that Wilmot is their "benefactor," the term connoting Wilmot's newfound position of patriarchal power to bestow wealth upon the children in contrast to the ruin of Ellison, their biological father (II. 121). When Hannah returns to Elfrida to give her news of having seen Wilmot, her reduction of his goodness to the facile adage, "a friend in need is a friend indeed" reduces him to the two-dimensional figure that he himself acts out now that he is empowered with wealth. Elfrida, equally facile in her pious and chaste praise, says of Wilmot, "Noble and good ... he was" and that she hopes "Heaven ... would reward him" (II. 128). When Hannah suggests the only reward for Wilmot would be marriage to Elfrida, the latter cuts her off to say, "[R]ecollect I am Mr. Ellison's wife, always recollect that, when you mention Mr. Wilmot to me, and you will not say what is improper for me to hear" (II. 128). Gibbes underscores the double standard regarding the profligate Ellison, forgiven by Wilmot, and the expectation of monogamous virtue for Elfrida, whose sexual repression is to become yet more pronounced with the events to come.

To Overbury, who expresses remorse over his responsibility for his daughter's new state of poverty, Elfrida now refers to herself as "Ella" for the first time: "You will soon find that Ella Overbury ... was *made* for poverty" (II. 130). Not only is she using the name Ella, but she refers to herself as "Overbury," suggesting that her marriage to Ellison may legally make him her husband, but her identity is one destined for poverty despite her father's ambition. Gibbes complicates the patriarchal appropriation of women as objects of negotiation when Elfrida is now not only impoverished by her husband's profligacy but is victimized by his "false friend" who, "knowing she was young, handsome, and in deep distress ..., flattered himself he should purchase her with her own money" (II. 130–31). The idea of detection is significant here, the hermeneutics of moral compunction likened to a business. The "gentleman" would clearly not have offered a "refund" if he had not been discovered. When Wilmot accepts the "refund," he worries about "the danger of Elfrida's penetrating the fraud," and therefore, attempting to spare her knowledge of her having been tendered, "like a faithful steward, brought it to Mr. Overbury" (II. 132). Wilmot simply shifts how Elfrida is being bartered between men. One form of transaction—between Ellison and the "gentleman"—considered evil, the other—between Wilmot and Overbury—considered virtuous. In Gibbes's ultimate subversion of the sentimental novel in Volume III, Elfrida's choice to act on her own behalf takes a yet more tragic turn when Elfrida appears to have compromised both marriages.

At this point in Volume II, however, the sequence underscores what appears the inevitability of patriarchy, whether that of the old or new money: while the "gentleman" finds himself "detected," he produces the money; worrying about Elfrida's detection of the source of the money, Wilmot gives it to her father rather than directly to her. The outcome of the elaborate transaction is that Ellison's children are now in the custody of Elfrida's father. Wilmot's actions, from acquiring wealth in India to the subsequent actions that wealth enables—including his rescue of Ellison; his defiance of Ellison's "false friend"; and his interception of the money of two rightful female owners, the unnamed mother of the children and Elfrida— all suggest that even the new wealth acquired through colonial ventures rather than inheritance, circulates among men, victimizing women.

Elfrida's talents and emolument

As a turning point in the novel's marriage plot, this complex sequence of transactions exemplifies the novel's anticipation of free indirect discourse, a narrative device attributed to nineteenth-century fiction.[25] Elfrida does not let her mother forget "how unnecessary our cruel separation to make me rich" is; poverty, she tells her mother, "the very evil that others torture themselves so much about, sits quite easy upon my feelings" (II. 133). Elfrida sets about rising above poverty by using her talents: "[T]his is the age of liberality, and my pencil shall bring its industry decent rewards .... O insult me not so far as to call it degrading ... to defend myself against the daemon poverty" (II. 134). While Gibbes portrays Elfrida's powerful new level of subjectivity, her father can only turn to his wife and create of Elfrida a tableau of tragedy: "Patience on a monument ... smiling at grief" (II. 134). Gibbes sets Overbury's objectification of his daughter as a monument to grief against Elfrida's own thoughts, words, and actions.

Far from an immobilized monument to grief, Elfrida quickly acts to sell all the accoutrements of both her upbringing with the Cluwyds and her marriage to Ellison, disposing "of her whole wardrobe and little ornaments, which her fall from affluence, she said, had made idle possessions to her" (II. 135). Wilmot is not only baffled but apparently emasculated by Elfrida's embracing of the poverty that requires her to use her talents: her "idea of working for her living, as she calmly called it, made him frantic; yet with the whole Eastern world at his feet, it would have been impossible, as she was situated, to impart any portion of it to her" (II. 135). His conquest of the East is meaningless for Elfrida, whose independent notion of earning a "living" refuses gifts gotten through the imagined East prone at his feet in feminized passivity. While Wilmot's eastern adventure has made him more "manly" in the eyes of others, Elfrida's newfound independence gives her a voice of authority that cannot be equivalently gendered when she calls upon Wilmot "to entreat" him to invest her money in "the best emoluments in India, and I will thankfully receive from you the genuine profits" (II. 137). Is Elfrida tapping into the "mercantile advantage" of English imperialism, or is her investment a means of recirculating the wealth, as it is in *Zoriada*? What does it mean for an English woman, herself treated as an "emolument," to capitalize on the western plunder of India? By having Elfrida invest her money in Wilmot's India venture, Gibbes suggests the plot has the potential at this point to turn in any of several directions regarding the equation of the East with victimized women.

The question of Elfrida's motivation in wishing to invest in Wilmot's Indian venture can best be addressed through her attitude towards Hannah. For the first time, Elfrida addresses Hannah formally now as "Mrs. Jenkins," perhaps to remind Hannah, extolling Wilmot's great merits, of both women's married status and to formalize their relationship. She thus cuts off Hannah's statement, "If ever there was—" by saying, "Come, come, Mrs. Jenkins ..., it is not at this time of day that I am to learn either Mr. Wilmot's merits, or your high sense of them" and, with that, she gathers up "the ninety pounds, and, highly pleased with her morning's transaction, left Hannah to finish her harangue alone" (II. 138). The former sensibility shared between Elfrida and Wilmot has been transmuted into a business relationship. Wilmot understands the "generosity of what Elfrida call[s] her self-interested conduct" when she tells her father, "[L]et us not despair; are we not very comfortable? And is not that a gigantic step towards happiness?" (II. 139). Gibbes creates a chasm between Wilmot's extolling her "angelic purity" and her own self-described "self-interest": Elfrida simultaneously attempts to teach her father the value of happiness in the face of poverty while she distances herself from Wilmot by transforming their former affection to friendship based on transaction.

Wilmot thus continues turning Elfrida into a saintly object of adoration whereas she rises above her former sensibility to becomes financially independent. While this is not the end of their story, one can return to Gibbes's anticipation of Wollstonecraft's *VRW* to note the distance Gibbes has proleptically brought her heroine, even at this midway point of the novel. While she speaks of her happiness and "self-interest," Wilmot, who is never far from his paternal roots in the rectory, muses sanctimoniously that "the kind Gods had given her to Ellison, and he could only lament and adore"

(II. 140). Elfrida, meanwhile, "seemed to lose herself, and all her disappointments, in the prosecution of her industry," of which she tells her mother, "O, I have often told you how well it would agree with me to be poor" (II. 140).

Despite Elfrida refusing both her father's and Wilmot's pathos, both men continue objectifying her as "My beautiful, my most injured Elfrida," in the words of Overbury, who regrets having forced her into the world of the Cluwyd cousins and ultimately Ellison. Speaking of himself in third person as he voices his regret over his "paternal ambition" that led to Elfrida's marriage to Ellison, Overbury's entangled terms of sensibility and commerce underscore his lack of self-awareness regarding his continuing objectification of Elfrida, shifting her from one man to another:

> [H]ad your father not been deaf to the voice of nature and the pleadings of truth, instead of the widowed wife he has rendered you, after every violence your tender mind must have sustained, you would now have been enabled to unite yourself to the object of your infant election, whose spirit and integrity, in the execution of his East Indian commission, has done away the only objection that could be set up against him. (II. 140–41)

Indeed, before Wilmot departs again for India, he meets Overbury "every evening" at a coffee-house, "under pretence [sic] of business," because the presence of Elfrida "always threw him into ... discomposure ... which he was unable to conceal" (II. 142). "Tender" feelings give way to "tendering" property: Wilmot proposes that the Grange be sold to an East India Company agent rather than a "stranger" since it is the patriarchal home of the elder Ella. Now expressing regret only because he knows that Wilmot has made his fortune in India, Overbury has clearly learned nothing through the effects of his "paternal ambition" regarding Elfrida's subjectivity.

Just as Overbury has failed to absorb the role of his patriarchal aspirations in his daughter's suffering, Wilmot mistakenly believes he knows "the full force of [Elfrida's] situation upon his heart" as soon as he loses "sight of England" (II. 145). Wilmot justifies his appropriation of wealth due to his plundering of India as ordained by God: "[W]hatever wealth Heaven is pleased to pour into my lap, shall, by some happy devise, be rendered useful to her" (II. 146). Again anticipating the free indirect discourse attributed to later writers, Gibbes distinguishes the views of others regarding Elfrida's state of mind and Elfrida's own by having the narrator interject,

> The truth was, that Elfrida did not think it strictly proper, in her state of affairs, to have Wilmot always in her heart, or to spend her life in the recollection of past scenes, which, though innocent as the dreams of infancy, were not, she conceived, unisons to the feelings of an unhappy wife, as they held up perpetually to her eyes the unfavorable contrast between the husband,

whom her father had given her, and the friend she had lost, but even this was a piece of self-denial, a sacrifice to the world's opinion, and the world's customs. (II. 148)

The narrator's access to Elfrida's mind is important, looking ahead to the interiority of Austen's use of free indirect discourse in *Persuasion*. Gibbes complicates Elfrida's subjectivity by contrasting Elfrida's emotional vacillation with what Overbury, Ellison, and Wilmot, among the other characters, project upon her. By showing that Elfrida follows her own "satisfaction," Gibbes lets the reader glimpse the underlying concern Elfrida has that she is making choices based on how she is seen by others, an important stage in her emerging autonomy.

While Elfrida ambivalently follows her "satisfaction," Hannah is her foil as "the ignorant, though well-meaning and good creature" who looks "upon all approbation of the other sex, to verge naturally and finally towards love and matrimony; she was, therefore, fearful, lest being mistaken, she might be harmlessly misrepresented by her, and her hitherto spotless fame contract an undue shade" (II.148–49). Hannah is both a stand-in for the reader of the sentimental novel, with her simple desire to have her facile notion of love end in marriage, as well as a means for Elfrida to acknowledge her more complex though repressed feelings, "abstracted from the preference she imbibed for him in her infancy" (II. 149).

The procuress and a foiled stratagem

Overbury's relationship with his daughter has thus far emerged as one of both "tenderness" and "tendering." Overbury is tested when Ellison's "gentleman" creditor, the rapacious Lord S., appears at Overbury's door in an overt attempt to use Ellison's gambling debt as a transaction for "buying" Overbury's child. This transactional meeting signals a yet darker turn in the repercussions of Ellison's downward spiral and Overbury's paternal ambition. Overbury's sudden awareness of the connection of this Lord to Ellison resonates with the ironic diction that Gibbes has woven through the novel, Overbury exclaiming, "Heavens … is he not the wretch that would have bought my child of her own husband?" (II. 154, 155). Gibbes makes her indictment of patrimony clear as she suggests Overbury's hypocrisy in having "sold" Elfrida as a child to the Cluwyds. She sets this patriarchal child-marketing against the matriarchal line that insists on Elfrida's happiness derived from her own "industry." This new sense of a female lineage that transcends patriarchy culminates with Ella Overbury and Elfrida giving the name of Ella to Ellison's illegitimate and rejected daughter, now under the care of Ella Overbury.

Lord S.'s next scheme thus brings his previously euphemistic "seductions" to the surface as full-blown prostitution. On a stagecoach ride to Portsmouth, the Overburys befriend an "elderly lady" who introduces herself as Mrs. Felton, whom Gibbes reveals to be a "procuress" involved in an elaborate lie with Lord S. to which Overbury falls prey (II. 157). In his efforts to protect his daughter, the naive Overbury sends Elfrida into greater danger. Six months pass in which this procuress is able "to pass herself off for a very good sort of a woman," paying "close court" to the besotted Overbury (II. 164). Lord S., however, complains to Mrs. Felton that he fears Elfrida's "mind, like another Troy, would stand a ten years' siege, but would not be won at last" (II. 158). Instead of comparing Elfrida to Helen as the traditional object of seduction, Lord S. acknowledges the power of Elfrida's intellect when he compares her mind to Troy itself.

Mrs. Felton is flummoxed when she happens upon Elfrida: "You work for your living ... and not for your amusement ...! You who would do honor to a coronet!" (II. 163). Elfrida offers a corrective to Mrs. Felton's binary assumption about Elfrida's beauty, explaining that Mrs. Felton's imputing "ease [and] elegance" to her "manner and appearance" is faulty (II. 163). The discovery that Elfrida "not only dared to be poor, but delighted in employment" makes Mrs. Fulton "deranged" and Lord S. enraged to find a "lovely woman" whose soul, as Mrs. Felton tells him, "is as free from ambition, folly and vanity, as her face is from blemish" (II. 165). Mrs. Fulton tells Lord S. that Elfrida is beyond reproach, but he is desperate, whether "by stratagem or violence," to "have her in [his] possession" (II. 166).

With the disclosure that Mrs. Felton is a procuress, Gibbes brings the tendering of women to the surface. Besides playing on "tender" as both sensibility and an object of financial exchange, Gibbes adds a the third meaning of "tender": the nautical connotation of either a boat used to transport people or cargo or being capable of overturning.[26] Thus, with his new strategy of unmitigated violence in which rape is no longer disguised euphemistically as seduction, Lord S. tells Mrs. Felton he will "bear [Elfrida] to some happy spot, and, perhaps, without so much as asking her consent, draw her into a little trip to France, in all which, you, Mrs. Felton, must accompany us" (II. 167). Deciding to take the gullible Hannah for the sake of appearances, Mrs. Felton "artfully" fills Hannah's head with "pleasure-parties" and "sea expeditions" (II. 168). The naive Hannah thus encourages Elfrida to go with Mrs. Felton. Elfrida's only concern is that they need to "have the likeness of a man to attend us," yet Overbury, "not fond of the water," refuses to go. Overbury thus gives Elfrida his characteristic and misguided blessings as he sends her, unprotected, into danger (II. 169).

When the day of the planned abduction arrives, Elfrida dresses in "virgin white," creating the chaste "emblem of the golden age" (II. 171). Framing

Elfrida as an icon of chastity is the boat that "tenders" her in both nautical senses, endangering her in its precariousness while transporting her as merchandise (II. 171). As soon as the boat is out of sight of land, Lord S. begins to make sexual advances towards Elfrida, who "dreamed not of her danger" (II. 172). Naively concluding that "the young man might not be quite sober," Elfrida demurely changes her seat (II. 172). She becomes increasingly alarmed, however, when his aggressiveness intensifies, at which Hannah gives "him an honest and smart box on the ear," Lord S. dropping any pretense of civility: "We shall humble your mistress' pride ... and revenge that blow before tomorrow morning" (II. 173). Giving Elfrida the ultimatum to be "queen or vassal," Lord S. creates a binary suggesting a duplicitous distinction between Petrarchan seduction and rape. Yet despite fearing she has no recourse, even contemplating "throw[ing] herself into the sea," Elfrida uses her cunning to twist his own logic, saying that they should wait till they are ashore: "[L]et me then owe you the obligation of not betraying your success to the world" (II. 175, 176–77).

Urging the ship's Pilot to help them, Hannah uses Wilmot's newfound imperial power to bribe him, saying that, as a "school-fellow" of Elfrida, Wilmot has "gone to the East-Indies" and will come back with plenty of money that he will be "free to part with" (II. 178). Whether due to Hannah's bribe or the unlikely plot twist in which the Pilot claims to know and admire Wilmot who "came home in the same ship with him from India," the Pilot vows to protect Elfrida (II. 179). Noticing a ship in the distance, the Pilot signals the boatswain of the sloop, whose captain, Venables, in yet another unlikely twist, recognizes Lord S. as a scoundrel "through all his disguise," thus pulling Elfrida and Hannah to safety (II. 181). The name "Venables" suggests an elision of "venerable," the moral rectitude he comes to embody. He and the infamous Lord D., volleying Elfrida between them, create a more facile, caricatured version of the novel's love triangle with the more complex figures of Ellison and Wilmot (II. 182).[27]

Despite his moral rectitude, however, Venables delivers the critical misinformation to Elfrida upon which the unfolding plot hinges, namely, that Ellison has died in America: "It was his destiny ... to be sent out upon a reconnoitering party, when some Indians surprised them, and they died to a man," Venables tells her, information Gibbes delays disclosing as false until later (II. 184). Elfrida's response to the discovery of Ellison's apparent death is tepid: "Mrs. Ellison was astonished, her tenderness, indeed was unwounded, though her humanity felt for him (II. 184).[28] Not long after their return to the apparent safety of the patriarchal home of the Overburys, Venables explains that his source "thought he had seen" Ellison's name "in the returns of the killed," another of the many hermeneutical missteps by men creating tragedy for Elfrida (II. 189). She continues to be buffeted among the men who manipulate her fate. Despite being engaged, Venables falls in love with Elfrida, objectifying her as has every other man who has beheld her. Gibbes uses free indirect discourse to underscore the dismantling of sentimentality that has surfaced by this point, the end of Volume II. Venables expresses his weakness for rescuing a beautiful woman: "There is something so touching in the distress of a young, beautiful, and virtuous woman, that the man who has the happiness to rescue her from danger, is very apt to lose his heart for his pains" (II. 186–87). Venables, a caricature of heroic manliness, is complicit in Elfrida's tendering. Nevertheless, he is engaged to "a very worthy woman," who will play a role in Elfrida's recovery in Volume III. The narrator here comments upon Venables's virtue in honoring the "rules of romance" a code that would dictate his pursuit of Elfrida as "violat[ing] truth" (II. 187).

With free indirect discourse as a technique by which Gibbes's narrator can move in and out of the perspectives of various characters, Gibbes subverts the binaries underlying the traditional sentimental novel even as the narrator upholds them. Gibbes's erosion of her narrator's sentimentality is immediately underscored by Overbury's reaction upon discovering his daughter has been nearly abducted and that his son-in-law, Ellison, has apparently been killed in America: "Captain Overbury remarked, how wonderfully Providence had brought that event to their knowledge, which, from distance of situation, might have remained undiscovered, or, at least, unascertained, to the end of their lives" (II. 189). The hermeneutical process proves to be flawed, evidence not proving to be as it appears. When Ellison's "unascertained" death is later investigated, it is falsely confirmed, thus further complicating the plot with another layer of misinformation (II. 189). The more immediate irony, however, is Overbury's celebration of a twofold "Providence": the one that the characters believe is ruling their destinies, and the puppet master Gibbes as authorial "Providence" who throws her characters into situations that challenge their assumptions, casting light upon their shortcomings.

Eager to have Wilmot know of Ellison's death and thus Wilmot's apparently unimpeded path to marry Elfrida, Hannah writes to Wilmot, whose response is to send money. With the new world order of capitalism supplanting inherited wealth, Gibbes suggests that one form of paternalism has merely replaced another. In the aftermath of the aborted abduction, Lord S. writes to Overbury, attempting to assure Overbury of his "high respect and veneration for his lovely daughter"; Lord S. concludes with "an offer of his hand and fortune, which he would have tendered sooner" (II. 197). Here again, the word "tender" brings together the multiple levels of irony implicit in the layering of sentimentality and the business negotiations of patriarchy in this novel.

At the end of Volume II, Hannah writes to Wilmot, "pour[ing] her heart out upon paper" about her and Elfrida's near abduction, their rescue, and the news of Ellison's death (II. 202). She warns Wilmot of the danger to those who, "making themselves miserable, let love steal upon their hearts," using the metaphor of "infektion" [sic], a motif Gibbes had introduced earlier with the small-pox episode (II. 203). The narrative significance of Gibbes devoting so many pages to Hannah's reiterating these events is that Wilmot never gets the letter. Hannah's narrative voice thus provides an alternate, comic narrative voice to that of the third-person narrator of the novel:

> [T]hough it was your name that was the great means of saving us, it was I, myself I, from the lessons I had learned of *that quack-doctor* Ellison, that might be said to do the business, for, finding how matters went, by this Lord almost devouring *your* (yes, she shall yet be *your*) Elfrida's hands, what did I? I wish you could have seen me, but put on the downright hypocrite, and seemed glad she had got a lover, when I could have stabbed him to the heart. (II. 207)

Gibbes distinguishes her authorial voice from that of the narrator, through whom these events are told in real time. Hannah's pastiche of illiteracy, superstition, and wisdom anticipates by four years Wordsworth's 1800 Preface to *The Lyrical Ballads*, in which he claims that poetry derives from rustic folk whose "essential passions of the heart find a better soil in which they can attain their maturity, are less under restraint, and speak a plainer and more emphatic language" (78).[29] Though the reader laughs at the image of Hannah rescuing Elfrida with a sword, her role-playing had been instrumental in the rescue. Hannah's vividly imagined cross-dressing echoes Charlotte in *Francis Clive*, Charlotte disguising herself as a soldier to rescue her husband from Penelope the prostitute.[30]

When Wilmot returns to London, Overbury is so overjoyed that he "caught him in his arms," describing his "happiness unspeakable" (II. 212). Wilmot observes that, by contrast to Overbury's ardor, Elfrida is tepid at seeing him again, Wilmot ironically seeing her as "the same sacred character he had left her" (II. 213). Though Wilmot is glad that she regards him "with less discomposure than formerly," the use of litotes underscores Wilmot's underlying disappointment at her discomposure (II. 213). Receiving the news of Ellison's supposed death, Wilmot's first reaction is to say, "I was almost deprived of my senses," followed immediately by repressing such glee when he asks Overbury, "[M]ay I hope, if your Elfrida should prove propitious, you will accept me for your son?" (II. 215). The transactional discussion underscores Wilmot's transformation into a man of commerce during his absence. Elfrida talks business with Wilmot regarding the money she had asked him to invest in India, at which he "looked around him with an air of self-satisfaction" (II. 217). When Wilmot heaps gifts from India upon Hannah and the Overburys, Elfrida remarks with cutting irony that he will "give our habitation the appearance of an Indian palace," her sardonic view of cultural appropriation (II. 220). Wilmot responds that only one "event" would "occasion me another voyage, but that would be a decisive one, for I would never see England more" (II. 220). Elfrida is not "unconscious of his meaning," hoping that her receiving him "with the chearful [sic] warmth of friendship ... would testify for her, that she had no expectation of his addressing her as a lover" (II. 220).[31]

Reuniting Elfrida and Wilmot, Gibbes reveals the shift in their gender roles since they had parted. With rational detachment, Elfrida makes clear that, though the "pleasures" of their "infancy" were abundant, they "can never be renovated, and we must adopt such as are suited to the maturity we have attained," telling him to "sit down, and let me discuss the point with you" (II. 221).[32] These cool-headed lovers have repressed the passion towards each other they had been free to feel and to communicate as children, Elfrida now observing in stolen glances that "the lines of distress which had cut him to the heart, before he went to India, were softened into lines of tranquillity [sic]" (II. 216). Elfrida confesses to Wilmot that he had been "the first object" of her "affectionate attachment," and that if Ellison had died before they married, she would "have readily consented to unite [her] fate with [his]"; however, suggesting that such repression of her sensibility comes with a cost, she adds an odd description of her mental state: "[S]ince that time, my mind has ... been greatly deranged" (II. 222). That she appears as the model of serene and rational maturity yet confesses that she has been "deranged" by the situation underscores her complexity: she is neither the saint nor the businesswoman she projects to others. Wilmot argues that she is of "sound understanding," and suggests that it is the "idle opinions" of others that influence her self-diagnosis as "deranged."

Volume II ends with Wilmot attempting to convince Elfrida that the only difference that marriage would entail for her would be her "change of name," a statement whose irony the reader can appreciate since the novel has suggested that for a woman, a name change is anything but simple: beginning with Elfrida's childhood, she is first named after her mother, then taken away and renamed as a means to have an entitled existence, only to have that entitlement taken with her marriage—and another name change—to a man who squanders that very inheritance. Overbury's calling Wilmot their son suggests that Volume II ends much as the novel began, with the expectation that Elfrida should "disappoint not" her parents' "high-raised hopes of happiness, from seeing [her] united" with the man they choose for her (II. 223).

The legal, social, and emotional obstacles that have slowed the arc of the marriage plot in the first two volumes return and intensify with Elfrida's bigamy in Volume III. By the conclusion of the novel, Elfrida realizes that her identity is a cipher behind the many illusory names she has, from Ella to Elfrida, from Mrs. Ellison to Mrs. Wilmot, an ending reminiscent of *Zoriada* in which the heroine's name is never revealed even to the reader.[33] However, to get to that realization, Elfrida will need to confront patriarchy's repression that the names of her birth, adoption, and marriage represent.

Volume III begins with Elfrida's virtuous refusal of Wilmot's advances without proof of Ellison's death. Having become increasingly rational—to a fault from Wilmot's perspective—Elfrida expresses her irritation at his "importunity" and her inability to meet "the particular intimacy you solicit" (III. 1). She complains that it is impossible "to have so elastic a turn of mind, as to lose and receive impressions with such rapidity" (III. 1). Though she had referred to her "derangement" at the end of Volume II, and now to her lack of mental elasticity that would make it possible for her to shift from being the wife of Ellison to that of Wilmot, her ability to articulate such a state speaks to a rationality that appears willfully to refuse such elasticity. She is determined to be a virtuous friend to Wilmot while living with the lack of evidence proving Ellison's death.

Wilmot, however, attempts to convert Elfrida to his perspective by giving her a distorted rendition of the *Odyssey*. In his retelling, Wilmot figures as Ulysses, having returned from his epic journey to Elfrida, whom he thus likens to Penelope. According to Wilmot, "[W]hen finessing with her suitors," Penelope "made a respectable figure"; in Wilmot's rendition, he, Wilmot, figures as "Ulysses ... the husband of her tenderest affection, her first and only choice," Wilmot speaking with apparent sympathy towards Penelope's "anxieties of a peculiar nature upon her heart" (III. 2). Wilmot not only presents his Homeric version of Elfrida's story but asks her in third person, "what shall we say in my Elfrida's situation, for thus trifling with her honest Wilmot?" (III. 2). However, it is no mere trifle: the "decease" of her actual husband—not a mere interloper in Ithaca—she says, "ought to be well assured" before she "has the courage to enter into a second marriage" (III. 2–3).

To find evidence of Ellison's death that will satisfy Elfrida, Wilmot volunteers to go West rather than to his well-trodden path to the East Indies, Wilmot making Elfrida promise that she will agree to marry him if he succeeds. He interrupts her when she begins, "I was born," anticipating and overriding her words, namely, to have her "peace [be] the unending prey of painful solicitation"; when he pauses, she is silent (III. 3). When Wilmot badgers her about "the construction which your silence admits of," Elfrida protests, "[Y]ou are not my Wilmot, the gentle, the generous, and the good, but quite a man of the world, capable of laying traps for approbation and bearing down all before you by implied success" (III. 4). All her life, Elfrida's voice has been taken by those around her. As the would-be sentimental hero Wilmot is yet another iteration of such silencing and thus most disturbing.

Gibbes makes clear that a second marriage is not Elfrida's choice, just as the first was not, despite the "grave faces" of her family and Wilmot. She tells them again that if Ellison had "expired in England, most cheerfully would I have [waived] my disinclination for marrying a second time, to have made you all happy" (III. 9). Considering her "delicate apprehensions" as "sacred," Wilmot promises not to "press [her] farther, until [they] have written letters to, and received answers from, America" (III. 9). Elfrida's response is coldly transactional: "This hand ..., if Mr. Ellison's death is confirmed, shall be your's [sic]" (III. 10). Her internal conflict is unmistakable when, for a fleeting moment before she "resum[es] her accustomed complacency," she "wip[es] away her tears," thus "tendering" herself as she represses the tenderness she feels (III. 10).

Volume III thus furthers the novel's trajectory into the shift from the old patrimony into the new capitalism in two ways. First, although a period of albeit superficial happiness ensues in which Wilmot gives up "every idea of returning to India," young Frederic, the biological son of Ellison but raised by Overbury and Wilmot, having gone with Wilmot to India was "delighted with a sea-life" and wants to return (III. 10–11). Through the larger perspective of the novel, Frederic, Jr. represents the complexity of this third generation of men who will negotiate their place in the world through imperialism, with entitlement no longer a promise of security. Frederic thus assures the uneasy Overbury about his plans, saying that he will hear "how well I have behaved, and how rich I am likely to become" (III. 11).

The second way the new capitalism emerges in Volume III is when Wilmot tells Overbury that he has purchased the Grange, the ancestral home of the Cluwyds and, therefore, of Ella Overbury, with the wealth he has appropriated in India. He displays an aggressive egocentricity to Overbury when he boasts of the purchase, comparing his "presentiments" to those of Elfrida, whose "are all of a distressing, mine of a flattering complexion"; what his "flattering presentiments" suggest to him is that his purchase of the Grange will bring "back to [Ella, Sr.'s] fortune" the wealth she had lost in marrying Overbury (III. 12). The trajectory from Wilmot's perspective is towards a happily-ever-after ending, with him as the hero rescuing not only Elfrida but her family's wealth. His boast is implicitly that the landed aristocracy represented by Ellison is dead, while he, Wilmot, can return it to its rightful heir, paradoxically, by purchasing it. However, Gibbes's larger perspective in the novel shows what Wilmot omits, namely, the matriarchal line that must win back not just the Grange but the notion of an "Arcadia" coopted by the Cluwyd cousins, doppelgangers to the rightful matriarchy. Thus, the novel must resolve the remaining problems in bringing matriarchy to its fullest realization.

When Wilmot asks why Elfrida has not asked for the "returns" of her "venture" in his India business, she replies simply, "I do not ... want money at present" (III. 13). Gibbes leaves the reader little time to absorb her words on their own terms before Overbury completes her statement: "And, therefore ..., chooses to leave her property in your hands, Wilmot, to prevent future transfers" (III. 13). If one takes Elfrida's statement at face value, it is free of any financial strategizing: she has no need at present for his money. However, Overbury is quick to assure Wilmot that he will be the patriarchal figure who will protect Elfrida's money from "future transfers" that imply Ellison or other nefarious men like Lord S. taking advantage of Elfrida. Yet Elfrida will not compromise, even after Wilmot says that she "may wish to hear its amount ... if it even is your intention, Elfrida, to make me premature master of it," Elfrida says simply, "I will have nothing to do with either of you ... for you will read my meaning as you please, and seem to make a point of encouraging each other to mistake both my words and actions" (III. 14). Gibbes here makes clear that her heroine has no intention of allowing either her father or Wilmot to decide her fate or her property, refusing even to speak more to them since—as just witnessed—they manipulate her words to serve their paternalistic objectives.

The hermeneutical problem behind the marriage plot intensifies when a letter from Ellison's captain arrives, appearing to confirm Venables's claim of Ellison's death. The captain encloses with his letter "the returns, where his name was inserted in the slaughter-list," the term "returns" echoing Wilmot's question to Elfrida about her not wishing the "returns" on his India business, noted above. Now that the term is used to denote confirmation of Ellison's death, Wilmot's response is immediate and businesslike. Gibbes's use of the passive voice underscores Wilmot's cold formality regarding his legalistic approach to their contract: "Elfrida *was called upon* by Wilmot for the performance of her promise, and, like a woman of honor, met him"; the marriage ceremony taking place in a half-sentence in which Gibbes notes that Hannah is "the only female, besides herself, of the party" and that Elfrida was, "with equal pleasure and privacy, *given, by her father, to her most worthy lover*" (III. 15, italics added). Gibbes has underscored the repression of tenderness in what would be the traditional marriage plot's culmination. Wilmot's happiness is described in financial terms: "If happiness, as Wilmot would sometimes say, was greatly in arrears to this family, they were now repaid both in interest and principal" (III. 16). The passive voice is telling once again: what subject has repaid the family? The implication is that Wilmot has, through his attainment of wealth in India, Ellison has, by apparently dying, and Elfrida has, by marrying Wilmot and bearing three "beautiful" children (III. 16). Elfrida, however, evolves through motherhood to become the prototype of Wollstonecraft's ideal woman, the narrator noting that Elfrida would "amuse, regulate, compassionate, instruct, serve and sympathize" (III. 17).[34]

It appears that the old patrimony is restored when the Overburys reconcile with the elder Cluwyd, Ella Overbury's father. However, Overbury, who has had a similar reconciliation with Wilmot, lets Cluwyd know that he, Cluwyd, not only has his own daughter, Ella, to embrace "but even great-grandchildren to play around [his] knee. Your Ella has an Elfrida, the parent stock of the young ones," he says, recognizing the matriarchal lineage of Ellas (III. 22–23). Cluwyd thus restores "Arcadia" to the family, saying, "my power will gain strength from alienation" (III. 24). The term "alienation," first appearing at the opening of the novel when Overbury sends Elfrida to live with the Cluwyds, returns with yet another layer of meaning, since it now reverses the earlier alienation: Elfrida's grandfather, the patriarch, now says his own power comes from his alienation, the meaning here being purely financial, at odds with the sentimental notion of his resolving his earlier emotional alienation from his family. The ritualized entrance of the family to meet their "Patriarch," Cluwyd, is revealing: the males, led by young Overbury, come first, and then the females. Elfrida and Wilmot's elder son, named after his grandfather, Overbury, says, "as if by instinct, 'What Sir, have I more papas than ever?'" (III. 26). The comment could well be a humorous reflection of the dizzying iterations of names in the novel's complex lineage, patriarchal and matriarchal. Yet the narrator interrupts young Overbury's voice to point out that "Elfrida and the two other infants were now admitted—what a subject for the pencil! The pen is not capable of doing it justice"; the younger son, the reader discovers, is named after Venables, and his sister, not Ella as they named Ellison's daughter, but Elfrida. Overbury declines his military commission now that he is "an affluent man, by the bounty of his wife's father." The irony vis-à-vis the opening of the novel is pointed, for Overbury now has regained Ella, Sr.'s inheritance for which he had originally given Elfrida to the Cluwyd cousins.

Elfrida as fugitive: the new Romantic wanderer

This ostensibly idyllic family life with Elfrida at its angelic center is not the end of the novel, for the surface level of domestic harmony unravels when news arrives that Ellison is alive. All that had appeared legitimate is now "illegal" and immoral from the view of institutional patriarchy to which Elfrida too readily acquiesces. She now sees herself as an adulterer and, after telling Wilmot to leave with the children, realizes that she herself must go and leave Wilmot behind with the children. When Elfrida tells the children she has an "incurable ... disease," Gibbes signals a return of the metanarrative level of contagion infecting patriarchy, as seen in Volume I with the outbreak of smallpox. Elfrida thus becomes "fugitive" so that she will not infect the family (III. 51).

Frustrated that he cannot play the traditional hero and save Elfrida, Wilmot's response to her is devoid of sympathy, Wilmot saying, "Your mind ... is cruelly disordered, do not augment it," while Elfrida sees herself as no less than "the outcast of creation" (III. 42). When Elfrida describes herself as bearing "a mark of wretchedness," Gibbes anticipates and complicates the high Romantic trope of the exiled wanderer, as canonical Romantic poets describe their Cain-like personae. Setting Elfrida's new life of wandering against the chosen foreign adventures of Wilmot and Ellison, Gibbes genders the outcast as a woman considered mad by her lover, thus gesturing beyond the masculine subjectivity of the Romantic wanderer to represent the tragic outcome of a woman bound by the laws of institutional patriarchy.[35] The revelation is an existential blow to Elfrida, forcing her to ask who she is as she feels she must leave behind all the roles that have represented her identity: mother, daughter, and wife—all appear canceled, legally and morally.

Joined by Ella, the illegitimate daughter of Ellison, Elfrida is now on the road for the first time. Gibbes suggests an alternative set of adventures based on gender and, specifically, the lineage of men and women, by paralleling the wandering of Ella and Elfrida with the chosen adventure of Wilmot and young Ella's brother, Frederic, travelling to India. Gibbes underscores the contrast between the pairing of Wilmot and Frederic, whose trip to India is a masculine rite of passage involving global domination and the acquisition of wealth, and the pairing of Elfrida and Ella, who insists on accompanying Elfrida as an act of love and self-sacrifice: "I will die with you, Madam .... I will follow you wherever you go .... I am an innocent sufferer in this bad world as well as yourself" (III. 51). Though Ella, named by Mrs. Overbury, suggests that her choosing the Ella/Elfrida lineage is one of choice rather than birth, Elfrida herself underscores her bafflement about her own identity, asking, "What name must I give myself ...? Ellison and Wilmot are equally guilty ones"; rejecting both married names, she settles on her birth-name, Overbury, for, she says, it is "unblemished," although her father's name represents his ambivalence from the beginning of her life in offering her to the Cluwyds (III. 52).

"If you will not let me decorate, I cannot tell my story": metanarrative and the legal ethics of Hannah as storyteller

As noted in the earlier chapters of this study, Gibbes complicates the traditional narrative voice of the sentimental novel through metanarrative that manifests in various forms of storytelling beyond the third-person narrator. Gibbes thereby forces the reader to engage in hermeneutics beyond traditional plot revelation. Thus, at the climactic moment in *Elfrida* in which characters and reader want to know how Ellison could be alive, Gibbes chooses to have Hannah convey Ellison's story of his adventures through his letter to Hannah. As she reads the letter to the family, Hannah mediates the reader's relationship to the story that Ellison himself tells, explaining for the first time how his name had appeared on the list of the dead. However, complicating this doubly mediated storytelling, Ellison proves to be a most unreliable storyteller, which is as important as the questionable story he is telling. Thus, he describes the slaughter of his "reconnoitering party," his clothes put on one of the murdered prisoners, Ellison claiming that this "wanton cruelty" was to make him live with the confusion of identity through which, he says, "I was buried ... by proxy" (III. 61).[36] Ellison hyperbolically describes the "savage captivity" in which he was forced to be "the husband of an [sic] horrid creature, the daughter of the chief, whose prisoner I was, and whose death at length set me free" (III. 62). The story is dubious—including the dying woman's request to her father that Ellison should have his liberty, Ellison saying "it would disturb her in her grave, if I took another wife in that quarter of the world" (III. 62). Whether or not the reader is meant to doubt the veracity of the story, the double standard that continues to inform the novel reaches a new level of irony in which Ellison considers Elfrida's marriage to Wilmot to be adultery, whereas neither his having fathered two children with the nameless woman earlier nor his "marriage" to the Indian woman affords him compassion for Elfrida. Further, Ellison tells Hannah in his letter that the Indian chief's "enriching" him with gifts was the result of "plunder and rapine," savagery neither Wilmot nor Ellison admit to committing in their own descriptions of their exploits abroad.[37]

Gibbes thus reminds the reader again of the artificiality of storytelling, connecting unreliable storytellers to her own sly references to "providence" guiding the lives of her characters. Gibbes is psychologically, politically, and socially acute in having the picaresque qualities of the novel serve its message of the tendering of women in patriarchal society. Especially absurd about Ellison's story is that he represents himself as the sexual plaything of the Indian woman who saves his life because she has fallen in love with him: this Indian woman can be seen as his parodic creation of the novel's story of four generations of Ellas struggling to evolve in a patriarchal world. From his farfetched description of his escape from the Indians, therefore, Ellison immediately turns to worry that the "whining Wilmot" has "built his happiness upon the poor prodigal's ruin"; his self-deception is blatant, threatening that "no second marriage can rob me of my claims" (III. 63). As noted earlier in the study, Gibbes plays upon the biblical story of the prodigal son throughout her career; in this case, Ellison speaks of himself in the third person as the "prodigal," a ludicrous reference, as he has spent Elfrida's money, fled England following his murder of a man, fathered two children out of wedlock, and offered his wife sexually to his creditor as payment for his gambling debt.[38]

Agreeing to meet Ellison when he returns to Arcadia, Hannah does not recognize this "young man of a fierce and bloated aspect" (III. 66). Ellison's appearance has grown incrementally more repulsive in the novel, with the earlier scars left by smallpox and now the years of gambling and exploits in America only known to the reader through his unreliable narration. Hannah tells Ellison that Elfrida has married the anonymous "hero" who had saved him from being charged with murder after the duel, not immediately revealing Wilmot's identity. Despite having called this hero "godlike" in having saved him, Ellison threatens violence, not only to the man but to Hannah, the storyteller, whom Ellison pressures to reveal the identity of the man who has married Elfrida. Gibbes appears to enjoy giving Hannah the metatextual reins as storyteller who, refusing to let Ellison—or the reader—rush her, says, "if you will not let me decorate, I cannot tell my story"; Ellison's response is "You are a strange woman—but go on" (III. 71). When Ellison threatens Hannah, demanding that she "cut the matter short, and tell me at once," she refuses, saying, "I can tell you no way but straight forwards … and if that does not please you, Sir, I must even be silent, though you should scare me in fits with your horrid sword" (III. 71). Adding a deeper layer of significance to this exchange, Hannah is as heroic as either Wilmot or Venables in her response to his threats, defying Ellison when he brandishes his "naked sword" at her (III. 70). For Hannah, being storyteller involves nothing less courageous than laying her life on the line. Of course, her claim that she must tell the story "straight forwards" contradicts her earlier comment that she must "decorate"; she has the power of the raconteur to tell the story as she wishes. Hannah makes the reader aware of the extemporaneous means of preserving her life with the knowledge that Ellison will erupt in fury when he discovers Wilmot to be the husband of Ellison's wife.

Gibbes contrasts Elfrida's unemotional performance of the dutiful wife, mother, and daughter with the dramatic storytelling of Hannah as the scene shifts back to the family who rely on Hannah to tell Ellison about his children, Ella and Frederic, that he fathered with the nameless woman. Hannah responds to the request that she tell Ellison of their existence "with all the pathos ... she was mistress of," telling Ellison of Wilmot's protecting and providing for and then putting them in the care of the Overburys (III. 98). He appears to feel chastised by Hannah's moving tale, responding, "I shall feel the parent, and learn to pity even Wilmot," when she reminds Ellison that he had earlier claimed Wilmot to have fathered his own "spurious offspring" (III. 99, 98). Gibbes thus endows the lower-class, illiterate Hannah with the gift for storytelling, Ellison held in Hannah's thrall.

Ellison is confounded not only by Elfrida having married and borne children in his absence, but by the traditional patriarchal lineage having been replaced by what may be the first modern idea of the blended family, as Hannah herself refers to them: "I hope you see how much you have to be thankful for—the families are, as Mr. Overbury calls it, blended together" (III. 105). Ellison, however, has no capacity for such reform, as he "could not forbear relapsing" into his paranoid rivalry with Wilmot, proclaiming, "They shall not meet again on earth ... and there need not be a worse hell prepared for me, than to see them meet in heaven" (III. 106–07). The mild-mannered Wilmot hears about Ellison's plan for revenge from Hannah who tells him, "He will butcher you" (III. 107). Wilmot thus attempts diplomacy, his first words to Ellison being, "[In] this chain of unforeseen and inevitable events, you and I are fellow-sufferers [sic] in the same cause"; Wilmot pleads for Ellison's compassion: "[I]s there a pang your heart has felt that has not been equaled by mine?" (III. 108).

Lest the reader forget, however, Gibbes shows even here that Wilmot and Ellison are two sides of the same patriarchal coin that objectifies Elfrida. Wilmot implicitly reminds Ellison of his crime that caused him to flee England, Wilmot saying, "You know how I obtained her" (III. 109). Promising Ellison that he will leave England, Wilmot asks Ellison to keep secret his intention to go to America rather than the East, as it is "the present theatre of war and bloodshed" (III. 110). Wilmot explains that he will not return to the East because he is "unfitted for business, unfitted for company, and must wander at large, or mix with the labors of the moment—it is not for a mind, deranged as mine is, to draw out straight lines of conduct" (III. 110). It is an odd rationale for Wilmot's choice: by claiming his mind is deranged and therefore fitted not for business but for war and bloodshed, Wilmot emulates Ellison in rushing to war in America because of a deranged mind. Ellison, in turn, hopes that Wilmot will die and thus nullify Wilmot and Elfrida's marriage: "If he dies ...[,] Elfrida may be mine—may—she must—she shall—she is—for our marriage was never invalidated"

(III. 110). Despite his acting the part of the noble warrior in the "present theatre of war and bloodshed," Wilmot appears less than heroic, his mirroring of Ellison suggests his equal participation in the patriarchal justification of male adventure.

Towards a new lineage: Ella Ellison and Elfrida Overbury emerging from patriarchy's bondage

Revealing how far she has repressed her sensibility and therefore compassion, Elfrida insists that the young Ella meet her father when Ellison sends for her, despite young Ella's expression of intense dread. Elfrida says to her, "Ella, my good girl ..., you must not entertain these illiberal notions of so near a relation as your own father—Hannah has, I perceived, poisoned your infant mind with unjust prejudices" (III. 113–14). After Elfrida's pious lecture for her to be patient, this third-generation Ella, daughter of Ellison, must confront her abusive father on her own. Ellison tells her that he wishes she were not a teen but an infant—literally without language, a term that echoes Elfrida's own accusation that Hannah had poisoned Ella's "infant mind." Young Ella's response to Ellison reveals that she has indeed found her voice: "It is not my fault ... that you did not know me when I was an infant" (III. 118). The first Ella, Mrs. Overbury, reacts to what she sees as Ellison's "barbarous" treatment of his daughter, yet claims that "there was no interfering" (III. 119). Both Ella, Sr. and Elfrida are fearful of inciting Ellison's wrath. When young Ella pleads with them, saying, "I shall die, Madam ... if my father is to torment me thus," Mrs. Overbury tells her it is her "duty to pity and to obey him" (III. 119). Ellison demands his daughter tell him where Elfrida is, Ella responding, "You may kill me, Sir ..., if it is your pleasure ... but from me you shall never know this secret" (III. 121). This third-generation Ella gives promise of a new age of women unafraid to stand their ground against patriarchal oppression.

For all his account of being held captive in America, Ellison returns to England with wealth that he tells Overbury will be for Ella and Frederic, the children whom he finally accepts as his. Born into wealth he had squandered through gambling, Ellison rejects Overbury's offer to support Ellison's children so that Ellison can, in Overbury's words, "guard [his] inconvenience at all points" (III. 127). Ellison gives a self-pitying description of his future as "a miserable wanderer over the face of the globe," yet, characteristically, he qualifies this image of the self-exile by saying, "[T]he laws of my country would have restored Elfrida to my claims" (III. 127). Overbury responds to Ellison's claims by saying, "Talk not of laws .... Our Elfrida lives to her own heart, and would be buried quick in the earth, rather than, knowingly be an adultress [*sic*]" (III. 127). Ellison leaves for New York, "complimenting himself upon his lenity, his forbearance, his most heroic resolution," yet vows "by every power, both celestial and infernal" to take Elfrida if he outlives Wilmot (III. 136).

When Elfrida returns to Arcadia, she acquires "all the outward signs of tranquillity," repressing any possible return to the happiness of her life before Ellison's return; she thus urges Hannah to "never name [Wilmot] when [she is] present" (III. 140). When Hannah asks what Ellison's children should call her, Elfrida answers, "the Lady ... Mrs. Overbury's daughter, their friend" (III. 140). Elfrida thus represses not only happiness but her identity as mother. One may hear in Gibbes's tone her mixed tenderness and irony towards Elfrida's stoicism: "Thus lived Elfrida, in the bloom of years (for she was not eight-and-twenty) the innocent victim of sorrow and the uncomplaining daughter of grief" (III. 142).[39]

Alienation, the French and Indian War, and the globetrotting denouement

When Ellison arrives in New York, he is described as a "self-tormentor" with elements of a Jacobean villain in this "theatre of war" (III. 110), including even "furious soliloquies": "Should I discover ... that he has deceived me, nothing but his heart's-blood shall appease my resentment," he soliloquizes about his desire to destroy Wilmot (III. 143).[40] He joins a party of Venables's acquaintances in Philadelphia, and when he hears them toasting "Elfrida Wilmot," he explodes in "an agony of rage" (III. 145). With Ellison's and Wilmot's paths intersecting, Wilmot again attempts diplomacy, though he is under suspicion until his friends vouch for him. Once Ellison cools off, they reconcile, Wilmot naively praising Ellison for conduct that "is noble, humane, and benevolent, for you have given happiness to the deserving"; though the narrator appears impressed by Ellison's "sincerity," Gibbes has exposed Ellison's dark "soliloquys," thus making the unreliable narrator appear the more naive in idealizing Wilmot's own naivete (III. 147).

Wilmot thus urges Ellison to drop his antagonism in the name of "the carnage of war," which, he adds, "seems to be the convulsion of nature—To behold beings, not only of the same form but of the same religion, climate, family, slaughtering each other to gratify the wild passions of ambition, anger, and pride, is an absolute alienation of both benevolence and reason" (III. 149). The word "alienation" has accrued multiple layers of meaning by this point that now crystalize the complexity of Wilmot's double role in extending Overbury's "alienation" of Elfrida even as he decries war and oppression.[41] In decrying masculinist violence, Wilmot's tenderness to which

Elfrida had been attracted in her youth now resurfaces. Gibbes thus complicates Wilmot by overlaying the lifelong rivalry between Elfrida's lovers with the war in America, Wilmot growing to deplore the "rending asunder every soft, gentle, and endearing tie, and leaving widows, orphans, and childless parents, to people the world, and to deluge it with tears," even using the language of economics to describe the "agonizing woes, by which our best victories are purchased" (III. 149–50).

Wilmot's speech has a powerful effect on Ellison, who volunteers to go into battle for Wilmot. Ellison tells Wilmot that his own "fierceness ... shuts the door of every heart against me—whilst you, Wilmot, from your gentleness and goodness, are universally esteemed" (III. 151). He confesses that he came to America with the intention of assassinating Wilmot, but it is "Heaven and your merit" that have changed him (III. 151). When they come to the realization that one of them will likely be killed, they speculate on the legal and economic ramifications regarding to whom Elfrida will "belong"; in spite of the narrator praising the "honest, credulous, liberal Wilmot," he still engages in the masculinist enterprise of bidding for ownership of Elfrida through marriage for, as he tells Ellison, "[D]eath is the business of life" (III. 152–53). Ellison says, "I cannot unmake myself" regarding his volatility, while Wilmot observes that Ellison's "great mind" has been compromised because Ellison has not learned "to regulate [his] passions" (III. 153–54). Typical of Gibbes's presence behind her narrator, there is a decided split between the narrator's own admiration of Wilmot's sensibility and Gibbes's indictment behind it: even as Ellison walks away from Wilmot, Ellison says snidely, "This fellow ... would have made a most excellent Methodist Parson—for he can whine with any he that was ever most celebrated for whining" (III. 155).

While a deserter saves Wilmot, a poison arrow on the battlefield wounds Ellison, the latter a fitting retribution by an indigenous American towards Ellison's colonial pretensions. Yet Wilmot's rescue by a deserter compromises his own claim for heroism. Adding to this subversion of Wilmot's role as the hero of a sentimental novel is his eagerness to carry Ellison off the battlefield. Though he does so presumably to save Ellison, Wilmot's motives are less than noble. Assuming Ellison will die, Wilmot agrees with Ellison that his remains should be carried to England, for, as Ellison himself says, "Elfrida will not believe even your report, if my bones are left in a foreign land" (III. 160). Despite Wilmot being convinced that Ellison would not survive his wound, the surgeon informs him that "he might be years in dying" (III. 161). With the surgeon's news that the poison will consume Ellison slowly and painfully, Gibbes once again interjects her providential role, Wilmot exclaiming, "If I ask not too much, All-gracious Author of my experience ... , let me convey this unhappy man to the village of his nativity, and grant him there to depart, in the midst of those, whose sufferings his life has occasioned, and whose hearts can alone know tranquillity [*sic*] by his decease—grant me this, and of my own destiny, I will not have one anxious thought" (III. 161). Wilmot's wish for Ellison to die in England is less patriotic than it is a wish for Elfrida and the rest of the family to experience the "tranquillity" that would come from unmitigated proof of his death.

Though the providential Gibbes grants Wilmot's wish, she does not make it easy. The globetrotting reaches its denouement, having extended into the next generation with Ellison's son, Frederic, Jr. Returning from India, young Frederic is concerned about both Wilmot's safety and meeting his father, Ellison, for the first time. The poison metaphor now expands to include Ellison's engagement with those waiting at the Grange. Ellison is at first polite and complimentary towards Frederic, Jr., though once Ellison hears that Hannah has remained with Elfrida and the others, his mind is set "on edge," for he believes Hannah has convinced his daughter, Ella, to hate him (III. 166). The literal poison runs a parallel course to his self-consuming paranoia, intensifying as Ellison accuses young Frederic of lying when he tells Ellison that the others have only spoken kindly of Ellison. Once Ellison sparks his own rage, it continues unabated so that, when Frederic, Jr. refers to Elfrida by name, Ellison demands, "And who taught you ... to call Mrs. Ellison Elfrida?" (III. 168). This moment is a culmination of the crisis the novel has developed from the start regarding Elfrida's identity, beginning with Overbury changing his daughter's name so that she could inherit the wealth her mother gave up in marrying Overbury. The issue of patriarchal naming intensifies when Frederic informs his father, Ellison, that the last name of Elfrida's children is Wilmot. Gibbes inscribes the moment with irony, the patrilineal name suggesting that, regardless of women's choices, all social strata are defined by patrimony as the three generations of Ellas react with dismay upon learning of Ellison's return to the Grange.

Elfrida has thus evolved into a sharp and damning portrayal of legal, social, and religious patriarchy as it is perpetuated in the traditional sentimental novel. Ellison bitterly states, "I am always wrong and others always right" in the "old story," one that Gibbes subverts through metatextuality. The old story is founded on binaries of good and bad men vying for the idealized woman, object of their competing desires (III. 171). Thus, while Gibbes couples Ellison's psychological illness with his literal poisoning, Wilmot, in London, appears to be going mad. Although he recognizes that everyone fluctuates between lucidity and irrationality, Wilmot does not see his own commonality with Ellison, the novel having spared neither of the rivals the contamination of patriarchy. Yet by muddying the line between the two poles that Wilmot and Ellison represent, Gibbes not only complicates Wilmot but gives Ellison this moment for the reader to imagine Ellison's struggling humanity behind his life of entitlement, abuse, and ultimate madness.

Though Ellison cannot be redeemed, Gibbes grants Frederic, Jr. an increasingly important role in the final movement of the novel, ironically suggesting that patriarchal lineage may be redeemed through the illegitimate son of the entitled scion. Frederic, Jr.'s respect and gratitude for his adoptive family is implicit in the new meaning his name suggests: he is not "Ella's son" but that of a woman to whom Ellison was not married. Though it appears that Gibbes has offered through Frederic, Jr. a hope for male redemption beyond both the overt oppression of Ellison and the more insidious masculinity of Wilmot, we are reminded that Frederic, Jr. retains his connection to Anglo-India when he asks Ellison's leave to do business with "one of my East India Captains" (III. 180). Gibbes thus leaves open the possibility that Frederic may be among the next generation of men to colonize the East.

The novel circles back to the opening, with Overbury attempting to claim for his wife, Ella, the inheritance taken by the Cluwyd sisters and now in the clutches of Ellison, who refuses to leave his own children anything in his will. Elfrida herself is a "prisoner of herself," struggling to rationalize her desire that Ellison die before Wilmot. When Elfrida concludes that "she was as humane as another and had as tender a heart," Gibbes's recurrence to Elfrida as "tender" suggests the moral quandary she faces regarding the rivalry of the two lovers: she is the "tender" for whom they negotiate even as she is concerned about her ethical duty to feel tenderness towards a dying man (III. 196). Realizing he is "going fast," Ellison decides to "make his will," negotiating with Overbury over whether Elfrida owes Ellison "some recompence," Ellison insisting he is "not culpable" for having fallen "into the dissipations of the age" (III. 200–01). Overbury responds by acknowledging his own guilt regarding "whatever injustice has been done"—not only to Elfrida but to Ellison himself, Overbury claiming he has been

> the first, and melancholy cause of all my child has smarted under—she would not have married you, Sir, if I had not commanded her—you knew her reluctance better than I could do, yet you would solicit, and I would bestow her upon you—You talk of recompence—that idea misled me into espousing Wilmot's pretensions—Elfrida besought us to spare her—an attempt to repair the errors of my conduct, induced me, a second time, to exert my authority. (III. 202)

Overbury's apparently gracious act towards Ellison now reveals itself to be Overbury's deeper recognition of his own "criminal" behavior towards his daughter. As Overbury defends Elfrida, Ellison becomes increasingly enraged, entrenched in the patriarchal gender binary: "[S]he is my wife, and I would know whether she means to pay me the last duties as such—or if I am to imagine her capable of revelling upon my grave" (III. 203).

This moment is nuanced in its psychological depth, with all the women present, "silent as death" (III. 211). Ellison commands them to kneel and pray for him, yet he dies without getting a promise from Elfrida "never more to reunite herself" to Wilmot, "for neither powers nor time was left him to accomplish his own intentions" (III. 212). Gibbes creates a dramatic contrast between the shocked silence of Elfrida at witnessing Ellison's death and Hannah's "not unpleasant soliloquy," as she speculates, "[W]hat a nutshell have we contracted ourselves into, to avoid this strange man's brow-beatings, who, because he could not be happy himself, took unending delight in destroying the happiness of others"; Hannah provides comic relief through her ironic appreciation of Ellison's thoughtfulness "to come and die amongst them, to prevent all doubts and demurs hereafter" (III. 213). Hannah once again presents the metafictional counter to Gibbes as storyteller when she adds, "Ah me, though, if poor Mr. Wilmot should be dead, what a heartbreaking thing it would be, now all evil impediments are removed" (III. 213). Behind Hannah, Gibbes reminds the reader that the story is not over.

Not telling any of the characters of his return to England until he can "settle a proper plan," Wilmot dramatically orchestrates his centrality to the novel's end with his homecoming. Gibbes, however, gives the novel's final chapter, "A Jubilee," to Hannah, who has free narrative rein not only to tell her story but to choreograph with the children the festival they are creating for the return of Wilmot to Arcadia: "[W]e will dance, and sing, and huzza, and never, no never be sad again," the narrator adding that "this fine story was told regularly every day by Hannah in the nursery ... but it was all amongst themselves" (III. 214–16). The return to Arcadia signals the novel's promise of a return to innocence, empowering the working-class Hannah to imbue the denouement of the novel with a postlapsarian return to innocence. However, Gibbes does not dismiss the multi-generational Ellas' struggles against patriarchy. When the dazed Elfrida asks, "What will become of me?" Gibbes reminds the reader that she has postponed the fulfillment of the marriage plot to make the question more than rhetorical: the question is another iteration of Elfrida's prodigality in her lifelong questioning of her identity (III. 223).

The ending, however, is sheer comedy, complete with Hannah's and the children's malaprops. Gibbes takes the notion of the comedic even further into the return to nature that was to be associated with high Romanticism. Hannah's celebration is not only of the rustic life and landscape but of a refusal to betray one's own nature, her words recounted by Overbury:

> I ... asked Hannah ... what could put it in her head to behave so wildly; she answered, nature ... for Mr. Wilmot, God bless him, would let every body

follow their own head—and not seek to make a velvet purse of a sow's ear, as her mistress had so often done—wanting to teach her sentimentals and *dickorums* [sic]—and not to be joyful when she was glad, and sorrowful when she was afflicted—or angry when she was misused—or to hate her enemies, all of which was against nature, law and conscience. (III. 225–26)

By having Overbury "obliged to be his own messenger," Gibbes offers the titular patriarch redemption through his role reversal with Hannah. Thus, the first two generations of Ellas—Mrs. Overbury and Elfrida—"whose muscles were such strangers to risibility, not only relaxed, but a most hearty fit of laughter did they enjoy"; watching Hannah and the children's "numberless little antics," Elfrida walks with "the dignity of a tragedy-queen ... but being ready to tumble at every second step, from the incumbrance of an hoop, and the impediments of her train" (III. 227). Catharsis comes ambivalently through the laughter of tragicomedy.

Hannah's drama thus eclipses Wilmot's arrival, the object of this jubilee. After he has "tenderly embraced the children ... and spoken kindly to Hannah" in the bland language of "his good wishes and his gratitude," Hannah responds in colorful contrast, "I never felt anything like this day's pleasure in all my life—nor has the best fine lady among them all, half the satisfaction in their kickshaw notions, as I have in an honest and plain heart, which I am not ashamed to shew to all the world" (III. 230). Gibbes has anticipated the reunion of Wilmot and Elfrida, an anticlimax since they had wed and borne children long before. Another layer of anticlimax manifests through Hannah's storytelling/playacting: when Elfrida sees Hannah arriving without the children, she is alarmed but smiles, finding it "hard ... to condemn such well-meant kindness—but it would, surely, have been better, for you to have gone up with them to the house, than to have hoisted them over the park-wall" (III. 231–32). To this criticism of Hannah's spontaneously joyful choreography, Hannah responds, "It might have been more *politer* [sic] ... but it would not have been half so affectionate—for affection knows nothing of whims and forms, but, like hunger, would break through stone walls" (III. 232). Gibbes thus concludes the novel by elevating Hannah's malaprops to poetry.

Gibbes underscores the anticlimax of the lovers' reunion: though Elfrida, acting the part of the sentimental heroine, "preserved herself from fainting" with "the assistance of her smelling-bottle" in anticipation of Wilmot's arrival at the house, her mother, Ella Overbury, is concerned that "the world's eye will be upon" them, Ella, Sr. worrying that Ellison's "death must have its proper effect upon our minds" (III. 233). She says they must "meet a second time at the altar" despite her "detest[ing] forms—but decency must not be violated" (III. 234). This anticlimax is pointed as Ella, Sr., the matriarch, announces that Elfrida and Wilmot are "now at liberty to re-choose each other" (III. 235).

The novel's final paragraphs return not only to the opening frame with Mr. and Mrs. Overbury, whose present happiness is "like a dream from which they were afraid to wake," but to Hannah, now free to "do and say whatever she pleased," and to Frederic, who has "bid a final adieu to sea-life" now that he is "so miraculously restored" to friends "he held so dear" (III. 236). The novel's conclusion thus returns from its expansive geography to the provincial lives of the family at the Grange. Gibbes fulfills the promise that Ella, Sr. can return to her home now as matriarch, honoring Hannah's ebullience and, with young Frederic finding contentment at home, quieting his impulse for global domination, at least temporarily.

Notes

1 See Franklin xvi.
2 The details and significance of Ella's name change to Elfrida are taken up later in this chapter.
3 Ellison's rejected lover and offspring are discussed later in this chapter.
4 In order both to bring this naming chaos to the surface and to help make sense of it, this chapter will distinguish among the Ellas—if not apparent from context—as either "Ella, Sr." (Mrs. Overbury, Elfrida's mother); "Ella, Jr." (Elfrida, the protagonist who becomes Mrs. Ellison and then Mrs. Wilmot); and the third generation Ella (not the birth daughter of Elfrida, she is the bastard daughter of a young woman who has died because of her abject poverty, abandoned by her lover who is the wealthy Frederic Ellison, the rival lover in the triangle with Elfrida and Wilmot). Elfrida's father, Lt. Overbury, forces her to marry Ellison before Overbury recognizes the depth of Ellison's depravity. Overbury's "paternal ambition" of the novel's subtitle leads to generations of tragedy in the novel.
5 See April London's detailed Introduction to her study of women and property in the eighteenth-century novel (pp. 1–11).
6 According to the *OED* the double meaning of "alienation" as a transference of property (which would include women); and a "state of madness to estrangement" appeared as early as the thirteenth century. www.oed.com/view/Entry/4999?redirectedFrom=alienation#eid. Accessed September 15, 2024.
7 Elizabeth Norton. www.historyanswers.co.uk/kings-queens/elfrida-mother-murderer-and-englands-first-crowned-queen/. This study does not take up the relationship of this novel with William Mason's 1752 dramatic poem, *Elfrida*.
8 See the references to Othello in the previous chapters. Though the references to the play are ubiquitous in Gibbes's fiction, she uses the same quotation in *The American Fugitive*. The phrase "out of doors" took on figurative meaning suggested in the sixteenth century and lasted into the eighteenth century, as seen in the *OED*'s citations. www.oed.com/view/Entry/56820?rskey=RkSunj&result=1&isAdvanced=false#eid126392681. Accessed September 15, 2024. P4.

out (†forth) of door (also *doors*): out of the house; in the open air, abroad; hence *figurative* out of place, lost, abroad, irrelevant, worthless (*obsolete*).
1574 St. Avstens Manuell in <u>Certaine Prayers S. Augustines Medit.</u> sig. Qvij^v Love driveth feare out of doores.
1581 G. PETTIE tr. S. Guazzo <u>Ciuile Conuersat.</u> (1586) III. 156 Some fathers will not suffer their Daughters to set their foote foorth of dores.
1595 E. SPENSER <u>Colin Clouts come Home Againe</u> sig. D2^v Out of doore quite shit.
1658 T. BURTON <u>Diary</u> (1828) II. 456 All precedents are out of doors in this case.
1699 J. COLLIER <u>Second Def. Short View Eng. Stage</u> (1730) 324 A Place where Thinking is out of Doors.1719 D. DEFOE <u>Farther Adventures Robinson Crusoe</u> 355 That Objection is out of Doors.

9   Iago's ruin of Cassio is swift in the play, Cassio saying, "Reputation, reputation, reputation! Oh, I have lost my reputation! I have lost the immortal part of myself, and what remains is bestial," Iago responding, "Reputation is an idle and most false imposition, oft got without merit and lost without deserving" (II. iii. 281–95).

10 This authorial presence suggests Gibbes as both a precursor to the free indirect discourse of Austen and later writers, as the Conclusion to this study discusses in greater detail.

11 Ella's inability to testify looks ahead to Mary Shelley's ironic use of the term regarding the trial of Justine in *Frankenstein*, in which Elizabeth's extolling of Justine's virtues is used against Justine, and so her own testimony is used against Justine. The term's etymology, showing one's virility in court, shows the phallocentric language associated with the patriarchal court system.

12 *Elfrida*'s metanarrative message about the ill effects of the sentimental novel on young people is yet more radical than Wollstonecraft's argument for women's education in *VRW*. Because of her desire to sway the patriarchal powers controlling women's education, Wollstonecraft felt politically constrained from being more overt about her desire for women's independent agency, advocating for their education by arguing that it would make them better mothers and wives. Gibbes, by contrast, dismantles the patriarchal foundation of marriage itself as the problem of female identity. See Franklin on Gibbes's anticipation by forty years of "the social protest of novelists such as Mary Hays, Mary Robinson, Anna Maria Bennett, and Mary Wollstonecraft" (xv). Chapter 13 of Wollstonecraft's *VRW* focuses on the detriment of sentimental novels for young women whose "minds were quiescent, and when they were not roused by sensible objects and employments of that kind, they were low-spirited, would cry, or go to sleep" (194). Wollstonecraft appears to have been at the threshold of realizing that fiction would be a more powerful means of communicating to the women she wished to reach, her novel *Maria* unfinished at the time of her death. It is indeed tantalizing to speculate on the direction Wollstonecraft may have pursued had she lived.

13 My introduction to *Rethinking Romanticism* discusses the influence by women writers on the canonical male poets' sensibility. See also this study's Chapter 2 regarding the feminine qualities of Lord D. in *The American Fugitive*.

14 According to the *OED*, the term "entitle" and its variants were evolving during this period: besides its original meaning as having a legal right to property, by 1817, the derogatory adjective, "entitled" as "spoiled" becomes part of the lexicon, anticipated here by Gibbes's characterization of Ellison. www.oed.com/search/advanced/Entries?textTermText0=entitle&textTermOpt0=Etymology&dateOfUseFirstUse=false&page=1&sortOption=Frequency. Accessed March 9, 2024.

15 This early moment of the narrative entering Elfrida's interior state anticipates the free indirect discourse of Austen, as discussed in the Conclusion to this study.

16 Elfrida's creating for herself rather than for either young man demonstrates Gibbes's assertion of a woman's education for herself rather than her husband, a message that Wollstonecraft cannot pursue in *VRW*, as noted in the Introduction to this study.

17 Though Wilmot calls Elfrida "Ella" since she had asked him to do so earlier, this chapter will continue referring to the protagonist as Elfrida to avoid confusion.

18 Gibbes's use of *Werter* to suggest a new, tender masculinity predates Mary Shelley's use of in *Frankenstein* (1818); the novel's "gentle and domestic manners … combined with lofty sentiments and feelings" fill the creature with "speculation and astonishment" (89).

19 See the Introduction to this study for a detailed discussion of the disjunction between the persona Wollstonecraft creates in her polemical prose and that of her letters and the woman known by her close circle, including William Blake.

20 Pun intended.

21 See the Conclusion to this study for the role Bath plays in the relationship between class and gender with the struggling subjectivities of both Elfrida and Austen's Anne Elliot in *Persuasion*.

22 See the Conclusion for the connection between Ellison and Sir Walter Elliot in *Persuasion* regarding the lure of London to a man with uncontrollable spending habits.

23 Though this moment hearkens back to the discussion of *Francis Clive* in Chapter 1, in which Penelope the prostitute disparages Mrs. Charlotte as "an ice-piece," the attack on the wife as sexually frigid comes from two very polarized figures of England's class structure (*Francis Clive*, II. 68).

24 As discussed earlier, this attack on novels occurs in *VRW*, ch. XIII.

25 See the Conclusion to this study for a more detailed discussion of this novel's anticipation of Austen's use of free indirect discourse in *Persuasion*.

26 See *OED*: Adj #10e; of a ship; capable of overturning; n: small boat used to convey passengers, cargo to/from ship. This triple pun is discussed in greater detail in the Conclusion as a commonality between *Elfrida* and Austen's *Persuasion*.

27 Venables is also the name of Maria's husband in Wollstonecraft's 1798 novel, *The Wrongs of Woman, or, Maria*, perhaps suggesting Wollstonecraft's influence by Gibbes.

28 As discussed later in this chapter, by V. III, Ellison is revealed to be alive, though only after he is assumed dead because of his clothes discovered on the dead body and Ella's marriage to Wilmot and their bearing of three children.
29 By giving Hannah the means to write her emotional message, thus endowing her with subjectivity, Gibbes gives her agency that Wordsworth never grants his rustic figures.
30 See Chapter 1 for discussion of the episode in *Francis Clive*.
31 The phallocentric etymology of the word "testify"—asserting one's masculinity in court—suggests that her words derive from the language of patriarchy that has repressed her own feelings. Mary Shelley uses the term to great effect in *Frankenstein*, when Elizabeth's "testimony" in the trial of Justine is used against rather than her intended defense of Justine, who is then executed. The message is clear: the judicial system is patriarchal and women who try to "testify" will not be heard (Shelley 56).
32 Gibbes here looks ahead to the nostalgia of Wordsworth's desire to return to childhood; even the word "renovating" is uncanny since it is a word Wordsworth would come to after multiple revisions of *The Prelude*'s "spots of time" passage. Gibbes nevertheless complicates the lament in the "Intimations Ode" that "nothing can bring back the hour of splendour in the grass" by countering the contrary subjectivities of Elfrida and Wilmot regarding their memories of "Arcadia."
33 See Chapter 3 for discussion of Zoriada's namelessness as well as the significance of her pseudonym.
34 Wollstonecraft, for instance, imagines a scenario of motherhood in which, she says, "I see her surrounded by her children, reaping the reward of her care. The intelligent eye meets hers, whilst health and innocence smile on their chubby cheeks, and as they grow up the cares of life are lessened by their grateful attention. She lives to see the virtues which she endeavoured to plant on principles, fixed into habits, to see her children attain a strength of character sufficient to enable them to endure adversity without forgetting their mother's example" (*VRW* 55).
35 See, for instance, Byron's and Percy Shelley's many personae based on the biblical figures of Cain and Ahasuerus. Gibbes's Elfrida is closer to Blake's Oothoon in *Visions of the Daughters of Albion* who, bound to her abuser and rejected by her lover after her rape, recognizes the larger social plight into which marriage forces women:

Till she who burns with youth, and knows no fixed lot; is bound
In spells of law to one she loaths; and must she drag the chain
Of life, in weary lust! must chilling murderous thoughts obscure
The clear heaven of her eternal spring! to bear the wintry rage
Of a harsh terror, driv'n to madness, bound to hold a rod
Over her shrinking shoulders all the day; & all the night (ll. 21–26).

36 The corpse with his uniform suggests a parody of the narrative ploy of women cross-dressing as soldiers, seen for instance in Charlotte Clive's rescue of her

husband, and in the escape of the young women from the convent in *The American Fugitive* by way of dressing in the clothes of the boys who had died of the plague. Regarding the *Clive* reference, see Chapter 1; for the *American Fugitive* escape, see Chapter 2.

37 Regardless of whether Gibbes was aware of Aphra Behn's 1690 tragicomedy, *The Widow Ranter*, Behn's play may have made possible this episode in *Elfrida*, in which Ellison, in America during the Seven Years' War, claims he was nearly forced into marriage with an indigenous woman of a tribe that butchered his army. See Eastwood's historical contextualization of Behn's play as well as its generic complexity, in which "the tragic plotline featuring Bacon is balanced in the play by a comic one featuring the hard-drinking, tobacco-smoking Widow Ranter, who woos and wins Bacon's first lieutenant … by dressing as a soldier" (12).

38 See this study's Introduction for a detailed discussion of the evolution of the term "prodigal" during the long eighteenth century.

39 Like Austen's Anne Elliot in *Persuasion*, Elfrida is twenty-seven; yet Elfrida is in the "bloom of years" whereas Anne has prematurely "lost her bloom"; see the Conclusion to this study for a comparison between the two novels.

40 The chase around the globe looks ahead to Frankenstein's maniacal pursuit of the creature.

41 As noted earlier in this chapter, according to the *OED* the double meaning of "alienation" as a transference of property (which would include women); and a "state of madness to estrangement" appeared as early as the thirteenth century. www.oed.com/view/Entry/4999?redirectedFrom=alienation#eid. Accessed September 15, 2024.

Conclusion: affect, globalism, and modernity from the Seven Years' War to Waterloo

This study began by framing Gibbes's career through her literary inheritance from such late seventeenth- and early eighteenth-century writers as Aphra Behn, Charlotte Lennox, and Eliza Haywood. The hindsight of the preceding chapters offers an opportunity to reappraise the periodization-driven lacuna between the two poles of the long eighteenth century by returning to Janet Todd's provocative pairing of Behn's satire and Wollstonecraft's polemical prose: "Behn and Wollstonecraft differ mostly in the power to laugh and mock. There are problems in laughter—it does not move people to act. Wollstonecraft's seriousness leads towards change. But one might argue that the change was premature because there had been a failure in analysis of the construction of femininity, sexuality and power that needed shaking" ("Aphra Behn" 158). Because of the recovery of much of Gibbes's oeuvre since that essay was written in 1995, and knowing that Wollstonecraft had favorably reviewed Gibbes's fiction, it is instructive to substitute Gibbes for Behn in the subsequent statement of Todd's essay, to which I add the following clause: had Wollstonecraft lived longer, we can thus surmise that [Gibbes] might have "taught [Wollstonecraft] to rally rather than rail and to watch from some distance what Behn described as 'the hot brute' drudging on" ("Aphra Behn" 158). In this way, "the change was [not as] premature" as it seemed even thirty years ago. That Wollstonecraft died before she could finish her novel, *Maria, or the Wrongs of Woman*, suggests her potential for entering a new phase of a career that was recognizing the power of fiction to enact change.[1]

When she praised Gibbes, therefore, Wollstonecraft may have recognized implicitly that Gibbes was able to use fiction to subvert the sentimental, holding in tension such polarities as psychological realism and the polemical. Yet regardless of whether Wollstonecraft drew inspiration from Gibbes's complication of what for Wollstonecraft had not yet fully evolved beyond the polemical, Gibbes's fiction realizes what Jill Campbell has described as the potential of a single novel to "bridge the gap between the individual experience related in its fictional narrative and the depiction of general wrongs to a social group" (163). To blend individual experience in narrative with commentary on such "general wrongs," Gibbes reconceptualizes such fundamental elements of fiction as character, plot, and narration. As the preceding chapters have detailed, Gibbes's authorial voice emerges often at odds with her narrators through metanarrative strategies including a range of untraditional storytellers: prostitutes, cross-dressing wives, illiterate servants, and, in the case of Zoriada, an Indian woman whom Gibbes situates in provincial England and empowers with an identity that eludes even her reader.

Two narratives of the tendered wife: Gibbes's 1786 *Elfrida* and Austen's 1818 *Persuasion*

As Gibbes's fiction bridges the writings of Behn and Wollstonecraft, so too does Gibbes extend her reach to Austen, thereby providing a link in the evolution from satire to a new irony in fiction that bridges the polemical and the psychological. To provide an end frame for discussing Gibbes's fiction as a lynchpin in this legacy of women writers in an emerging modernity, therefore, this Conclusion draws upon multiple commonalities between *Elfrida* and *Persuasion*. Though thirty-two years of literary and sociopolitical change stand between these two novels, they share plot devices and diction often uncanny in their similarities, thrusting together gender, economy, and social class to destabilize the traditional formula of the sentimental novel. This Conclusion aims not to argue that Gibbes influenced Austen, though this may have been the case.[2] The objective of exploring the relationship between the two novels is rather to reflect on their remarkable commonalities, including the literal and figurative sea changes their two female protagonists undergo and, from these commonalities, to trace larger patterns in women's writing across the long eighteenth century.

Austen's position as a culminating female novelist during the long eighteenth century belies the reductive emphasis on canonical poetry in traditional periodization. *Persuasion* has long been considered Austen's most "romantic" novel, with Anne Elliot as the first of Austen's heroines to step out of drawing rooms into landscapes reflective of her interiority.[3] Focusing on the relationship of Austen and Gibbes is not intended to diminish the impact of canonical Romanticism on Austen's new landscape as a "structure of feeling," but rather to complicate the idea that *Persuasion*'s representation of nature is due wholly to the influence "by the new Romantic poetry of the nineteenth century" (Litz 153). The purpose of the comparison, then, is rather to expose the legacy of women writers behind Austen's narrative voice that balances irony and sentiment, a voice that accesses Anne's subjectivity through free indirect discourse (FID) as it modulates satire to irony in representing the intersection of gender, patrimony, and empire.[4]

Persuasion, whose two slender volumes epitomize Austen's elegant narrative brevity and limited spatial movement, presents an odd pairing with *Elfrida*, a triple-decker novel of global expanse across several generations. Yet both novels represent the central female subjectivity of their protagonists at the crossroads of a shifting patriarchal social structure. Through a tension between satire and sentimentality that evolves across the long eighteenth century, both Gibbes and Austen, each in her respective historical context, attain a new level of authorial irony whose nuanced voice emerges behind the third-person narrator. Though Austen has long been recognized for using FID, therefore, this narrative voice can be traced to Gibbes's metanarrative and further back to Behn's late exploration of the connection between her earlier use of metadrama in her plays and in her pioneering narrative voice late in her career. As noted in Chapter 4 of this study, for example, echoes of Behn's 1688 play, *The Widow Ranter*, appear in *Elfrida*, with Ellison's outlandish claim to having been forced to marry an indigenous woman whose tribe, he claims, had massacred his army in America during the Seven Years' War (III. 61–62). The same year Behn wrote the tragicomedy, *The Widow Ranter*, she wrote *Oroonoko*, a narrative of slavery in Surinam in which Behn grafts travel narrative and fiction.[5] Both play and narrative rest on Behn's albeit ambivalent representation of British depredations in the New World, a complex network of genres and voices.

From Behn to Gibbes, then, a multilayered authorial voice emerges in charting the gradual shift in women's fiction towards a more nuanced irony from the polarities of satire and sentimentality—or between satire and polemicism, depending on which writers are chosen to represent their eras. The importance of gender in contributing to the advent of modernity is thus not confined to women writers representing patriarchy as an isolated sociopolitical phenomenon. Recent scholarship on the long eighteenth century has applied affect theory to engage with both the political and domestic subjugation of women as foundational to the rise of the sentimental novel.[6] Katie Barclay, for instance, refers to the rise of the "affective family" as patriarchal power shifts from inherited entitlement to capitalism.[7] This interest in the connection between affect and women's writing began in the 1980s with such pioneers in the recovery of women poets of the late eighteenth century as Stuart Curran, whose essay first refers to the "cult of sensibility" ("The I Altered" 195). Scholarship of the long eighteenth century has evolved both to hone and broaden the implications of affect for women writing a century before late eighteenth- and early nineteenth-century poets such as Charlotte Smith and Mary Robinson. Expanding the revolutionary context through the range of women writing in diverse genres, this scholarship has traced the connection of gender and affect to the shifting of patriarchy away from patrimony within England to the global expansion of the British empire. Comparing *Elfrida* and *Persuasion* thus demonstrates the evolution of affect during the long eighteenth century as more than what Isobel Armstrong's influential study refers to as the "gush of the feminine."[8] Exploring the commonalities between the two novels helps qualify the claim that Austen's interiority in *Persuasion* is due exclusively to her influence by canonical poets, themselves influenced by such poets as Charlotte Smith. Gibbes and Austen contextualize their narratives through revolutionary upheaval, simultaneously challenging the sentimental tradition through metanarrative's self-referentiality. As Austen's final work, *Persuasion* paradoxically reaches back to a female legacy that in turn ushers in the modern novel's tension between interiority and an external world that is both provincial and global.

Devices that subvert the sentimental: anticlimax and the love triangle

Despite their many differences, the two novels represent common concerns through similar plot devices that conspire to complicate, if not dismantle, the sentimental novel's trajectory towards the marriage of the heroine and hero. Before delving into the comparison of the two novels, a brief overview of each plot will help contextualize both their commonalities and differences detailed in the discussion that follows.

Elfrida begins before the birth of the eponymous heroine, with her father, Lieutenant Overbury, a poor but ambitious English military hero who falls in love with Ella Cluwyd, born into Welsh aristocracy. When the untitled Overbury asks for Ella's hand in marriage, the Cluwyd patriarch disinherits his daughter. The couple elopes to London where they live in poverty, eventually with their daughter, Ella, who becomes Elfrida when a wealthy cousin of Ella, Sr. pressures the Overburys to give her custody of the infant so that she may regain her mother's lost wealth. Ella, Sr. grieves the loss of her daughter but acquiesces to her husband's "paternal ambition," the novel's subtitle. The upheaval this adoption creates takes three generations to resolve. Some of *Elfrida*'s plot points discussed in Chapter 4 regarding the love triangle are here reframed since they are salient to the comparison with *Persuasion*: Gibbes's love triangle begins during Elfrida's childhood on the Cluwyd estate. She soon becomes the object of a rivalry between two boys: Wilmot, the son of the humble rector on the Cluwyd estate, with whom she develops an intimate friendship, and Ellison, the aristocratic and haughty son of the Cluwyds' neighbor, whose resentment of Elfrida and Wilmot's bond becomes Ellison's lifelong obsession. As the three enter adolescence, Elfrida's father, Lieutenant Overbury, who had been rejected by his own father-in-law, rejects even Wilmot's friendship with Elfrida, forcing her into an unhappy marriage with the nefarious and profligate Ellison who gambles away their inheritance. Following a false report of Ellison's death abroad, Overbury pressures Elfrida to marry Wilmot, who has earned wealth through colonial ventures in the East. When Ellison turns up alive several years later, Elfrida leaves Wilmot and their children. They are reunited after Ellison's actual death that coincides with Elfrida's newfound self-awareness and the promise of redemption for both Overbury and Wilmot beyond patriarchal authoritarianism.

In its far more compressed timespan, *Persuasion* begins with Anne's father, a baronet named Sir Walter Elliot who has squandered the family estate despite his two preoccupations that the novel interweaves: his legacy of siring only daughters and his repulsion at the victorious navy men bringing new wealth to provincial Somersetshire. Sir Walter is advised that the most viable solution to his debt is letting the patriarchal estate to one of the navy men, Admiral Croft, who has returned from the victorious Battle of Trafalgar. Croft's brother-in-law, Frederick Wentworth, also returns to Somersetshire as a naval war hero. Only after the focus on Sir Walter in the opening chapters does the reader discover that, before the time of the novel, Anne had broken off her engagement with Frederick at the urging of her deceased mother's friend, Lady Russell. The love triangle emerges with another return: the heir to the Elliot estate, William Walter. Lady Russell tempts Anne to take her mother's place by urging Anne to marry him. Anne overcomes this iteration of persuasion, rightly suspecting her cousin of nefarious motives. Thanks to a warning from her old friend, Mrs. Smith, whose husband was cheated out of his property in the West Indies by William Walter, Anne's suspicions are confirmed. William Walter nevertheless rejects the patrimonial inheritance, and Anne marries Frederick after a sequence of awkward meetings. The novel ends with Anne anticipating an uncertain future as a sailor's wife.

Laying the groundwork for the two novels' connection, the love triangle is how each represents the socioeconomic triangle among patriarchal bloodlines, marriage, and property. Gibbes and Austen use the love triangle to explore the tension between the waning of patrimony and modernity's more complex and often insidious patriarchy founded on its expanding empire. *Elfrida*'s love triangle involves the mercenary Ellison, who spreads his infection—literally and symbolically—across the globe, and Wilmot, who ultimately rejects his own colonial aspirations; Austen's love triangle involves William Walter Elliot, the heir to the Elliot baronetage, and Wentworth, who earns the wealth and admiration of provincial Somersetshire through his naval victories.

Besides the love triangle, both novels use anticlimax to unite hero and heroine prematurely, forcing them to separate until they individually come to terms with their patriarchal entanglements involving the heroine's father and the hero's entitled rival. Gibbes and Austen end with the newly reunited couple radically transformed. Both gesture towards a revolutionary, though flawed, new social structure that promises the ascendency of female agency in a new sociopolitical climate. *Elfrida*'s love triangle and anticlimax sketched above thrust the eponymous heroine into a growing awareness of her selfhood beyond her familial roles. Elfrida evolves from seeing herself as the "outcast of creation" following the revelation of her bigamy. This existential blow forces her to claim her subjectivity, temporarily leaving behind her roles as mother, daughter, and wife, all suddenly and legally jeopardized. Austen's Anne must likewise turn inward, a result of having been persuaded to break off her engagement to the lower-class Wentworth before the novel begins. Anne comes to recognize the necessity of "knowing our own nothingness beyond our own circle" (40), discovering her "happiness from within" (175). By the novel's end, Anne turns outward to assert her autonomy in her reunion with Wentworth (212). Though the novel's end for each heroine promises liberation from "paternal ambition" and from the passivity expected of them as daughters and wives, both novels suggest the fragility of such a promise during the long eighteenth century. Central to the crisis for both heroines is that they must reckon with and overcome their mothers' legacy as passive wives. Just as the heartbroken Ella, Elfrida's mother, defers to her husband with little more than a sigh when he surrenders the infant Elfrida to the Cluwyd cousin at the opening of Gibbes's novel, the specter of Anne's unhappy mother haunts Austen's novel.[9]

The grown Elfrida, like her mother, passively accepts her role as object of negotiation when her father chooses first the wealthy Ellison and then the newly wealthy Wilmot for Elfrida's marriages. Elfrida surpasses her mother's docility towards both father and husband by confronting and even embracing the poverty in which Ellison has left her. Using her talents to support herself, she tells her mother, "[M]y pencil shall bring its industry decent rewards .... O insult me not so far as to call it degrading ... to defend myself against the daemon poverty" (II. 133–34). Yet Elfrida, like her mother, submits in silent stoicism when Overbury pressures her to marry Wilmot despite her doubts about the authenticity of the first announcement of his death.

The naming chaos is significant in both novels beyond its satire of the generations of patriarchs with names such as Charles. In *Elfrida*, it begins with an early reference to Overbury's ancestor as a victim of Charles II, while *Persuasion* includes the upwardly mobile Charles Musgrove and Charles Hayter. In a chapter early in Elfrida's first volume, "Paternal Folly," Gibbes traces the origin of the overweening ambition that Overbury projects onto his daughter, namely, his descent from the paradoxically broken lineage of a Royalist whose estate was taken at the Civil War, one of "the many sufferers in Charles the Second's cause, who were unrequited at the Restoration; but, being a Royalist upon principle, his great grandfather brought up his son in the same political faith with himself, and pointed out the army as his natural and sole inheritance" (I. 17).

Persuasion's love triangle insinuates itself gradually and obliquely, connecting the hero's rival, William Walter Elliot, with Anne's conflict with her dead mother. Though Lady Elliot, unlike Elfrida's mother, had died before the opening of the novel, her unhappy marriage to Sir Walter, Anne's "conceited, silly father," looms over Anne throughout the novel. Its opening pages describe her mother as having "humoured, or softened, or concealed [Sir Walter's] failings, and promoted his real respectability for seventeen years; and though not the very happiest being in the world herself, had found enough in her duties, her friends, and her children, to attach her to life" (6). Austen connects the tepidness of Lady Elliot's life to her role in promoting Sir Walter's "real" respectability, a phrase that ties her to his patrimonial worth. Such an articulation positions Austen at the cusp of modernity characterized by women emerging from the foundation of their identity in patriarchal forms of economy.

When the late Lady Elliot's close friend, Lady Russell, attempts to persuade Anne to marry William Walter, the conflict among Lady Elliot's insipid married life; Anne's nostalgia and longing for her mother; and the prospect of Anne living her mother's life coalesce. Lady Russell, who had persuaded Anne to break off her engagement with the untitled Wentworth before the time of the novel, conjures the image of Anne "taking her mother's place; Lady Russell tells Anne, "You are your mother's self in countenance and disposition; and if I might be allowed to fancy you such as she was, in situation, and name, and home, presiding and blessing in the same spot!" (II. v. 150).

This vision of becoming her mother has a powerful effect on Anne: "For a few moments her imagination and her heart were bewitched. The idea of becoming what her mother had been; of having the precious name of 'Lady Elliot' first revived her herself; of being restored to Kellynch, calling it her home again, her home for ever, was a charm which she could not immediately resist" (II. v. 150–51). The terms "bewitched" and "charm" are those of seduction, ironically suggesting that the marriage plot teases the reader not with the promise of happiness nor of union with the sentimental hero but of the anticlimax of reliving the half-life of one's mother. Yet resist Anne does, trusting her own power of discernment to distrust her cousin, whose cruelty is exposed in the subsequent chapters.

Empowering Anne to reject her mother's acquiescence to a loveless marriage, Austen thus refuses to capitulate to the sentimental novel's trajectory—namely, for Anne to choose to become the next Lady Elliot. Two earlier scenes mark a trajectory to this moment of triumph for Anne. The first is a brief, nonverbal tableau of the love triangle. Anne and Wentworth's path crosses that of a stranger they later discover to be William Walter. Wentworth eyes the stranger whom Wentworth does not realize is Anne's cousin, who is in turn eyeing the attractive young woman whom William Walter does not know to be Anne. Through the stranger's eyes, Wentworth now reappraises Anne as more valuable than he had estimated on his return to Somersetshire after seven years. Wentworth's new regard for Anne through the stranger's perspective threatens the hero/villain binary. Despite the opposition between Wentworth as navy man and William Walter as patrimonial heir to the Elliot estate, both objectify Anne through this wordless appraisal.

The second scene leading to Anne's refusal of Lady Russell's attempted persuasion to marry William Walter occurs just after the above tableau. Louisa Musgrove impetuously refuses Wentworth's assistance as she jumps over a stile and falls, losing consciousness. Except for Anne, everyone—including the young military men—is paralyzed by Louisa's fall. Anne's brother-in-law, Charles, desperately asks Anne, "What, in heaven's name, is to be done next?" The scene even more dramatically reverses the former roles of the heroic Wentworth and the apparently passive Anne: "Captain Wentworth's eyes were also turned towards her" (I. xii. 103). Anne rises to the heroic while Wentworth and the other men, rendered helpless, defer to her. The sequence underscores that, for Anne and Wentworth to be rejoined, they will have to meet each other's gaze. In her revised ending of the novel, Austen represents their nascent intersubjectivity with brilliant irony, Anne's indirect message to Wentworth through her conversation with Harville coalescing with Wentworth's letter to Anne revealing his feelings.[10]

Yet both Gibbes and Austen put their romantic heroes through emotional ordeals to have their worthiness evolve. Thus, before the two novelists allow the culmination of the marriage plot, both threaten to collapse the binary between hero and rival. For Gibbes, this crisis arrives at the pivotal midpoint of *Elfrida*, through Wilmot's growing opportunism and aggression as he vies for Overbury's admiration. Regarding Austen's placing an entitled rival in the heroine's path, Gillian Beer notes the potentially "endogamous" marriage to William Walter Elliot by which Anne would take her mother's place (xx). Though the same potential endogamy can be applied to *Elfrida*, Gibbes complicates this anthropological approach by contextualizing Elfrida's marriage to Ellison across generations, in which entitlement becomes increasingly fluid (xx).[11] Thus, both Wilmot and Ellison have mercenary motives for participating in the British enterprises of the Seven Years' War and empire-building in India. While Ellison fights in America to free himself of debt, Wilmot trades off the two forms of patriarchal aggression—war and colonialism—in his quest to fulfill the paternal ambition of Elfrida's father. Wilmot first participates in the plunder of India to prove himself worthy of Elfrida, then goes to America to track Ellison down, joining the army and fighting as his ploy. Though he carries the wounded Ellison off the battlefield in what looks like a selfless act, Wilmot does so because, after the earlier false report of Ellison's death, he wants to return to Elfrida and Overbury with the dying Ellison as proof of his demise, Ellison himself admitting, "Elfrida will not believe even your report, if my bones are left in a foreign land" (III. 160).

Following the false news of Ellison's death in America, Wilmot's transactional diction when talking to Overbury about his proposed marriage to Elfrida echoes Ellison's exploitation of Elfrida, thereby threatening Wilmot's position as romantic hero. In a tone remarkably arrogant for the sentimental hero whose humility had formerly been praised by Elfrida, Wilmot tells Overbury that Ella, Sr. will be brought "back to her fortune" with his purchase of the Cluwyd estate (III. 12). Wilmot's financial terms to describe his emotional response underscore the contamination of the hero by the villain: "If happiness, as Wilmot would sometimes say, was greatly in arrears to this family, they were now repaid both in interest and principal" (III. 16). Equally troubling is Wilmot's response to Ellison who, having been discovered alive, discovers Wilmot has married his wife. Wilmot tells Ellison cryptically, "You know how I obtained her" (III. 109). Wilmot's objectification of Elfrida here is literal in his reminder to Ellison that Wilmot has won Overbury both through Ellison's having squandered his inheritance and through the wealth Wilmot himself had acquired in India, thereby inserting himself into the patrilineal system through plundered riches.

Like Gibbes's Wilmot, whose eastern riches allow him to buy the ancestral Cluwyd estate that Elfrida's mother was denied when she married Overbury, the navy men in *Persuasion* can rent patriarchal estates, humiliation enough for Anne's baronet father despite the fact that it allows the family to keep Kellynch. Wilmot's new wealth anticipates Austen's representation of the unchanged patriarchal hegemony behind the shift to capitalism from aristocratic entitlement. However, unlike Gibbes's tracing of the potential downfall of Wilmot as romantic hero, Austen complicates Wentworth's heroic position from the start of *Persuasion* through her use of free indirect discourse. Austen's reader learns the background of Anne and Wentworth's broken engagement at the start of the novel from Lady Russell's perspective of Wentworth as "a young man, who had nothing but himself to recommend him, and no hopes of attaining affluence, but in the chances of a most uncertain profession" (I. iv. 27). By the end of *Persuasion*, the third-person narration is filtered through Anne's rejection of Lady Russell's second attempt at persuasion, this time with her desire for Anne to take her mother's place by marrying William Walter. With Anne embracing the prospect of their married albeit "uncertain" life at sea, the narrator wryly returns to Lady Russell's earlier perspective: "[H]ow should a Captain Wentworth and an Anne Elliot, with the advantage of maturity of mind, consciousness of right, and one independent fortune between them, fail of bearing down every opposition .... Captain Wentworth, with five-and-twenty-thousand pounds, and as high in his profession as merit and activity could place him, was no longer nobody" (II. xii. 232).

The uncanny similarities of Gibbes's and Austen's transactional diction merit closer attention, echoes that do not overrule the larger differences between the authors or the shifts between their historical contexts but rather gesture towards overlooked continuities. Both play on double and even triple meanings of words such as "alienation" and "tender" to interweave patriarchy's financial transactions with the existential estrangement of daughters and wives. The two heroines' fathers are preoccupied with "alienation," or the transference of property in which their paternal identity is deeply engrained. For their wives and daughters, however, "alienation" comes to mean estrangement from their families and, more important, themselves due to their fathers' obsession over property and entitlement. Thus, for instance, Gibbes's novel opens with Ella, Sr. referring to the "alienation of their child" when Overbury agrees to give custody of Elfrida to the Cluwyd cousin (I. 18). The two meanings of alienation come together again when Elfrida, tethered in marriage to the dissipated Ellison, becomes "alienated," or depressed, "unconcerned for the future, and uninterested by the present" (II. 55). Soon after, Ellison takes Elfrida to court "to alienate her dower," thereby enabling him "to do as he pleased with his whole estate" (II. 60). In *Persuasion*'s early retrenching scene, Sir Walter refuses to sell his estate, even if "every acre [had] been alienable." Later, Anne's emotional alienation is implicit when Lady Russell attempts to persuade Anne to marry William Walter. Underscoring the double meaning of "alienation," Anne rejects both her parents' perpetuation of patrimony: Sir Walter's wish that the "Kellynch estate should be transmitted whole and entire, as he had received it," and Lady Elliot's "promot[ing] Sir Walter's real respectability" (I. i. 11).

The two novels share a yet more complex play on the word "tender" to underscore the economic exploitation of women by fathers and husbands. Just as Overbury "tenders" his daughter to regain his wife's wealth, Ellison "presse[s Elfrida's] hand [,] proof positive of his tender intentions," Ellison following with another double use of "tender" that suggests the transactional behind his profession of love: "He made a tender of himself in form, and was in form accepted" (I. 231). Both novels suggest an uneasy relationship not between only tenderness as feminine delicacy or vulnerability and tendering as offering payment, but also among these definitions and the third meaning of "tender": a ship's foundering. A pattern of nautical hazards for women extends through the three volumes of *Elfrida*, beginning with the attempted abduction of Ella by boat; echoed a generation later with the same boat that Ellison unmoors and that subsequently capsizes with Elfrida aboard; followed by parents dying in a ferry accident; and culminating in Ellison's creditor kidnapping Elfrida aboard a ship (II. 51–52).

Austen too suggests the fragility of naval life, with England poised between two battles with France that she symbolizes through the foundering of old ships such as Wentworth's *Asp*. Yet Wentworth and Anne ultimately embrace naval life despite its risks. Mrs. Croft, having accompanied her husband on his naval ventures, claims, "Women may be as comfortable on board, as in the best house in England .... I know nothing superior to the accommodations of a man of war" (I. viii. 64). Mrs. Croft thus prepares for Anne's nautical release from the provincial dreariness of her mother's life.

In *Persuasion*'s final paragraph, the three meanings of "tender"—emotional delicacy, economic transaction, and naval 'foundering"—suggest a fragile equipoise:

> Anne was tenderness itself, and she had the full worth of it in Captain Wentworth's affection. His profession was all that could ever make her friends wish that tenderness less; the dread of a future war was all that could dim her sunshine. She gloried in being a sailor's wife, but she must pay the tax of quick alarm for belonging to that profession which is, if possible, more distinguished in its domestic virtues than in its national importance. (II. xii. 236)

With his rejection of the masculinist conquest and violence in which he had participated, Wilmot is reunited with Elfrida at the end of Gibbes's novel. He embraces traditionally feminine tenderness to decry the violence of war and empire, "rending asunder every soft, gentle, and endearing tie ..., leaving widows, orphans, and childless parents to people the world, and to deluge it with tears"; Wilmot now redeems (pun intended) transactional diction as he describes the "agonizing woes, by which our best victories are purchased" (III. 149–50). Yet, unlike the conclusion of *Persuasion*, in which Anne escapes the traditional return of the daughter to the patriarchal estate through marriage to Wentworth, Elfrida returns with Wilmot to reclaim her mother's estate. It is the matriarch, Ella Cluwyd Overbury, who announces that Elfrida and Wilmot are "now at liberty to re-choose each other" (III. 235). While Gibbes affords Elfrida's living mother an opportunity to witness and even partake in the new social order, Lady Elliot dies before she herself can evolve past her duty to soften and conceal her husband's failings or to learn from her daughter, as Ella Overbury does from Elfrida. Anne, therefore, rejects the specter of her dead mother's place as matriarch of Kellynch Hall, embarking on her married life at sea.[12] The uneasy peace offers an unsettling prospect, entwining the economics of eros and the eros of economics.

The two novels thus share three sites of masculinist violence: waging war abroad; empire-building; and violence against women both at home and, especially in the case of *Elfrida*, abroad. Anticlimax allows Gibbes and Austen to problematize the linear trajectory of the sentimental novel that, as a variant of the bildungsroman, leads to the heroine's marriage to the man she loves. Both heroines' crises involve more than their erotic entanglements: their very sense of self is at stake in their need to extricate themselves from their fathers' ambition and their mothers' acquiescence to their husbands.

Female prodigality: the paradox of the matriarchal lineage in the long eighteenth century

In her 1984 *The Proper Lady and the Woman Writer*, Mary Poovey laid a foundation for the critical awareness of Austen's shift towards modernity's interiority in this last novel through its protagonist's "turbulent consciousness" (229). Underscoring the nuanced psychological dimension that comes with Austen's shifting authority from third-person narrator to Anne's subjectivity in Austen's use of free indirect discourse, Poovey notes the shift from *Emma* as the novel's immediate predecessor to *Persuasion*, in which Anne's subjectivity influences narrative authority "punctuated by dramatic changes of locale" (224). As this study has sought to demonstrate, Gibbes anticipates such a notion of modernity through both an increasing attention to interiority, and by representing the conflict between the forces of patrimony, nationalism, and colonialism through the lens of her female protagonists.[13]

With the hindsight of the preceding discussion of the three stages of Gibbes's career and Gibbes's anticipation of Austen, the epigraph to the introduction from Behn's *The Rover*, in which Blunt describes English women as "prodigal whores," takes on a new level of significance. The meaning of "prodigal" regarding gender was shifting during the long eighteenth century. The *OED* gives only one reference to a prodigal woman, a 1796 letter Austen wrote to her sister, Cassandra: "My Father will be so good as to fetch home his prodigal Daughter from Town." In the context of this letter, the possibility of Austen's erotic interest in a young man suggests an undercurrent in her use of the term "prodigal" in projecting her father's perspective of her.[14] Regardless of the biographical implications of

Austen's usage, however, describing herself as prodigal from her father's perspective—albeit with light irony—regarding her being away from home, has important implications for *Persuasion*'s relationship to its predecessors beginning with Behn's seventeenth-century usage. *Persuasion*, like *Elfrida*, deploys its female prodigality nautically, representing the double standard of men and women in embracing a seafaring life, boldly articulated by Mrs. Croft in *Persuasion*.

Whereas Behn's *The Rover* leaves no ambiguity about Blunt, for whom English women are stingy with their sexuality by contrast to the European women, for Austen, writing at the end of the period, sexuality is implicit in such diction. During the late eighteenth century, further layers of female prodigality emerge to suggest another set of double meanings: "freak" and "genius," a double-sided repudiation of female creativity.[15] Not until the twentieth century would the thwarting of female genius be explicitly articulated, with Virginia Woolf imagining the inevitable suicide of "a woman in Shakespeare's day" who "had had Shakespeare's genius" (*A Room of One's Own*). Returning to Austen's seemingly offhand remark in her letter to her sister from the hindsight of Woolf suggests the paternal projection of an entangled deviance between female authorship and sexual promiscuity, Austen's fiction representing Anne's ultimate prodigality in rejecting the inheritance of her mother's staid life in the paternal home.

Gibbes connects her prodigal sons—including Francis Clive, Jr. and the younger Frederic Ellison, the offspring of Ellison and the unnamed woman of *Elfrida*—through their ambivalence in redeeming their fathers' prodigality. She sets such prodigal male homecomings against female wanderers whose prodigality is a stigma. These women are charged with sexual and creative deviance, from the prostitute in *Francis Clive* to Arabella Smith, the eponymous American fugitive who scandalizes the French convent by embodying American wildness, to Elfrida who emerges from self-exile for having committed bigamy to a new agency that promises an end to the generational cycle of patriarchal oppression, to Zoriada, who overcomes the xenophobia and misogyny of the provincial English village through a subjectivity that promises the emergence of a larger global community, a hoped-for redemption, perhaps, of a transnational Anglo-India.

Through her fiction's challenges to assumptions regarding gender, race, and culture, Gibbes thus subverts the commonplaces of prodigality and homecoming. She stands at the center of a lineage begun by Behn, who represents female agency through satire of its masculinist repudiation in the name of female prodigality. That lineage culminates with Austen's prismatic representation of Anne's consciousness navigating a shifting patriarchy during the rise of modernity. Ending in uncertainty, *Persuasion* embraces the belated prodigality of Anne who refuses to return to the patriarchal home.

By connecting women writers previously marginalized and, in turn, segregated from each other through the traditional canonical periodization, scholarship devoted to the long eighteenth century has the potential to do more than realize Woolf's wish for a future of women writers carrying on Behn's legacy. One can see that legacy transmuted by individual women writing in the revolutionary period who actively shaped both their craft and their historical contexts. The connections among women writing from the late seventeenth through the early nineteenth centuries, individually and collectively, lay a foundation for the literary production of an increasingly complex modernity. At the turning point in the long eighteenth century, Gibbes's imagined worlds represent possibilities for women to emerge from oppression with a lineage that ultimately triumphs over their prescribed role in marriage as passive instruments of patriarchy. The evolving agency of Gibbes's female characters shapes their world for the better, both morally and creatively.

Notes

1 Wollstonecraft's literary vocation had begun with her 1788 *Mary, A Novel*, influenced by Rousseau whom she went on in *VRW* to attack for his misogyny, and ended with the incomplete *Maria*. This trajectory suggests a need to refocus scholarly discussion of Wollstonecraft beyond the attempt to limit her voice to that in her polemical prose.

2 It is not surprising, of course, that Austen does not mention Gibbes: as recently as 1990, the authorship of *Elfrida* is listed as "A Lady." See the entry in Judith Pascoe's compilation of women and anonymous writers, 1770–1830 (PR/3991/A6/L317/1786b S-M). Though we know that Austen admired such early novels as Lennox's *The Female Quixote*, to date there is no evidence that she knew Gibbes or her fiction under other authors' names (see Copeland on Austen's reading of Lennox's novel, 198). While *Persuasion* has enjoyed the canonical status that over a century of scholarship has generated, reflecting a variety of literary approaches to the novel's place in the history of the genre, Gibbes has not garnered this level of scrutiny largely because she published anonymously or simply as "A Lady." For the scant details known about Gibbes's life, see Franklin's "Introduction" to his 2019 edition of *Hartly House, Calcutta*. Relevant to *Elfrida*, Franklin notes that Elfrida's husband, Ellison, who "gambled away the family fortune," may have been based on Gibbes's "similar reversal," a "continuing and necessary reality" from 1764 to at least 1789 (xi). Only since about 2014 has archival research revealed "a substantial increase in our knowledge" of Gibbes life (Franklin 2019, xii).

3 Woolf first observed that, in writing *Persuasion*, Austen is "beginning to discover that the world is larger, more mysterious and more romantic than she had supposed" (*Common Reader*).

4 Kornbluh details the permutations of scholarship on free indirect discourse, including the development of the term itself (p. 36, n. 1).
5 *The Widow Ranter* was performed posthumously in 1689. See Visconsi's detailed discussion of the relationship between *Oroonoko*, a precursor to the genre of the novel.
6 As noted in the Introduction to this study, Lauren Berlant coined the phrase "cruel optimism" regarding modernist and postmodern literature. Applying affect theory to this earlier period, with Gibbes at the center, brings into focus the shift from providential thinking as religious to providential thinking as socioeconomic. Also noted in the Introduction, though the female writer emerges albeit peripherally to create a new social order through metanarrative, Ahern rightly voices concern about applying affect theory to eighteenth-century literature, because "such a focus may vacate potentials for political agency beyond mere celebration of immediate ... affective engagement," ultimately "reinforc[ing] rather than "interrogat[ing] a metaphysics of presence that both the writer of sensibility 200 years ago and the affect theorists now would seem to embrace" (281). On precarity, see Hsu: "We like to imagine that our lives follow some kind of trajectory, like the plot of a novel, and that by recognizing its arc we might, in turn, become its author" but instead experience "precariousness."
7 See the Introduction to this study for more on Barclay's discussion of the relationship between the "strict settlement" debate and the history of emotions that extended from 1650 into the eighteenth century.
8 Armstrong's pioneering study of noncanonical poetry suggests that affect becomes the female poet's way of thinking through her relationship to knowledge by using "the customary 'feminine' forms and languages," but turning them "to analytical account" and using them "to think with" (15). Wordsworth wrote of Smith in the 1830s that she was "a lady to whom English verse is under greater obligations than are likely to be either acknowledged or remembered" (*Poetical Works*, 7. 351 qtd. in Zimmerman).
9 Beer's discussion of the "kinship plot struggle" in *Persuasion* regarding the "benefits and hazards of marrying within the kin-group or outside it, endogamy and exogamy" can be extended to Gibbes. The alternative matriarchy in *Elfrida* plays out through the lineage of Ellas threatened by Ellison, who insists on his patriarchial entitlement to Elfrida. While their union does not produce offspring, Elfrida's with Wilmot does. Ellison's proclaimed entitlement is pronounced in his relationship to the next generation: he denigrates his two biological children, born of his "seduction" of a poor woman, as he hypocritically seethes over Wilmot and Elfrida's three children.
10 Though Austen's anticlimax will be seen to subvert the sentimental formula as radically different from that of Gibbes, they are related in important ways. Austen's struggle with the ending of *Persuasion*, familiar to the modern reader through editions that reproduce her revised manuscript of the final two chapters, shows her "dissatisfaction with the reunion of Anne and Wentworth" (Southam xiii). See also Anne Mellor on Austen's admiration of Wollstonecraft;

among Austen's novels that Mellor uses as evidence, *Persuasion* is important to Mellor's argument, with Anne embodying the principles of *VRW* (157).
11 As noted in Chapter 4, by the early nineteenth century, the etymology was shifting away from the literal origin of the term to the meaning extant today of being spoiled.
12 Pun again intended.
13 See Kornbluh regarding the critical debate over FID, noted in the Introduction to this study.
14 See the link to the complete letter in this study's bibliography. According to Baron Brabourne, the early editor of Austen's letters, "The most interesting allusion … is to her 'young Irish friend,' who would seem by the context to have been the late Lord Chief Justice of Ireland, though at the time of writing only 'Mr. Tom Lefroy.' " See also the full *OED* entry for the other definitions of prodigal.
15 According to the *OED*, the term "freak," like "prodigy," had both implications of a monster and one with "exceptional qualities or abilities" in the eighteenth century.

Bibliography

Novels of Phebe Gibbes

The life and adventures of Mr. Francis Clive. In two volumes. ... Vol. 1, printed for E. Watts, J. Potts, A. M'culloh, and J. Williams, M,DCC, LXIV. [1764]. *Eighteenth Century Collections Online*, link.gale.com/apps/doc/CW0109995693/ECCO?u=miami_richter&sid=bookmark-ECCO&xid=03efde4f&pg=1. Accessed March 13, 2023.

The life and adventures of Mr. Francis Clive. In two volumes. ... Vol. 2, printed for E. Watts, J. Potts, A. M'culloh, and J. Williams, MDCC, LXIV. [1764]. *Eighteenth Century Collections Online*, link.gale.com/apps/doc/CW0109995820/ECCO?u=miami_richter&sid=bookmark-ECCO&xid=7c19392c&pg=1. Accessed March 13, 2023.

The history of Lady Louisa Stroud, and the Honourable Miss Caroline Stretton. In two volumes. ... Vol. 1, printed for, and sold by, F. Noble, at his Circulating Library, opposite Grays-Inn-Gate, Holborn: and J. Noble, at his Circulating Library; in St. Martin's Court, near Leicester Square, MDCCLXIV. [1764]. *Eighteenth Century Collections Online*, link.gale.com/apps/doc/CW0111569225/ECCO?u=miami_richter&sid=bookmark-ECCO&xid=e4ed5f84&pg=1. Accessed March 13, 2023.

The history of Lady Louisa Stroud, and the Honourable Miss Caroline Stretton. In two volumes. ... Vol. 2, printed for, and sold by, F. Noble, at his Circulating Library, opposite Grays-Inn-Gate, Holborn: and J. Noble, at his Circulating Library; in St. Martin's Court, near Leicester Square, MDCCLXIV. [1764]. *Eighteenth Century Collections Online*, link.gale.com/apps/doc/CW0111569225/ECCO?u=miami_richter&sid=bookmark-ECCO&xid=e4ed5f84&pg=1. Accessed March 13, 2023.

The History of Miss Pittborough. In a series of letters. By a Lady, 2 vols. (London: Printed for A. Millar, and T. Cadell; and J. Johnson and Co., 1767).

The History of Miss Sommerville, Written by a Lady, 2 vols. (London: Newbery and Carman, 1769).

The fruitless repentance; or, the history of Miss Kitty Le Fever. In two volumes. ... Vol. 1, printed for F. Newbery, the Corner of St. Paul's Church Yard, MDCCLXIX. [1769]. *Eighteenth Century Collections Online*, link.gale.com/apps/doc/CW0116698051/ECCO?u=miami_richter&sid=bookmark-ECCO&xid=a96def55&pg=1. Accessed March 13, 2023.

The fruitless repentance; or, the history of Miss Kitty Le Fever. In two volumes. ... Vol. 2, printed for F. Newbery, the Corner of St. Paul's Church Yard,

MDCCLXIX. [1769]. *Eighteenth Century Collections Online*, link.gale. com/apps/doc/CW0116698266/ECCO?u=miami_richter&sid=bookmark-ECCO&xid=24d85c82&pg=1. Accessed March 14, 2023.

The History of Miss Eliza Musgrove, 2 vols. (London: Johnston, 1769). *Modern Seduction, or Innocence Betrayed; Consisting of Several Histories of the Principal Magdalens*. By the author of Lady Louisa Stroud, 2 vols (London: Printed for F. Noble, near Middle-Row, Holbourne; and J. Noble, in St. Martin's Court, near Leicester-Square, 1777).

Friendship in a nunnery: or, The American fugitive. Containing a full description of the mode of education and living in convent schools, both on the low and high pension. The manners and characters of the nuns; the arts practised on young minds; and their baneful effects on society at large. By a lady. In two volumes. Vol. 1, printed for J. Bew, in Pater-Noster-Row, MDCCLXXVIII. [1778]. *Eighteenth Century Collections Online*, link.gale.com/apps/doc/CB0128271549/ECCO?u= miami_richter&sid=bookmark-ECCO&xid=f5280cc9&pg=1. Accessed March 13, 2023.

Friendship in a nunnery: or, The American fugitive. Containing a full description of the mode of education and living in convent schools, both on the low and high pension. The manners and characters of the nuns; the arts practised on young minds; and their baneful effects on society at large. By a lady. In two volumes. Vol. 2, printed for J. Bew, in Pater-Noster-Row, MDCCLXXVIII. [1778]. *Eighteenth Century Collections Online*, link.gale.com/apps/doc/CB0128271812/ECCO?u= miami_richter&sid=bookmark-ECCO&xid=d0637bf9&pg=1. Accessed March 13, 2023.

Elfrida; or, paternal ambition. A novel. In three volumes. By a lady. ... Vol. 1, printed for J. Johnson, No. 72, St. Paul's Church-Yard, M.DCC.LXXXVI. [1786]. *Eighteenth Century Collections Online*, link.gale.com/apps/doc/ CW0110191740/ECCO?u=miami_richter&sid=bookmark-ECCO&xid= e64df9ce&pg=1. Accessed March 13, 2023.

Elfrida; or, paternal ambition. A novel. In three volumes. By a lady. ... Vol. 2, printed for J. Johnson, No. 72, St. Paul's Church-Yard, M.DCC.LXXXVI. [1786]. *Eighteenth Century Collections Online*, link.gale.com/apps/doc/ CW0110192005/ECCO?u=miami_richter&sid=bookmark-ECCO&xid= bcff4b80&pg=1. Accessed March 13, 2023.

Elfrida; or, paternal ambition. A novel. In three volumes. By a lady. ... Vol. 3, printed for J. Johnson, No. 72, St. Paul's Church-Yard, M.DCC.LXXXVI. [1786]. *Eighteenth Century Collections Online*, link.gale.com/apps/doc/ CW0110192229/ECCO?u=miami_richter&sid=bookmark-ECCO&xid= 6e545aec&pg=1. Accessed March 13, 2023.

Zoriada: or, Village annals. A novel. In three volumes. Vol. 1, printed for T. Axtell, Royal Exchange, MDCCLXXXVI. [1786]. *Eighteenth Century Collections Online*, link.gale.com/apps/doc/CB0130616357/ECCO?u=miami_richter&sid= bookmark-ECCO&xid=b866cede&pg=1. Accessed March 13, 2023.

Zoriada: or, Village annals. A novel. In three volumes. Vol. 2, printed for T. Axtell, Royal Exchange, MDCCLXXXVI. [1786]. *Eighteenth Century Collections Online*, link.gale.com/apps/doc/CB0130616555/ECCO?u=miami_richter&sid= bookmark-ECCO&xid=7cb57467&pg=1. Accessed March 13, 2023.

Zoriada: or, Village annals. A novel. In three volumes. Vol. 3, printed for T. Axtell, Royal Exchange, MDCCLXXXVI. [1786]. *Eighteenth Century Collections*

Online, link.gale.com/apps/doc/CB0130616717/ECCO?u=miami_richter&sid=bookmark-ECCO&xid=23d8d714&pg=1. Accessed March 13, 2023.

The niece; or, the history of Sukey Thornby. A novel. In three volumes. .... By Mrs. P. Gibbes, Author of the History of Lady Louisa Stroud. Vol. 1, printed for F. Noble, At his Circulating Library, No. 324, Holborn, 1788. *Eighteenth Century Collections Online*, link.gale.com/apps/doc/CW0114411825/ECCO?u=miami_richter&sid=bookmark-ECCO&xid=ffc9d119&pg=1. Accessed March 13, 2023.

The niece; or, the history of Sukey Thornby. A novel. In three volumes. .... By Mrs. P. Gibbes, Author of the History of Lady Louisa Stroud. Vol. 2, printed for F. Noble, At his Circulating Library, No. 324, Holborn, 1788. *Eighteenth Century Collections Online*, link.gale.com/apps/doc/CW0114412065/ECCO?u=miami_richter&sid=bookmark-ECCO&xid=c0ab661c&pg=1. Accessed March 13, 2023.

The niece; or, the history of Sukey Thornby. A novel. In three volumes. .... By Mrs. P. Gibbes, Author of the History of Lady Louisa Stroud. Vol. 3, printed for F. Noble, At his Circulating Library, No. 324, Holborn, 1788. *Eighteenth Century Collections Online*, link.gale.com/apps/doc/CW0114412305/ECCO?u=miami_richter&sid=bookmark-ECCO&xid=5eae5abd&pg=1. Accessed March 13, 2023.

Hartly House Calcutta [1789]. Ed. Michael Franklin. Manchester: Manchester University Press, 2019.

Jemima: A Novel (London: Printed for William Lane, at the Minerva-Press, Leadenhall-Street, 1795). Attributed in its printing to "the author of Zoriada: or, Village Annals."

Heaven's Best Gift. A Novel, 4 vols. (London: Printed for the Author, and Sold by W. Miller, n.d. [1798]); also attributed to Mrs. Lucius Phillips.

Gibbes's contemporaries and precursors

Austen, Jane. *Persuasion*. Ed. Gillian Beer. New York: Penguin, 1998.

———. *Letters to Her Sister, Cassandra, 1796*. Ed. Edward Hugessen Knatchbull-Hugessen (1829–93). https://pemberley.com/janeinfo/brablet1.html#letter7. Accessed August 6, 2022.

Baillie, Joanna. *The Tragedy of Count Basil. Plays on the Passions*. Ed. Peter Duthrie. Orchard Park, New York: Broadview, 2001.

Barbauld, Anna. "The Rights of Woman." www.poetryfoundation.org/poems/43615/the-rights-of-women. Accessed March 15, 2023.

Behn, Aphra. *The Rover and Other Plays*. Ed. Jane Spencer. New York: Oxford University Press, 1995, 2008.

———. *The Widow Ranter*. Ed. Adrienne L. Eastwood. Tonawanda, New York: Broadview, 2022.

Blake, William. *Visions of the Daughters of Albion*. In *Blake's Poetry and Designs*. Ed. Mary Lynn Johnson and John E. Grant. 2nd ed. New York: Norton, 2008, 1979, pp. 56–65.

De Pizan, Christine. *The Book of the City of Ladies*. Trans. Renate Blumenfeld-Kosinski and Kevin Brownlee. New York: Norton, 1997, pp. 119–55.

Fay, Eliza. *Original Letters from India: 1779–1815*. Ed. E.M. Forster. New York: Harcourt, Brace and Co., 1925. Print.

Bibliography 227

Godwin, William. *Memoirs of the Author of* A Vindication of the Rights of Woman. Orchard Park, New York: Broadview, 2001.

Haywood, Eliza. *Fantomina, or Love in a Maze*. https://digital.library.upenn.edu/women/haywood/fantomina/fantomina.html. Accessed June 7, 2021.

Jonson, Ben. *Every Man in his Humor*. www.gutenberg.org/files/5333/5333-h/5333-h.htm. Accessed June 18, 2021.

Lennox, Charlotte. *The female Quixote: or, the adventures of Arabella. In two volumes*. ... Vol. 1, printed for J. Smith, at the Philosophers-Heads on the Blind-Quay, MDCCLII. [1752]. *Eighteenth Century Collections Online*, link.gale.com/apps/doc/CW0102845247/ECCO?u=miami_richter&sid=bookmark-ECCO&xid=f0c44878&pg=1. Accessed March 13, 2023.

Macaulay, Thomas. "Minute on Indian Education." *Macaulay: Prose and Poetry*. Ed. G.M. Young. Cambridge: Harvard University Press, 1967, pp. 719–30. Print.

Mason, William. *Elfrida, a dramatic poem. Written on the model of the ancient Greek tragedy. By Mr. Mason*. 3rd ed., printed for J. and P. Knapton, in Ludgate-Street, MDCCLII. [1752]. *Eighteenth Century Collections Online*, link.gale.com/apps/doc/CW0110375219/ECCO?u=miami_richter&sid=bookmark-ECCO&xid=a1c112b0&pg=22. Accessed March 13, 2023.

Philips, Katherine. "A Married State." www.poetrynook.com/poem/married-state. Accessed June 8, 2021.

Shakespeare, William. *Othello*. https://shakespeare.folger.edu/downloads/pdf/othello_PDF_FolgerShakespeare.pdf. Accessed April 14, 2021.

Shelley, Mary. *Frankenstein*. Ed. J. Paul Hunter. New York: Norton, 2012.

Sheridan, Frances Chamberlaine. Memoirs *of Miss Sidney Bidulph, extracted from her own journal, and now first published. In three volumes*. ... Vols. 1–3, printed for R. and J. Dodsley, in Pall-Mall, M.DCC.I.XI. [1761]. *Eighteenth Century Collections Online*, link.gale.com/apps/doc/CW0101744011/ECCO?u=miami_richter&sid=bookmark-ECCO&xid=33b5abb2&pg=1. Accessed December 12, 2022.

———. *Conclusion of the memoirs of Miss Sidney Bidulph, As prepared for the press by the late editor of the former part. Volume IV*. Vol. 5, printed for J. Dodsley, in Pall-mall, MDCCLXVII. [1767]. *Eighteenth Century Collections Online*, link.gale.com/apps/doc/CB0129193007/ECCO?u=miami_richter&sid=bookmark-ECCO&xid=0823b67e&pg=1. Accessed December 12, 2022.

Shirley, James. *The Gamester*. https://quod.lib.umich.edu/cgi/t/text/text-idx?c=eebo;idno=A12137.0001.001. Accessed September 30, 2022.

Smith, Charlotte. "Thirty-eight." In *The Poems of Charlotte Smith*. Ed. Stuart Curran. New York: Oxford University Press, 1993, p. 92.

Smollet, Tobias. *Humphrey Clinker*. Ed. Arthur Machen. New York: Modern Library, 1929. https://babel.hathitrust.org/cgi/pt?id=pst.000027627129&view=1up&seq=6. Accessed December 12, 2022.

Spenser, Edmund. *The Faerie Queene*. Ed. Thomas P. Roche, Jr. New Haven: Yale University Press, 1978.

Williams, Helen Maria. *Letters from France: containing a great variety of interesting and original information concerning the most important events that have lately occurred in that country, and particularly respecting the campaign of 1792*. ... Vol. 3, printed for G.G. and J. Robinson, Paternoster-Row, M.DCC.XCIII. [1793]. *Eighteenth Century Collections Online*, link.gale.com/apps/doc/CW0100840899/ECCO?u=miami_richter&sid=bookmark-ECCO&xid=c508c012&pg=1. Accessed March 13, 2023.

Wollstonecraft, Mary. *A Vindication of the Rights of Woman.* Ed. Deidre Shauna Lynch. 3rd ed. New York: Norton, 2009.
———. *Maria or the Wrongs of Woman.* www.gutenberg.org/cache/epub/134/pg134-images.html. Accessed May 24, 2023.
———. *Mary, A Fiction.* www.gutenberg.org/cache/epub/16357/pg16357-images.html. Accessed May 24, 2023.
Wordsworth, William. "Preface" to *Lyrical Ballads.* In *Wordsworth's Poetry and Prose.* Ed. Nicholas Halmi. New York: Norton, 2014, pp. 75–96.

Criticism and historical references

Ahern, Stephen. "Nothing More Than Feelings?: Affect Theory Reads the Age of Sensibility." *The Eighteenth Century*, vol. 58, no. 3, 2017, pp. 281–95. JSTOR, www.jstor.org/stable/90013399. Accessed June 11, 2022.
Ancient Origins. "Armillary Spheres: Following Celestial Objects in the Ancient World." www.ancient-origins.net/artifacts-ancient-technology/armillary-spheres-following-celestial-objects-ancient-world-004025. Accessed July 27, 2022.
Anderson, Benedict. *Imagined Communities: Reflections on the Origin and Spread of Nationalism.* New York: Verso, 1983, 1991. Print.
Anthony, Frank. *Britain's Betrayal in India: The Story of the Anglo-Indian Community.* Bombay: Allied Publishers, 1969. Print.
Armstrong, Isobel. "The Gush of the Feminine: How Can We Read Women's Poetry of the Romantic Period?" In *Romantic Women Writers: Voices and Countervoices.* Ed. Paula Feldman and Theresa M. Kelley. Lebanon, New Hampshire: University Press of New England, 1995, pp. 14–32.
Ballaster, Ros. "Fakiry: The Oriental Tale." *Great Writers Inspire.* Licensed as Creative Commons BY-NC-SA (2.0 UK). http://writersinspire.org/content/fakiry-oriental-tale. Accessed July 27, 2022.
Ballhatchet, Kenneth. *Race, Sex and Class under the Raj: Imperial Attitudes and Policies and Their Critics, 1793–1905.* New York: St. Martin's Press, 1980. Print.
Barclay, Katie. "Natural Affection, the Patriarchal Family and the 'Strict Settlement' Debate: A Response from the History of Emotions." *The Eighteenth Century*, vol. 58, no. 3, 2017, pp. 309–20. JSTOR, www.jstor.org/stable/90013401. Accessed June 11, 2022.
Basham, A.L. "Sophia and the 'Bramin.'" *East India Company Studies.* Ed. Kenneth Ballhatchet and John Harrison. Hong Kong: Asian Research Service, 1986, pp. 13–30.
Batchelor, Jennie. *Women's Work: Labour, Gender, Authorship, 1750–1830.* Manchester: Manchester University Press, 2010.
——— and Cora Kaplan. "Introduction." *British Women's Writing in the Long Eighteenth Century: Authorship, Politics and History.* New York: Palgrave, 2005, pp. 1–16.
Berkeley, Richard. *Coleridge and the Crisis of Reason.* New York: Palgrave Macmillan, 2007.
Berlant, Lauren, and Lauren Gail Berlant. *Cruel Optimism.* Durham, NC: Duke University Press, 2011. ProQuest Ebook Central. http://ebookcentral.proquest.com/lib/miami/detail.action?docID=1172993. Accessed June 20, 2022.
Binhammer, Katherine. *Downward Mobility: The Forms of Capital and the Sentimental Novel.* Baltimore, MD: Johns Hopkins University Press, 2020.

Blain, Virginia, Patricia Clements, and Isobel Grundy, eds. *The Feminist Companion to Literature in English: Women Writers from the Middle Ages to the Present.* London: Batsford, 1990.

Cayton, Andrew R.L. "The Authority of the Imagination in an Age of Wonder." *Journal of the Early Republic*, vol. 33, no. 1, 2013, pp. 1–27. https://doi.org/10.1353/jer.2013.0009. Accessed June 19, 2022.

Clarke, Norma. *Ambitious Heights: Writing, Friendship, Love—The Jewsbury Sisters, Felicia Hemans, and Jane Carlyle.* New York: Routledge, 1990.

Clemit, Pamela and Gina Luria Walker. *Memoirs of the Author of A Vindication of the Rights of Woman. By William Godwin.* Orchard Park, New York: Broadview, 2001.

Clough, Monica. "Introduction to the 1989 Edition" to *Hartly House Calcutta: A Novel of the Days of Warren Hastings.* (Anon.) Winchester, MA: Pluto Press, 1989, pp. vii–xix.

Copeland, Edward. *Women Writing About Money: Women's Fiction in England, 1790–1820.* New York: Cambridge University Press, 1995.

Crane, Ralph J. and Radhika Mohanram. *Imperialism as Diaspora: Race, Sexuality, and History in Anglo-India.* Liverpool: Liverpool University Press, 2013.

Curran, Stuart. "The I Altered." *Romanticism and Feminism.* Ed. Anne Mellor. Bloomington: Indiana University Press, 1988, pp. 185–207. Print.

Curran, Stuart, ed. *The Poems of Charlotte Smith.* New York: Oxford University Press, 1993.

Dale, Amelia. *The Printed Reader: Gender, Quixotism, and Textual Bodies in Eighteenth-Century Britain.* Lewisburg, PA: Bucknell University Press, 2019.

Duthrie, Peter. "Introduction." *Plays on the Passions.* By Joanna Baillie. Ed. P. Duthrie. Orchard Park, New York: Broadview, 2001, pp. 11–57. Print.

Dziennik, Matthew P. "Scotland and the American Revolution." *Journal of the American Revolution.* October 14, 2013. https://allthingsliberty.com/2013/10/scotland-american-revolution/. Accessed April 13, 2021.

Eastwood, Adrienne, ed. "Introduction." *The Widow Ranter.* Tonawanda, New York: Broadview, 2022, pp. 7–14.

Farago, Jason. "The Myth of North America in One Painting." *New York Times*, November 25, 2020. www.nytimes.com/interactive/2020/11/25/arts/benjamin-west-general-wolfe.html?fbclid=IwAR36WxaHDnZMzAK5nITGdY8UgfznppwUVlHAoBaJ9kEiPXrbceq9JKsYc80. Accessed April 9, 2021.

Foster, William. "Who Wrote *Hartly House*?" *Bengal Past and Present*, vol. 15, pt. 2, no. 30, 1917, pp. 28–29.

Franklin, Michael. "Radically Feminizing India: Phebe Gibbes's *Hartly House, Calcutta* (1789) and Sydney Owenson's *The Missionary: An Indian Tale* (1811)." *Romantic Representations of British India.* Ed. Michael Franklin. New York: Routledge, 2006, pp. 154–79.

———. "Introduction." *Hartly House, Calcutta.* Manchester: Manchester University Press, 2019, pp. xi–lvi.

Freeman, Kathryn S. *British Women Writers and the Asiatic Society, 1785–1835: Re-orienting Anglo-India.* New York: Routledge, 2014.

———. *A Guide to the Cosmology of William Blake.* New York: Routledge, 2017.

———. "'A little earthly idol to contract your ideas': Global Hermeneutics in Phebe Gibbes's *Zoriada, or, Village Annals* (1786)." *Romantic Automata: Exhibitions, Figures, Organisms.* Ed. Christopher Clason and Michael Demson. Lewisburg, PA: Bucknell University Press, 2020, pp. 146–64.

———. *Rethinking the Romantic Era: Androgynous Subjectivity and the Recreative in the Writings of Mary Robinson, Samuel Taylor Coleridge, and Mary Shelley*. New York: Bloomsbury, 2021.
Freud, Sigmund. *The Psychopathology of Everyday Life*. www.stmarys-ca.edu/sites/default/files/attachments/files/Psychopathology.pdf. Accessed June 14, 2021.
"Front Matter." *The Eighteenth Century*, vol. 58, no. 3, 2017. JSTOR, www.jstor.org/stable/90013397. Accessed June 11, 2022.
Gallagher, Catherine. "Who Was That Masked Woman? The Prostitute and the Playwright in the Comedies of Aphra Behn." *Rereading Aphra Behn: History, Theory, and Criticism*. Ed. Heidi Hutner. Charlottesville: University Press of Virginia, 1993, pp. 65–85.
Gravil, Richard. "Helen Maria Williams: Wordsworth's Revolutionary 'Anima.'" *The Wordsworth Circle*, vol. 40, no. 1, 2009, pp. 55–64. JSTOR, www.jstor.org/stable/24045265. Accessed March 14, 2023.
Green, Katherina Sobba. *The Courtship Novel 1740–1820: A Feminized Genre*. Lexington: University Press of Kentucky, 1998.
Grundy, Isobel. "'the barbarous character we give them': White Women Travelers Report on Other Races." *Studies in English Eighteenth Century Culture*, vol. 22, 1992, pp. 73–86.
———. "(Re)discovering Women's Texts." *Women in Literature in Britain, 1700–1800*. Ed. Vivien Jones. Cambridge: Cambridge University Press, 2000, pp. 179–96.
Grundy, Isobel and Susan Wiseman, eds. *Women, Writing, History 1640–1740*. London: Batsford, 1992.
Gunn, Daniel P. "Free Indirect Discourse." *Oxford Research Encyclopedias*. June 25, 2019. https://doi.org/10.1093/acrefore/9780190201098.013.1020. Accessed July 11, 2022.
Haydon, Colin. *Anti-Catholicism in Eighteenth-Century England, c. 1714–1780: A Political and Social Study*. New York: Manchester University Press, 1993.
Hernandez, Alex. *The Making of British Bourgeois Tragedy*. New York: Oxford University Press, 2019.
Hsu, Hua. "That Feeling When." *The New Yorker*, vol. 95, no. 5, March 25, 2019, p. 61. Gale Academic OneFile, link.gale.com/apps/doc/A581882277/AONE?u=miami_richter&sid=bookmark-AONE&xid=badf20c2. Accessed June 20, 2022.
Hultquist, Aleksondra. "Introductory Essay." *Emotion, Affect, and the Eighteenth Century. The Eighteenth Century*, vol. 58, no. 3, Fall 2017, pp. 273–80. JSTOR, www.jstor.org/stable/10.2307/90013398. Accessed March 14, 2023.
Hutner, Heidi. *Rereading Aphra Behn: History, Theory, and Criticism*. Charlottesville: University Press of Virginia, 1993. Print.
"James Wolfe." *Encyclopedia Britannica*, January 1, 2021. www.britannica.com/biography/James-Wolfe. Accessed April 9, 2021.
Kelsall, Malcolm. "'Once did she hold the gorgeous East in fee': Byron's Venice and Oriental Empire." *Romanticism and Colonialism*. Ed. Tim Fulford and Peter Kitson. Cambridge: Cambridge University Press, 2009, pp. 243–60.
Kornbluh, Anna. "Freeing Impersonality: The Objective Subject in Psychoanalysis and *Sense and Sensibility*." *Knots*. Chapter 2. Ed. Anna Kornbluh and Jean-Michel Rabaté. New York: Routledge, 2020, pp. 35–54.
Lee, Christina. "The Legend of the Christian Arab Madonna in Cervantes' *Don Quijote*." *Revista Canadiense de Estudios Hispanicos*, vol. 32, no. 1, Autumn 2007, pp. 105–21.

Litz, A. Walton. *Jane Austen: A Study of her Artistic Development*. New York: Oxford University Press, 1965.

London, April. *Women and Propriety in the Eighteenth-Century English Novel*. Cambridge: Cambridge University Press, 1999.

"Lute." *Encyclopedia Britannica*. www.britannica.com/art/lute. Accessed July 27, 2022.

Marsden, Jean I. "Affect and the Problem of Theater." *The Eighteenth Century*, vol. 58, no. 3, 2017, pp. 297–307. *JSTOR*, www.jstor.org/stable/90013400. Accessed June 11, 2022.

Marx, Karl. *The Eighteenth Brumaire of Louis Bonaparte*. 1852. www.marxists.org/archive/marx/works/1852/18th-brumaire/ch01.htm. Accessed March 20, 2023.

McKeon, Michael. *The Origins of the English Novel, 1600–1740*. Baltimore: Johns Hopkins University Press, 1987, 2002.

Medoff, Jeslyn. "The Daughters of Behn and the Problem of Reputation." *Women, Writing, History 1640–1740*. Ed. Isobel Grundy and Susan Wiseman. London: Batsford, 1992, pp. 33–54.

Mellor, Anne K. "Mary Wollstonecraft's *A Vindication of the Rights of Woman* and the Women Writers of Her Day." *The Cambridge Companion to Mary Wollstonecraft*. Ed. Claudia L. Johnson. Cambridge: Cambridge University Press, 2002, pp. 141–59. doi:10.1017/CCOL0521783437.009.

Messenger, Ann. *His and Hers, Essays in Restoration and Eighteenth-Century Literature*. Lexington: University Press of Kentucky, 1986.

Molesworth, Jesse. *Chance and the Eighteenth-Century Novel: Realism, Probability, Magic*. New York: Cambridge University Press, 2010.

"Niobe." *Encyclopedia Britannica*, May 15, 2020. www.britannica.com/topic/Niobe-Greek-mythology. Accessed April 13, 2021.

Nobus, Dany. "The Sculptural Iconography of Feminine Jouissance: Lacan's Reading of Bernini's *Saint Teresa in Ecstasy*." *The Comparatist*, vol. 39, October 2015, pp. 22–46.

Norton, Elizabeth. "Elfrida: Mother, Murderer and England's First Crowned Queen." www.historyanswers.co.uk/kings-queens/elfrida-mother-murderer-and-englands-first-crowned-queen/. Accessed September 15, 2024.

Nussbaum, Felicity A. *Torrid Zones: Maternity, Sexuality, and Empire in Eighteenth-Century English Narratives*. Baltimore and London: Johns Hopkins University Press, 1996.

O'Connell, Lisa. *The Origins of the English Marriage Plot: Literature, Politics and Religion in the Eighteenth Century*. New York: Cambridge University Press, 2019.

Owen, Kate Novotny. "Dramatic Entertainments of a Mixt Kind: The Form of Mixture in Early English Pantomime." *Eighteenth-Century Studies*, vol. 48, no. 4, Summer 2014, pp. 503–20. *JSTOR*, www.jstor.org/stable/24690308. Accessed May 26, 2022.

Pacheco, Anita. "Rape and the Female Subject in Aphra Behn's *The Rover*. *ELH*, vol. 65, 1998, pp. 323–45.

Parkin, Chris. "Animate It: The Armillary Sphere." Oxford University Museum of the History of Science. January 8, 2016. www.youtube.com/watch?v=AaWuJHQL-bQ. Accessed July 27, 2022.

Pearson, Jacqueline. "The History of *The History of the Nun*." *Rereading Aphra Behn: History, Theory, and Criticism*. Ed. Heidi Hutner. Charlottesville: University Press of Virginia, 1993, pp. 234–52. Print.

Poe, Edgar Allan. "The Imp of the Perverse." *The Raven: Tales and Poems*. New York: Penguin, 2013, pp. 233–39.

Poovey, Mary. *The Proper Lady and the Woman Writer*. Chicago: University of Chicago Press, 1984.

Potter, Tiffany. "Introduction." *Oroonoko*. Ed. Tiffany Potter. Tonawanda, New York: Broadview, 2020, pp. 7–10.

Pratt, Mary Louise. *Imperial Eyes: Travel Writing and Transculturation*. London: Routledge, 1992.

Rajan, Balachandra. "Feminizing the Feminine: Early Women Writers on India." *Romanticism, Race and Imperial Culture, 1780–1834*. Ed. Sonia Hofkosh and Alan Richardson. Bloomington and Indianapolis: Indiana University Press, 1996, pp. 49–72.

Raven, James. "A Wheel of Fickle Fortune: Britain's Last State Lottery." *The Independent*. February 18, 1994.

Reiman, Donald H., Neil Fraistat, and Nora Crook, eds. *The Complete Poetry of Percy Bysshe Shelley*. Vol. II. Baltimore: Johns Hopkins University Press, 2004.

Reynolds, Nicole. "Phebe Gibbes, Edmund Burke, and the Trials of Empire." *Eighteenth-Century Fiction*, vol. 20, no. 2, 2008, pp. 151–76.

Ross, Marlon. "Romantic Quest and Conquest." *Romanticism and Feminism*. Ed. Ann Mellor. Bloomington: Indiana University Press, 1988, pp. 26–51.

Rudd, Andrew. *Sympathy and India in British Literature, 1770–1830*. New York: Palgrave Macmillan, 2011.

Scott, Hamish. "The Seven Years War and Europe's 'Ancien Régime.'" *War in History*, vol. 18, no. 4, 2011, pp. 419–55. JSTOR, www.jstor.org/stable/26098283. Accessed July 8, 2022.

Sharpe, Jenny. *Allegories of Empire: The Figure of Woman in the Colonial Text*. Minneapolis: University of Minnesota Press, 1993.

Sim, Stuart. *The Eighteenth-Century Novel and Contemporary Social Issues: An Introduction*. Edinburgh: Edinburgh University Press, 2008. *ProQuest Ebook Central*. https://ebookcentral.proquest.com/lib/miami/detail.action?docID=343580. Accessed June 19, 2022.

Spencer, Jane. *Aphra Behn's Afterlife*. New York: Oxford University Press, 2000.

Spencer, Jane, ed. "Introduction." *The Rover and Other Plays*. Aphra Behn. New York: Oxford University Press, 1995, 2008.

Teltscher, Kate. *India Inscribed: European and British Writing on India 1600–1800*. Delhi: Oxford University Press, 1995.

Temple, Kathryn. "Heart of Agitation: Mary Wollstonecraft, Emotion, and Legal Subjectivity." *The Eighteenth Century*, vol. 58, no. 3, 2017, pp. 371–82. JSTOR, www.jstor.org/stable/90013405. Accessed June 11, 2022.

Todd, Janet. "Aphra Behn—Whom Mary Wollstonecraft Did Not Read." *The Wordsworth Circle*, vol. 26, no. 3, 1995, pp. 152–58. JSTOR, www.jstor.org/stable/24044554. Accessed June 14, 2022.

———. *Sensibility: An Introduction*. New York: Methuen, 1986.

——— and Marilyn Butler. *The Works of Mary Wollstonecraft*. New York: New York University Press, 1989.

Tolstoy, Leo. *Anna Karenina*. Trans. Constance Garnett. Project Gutenberg. www.gutenberg.org/files/1399/1399-h/1399-h.htm. Accessed June 20, 2022.

Turner, Cheryl. *Living by the Pen: Women Writers in the Eighteenth Century*. London: Routledge, 1992.

Visconsi, Elliott. "A Degenerate Race: English Barbarism in Aphra Behn's 'Oroonoko' and 'The Widow Ranter.'" *ELH*, vol. 69, no. 3, 2002, pp. 673–701. JSTOR, www.jstor.org/stable/30032038. Accessed August 16, 2022.

Whitehead, James. *Madness and the Romantic Poet: A Critical History*. Oxford, 2017; online edn, Oxford Academic, July 20, 2017. https://doi.org/10.1093/oso/9780198733706.001.0001. Accessed April 1, 2023.

Wolfson, Susan. "'Domestic Affections' and 'the spear of Minerva': Felicia Hemans and the Dilemma of Gender." *Re-visioning Romanticism: British Women Writers, 1776–1837*. Ed. Carol Shiner Wilson and Joel Haefner. Philadelphia: University of Pennsylvania Press, 1995, pp. 128–66.

Woolf, Virginia. *The Common Reader*. http://gutenberg.net.au/ebooks03/0300031h.html#C11. Accessed June 7, 2023.

———. *A Room of One's Own*. https://gutenberg.net.au/ebooks02/0200791h.html. Accessed June 14, 2022.

Zimmerman, Sarah M. "Smith [née Turner], Charlotte." *Oxford DNB*. www.oxforddnb.com/display/10.1093/ref:odnb/9780198614128.001.0001/odnb-9780198614128-e-25790;jsessionid=9E0F72ECEC098AF2D2CA49CD6F91ED5F. Accessed June 14, 2023.

Index

abortifacient 24, 62, 89
adultery 12, 24, 33, 40, 43, 48, 193
affect theory 6, 7, 19nn.22, 23, 71n.47, 210, 222n.6
alienation (multiple meanings) 15, 156, 157, 170, 171, 191, 197, 203n.6, 207n.41, 217
Anglo-India 10, 14, 73, 79, 80, 99, 115, 118, 128, 132, 137, 143, 151–52, 200, 220
 see also Orientalism
anticlimax 15, 27, 107, 202, 211, 213, 214, 219, 222n.10
Austen, Jane 2, 8, 13, 15, 128, 182, 207
 Persuasion 209–23
authorial voice 2, 7, 10–12, 31, 32, 45, 64, 80, 85, 88, 135, 140, 144, 165, 173, 186, 209, 210
 see also free indirect discourse; metanarrative; providence; storytelling

Barbauld, Anna 17n.14
Barclay, Katie 3, 6, 66n.8, 210, 222n.7
Behn, Aphra 1–8, 12–13, 21, 32, 45, 54, 58, 208–10, 221
 Oroonoko 138
 The Forced Marriage 7
 The Lucky Chance 15, 21, 56
 The Rover 219–20
 The Widow Ranter 210
Beer, Gillian 215, 222n.9
Berlant, Lauren 19n.22, 222n.6
bigamy 10, 15, 161, 164, 168, 188, 213, 220

binaries 7, 50, 116–20, 175, 185, 199
 gender 51, 53–54, 58, 76, 90, 116
 racial 138
 sociopolitical 73
Blake, William 17–18n.15, 205n.19, 206n.35, 116, 119, 133
British imperialism 9, 14, 73, 136–37, 146, 148, 180, 189

Catholicism 76, 82, 87
Cervantes, Miguel 42, 119
Cibber, Colley 64, 71n.48, 131
colonialism, British 7, 12, 14–15, 55, 73, 78–79, 99, 115, 125, 131, 134–36, 146–47, 154, 216, 219
comedy 2, 13, 15, 23, 53, 55, 58, 64, 132
 see also drama
contamination 102, 165–67, 174–75, 216
 see also disease
cross-dressing 2, 10, 13, 23, 34, 44, 51–54, 58–59, 87, 103, 186, 209
Curran, Stuart 6, 210

disease 80–82, 91, 104, 146–47, 155, 165–66, 169, 192
drama 2–3, 8–9, 12, 46, 53, 122, 162–63, 165, 194, 201–02, 215, 219
 metadrama and 64, 120, 210
 tragicomedy 31, 202, 210

Index

East India Company 14, 125, 132, 134, 136, 137, 140, 142, 148, 175, 181
education, women's 5, 9, 12–13, 21, 25, 30–31, 42, 47, 82, 97, 117, 131, 139, 162, 165, 174
elopement, eloping 36–37, 131, 185, 211
   multiple meanings in *American Fugitive* 91, 93, 95, 101–02
emotionalism, emotion 6, 25, 53, 122, 135–37, 144, 163, 169, 177, 182, 188, 191, 215–18
   Arabella as Niobe in *American Fugitive* 74, 76, 86, 97, 100, 104, 108
   see also affect theory
entitlement 9, 14–15, 101, 108, 124, 137, 155, 160–61, 163–64, 187, 189, 199, 215–17
epistolary novel 37, 72, 74, 83, 88, 101
   see also genre; Gibbes, *American Fugitive*

Franklin, Michael 133, 143–44
free indirect discourse 2, 11, 40, 48, 128, 179, 181–82, 185, 210, 216, 219
   see also authorial voice; narrative voice
French Revolution 14, 74, 105
Freud, Sigmund 12
   see also parapraxis
"frolic" [euphemism, sexual aggression] 22, 29–30, 39–40, 45–46, 56
   see also seduction

Gallagher, Catherine 4–5
generation 4, 8, 14, 24, 40, 65, 118, 128, 154–56, 158–65, 167, 176, 189, 194, 196, 199–202, 210–13, 215, 218, 220
   see also lineage; patriarchy; matriarchal
genre 8, 13, 21, 37, 115–16, 118, 210–11
Gibbes, Phebe, novels
   The Adventures of Francis Clive 9–13, 21–71, 72–74, 79, 81, 87, 89, 97, 101, 103, 115, 118, 186, 220
   The American Fugitive: or, Friendship in a Nunnery (Friendship in a Nunnery: or, the American Fugitive) 10, 13, 23, 60, 72–113, 115–18, 147, 220
   Elfrida; or, Paternal Ambition 13–15, 148, 154–207, 209–23
   Hartly House, Calcutta: A Novel of the Days of Warren Hastings 2, 10, 14, 116, 129, 133–51
   Lady Louisa Stroud and Caroline Stretton 73, 93
   Zoriada, or, Village Annals 10, 14, 60, 115–33, 137, 147–48, 155, 188, 209, 220
globalism 14, 116, 208–23
Goethe, Johannes Wolfgang von 167

Hartley, David 135
Haywood, Eliza 2, 8–9, 12, 21, 23, 32, 208
hermeneutics 32, 95, 116, 119, 122–25, 128–29, 133, 155, 163, 178, 193
Hindu, Hinduism 14, 116, 134, 145–47
Homer 9, 23, 91, 188
homosocial 29, 74, 76, 91–92
homoerotic, homoeroticism 75, 78, 80–81, 83–84, 88

interiority 11, 15, 182, 209, 211, 219
Islam 119
   Muslim 116, 118, 132
irony, authorial 13, 24–25, 32–34, 37, 39, 41–47, 51–56, 64, 76, 89, 99, 104, 108, 125–26, 140, 155–60, 164, 177, 185–93, 197, 215, 220
   satire and 11, 23, 54, 123, 209–10

Lennox, Charlotte 10–12, 42, 174, 208
lineage 2, 4, 8, 14, 136, 158–65, 191–200, 214, 219–21
   see also matriarchy; patriarchy

long eighteenth century 1–4, 6–8, 32, 58, 91, 116, 135–36, 144, 155, 208–11, 213, 219–21
  see also periodization

madness 49, 86, 98, 199
marriage plot 13, 22, 37–39, 49–51, 55, 59–60, 72–77, 83, 86, 96, 130–36, 141–48, 155–58, 160, 164, 170, 176, 179, 188, 190, 214
  see also sentimental novel
matriarchy 1, 7–10, 79, 155, 158–59, 165, 182, 189–91, 219
metanarrative 11–12, 21–22, 36–37, 40, 45, 50–51, 56, 55, 65, 79, 85, 88, 115, 118–19, 122–27, 136, 161–68, 176, 192–93, 211
  see also irony, authorial
miscegenation 133–43
modernity 2, 6, 8–9, 11–12, 208–21
  see also periodization

narrative voice 2–3, 11, 108, 128, 134, 186, 193, 209–10
  see also irony, authorial; free indirect discourse; subjectivity

Orientalism 135, 147

parapraxis, the perverse 11, 20, 32, 36, 48, 142–43
  see also Freud, Sigmund; psychology
patriarchy 4–10, 13–15, 76, 86, 99–101, 116, 148, 154, 157, 166, 177–79, 188, 196, 220–21
patrimony 6–7, 62–63, 155, 182, 189, 191, 199, 210–12, 217–19
periodization 1, 3, 208–09, 221
  see also long eighteenth century; Romanticism
prodigal 1, 3, 25, 55, 63, 101, 194, 220
prostitute 9–12, 22–23, 30–35, 37–39, 45, 47, 49–52, 56, 58, 72–87, 115, 186, 220
Protestantism 76, 82, 86

providence 12, 28, 31, 41, 60, 63, 80, 88, 92, 98, 103, 105, 146–47, 161, 185, 193
  see also authorial voice
psychology 11–12, 47, 135–36, 142
  see also Freud, Sigmund; Hartley, David; madness; subconscious

race 116, 137–38, 141–42, 146, 220
rape 6, 12, 22, 29, 36, 38, 40, 43, 45, 61, 65, 102, 124–25, 134, 146, 178, 183–84
religion 7, 81–85, 103, 116, 146, 197
  see also Catholicism; Hinduism; Islam, Muslim; Protestantism
revolution 3, 5, 8, 12, 72–110
  American Revolution 13, 73–74, 79, 92
  French Revolution 14, 74, 105
  Haitian Uprising 143
  see also Seven Years' War (French and Indian War)
Romanticism 2, 9, 11, 15, 86, 132, 201, 209
  canonical, noncanonical writers 1–2, 9, 15, 91, 116, 136, 162, 192, 209, 211, 221

satire 3, 6, 8–11, 13, 21–23, 32, 44, 54, 60, 73, 80, 87, 103, 120, 123, 137, 174, 209–10, 213
seduction [euphemism, sexual aggression] 6, 21, 28, 36, 41, 81, 154–57, 172, 178, 183–84, 214
  see also "frolic"
sentimental novel 5–6, 9–10, 21, 23, 25, 32, 50, 90–92, 105, 108, 117, 137, 145–48, 154, 156, 161–62, 175, 182, 185, 193, 198–99, 209–11, 215
  see also marriage plot
Seven Years' War 2, 8, 12–13, 72–73, 77, 79, 133, 210, 216
Shakespeare, William 87, 88, 96, 131, 135, 220
  Othello 90, 94, 123, 138–42, 146–47, 158
  Romeo and Juliet 93–98

Spencer, Jane 1, 3–4
Spenser, Edmund 87–88
storytelling 21–22, 30–32, 42, 45, 61, 64, 193–95, 202
  see also authorial voice, narrative
subconscious 99, 100, 107, 169
subjectivity, female 4, 7, 9, 13, 15, 23, 54, 73, 75, 84, 90, 107, 115–33, 135–42, 154–55, 165, 176, 213, 220
  see also free indirect discourse; narrative voice
suicide 97, 103, 141, 167, 220

tender, tenderness, tendering 15, 22–25, 30–36, 39, 48, 51–53, 57–59, 82, 90, 92, 94, 107–08, 116, 121, 125, 156, 160–76, 189–93, 197, 202, 209–18
Todd, Janet 4, 10, 208
tragedy 85, 95, 978, 104, 121, 132, 137, 158, 170, 176, 179, 184, 202
  see also drama

transnationalism 72, 105, 115–53
trepanning 99, 131
triangle (plot device) 15, 50, 81, 93, 124, 148, 154, 161–63, 171, 184, 211–15

violence 21, 36, 61, 107, 119, 125, 169, 171, 181, 183, 194, 197, 218–19
  see also rape

Wollstonecraft, Mary 2, 7–8, 10, 21, 30–31, 41, 44, 92, 98, 104, 106, 109, 135, 139, 161–64, 170, 173–75, 191
  review of Gibbes 5, 8, 135, 139, 208
  Vindication of the Rights of Woman (VRW) 4–6, 11, 58, 107, 117, 121, 164, 173, 180
Woolf, Virginia 1, 3, 220–21
Wordsworth, William 136, 186

EU authorised representative for GPSR:
Easy Access System Europe, Mustamäe tee 50,
10621 Tallinn, Estonia
gpsr.requests@easproject.com

www.ingramcontent.com/pod-product-compliance
Lightning Source LLC
LaVergne TN
LVHW050049200525
811683LV00004B/84